Politics in Modern Greece

Politics in Modern Greece

Keith R. Legg

Stanford University Press, Stanford, California   1969

x

Stanford University Press
Stanford, California
© 1969 by the Board of Trustees of the
Leland Stanford Junior University
Printed in the United States of America
L.C. 69–18495
SBN 8047–0705–7

1000493190

To Sue

Preface

Hopefully, this book will serve two purposes. First, it provides a description and analysis of the contemporary Greek political system. It is the culmination of an interest that goes back to a summer sojourn in 1956. This interest was rekindled and the present study undertaken in 1963, with the encouragement and guidance of Professor Ernst Haas. Second, a study of modern Greece may draw attention to a neglected but important category of contemporary political systems. Until recently, political scientists have been preoccupied with the developing nations of Asia and Africa, or with developed industrial states. Greece and similar countries in Europe and Latin America are set apart from the first group because they have long been independent; yet they remain very unlike the developed industrial states in their levels of economic development or the operation of their political systems. Perhaps the framework I have found useful for explaining Greek politics can be used elsewhere. More important, studies of political systems in this category can suggest other models of political development and regression.

Within the relatively short span of research and writing, there have been tremendous alterations in the Greek political system. The rapidity of political change has provided many opportunities and considerable incentive for constant reinterpretation and revision. The background work for the study was largely completed before the electoral victory of George Papandreou and the Center Union in November 1963. Field research in Greece began in the late summer of 1964 and was completed a month before the fall of the Papandreou government in the following summer. The first analysis of the data was completed before the coup of April 1967, and the original manuscript was submitted as a dissertation to the Department of Political Science at the University of California, Berkeley. The present book is a complete revision of that dissertation.

Field research was made possible through a Foreign Area Fellowship.

Additional assistance was forthcoming from the Graduate School of the University of California, Berkeley. The research in Greece would have been impossible without the friendship, guidance, and connections of many Greek friends. Mr. George Yemenakis, in particular, arranged interviews with members of parliament and other notables, and also acted as an interpreter. He was an unfailing source of information on contemporary political and social life in Greece.

I am also grateful to Professor Benjamin Ward, who, along with Professor Haas, read and commented on the original manuscript. Several of my colleagues—James Morrison, Rene Lemarchand, and the late Charles Farris at the University of Florida, and Joseph Schlesinger and Paul Abramson of Michigan State University—read and commented on individual chapters. Mr. Enrique Baloyra of the Political Science Data Lab at the University of Florida advised on statistical matters. Mr. Bill Brimmer did the map. I am also grateful to my editor, Mr. James Trosper; he made a sometimes garbled manuscript readable, and his attention to detail saved me from numerous errors and inconsistencies. The major typing chores were shared by Lorraine Viscardi at Gainesville and June Black at Berkeley. Mr. Augusto Quesada assisted in the final preparation of the manuscript.

Finally, special thanks go to my wife, Sue, to whom this book is dedicated. Her assistance—financial, scholarly, and otherwise—was very great indeed. Needless to say, I alone am responsible for the contents and the conclusions.

K.R.L.

University of Florida
June 23, 1969

Contents

Politics in Modern Greece

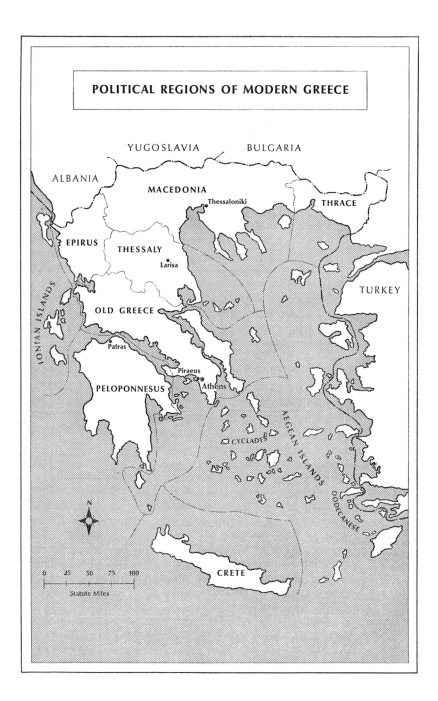

POLITICAL REGIONS OF MODERN GREECE

YUGOSLAVIA   BULGARIA

ALBANIA

MACEDONIA

Thessaloniki

THRACE

EPIRUS   THESSALY

Larisa

TURKEY

OLD GREECE

IONIAN ISLANDS

Patras

Piraeus

PELOPONNESUS   Athens

CYCLADES

AEGEAN ISLANDS

DODECANESE

N

0   25   50   75   100

Statute Miles

CRETE

Introduction

Greece hovers on the threshold between Europe and the non-Western world, between the "developed" and "developing" nations. Greece was the cradle of Western civilization, yet spent crucial centuries outside the pale of that civilization. Geographically, it is European, yet Greeks themselves speak of "going to Europe"; and depending on their purpose, the classifications imposed by foreigners make Greece a Middle Eastern, Balkan, or Mediterranean state. Greece possesses all the political institutions of modern democratic states. However, these institutions have not operated in the fashion of their Western European counterparts, and Greek parliamentary politics seem to be concerned with matters either settled or ignored in contemporary Western political systems. Even more disturbing to Western observers have been the periodic suspensions of representative institutions by the Greek military. On the other hand, Greece can scarcely be considered a typical "underdeveloped" country. By the usual indices of modernity, Greece ranks in the upper half of all nations.[1] One hundred years ago Greece was very like many Western countries, and her borrowed political institutions operated as their Western European prototypes did.

Greece represents a type of political system that emerged from colonial status or foreign subjugation in the nineteenth century but lagged behind Western Europe and the United States in economic development, ability to cope with social change, and the development of strong representative institutions. Many countries in Latin America would be included in this category; several Eastern European states (although their independence came later) would also have qualified before World War II. In a recent volume that used factor analysis to distinguish international regions, Greece was placed in a "Western community" category, even though she had a lower factor score for economic development than any other nation in that category.[2] In fact, the Greek score was much closer to the mean scores reported for a category of "semideveloped" Latins and for the Eastern European countries. One finds that descriptions of society and politics in nineteenth-century Greece do not differ substantially from contemporary accounts. Modern Greece may exemplify a failure of development, a retarded development, or a case of relatively permanent stagnation.

Political development is an elusive concept. It is far easier to note varying concepts of political development or to list the characteristics of developed polities than it is to rank actual states in terms of political "modernity." Some discussions assume modernization means eventual development of the characteristics found in a Western political system—rationalization of authority, orderly legal and administrative processes, differentiation of governmental structures, particular political infrastructures, widespread political participation, and some degree of governmental responsiveness.[3] Although these are very general attributes, the system envisioned is usually an open, constitutional democracy. However, particular institutional arrangements and values are not always associated with levels of economic development.[4] In reality, there is a great range of "more or less" in any of these characteristics in Western political systems, and an even greater range in developing ones.

Most political scientists now recognize that political development is not a unilinear or inevitable progression toward some predetermined goal, but is instead just one dimension of social change; the precise relationship of politics to other aspects of the social system will vary from system to system. It is perhaps most useful to view political development, like Alfred Diamant, as a "generic process of successfully sustaining new demands, goals, and organizations in a flexible manner."[5] Using this yardstick, Greece and the countries in her category are significant variants of the standard Western political model. Researchers in comparative politics have, until recently, tended to ignore this class of systems and have constructed their general models on the basis of experience in Africa, Asia, or the industrial West. This is unfortunate, since an examination of this class of "transitional" systems would be very useful in establishing the theoretical links between "developed" and "developing" countries. At the very least, the concepts of "transition" and "political modernity" could be far more accurately defined.

THE DEVELOPMENTAL PROCESS

There are a number of general models of political development that should, in theory, be applicable to all political systems, including that of Greece. However, many of these theoretical efforts are difficult to utilize in the study of an actual political system. Only a few are worked out in much detail; and in most cases there is a chasm between the conceptual framework and the data that must be organized and explained. More basically, the Greek political system simply cannot be understood using any single model of political development advanced thus far. Since the major effort here is an explanation of Greece rather than model building, I have pursued an eclectic course. In the following pages, I have derived a very general process model from the most complete developmental theories—those most directed toward transitional systems—namely, the theories of Gabriel Almond and G. Bingham Powell, David Apter, and Fred Riggs.* The elements and interrelationships of the general model are then refined to reflect the Greek situation. Recent classifications of the military and of political parties are used to specify the major actors, and a model proposed by Arend Lijphart to explain stability in fragmented Western democracies is revised to offer an explanation for the unstable pattern of Greek politics.

Despite differences in phraseology and emphasis, the three developmental models have a basically similar definition of development. For Apter, development is a "continuous process of differentiation and increasing complexity."[6] For Almond and Powell, a principal aspect of the development or transformation of political systems is also "role or structural differentiation."[7] Riggs, using optics as a heuristic device, views development in terms of the degree of "diffraction" in the society—that is, the increasing differentiation of structures and the number of roles held concurrently by members of the system.[8] For each author, differentiation is an index of development in a broad sense only; the major focus in each of the presentations is the explanation for this development and its ramifications, particularly in its political aspects.

Writers in comparative politics often distinguish between the developmental process in older nations and that in the new nations. However, the class of "transitional" countries that we are concerned with are left in an ambiguous positions. Apter and Riggs both pose two developmental paths, one characteristic of the West, the other of "developing" nations. Apter bases his division on the differences between industrialization and modernization. Industrialization is a process in which "the expansion of productive enterprises is the integrating factor in social life"; by itself, it creates certain structural and organizational uniformities. Modernization, a more general

---

* The discussion here is based on Riggs, *Administration in Developing Countries*; Almond and Powell, *Comparative Politics*; and Apter, *The Politics of Modernization*. The more recent formulation presented by Apter in "Political Systems and Developmental Change" is also used.

term, refers to the spread of roles originating in industrial societies to systems without industrial infrastructures.[9] In this context, pressures for change do not originate internally, but are produced by the international environment or the actions of the governmental elite. Riggs, without making an explicit distinction between modernization and industrialization, differentiates the new nations from the older ones by the sources of pressures for change. Endogenous societies, in his terminology, change because of internal pressures; exogenous (or exo-prismatic) ones change because of outside pressures.[10] Riggs bases further distinctions on the rate of change.

Almond and Powell also suggest that changes in a political system can be a response to pressures from the international environment, domestic society, or the local elites themselves.[11] However, they seem to consider societal changes as most crucial. They do not make an explicit distinction between developmental processes in the old and new nations, although on several occasions a divergence can be inferred. The system challenges recognized by these authors—state building, nation building, participation, and resource distribution, all of which lead to further structural differentiation and cultural secularization—are all based on European experience.[12] Presumably the same pattern and sequence occurs in non-Western settings. At one point Almond and Powell do suggest that some new states were provided with differentiated political infrastructures before they needed them, and before the new societies were ready for them; but these systems are then described as "historical accidents."[13]

The authors considered here all warn the reader that there is no inevitable trend in the direction of greater development. To Almond and Powell, it is "quite clear that regressions, or reversals, occur commonly in the development of political systems."[14] But in general, "When one variable in a system changes in magnitude or in quality, the others are subjected to strains and are transformed; the system changes its pattern of performance or the unruly component is disciplined by regulator mechanisms."[15] There is no further explanation of regression, and their typology of political systems only hints at the possibility. They recognize that a system might remain permanently underdeveloped at one point in their discussion, but this, too, is not pushed further.[16]

According to Apter, each level of development has an appropriate political system. Each political system eventually reaches a "ceiling," at which point system change is likely because the resources of development can no longer be redeployed.[17] Presumably, Western political systems "fit" their societies at various stages of development, since the political infrastructures developed along with the differentiation of roles; however, modern roles will not "fit" into a nonindustrial setting. "The goal of modernizing societies, i.e., industrialization, is a simple one, but the political problem, managing the complexities of role, becomes greater the closer a country moves toward the goal."[18] Modernization as a process may seem irreversible; but whether the normal result of Western industrialization can be induced through political action remains problematical.

The major burden of Riggs's work is to delineate one final outcome of the developmental process: a "prismatic" society that may fall far short of full economic development or political and social modernity as defined in Western terms. The prismatic society is usually found in a country where resources are scarce. It is not merely the midpoint between modern and traditional societies, but a special case, possessing unique features found in neither of the others—although Riggs does not suggest that every prismatic society must be like every other one. He does suggest several ways out of the impasse posed by a prismatic society, but he seems to discount the possibility of escape.* As Lucian Pye has noted, since the "logic of behavior in a 'prismatic' or 'transitional' society makes so much sense, why should we expect such societies to seek change and modernization?"[19] Riggs, in reality, projects a static model; retrogression to a traditional system is as precluded as advancement to a modern one.

TYPOLOGIES OF POLITICAL SYSTEMS

Logically, typologies as classificatory schemes follow observation and precede the devising of general propositions. The comparison that leads to a general theory is possible only after classification is completed. To be satisfactory in logical terms, the categories in any typology must be mutually exclusive, yet jointly exhaustive. Every object in the classification scheme must fall into one or another category.[20] However, social scientists have repeatedly argued that "problems and their answers are so closely linked to the categories and nomenclature adopted by the investigator that all these elements develop concurrently."[21] Unfortunately, the attributes of exhaustiveness and exclusiveness must be tied to empirical fact if the classification

---

* There are four possible strategies: a country could exploit colonial possessions, thus creating funds to use domestically; it might negotiate long-term loans with foreign powers; it might receive outright gifts from the same source; or finally, it might try to counter negative development by changing its economic policies and trying to accumulate internal capital. The very nature of a prismatic society seems to render any of these strategies hopeless.

scheme is to lead to useful generalization. Arend Lijphart suggests that a natural typology of political systems should perform two functions: "(1) It should facilitate comparison among different types and aid in the discovery of significant characteristics that are logically independent of the criteria defining the type but empirically associated with the different types. (2) It should also facilitate comparison within each type, with the attributes held in common by all of the systems within the type serving as the 'control' variables, or parameters."[22]

By and large, a typology that includes all political systems must be at such a high level of abstraction that its usefulness in classifying empirical systems is limited. Comparison is also hindered because the operational definition of the dimensions used in the classification scheme is often unclear. In one way or another, the political scientists discussed here have all constructed typologies to be used in the examination of all political systems, from traditional to modern. It is from these typologies that the conceptual frameworks associated with these men have been derived. There is relative agreement on the characteristics associated with "modern" and "traditional" political systems. However, the different authors vary in their operational definitions of each type, in the relationship that they acknowledge between types, and in the degree to which they are willing to make comparisons within each type. Even so, each theoretician is able to work with "traditional" and "modern" types. The major problems concern the "transitional" category. It is here that the specification of types is most difficult; yet it is in this category that most contemporary regimes in emerging nations seem to fall. Until the typologies suggested by the scholars discussed here, as well as those proposed by others, are refined to include this transitional category, comparison with the polar types and between transitional types will be difficult. All three systems have shortcomings in this respect. Riggs's classification scheme suggests three distinct types of polity, but its details of classification are not too precise. Apter's scheme is logically exhaustive and more or less empirically grounded, but it concentrates on political development and underrates the possibility of a static society. The model offered by Almond and Powell is very detailed, but it does not appear to satisfy the requirements of exhaustiveness and exclusiveness.

The primary concern of Riggs is to examine the particular relationships between structure and functions that will help us identify the essential differences between traditional, transitional, and modern political systems.[23] He places each of these on a scale of increasing "diffraction," or differentiation, of social structures: the lower extreme is the traditional "fused" structure, and the upper is the modern "diffracted" system; midway between the two is the transitional, or "prismatic," system. The first difficulty arises in specifying the variables used; another involves spelling out the exact relationships between the variables, as well as the relationship of each to political, social, and economic development.

Riggs views diffraction as the analog of development. Groups of variables are related in different ways to the degree of diffraction.[24] Some, such as marketization, are not important to development, but have a linear correlation with it. A distinguishing feature of Riggs's scheme is the group that he terms key variables, which both react to and influence development. The key variables comprise two types: strategic variables, which have an S-curve relationship to the degree of diffraction, and critical variables, which have a C-curve relationship. The strategic variables are primarily measures of individual and institutional behaviors—social mobilization, scope of individual responsibility, the basis of elite recruitment, underlying goals and myths of the society, the basis and scope of authority, and the level of political input and government output. The critical variables are measures of the relative proportion of traditional and modern elements in the society, such as the degree of equality, the mix of traditional and modern values, and the convergence of form and reality in institutions. Together, these key variables are measures of the style and performance of political systems. The fused and diffracted aspects of each dimension combine to produce a unique condition that is something more than the midpoint between them. The middle range on any variable is characteristic of a prismatic society. According to Riggs, the attainment of a high level on the strategic variables and a minimal level on the critical variables is necessary to political development.

Riggs then uses his selected variables to construct definitional and developmental models of both Western and non-Western prismatic systems. In the Western, or endo-prismatic, case internal pressures cause change. The differentiation of structures in the society is a general index of this change; other variables reflect more specific aspects. The impact of change on the intervening variables causes an advance in political, economic, or social development; the result is a modern, diffracted society. However, Riggs is primarily interested in the non-Western, or exo-prismatic, case. This has two major dimensions: a dependency syndrome, which concerns the relationship between the powerholders and the socioeconomic environment; and an interference complex, which arises from the mutual interrelations of different elite groups.[25] In an exo-prismatic society, external pressures cause change; the index of change remains the same, but the impact of this change on intervening variables causes retrogressive political, economic, and social development.

One earmark of a prismatic society is the importance of those occupying political roles. They are relatively unaccountable to the public at large or to other elite groups. In fact, they are able to use their political position to control wealth and prestige in the society. Economic transactions can be completed only through political influence. The entrepreneurial groups (largely foreign in Riggs's formulation) transfer wealth from the masses to the bureaucratic powerholders. The entrepreneurs themselves are unable to accumulate investment capital, and the powerholders, instead of investing it, use it for nonproductive purposes. Moreover, the predominant position held by those with political power retards the process of differentiation because achievement goals in the society revolve only about political position. In the prismatic society, there is a movement toward increased differentiation, but this tendency is associated with others that may disrupt the society: increasing personal insecurity, growing inequality, declining productivity, and decapitalization. "Thus, in the prismatic model, economic development is strongly linked with processes leading to political instability and social disorganization."[26]

To summarize, negative political development occurs when governmental structures expand more rapidly than do institutions of political control. Negative social development means increased social tensions. Negative economic development results from the failure of the entrepreneurial class or the elite to utilize wealth for productive purposes. The outcome of these processes is a prismatic society. However, this formulation is still unsatisfactory. For one thing, the division of transitional societies into the two categories of endo-prismatic and exo-prismatic is a gross oversimplification. Certainly, many supposedly "internal" pressures for change in European nations were externally inspired. Likewise, countries outside Europe cannot be so neatly categorized. For example, pressures for change in Greece were generated internally, but the country was in a formally subjugated condition corresponding to the exo-prismatic classification.

David Apter sets out to discover which type of political system is most appropriate for each level of development.[27] By implication, his concern is with political and economic development and the relationship between them. He proposes a series of types "deriving from a generalized theory of choice based on normative, structural, and behavioral dimensions."[28] These models are not constructed as ideal types, although they are used as such. The independent variable in the original formulation was the impact of modernization; recent reformulations make coercion and information the independent variables.[29] The intervening variables are two, related to the authority system and the value system found in the society. In the first category a distinction is made between pyramidal and hierarchical systems; in the second, consummatory and instrumental values are distinguished. These variables permit the construction of four possible models.* The dependent variable is the particular type of society. Apter argues that the political action required for the attainment of modernization goals at each level of development, given a particular model, will require a different political system. These systems are distinguished by the extent of coercion required to meet goals and the amount of information needed for decision making.

Apter suggests that two of his model systems are particularly suited to developing societies. The first is a "mobilization" system, involving consummatory values, or ideologies, and hierarchical authority. This system requires a regime whose leadership is committed to a thorough reorganization and redirection of society toward new values and loyalties. The other response to social transition is a "reconciliation" system, which combines pyramidal authority and instrumental values. In the reconciliation system, goals and legitimacy are defined by the representational principle. Here, power is dispersed among a number of separate units, and there is a tolerance of multiple loyalties. Either system may be useful as the framework of a society at the primary stages of modernization.[30] However, a mobilization system is particularly appropriate during the transition from extensive modernization to early industrialization, when a maximum of coercion is needed to cope with social disintegration.[31] The reconciliation system is more useful in a post-industrial phase, when information needs require decentralization of the control structures.[32] Each kind of political system—except, apparently, the reconciliation system in a post-industrial phase—reaches a "ceiling," at

---

* The distinction between hierarchical and pyramidal authority is made on the basis of accountability to the public: low accountability implies the first, high accountability the second. Hierarchical authority implies centralized decision making; pyramidal authority suggests semi-autonomous decision-making powers. Consummatory values are defined as empirical means germane to nonempirical ends (ideology), and instrumental values as empirical means germane to empirical ends (interest politics). The four possible models are identified as "mobilization," "reconciliation," "theocratic," and "bureaucratic." The theocratic model, based on consummatory values and pyramidal authority, is of historical interest only. (Apter, "Political Systems," p. 15.)

which point the resources for development at its disposal can no longer be redeployed.[33] For example, in a reconciliation system interest conflicts may be converted into value conflicts, and the groundwork laid for some alternative system.[34] If a mobilization system fails to meet the goals of industrialization for any reason, one of its subsystems may become increasingly crucial to its existence. At that point, the pattern of consummatory values may well give way to one of instrumental values.[35]

After dealing with models at this high level of abstraction, Apter suggests a different and more operational set of variables. In a reconciliation system, society now becomes the independent variable, and the government, as a mediator and coordinator, is the dependent one.[36] In a highly industrialized society, political and economic management requires information undistorted by coercion if the proper decisions are to be made; the major problems concern the surplus of information and its evaluation. A reconciliation system in a preindustrial setting, particularly one characterized by a low consensus, is likely to result in stagnation. Here, decision makers have no sure guide in determining the allocation of rewards, no matter how much information is available. Compromise based on the strength and persistence of existing blocs is the likely solution.[37] Stagnation can be avoided only if there is a dramatic increase in resources, or if the system has descended from a previous level that incorporated highly consummatory values, "according to which a 'New Jerusalem' had been defined in ethical terms."[38] In a mobilization system, government is the independent variable, and society the dependent.[39] Information is restricted, and decision making is easier but less accurate. A great deal of coercion is necessary if the system's predetermined goals are to be realized. Although these conditions may be tolerated at first, Apter suggests that low-information, high-coercion systems become increasingly dysfunctional as industrialization progresses. A bureaucratic system, involving instrumental values and hierarchical authority, is likely to result if a "ceiling" in the resources available for deployment is reached. In fact, the bureaucratic systems, although unstable, may be optimal for "intermediate" industrialization.[40]

Apter argues that "political development is no mere reciprocal of economic development, but rather a complex of factors that results in systemic coherence." Even if this coherence does not materialize, economic factors will "most frequently come to serve political and social needs."[41] In the mobilization model, economic development is the rationale for demanding complete allegiance; it is the goal of society. Coercion, the hallmark of such a system, is restricted only to the extent that it may interfere with the processes of economic growth. Hierarchical control ensures concentration on economic goals, permits tactical flexibility in meeting emerging problems, and enforces performance. A mobilization system can restrict demands and channel resources into productive investments. As suggested earlier, however, the costs of coercion as development commences may increase and thus slow economic growth. Eventually, some system change is likely. In the reconciliation system the public has greater influence in setting goals. A high proportion of the society's total resources is available for economic development, but the government cannot dictate resource allocation. Capital investment depends on the persuasive powers of the elite and the degree of self-discipline in the population. In general, reconciliation systems have slower economic growth than others, and are more liable to suffer social and political disorders. Another system is the modernizing autocracy, a variant of the general bureaucratic model, which can promote investment and economic growth for short periods but is not stable over time. Here, custom and precedent control the activities of both the leaders and the public. However, the traditional hierarchy is very flexible in this system, and can take a predominant role in technological innovation and in channeling resources to productive purposes. In the long run, this economic growth, resulting in a more highly differentiated society, creates pressures that undermine the political position of the modernizing oligarchs.

The two major models suggested by Apter, those of mobilization and reconciliation, are extremely general. Any number of empirical types might approximate either one. The intermediate bureaucratic type, though not spelled out in much detail, could also accommodate a wide range of actual systems. Both the reconciliation model and the bureaucratic one, as well as the relationship between them, suggest explanations for the developmental process in Greece and similar countries. However, if these models are to be useful, the types of regimes and the conditions of transformation must be more clearly set forth.

For Almond and Powell, the major sets of variables are conversion functions, capability functions, and maintenance or adaptation functions.[42] Conversion functions involve behavior within the system itself, and comprise the traditional legislative, judicial, and executive functions with new labels, plus three new functions—political communication, interest articulation, and interest aggregation. Capability functions relate the system to the environment.[43] Five types are suggested. The first four functions describe the pattern of outputs in the society: extractive capability (system performance in drawing human and material resources from the environment);[44] regulative capability (the political system's exercise of control over behavior); distributive capability (the allocation of goods, services, status, and opportunities); and symbolic capability (the symbol flow from the political system into the society and the international environment). A fifth function, the responsive capability, concerns the relationship between political inputs and governmental outputs. The last set of major variables, system maintenance and adaptation functions, is concerned with individual behavior.[45] Political socialization and political recruitment are related to the psychological dimension of the political system. This category comprises the political culture, "the attitudes, beliefs, values and skills which are current in an entire population."[46] These functions are so interrelated that a change in one will affect the others. Moreover, there is a general association between structural differentiation, cultural secularization, and the expansion of capabilities in a political system, all of which are involved in the "development" of the system.

Unlike the other theorists, Almond and Powell set forth an extensive classification of systems, which they base on differentiation of structures and degree of secularization; the variable of subsystem autonomy is added, but it is tied to a particular level of differentiation. Their types are cross sections taken at particular points on the continuum of development.[47] They provide two modern categories: mobilized and nonmobilized systems, distinguished by differing degrees of differentiation and secularization. However, they state that within these classes, and between them, the types merge into one another. The modern mobilized systems are divided into two sections, democratic and authoritarian, on the basis of variations in subsystem control. The democratic category is further divided into systems with high subsystem autonomy, those with limited autonomy, and those with low autonomy. The Anglo-Saxon states, Italy, and Mexico, respectively, are used as examples of these types. The authoritarian category is subdivided not on structural lines, but by the extent of mobilization; it includes authoritarian types and totalitarian types. These two types are subdivided, according to ideology, into conservative or modernizing authoritarian regimes and radical or conservative totalitarian regimes.

Almond and Powell suggest a time sequence of challenges that may lead to political development—namely, successive crises of state building, nation building, participation, and distribution. The manner in which these problems are solved is highly dependent on system capabilities. A system must have adequate capabilities of extraction before it can begin to distribute resources. The distribution involves not only economic resources, but also the structures and procedures of extraction. The regulatory capability involves intervention in social and economic life; presumably, complete allocation of resources is possible if this capability is highly developed. Structural differentiation and secularization are viewed as prerequisites for the development of higher levels of extraction and regulation. If transitional systems begin by emphasizing distributive and responsive capabilities, any sudden reversal is likely to shift the emphasis to regulative and symbolic capabilities.[48] This is similar to the relationship between coercion and information suggested by Apter; a concept not unlike his notion of "ceiling" is also implied.

The conceptual apparatus put forward by Almond and Powell is in part useful for our limited purposes here, but it has a number of serious defects. Although differentiation of structures is widely recognized as an index of modernization, the use of secularization as the developmental aspect of political culture seems dubious. Secularization may indeed be one dimension; but surely additional dimensions are needed to explain the differences between supposedly highly secularized states. Though useful, Almond and Powell's conversion variables are primarily descriptive categories drawn from Western political experience; like the categories of Rigg's system, they are essentially dimensions along which traditional, transitional, or modern systems may be placed. There is no empirical evidence that these variables are indeed the requisites of a political system, and the relationships between them are only suggested. Political socialization and recruitment are more specifically related to the political system as a whole, and seem far more general in application than the conversion functions. The discussion of capability functions, however, is useful, even though these functions are not logically exhaustive or of equal importance. Few models examine the question of regime performance so explicitly. More disappointing is the typology of systems.[49] The authoritarian-democratic division is much too simplistic. Some of the types noted seem marginal, some of the examples seem dubious, and other, more distinct, types are ignored.[50] Moreover, the typology lacks internal consistency. Degrees of subsystem control ought to be as appropriate a distinction among authoritarian regimes as among democratic; and democratic regimes might as easily be distinguished by political culture, as are authoritarian regimes.

These shortcomings create problems when system transformation is analyzed. Almond and Powell suggest that elite actions or the impact of the international or domestic environments create the impetus for change. These pressures create imbalances in the political system, forcing it to adjust to meet new challenges. If the change is gradual, increasing differentiation and secularization will eventually produce a modern society. However, this is not always the case. Sometimes the existing political system cannot handle the challenges; it may break down and give way to a new regime. The authors imply that something less than modernity will result in this case, although this is not apparent from the conceptual framework itself.[51]

From the foregoing formulations, a very general process model can be extracted for use in modern Greece and similar systems. Various pressures from the international system, the domestic environment, and elite action unbalance a political system; at the same time, their impact on certain intervening variables produces a new political system, the dependent variable. The character of the intervening variables and the rate of change usually distinguishes the old, developed nations from the several categories of underdeveloped nations. Apter provides logically derived developmental models, and relates the few variables considered in a satisfactory manner. However, although his descriptions of the reconciliation, bureaucratic, and mobilization systems are intellectually attractive because of their generality, this same feature makes their empirical application difficult. Riggs offers a set of descriptive categories tied to reality, but he is really describing only one of many possible systems. Modern Greece would fit his model of a prismatic society, but only for some periods of her history. Therefore, it is most useful to conceive of Riggs's model as a detailed explication of one possible prismatic society, and as one possible bureaucratic type of the kind suggested by Apter. Almond and Powell provide a number of categories that are useful in relating the political system to the environment. The discussion of capabilities, in particular, permits judgments to be made about performance levels and possible system transformations. In addition, these authors set forth several conditions for development that can be interpreted as intervening variables.

The reconciliation model, which seems most appropriate for modern Greece, can, in theory, accommodate bargaining systems of any type.

The reconciliation system, with its pyramidal authority, has retrospective and residual consummatory values that encourage compromise between groups expressing prevailing political objectives and views. Since reconciliation systems consist of single political units made up of constituent political units that have not lost their political identity, they can be relatively loose confederations that have a recognized structure or much more highly organized parliamentary regimes.[52]

It is clear that a variety of actual systems fall into this category. Regimes with functioning party systems fit, but so do any oligarchical regimes that have split along family, regional, ethnic, or religious lines. Moreover, any regime with subsystem autonomy would seem to be in this category. According to Almond, the major political actors in the type of reconciliation with which we are concerned are

organizations which perform other social or political functions but which, as corporate bodies or through groups within them (such as legislative blocs, officer cliques, higher or lower clergy or religious orders, departments, skill groups, and ideological cliques in bureaucracies) may articulate their own interests or represent the interests of groups in the society.[53]

Horacio Godoy and Carlos Fortín have described such a system in greater detail. The modern and the traditional parts of the society belong to the same economic, social, and political system. The whole system is dominated by the modern part, whose existence is "made possible by the existence of the archaic part." In essence, the traditional oligarchy and the newly emergent industrial and urban elites are allies. The traditional oligarchs concentrate economic, social, and political power, and the demands of the rural elements are articulated through them. However, they are less concerned with politics than with economic and social domination. In the modern part of society, a center comprised of the traditional oligarchy, the emerging middle classes, and a growing urban proletariat with varying degrees of participation is surrounded by a subordinated periphery, both urban and rural. The peripheral mass is integrated in the sense that it is articulate and possesses the possibility of direct political action. It may not actually participate, but the mere possibility of its political action makes it a potential source of power for other sectors.[54]

The bureaucracy and the military often have a dominant political role in developing countries because they are the only organized elements. Janowitz has suggested a typology of military types that includes three models rooted in Western European experience and an additional five drawn from the experiences of the military in the new nations. One of the second types, the civil-military coalition, is of interest because the military is an acknowledged actor in the political arena. "The military serves as an active political bloc in

its support of civilian parties and other bureaucratic power groups. . . . The
military may act as an informal, or even more explicit, umpire between competing political parties and political groups."[55]

A reconciliation system like this, composed of competing power blocs, is
fragile. The political infrastructure is weak, and alliances are unstable.
A military-dominated bureaucratic system is likely to develop because of the
organizational weakness of competing political institutions. The military
may intervene to preserve the system when the balance between competing
political groups is threatened, or when the modernization goals of the nonmilitary governing groups are not achieved. Of course, a tradition of political involvement by the military, like that existing in Greece, may provide
an additional excuse.[56] Janowitz suggests that even if modernization goals
are met, the military may inherit political power simply because its level of
organization and cohesion is so much higher than that of other social sectors.
However, the same qualities that make the military organization stronger
than its competitors reduce its ability to rule effectively. The military, regardless of its degree of involvement in the system, will be a poor agent of political change. Hence a military oligarchy will always be somewhat unstable.

The importance of the military and the bureaucracy in the reconciliation
system we are concerned with is directly related to the impotence of other
political organizations—namely, parties. The political party has become the
central institution of Western politics, and distinctions between systems are
made on the basis of party characteristics, often in terms of the number of
parties.[57] These classifications have usually been applied outside the developed areas on the assumption that sectors in conflict will organize along
party lines, and that competition between them must take place within a
party system. It is sometimes forgotten that the first parties in Western
Europe simply reproduced a pattern of open competition for power between
the different social sectors that had previously taken place in a different
framework. Only the open competition between different sectors of the
emerging bourgeoisie was actually confined to party struggles in a parliamentary setting.[58] Basically, the party is a creature of modern and modernizing political systems: "The political party emerges whenever the activities
of a political sytem reach a certain degree of complexity, or whenever the
notion of political power comes to include the idea that the mass public must
participate or be controlled."[59] These two conditions are related; only at a
certain degree of complexity are the old authority relationships sufficiently
eroded for new loyalties to take their place.

The term "party" is used to describe political organizations in many non-Western countries; it is nonetheless clear that there are few genuine parties and operating party systems outside the developed areas. Using a definition of party suggested by Joseph LaPalombara and Myron Weiner, genuine parties are easily distinguished from the "cliques, clubs and small groups of notables" that preceded them in the West, and from the small oligarchical groups that take the name of parties in many less developed countries.[60] By this definition, a party must have: (1) continuity in organization; the party's life-span must not be dependent on that of its current leaders; (2) a presumably permanent organization at the local level, with regular communication between local and national units; (3) a conscious determination of leaders at both national and local levels to capture and hold decision making power, either alone or in coalition with others; and (4) a concern on the part of the organization for seeking followers at the polls or in some manner striving for popular support.

By and large, parties in Greece and in similar countries have not advanced beyond the clique stage. The factors that were crucial for party development in Western systems have not been operative. In Western Europe "aristocratic" parties developed in existing parliaments when the legitimacy of representative institutions was being established.[61] In meeting crises of integration or participation, these groups developed into complex organizations that were genuine parties. Elsewhere representative institutions were usually accepted as legitimate almost automatically when a country gained its independence, and were considered a sign of political modernity. The initial struggles of these countries were directed against colonial regimes or foreign domination. There was, in most cases, no indigenous monarchical or aristocratic tradition. The elites that had led a country to independence could occupy the new parliamentary institutions, along with other seats of power, without a struggle; these institutions became no more than another arena for the usual bargaining for power. The elites who staff these parliaments and bureaucracies have generally not found it necessary to organize genuine parties. Formal suffrage requirements were often minimal, and the ruling elites were able to utilize their traditional authority to secure votes from the rural masses. There was no ground for a crisis of participation. More important, there were no great social and economic transformations to alter the existing social structure. Demands for meaningful participation, i.e., participation in decision making, were not made until relatively recently simply because economic and social development was slow. The older elites simply transferred their economic and social power to the political sector, and used their entrenched political position to maintain it.

Occasionally, mass parties that meet the LaPalombara and Weiner criteria have materialized in non-Western settings.[62] These parties are usually initiated by an articulate disadvantaged group (or by an elite representing it) that wants to participate in political decision making, at least to the extent of being involved in the social bargaining process. If the disadvantaged groups reach a stage of political awareness "before parties have been established and where the target of participation efforts is a non-party elite," they may well reject the existing regime.[63] Generally, these "combative" parties are urban based; they must rely upon organization and ideology to produce the cohesion and loyalty that the older elites can obtain through traditional ties to the population. Combative parties are no more likely than other political groups to view parliamentary institutions as the only center for the resolution of conflict. Extraparliamentary activities, such as strikes or demonstrations, are an important part of their quest for a share in political power. They are not committed to a competitive party system; if they tolerate political opponents, it is probably because they can not yet destroy them.

THE CONSOCIATIONAL SYSTEM AND THE BUREAUCRATIC MODEL

We can further refine the implications of the particular reconciliation system found in Greece by examining the exact relationships between her various political groups and the conditions that may lead to system change. A formulation proposed by Arend Lijphart to explain stability in the "fragmented" democracies of Western Europe can, I believe, be applied as well to regimes without party systems.[64] He labels as "consociational" those democracies with subcultural cleavage and with tendences toward immobilism and instability that are deliberately turned into more stable systems by the leaders of the major subcultures. He regards the representatives of the major subcultures as political parties; whether this is true or not, they do represent cleavages that cannot be managed by ordinary parliamentary methods. In the consociational democracies, bargaining between the major subcultures takes place outside the formal constitutional framework, through elite cooperation in the face of tendencies toward system disintegration. Since agreements are reached informally, or at least outside parliament, there is no reason to confine this formulation to democratic settings.[65] The major power blocs in the category of countries considered here include the church, the bureaucracy, and the military, as well as the older elites operating through traditional "parties" and the newer political organizations representing urban elements. All of these are antagonistic elements, even if they are not technically subcultures.

Lijphart suggests four prerequisites for the successful practice of consociational democracy, and these seem applicable to transitional systems. A consociational system can be considered as an empirically grounded type of reconciliation system, encompassing the civil-military coalition suggested by Janowitz. If the system is to be successful, the leaders of the rival subcultures must: (1) be able to recognize the dangers inherent in a fragmented system, and to follow the initial precedents of cooperation; (2) be at least partly committed to the maintenance of the system; (3) be able to establish effective contacts and communication with each other in spite of subcultural differences; and (4) develop institutional arrangements and "rules of the game" to accommodate their differing interests.[66]

A "consociational" label, however useful for describing a political system at one point in time, should not imply that the system is permanent. Unlike the consociational democracies examined by Lijphart, the consociational systems do not have a record of stability. Fundamentally, the elites in these settings do not have the four necessary attributes because their societies are not yet modern.* In Europe, the subcultures are relatively self-contained; by contrast, those in the developing countries are not "pillarized" but perform services for the whole system. In Europe, social mobilization is nearly complete, and each major subculture has a roughly equal chance of attracting new support. In the countries under consideration here newly mobilized elements are mostly attracted to only one or two of the major groups. The balance of power is inherently unstable in this setting. The leaders of each political group feel they have much to gain or lose by promoting instability or by blocking the actions of others.

Gerhard Lehmbruch, also concerned with consociational democracies, has suggested that the division of public offices among competing groups or the division of the system itself into more or less autonomous spheres of influence, on either regional or functional lines, can be useful in resolving conflicts.[67] But any effort on the part of new sectors to take power through elections is blocked by the old elite; yet these new groups may oppose con-

---

* Lijphart (pp. 25–30) offers a tentative list of social structures and cultural attitudes that favor the development of a consociational democracy: a distinct separation between subcultures, a balance of power among them, public toleration of a government by grand coalition, external threats to the system, and a moderate nationalism. Of these, the first two would seem to be the most important.

sociational bargaining as "undemocratic." There are no institutions or processes through which all the major groups are willing to settle conflicts. A change in the system, as Leonard Binder pessimistically notes in regard to the Middle East, depends on "the willingness and the ability of the military and bureaucratic elites ... to reject their own institutional orientations and to decide rationally and consciously to establish and work certain democratic institutions."[68] An implicit element in both consociational democracies and generalized consociational systems is the mutual possession of veto power, which is necessary if the elite representatives of all groups are to be induced to participate in bargaining. Essentially, the consociational system is kept running, as Irving Horowitz notes in reference to Latin America, only by "the peculiar socioeconomic symmetry in the distribution of power. ... Power is not exclusively lodged within any one social sector, but rather is so evenly distributed along Falangist lines that a cancellation effect occurs."[69] The system itself ultimately suffers; demands from newly mobilized sectors are not met. Economic change threatens the groups wedded to the status quo, but it is sufficiently impeded by them to retard the fullest expansion of system capabilities.

At this point, along the lines suggested by Apter, one sector, generally the military (with hierarchical organization and instrumental values) or an ideological political party (with hierarchical organization and consummatory values), takes over, either by design or in reaction to the activities of competing groups. Either one encounters problems. To be successful, the military generally has to create a mass following among civilians.[70] And up to this point, attempts to take power by ideologically oriented parties have been successfully resisted in most transitional nations. These lapses from the consociational system, however, do not solve problems; instead, they tend to mark readjustments between the political blocs. Eventually, a new equilibrium reasserts itself, and the consociational system is temporarily restored.[71]

THE INTERVENING VARIABLES

According to Lucian Pye, "Different types of systems are likely to have different patterns of modernization, while conversely, systems that have gone through different paths of development will be significantly different."[72] This gives great importance to the intervening variables that are part of the process model of development. This category is not especially well developed in any of the theoretical efforts discussed here. Riggs mentions "insensitive variables," which set limits to development but are not correlated with it. He mentions the rate of assimilation, moral values and other cultural elements, as examples, without further explanation.[73] However, the outcome of the developmental process that he describes is dependent on very specific intervening variables. Just as the standard Western model is characteristic of only one or two European states, the prismatic society, in the exact form Riggs specifies, could only develop in certain South and Southeast Asian states. Apter suggests that the definition and relative status of roles in a given system, the institutionalized criteria of the stratification patterns, and the recruitment patterns to the major groups that comprise the system must all be known before meaningful statements about change can be made.[74] Almond and Powell do not make direct reference to intervening variables, but factors and conditions that might be so classed are mentioned throughout their book: the kinds of problems faced by the system, the resources upon which the system can draw, development in others social systems and the international system, the functions of the political system itself, and elite responses to crises.[75] The precise relationship of these variables, however, is not clear. Finally, political culture itself, as defined by these authors, might be classed as an intervening variable.

Whether intervening variables are explicitly defined or not, they are crucial in determining possible models of political development.[76] First, the character of the society into which change is introduced should be fully examined. A tentative list might include the following: existing values, institutional structures, the styles of authority, the character of the economic and social systems, and the extent of national integration and political participation. Perhaps the most important single consideration, which encompasses many of the above factors, is the degree of domination in a society by some of its internal social formations. "This domination is determined by, and in turn affects, the particular form of dependence of the society as a whole and of the ruling groups on external sources of power."[77] Certain types of stratification systems may be more able to accept particular kinds of "modernizing" change. For example, a society like that of modern Greece, where patterns of reciprocal favors and mutual obligations between patron and client are common, can more easily be accommodated to a goal that defines modernity in terms of political structures (e.g., representative institutions) than to a goal of economic development.[78]

The activities of the elite are also determined by variations in the meaning of modernization according to time and place, and by the congruence of this particular image of modernization with the existing character of society. In the nineteenth century development was perceived primarily in terms of political institutions. The act of independence was the beginning and the end of political development, and modernization could be achieved by the adoption of a popular constitution and representative institutions. However, institutional modernization alone did not necessarily or immediately alter a society's stratification system. There was no imperative need to mobilize the entire population to some further end. In the twentieth century it has generally been assumed that economic development is a prerequisite to political development, and that all national elites are genuinely interested in this goal. As Hoffman notes, this may not be the case: "It is absurd to assume either that 'modernization' is the overriding, necessary concern of all political leaders or that the techniques of 'political development' as so clearcut and pre-determined that they force statecraft into a necessarily small number of distinct molds."[79] Obviously, the task of elites in developing societies is much greater than it is elsewhere, and the possibilities for failure are also greater. Of the three formulations considered here, only Apter's really stresses this factor.

A country's existence in an international system cannot be ignored. However, the authors whose model we are adapting, in common with many others, tend to consider each society as a closed system, and rarely mention the international environment after initial consideration of the origins of social change. Nevertheless, the existence of a particular type of international system at a given point in time may have severe ramifications on the internal politics of a state. The extent of government resources, the methods of mobilizing and distributing them, the parameters of policy, and the general manner of conducting public affairs—even the form of government or the holders of political office—may be influenced by external factors like war or international market collapse. James Rosenau has suggested that some societies may even become permanently "penetrated" systems, in which nonmembers of the society participate directly in either the allocation of resources or in the mobilization of support for national goals.[80] Other authors have paid more attention to this variable. Godoy and Fortín, in a Latin American context, view external dependence, particularly economic relationships with the outside world, as particularly crucial.[81]

A final intervening variable is the physical environment of the political system. Many theorists have assumed that political and economic development can occur in any geographical location if the proper achievement values exist or can be inculcated into the population.[82] Although it is often admitted that some region within a given nation may not be worth developing, the same attitude is rarely applied to the nation as a whole. This proposition neglects the fact that the absence of natural resources, and even a poor location, must be considered as restraints to development. The existence of energy resources and minerals is crucial for industrialization. In their absence, it is not always possible to fall back on a modernized agriculture. Climate, terrain, fertility of the soil, and population pressures all have a bearing on the possibilities for commercialization and mechanization of the agricultural sphere. The lack of resources for industrialization does not automatically mean that resources for agricultural specialization will exist. In other words, alternative paths to economic development are not automatic; not only the motivation for development, but the capacity for development must be considered. When this is recognized, one can see that some countries may never become "modern." Economic scarcity exacerbates traditional mistrust in the society, and this impedes cooperation and association outside of the immediate family. The normal pressures of an increasingly mobilized population on political institutions are compounded under these conditions, since all resources in the society must be authoritatively allocated.

The general model of political development to be used in the following chapters looks upon the impact of change, whatever its source, as the independent variable; this impacts acts on the intervening variables to produce a specific kind of system. Both kinds of variables differ from country to country. Several alternative models that fall into the reconciliation and bureaucratic categories of Apter have been suggested as especially appropriate for the analysis of Greece and similar countries: the "prismatic" society of Riggs is one; military oligarchies are another; and consociational systems with an unstable equilibrium among various political sectors would be a third. These do not represent all possible systems that might fit the Apter formulation. They are simply types that seem particularly appropriate to the class of countries under discussion, both in terms of description and in terms of explaining system transformation.[83] It must be remembered that these are fluid systems, most particularly because they are not yet "modern"; and that the existing constraints on their development may prevent them from ever being so. Modern Greece provides an interesting focus for the application of these eclectic models, especially since no systematic investigation of her politics has yet been attempted. The few works dealing with Greece are concerned with technical issues of economic development, polemical politics, or mere summaries of current events. The simplest systematic description would fill a lacunae in political studies.

POLITICAL RECRUITMENT

The primary focus of this study will be on the way in which the Greek political system has accommodated change over the long run, and particularly on the way in which this change is reflected in changing patterns of socialization and recruitment. The theorists who have provided our model recognize the importance of these processes, and can again provide some useful formulations.

The process of socialization can be divided into several parts. The basic socialization process introduces the individual to the values, skills, role relationships and common knowledge necessary for all adult roles in his society. Political socialization introduces the individual to the political world; specifically political knowledge is imparted, and specifically political attitudes and values are acquired.[84] Political recruitment is the process of socialization and induction into particular political roles. It both reflects and affects the political system. On the one hand, it expresses the values of the society, the system of social stratification, and the actual representativeness of the political system; on the other, elite recruitment can affect political participation, the status hierarchy, and policy making itself.[85] The maintenance of a consociational system as outlined above, is particularly dependent on the character and attitudes of the political elites.

Political change can arise from many different causes, but it is almost always reflected in socialization and recruitment.[86] New values precipitated by new religious beliefs, for example, or changes in the economic system (especially the process of industrialization) have political ramifications that can easily be charted in this way. Old values are eroded, and new ones take their places. Old structures atrophy, and new roles and structures appear. Demands from new groups are directed to political channels. Invariably, discontinuities occur in the socialization process, as new elites seek entrance to the political level. The reaction of the political system may range from cautious adaptation to cataclysmic change.

In some settings, the political elite may manipulate socialization and recruitment processes directly, in order to promote or retard change from the beginning. The role of the family or the schools in the socialization process may be altered. The content of education itself is usually planned to inculcate attitudes and values congruent with the goals of the elite. The basis of eligibility for political roles may be specified. At other times, elite actions in one sphere may have unplanned consequences elsewhere. For example, an expansion of educational facilities without the corresponding development of an economic infrastructure to provide employment may create serious political problems. In these cases, too, the recruitment patterns change, but this time in response to the situation.

Almond and Powell separate political socialization and political recruitment from other political functions, calling them system maintenance and adaptation functions, respectively.[87] Discontinuities in the socialization process, provoked by conflicting attitudes and values held by the different socializing agents, may result in individual role conflicts that eventually have a disastrous impact on the whole society. The uneven impact of modernization or the existence of antagonistic subcultures maintained by separate socialization processes can also produce political conflict. For Almond and Powell, recruitment in any political system is based on some combination of achievement and ascription; modern societies stress the first and traditional the second. Regardless of orientation, recruitment cannot be wholly separate from socialization because the incumbent of a political role cannot completely escape his earlier socialization experiences.

Apter handles socialization and recruitment in his discussion of stratification patterns; and the several models he elucidates handles these processes, or react to them, in different ways.[88] In the mobilization model, the stratification pattern, including the basic values and recruitment criteria, is determined by the goals of the system, and by the necessity of redefining the basis of legitimacy. Modernizing autocracies or neo-mercantilist systems, both variants of Apter's bureaucratic model, are able to integrate the antagonistic elites. This is done either by dividing labor along functional lines or by expanding existing roles. However, the acceptance of new values and of political recruits from sectors holding these values depends on the compatibility of these new values with those already characteristic of the system. In a reconciliation model, competitive bargaining is likely to lead to the maintenance of separate socialization processes and the perpetuation of conflict. According to Apter, the modern sectors in this system cannot expand educational and economic opportunities quickly enough to prevent the fragmentation of the society. In this model, recruitment to each sector is ascription oriented in order to prevent the incursions of other sectors. Finally, Apter suggests that a complete analysis of stratification patterns, in-

cluding socialization and recruitment, must answer the following questions. (1) What is the effect of overall government policy on the various
roles in the power and prestige hierarchies? (2) How are the qualifications
for power and prestige roles altered by specific government actions? (3)
How responsive is the government to demands for social mobility? (4)
How coherent is the hierarchy in terms of ideology?[89]

Riggs also notes that every society must provide means for socializing its
members and for recruiting them into social and political roles.[90] In his prismatic model, the rate of assimilation to the symbol system of the dominant
elite varies. Several communities tend to arise, based either on indigenous
cultural differences or on the uneven impact of modernization, to challenge
the dominant group. These "deviant" communities, because of different
socialization experiences, both natural and imposed, have no way of gaining elite status and therefore embark on various kinds of hostile action. Recruitment to the top political roles, which are central and dominating in this
society, is based on ascriptive criteria in the sense that only members of the
dominant community are eligible; however, the actual men in top positions
are selected on a performance basis. Riggs calls this an "attainment" orientation.

After describing the processes of socialization and recruitment in a prismatic society, Riggs offers several hypotheses about the ability of such a
society to maintain itself. The narrower the communal base of elite recruitment, the greater the potential base for combative parties led by counter-
elite groups. Conversely, when the communal basis of elite recruitment is
relatively broad, it is difficult for combative parties to overthrow the regime.
In such contexts, the "parties" become more narrowly communal; demands
tend to focus on autonomy, and on special rights to the maintenance of
non-elite value systems. In this way, the cohesion of the deviant community
is maintained, and there are more opportunities for a man to gain "sub-
elite" status.

If Greece indeed represents a class of political systems that vacillate between the "consociational" variant of a reconciliation system and the military subtype of a more general bureaucratic model, as suggested earlier, my
focus on socialization and elite recruitment is particularly appropriate. In
both these general models, elite behavior is a crucial variable. Discontinuities in the socialization process, for whatever reason, may fragment the society. The character of the value systems, the size of the various subcultures,
and the resources of the political system as a whole may all determine the

manner in which the demands of new groups are met. Under certain conditions, aspiring elite groups are accepted and integrated into the top political roles in the system; in other instances, they are rejected and begin to work against the established elites and the regime they represent. Many of these processes are evident in the history of modern Greece.

As a whole, this book is a case study, a description and analysis of socialization and recruitment in a country characteristic of those that fall somewhere between the developed Western nations and the underdeveloped "new" nations. By the methods outlined in Appendix A (pp. 319–23), specific "communities" or subcultures in the Greek system were identified. The extent and pace of mobilization since 1843 were traced by analyzing the recruitment data of cabinet members. The more specific patterns of socialization and recruitment for political life as a whole in the last several decades were examined by using records for parliamentary candidates and deputies, and by a series of interviews with members of the 1964 Parliament. In addition to this empirical data, I have offered a general description of contemporary Greek politics and society, and have tried to trace the connections between the patterns of social mobilization of specific groups and the access of these groups to the political system. The final chapter suggests some possibilities for Greece's future development.

I. The Background of Greek Politics

1. The Character of Greek Society

A distinguished Greek parliamentarian, in assessing the problems faced by his nation, said that until Greeks could learn to trust one another, and to trust the government, political life would continue to be chaotic.[1] He might have added that a pervasive mistrust can cripple economic development as well. In studies of national development, an absence of trust is most often blamed on a lack of voluntary associations or cooperative enterprise.[2] At the most general level, it can be argued that the lack of trust often noted in transitional societies arises from the "juxtaposition of modern organizations and institutions with a society where a modern system of social roles has failed to develop."[3] Moreover, the existence of mistrust further inhibits the development of these modern social roles.

One effect of social mistrust is a strengthening of kinship ties. Edward Banfield, describing the southern Italian village of Montegrano, suggests that its extreme backwardness and poverty can be explained "largely (but not entirely) by the inability of the villagers to act together for their common good, or indeed, for any end transcending the immediate, material interest of the nuclear family."[4] He goes on to suggest that this inability arises from "amoral familism," which is produced by a combination of three factors: a high death rate, local land tenure conditions, and the absence of the institution of the extended family. But Banfield does not really explain why the institution of the extended family failed to develop; moreover, he is apparently describing a special case. Sidney Tarrow has marshaled substantial evidence to show that "southern Italians are strongly oriented toward the extended family as well as the nuclear family."[5] He believes that nuclear-family solidarity, Banfield's "amoral familism," is caused less by traditional loyalties than by a fear of destitution.[6] This formulation explicitly ties mistrust, and the resulting importance of the family, to economic scarcity. Certainly, this connection seems plausible in the case of modern

Greece. However, Tarrow does not explain why the nuclear family is the focus in some societies, and the extended family in others.

Not all states are equally endowed with natural resources, to be sure, but this factor alone cannot account for differences in levels of economic development. Almond and Powell argue that there is a logic to the process of development.[7] A system has to have adequate capabilities for resource extraction and for the regulation of the society before it can begin to distribute resources. As modern roles and structures are transplanted into a society that lacks a supporting infrastructure, a rush of demands for distribution overwhelms the capabilities of the system. Whatever the potential supply of resources, those available for immediate distribution are usually severely limited in any developing political system; and large segments of the population find their demands unmet and come to believe that the resources of the society are scanty. The perception of scarcity breeds insecurity, and ultimately distrust; and this, in turn, diminishes the possibility of cooperation for economic betterment or the attainment of other public purposes. Although there may be a question about the potential for economic development in Greece over the long run, the Greeks have always believed that resources were scarce, and this has been a cultural factor of great importance. An opposite situation also seems to be possible. Banfield, in contrasting Montegrano with St. George, a village in Utah, noted that the latter had fewer natural resources; yet this did not prevent the community from flourishing. Community cooperation and association were everywhere in evidence. The differences in behavior might be attributed to a particular local ethos; but the fact that the residents of St. George were geographically mobile and lived in a society of plenty would seem most significant.[8] Certainly, a major explanation for community cooperation and organizational proliferation in the United States has been the notion of abundance.[9]

In a transitional society, the lack of trust and the resulting underdevelopment of secondary organizations supposedly characteristic of modern societies increase the importance of the family or produce an extension in the form of clientage relationships. The institutions transplanted from modern societies, as well as demographic pressures, all make life more difficult for the individual and his family. The old pattern of subsistence agriculture is altered, peasant attitudes are shattered, and aspirations increase. The problem of facing the outside world becomes incomparably greater than before. Family cohesion in this setting is in the self-interest of every family member, since the identity of each person is established by the family. Moreover, family roles predominate in the economic and political spheres: the economic unit is the family; and the individual uses politics, either as a politician or as a voter, for family advantage.

Although the immediate future is perceived in family terms, it is recognized that one cannot realize this future without assistance from outside. The problem of extending loyalty beyond the family in order to satisfy family goals has been solved in similar ways by several transitional societies. One solution has been to create binding obligations to non-kinsmen through a spiritual tie, generally that of godfather. Another has been through friendship ties, especially between individuals of different status. As J. A. Pitt-Rivers has noted of Andalusia, friendship implies mutual liking and mutual confidence, but it also involves mutual service.[10] Where there is economic inequality such friendship can be described as a condition of patronage: "The institution of friendship, based upon the moral notion of equality and the free exchange of favour, builds up, in situations of material inequality, a structure of patronage which links up the authority of the state through the economic power of certain individuals to the network of neighborly relations."[11]

In practice the spiritual roles and the less formal connections can coexist. To quote Pitt-Rivers again: "In the changing kaleidoscope of friendship, the *compadrazgo* is an irrevocable tie of mutual trust, stronger than that of kinship because it owes its existence to the free consent of both parties."[12] Later, he notes a situation where a man is both godfather and patron. It is the second role that is important; it is, "above all, his relationship to the powers outside the pueblo which gives him value."[13] Tarrow, although suggesting that the Italian *compare* system is less important than its equivalent elsewhere, notes that "the godfather in southern Italy is usually a friend of the parent who does not have business ties with the family. He is a protector and confidant to the godchild, but his role may extend to eventual economic or political patronage."[14] In southern Italy the patronage tie between landholder and peasant or employer and laborer is more important. In another village study in the Mediterranean region of France, Laurence Wylie records that families attempted to secure godparents who might be of some practical help to the child in later life, but that this quest was rarely successful.[15]

Certainly, the social and political system of modern Greece cannot be understood without a knowledge of family roles and the clientage system. "Clienteles belonged to the corporate tradition of the Ottoman Empire."[16]

During the centuries of Turkish rule, it was customary for a local notable in Greece to intercede with the authorities on behalf of his fellow citizens. This role gave him added prestige, power, and wealth; the villagers gained a sponsor and security. There was some reciprocity, since it was recognized that the notable had a call on the service or loyalty of those for whom he did favors. Conversely, the notable had an obligation to protect the interests of those who entered into this relationship; thus the client maintained a certain self-respect. Clientage relationships played a predominant role in nineteenth-century Greece and continue today, particularly in the rural areas but also among some parts of the urban population.

It seems more appropriate to tie social mistrust in Greece—and the consequent emphasis on family loyalty mitigated only by clientage relationships —to a general sense of insecurity, rather than to economic scarcity alone. In early modern Greece, particularly after the expulsion of the Turkish landlords, pressures on the land do not seem to have been great; yet the clientage system flourished in this period.[17] Jean Grossholtz, in discussing the essential role of the family in Philippine society and the importance of family ties and clientage relationships, does not intimate that this importance developed out of a situation of scarcity.[18] In the Philippines, apparently, and more certainly in Greece, the initial impetus for clientage ties and extended-family solidarity came from a desire to isolate the individual and the family from extra-community forces. In both cases the political ruler of the country was alien, although this would not seem to be a crucial factor. Later, as modern structures and roles entered the society, the ties that had once served to isolate and protect the family unit were used to tie the individual to the political system. The patrons found that their clientage networks were useful for the acquisition of modern roles in the political or social system. For the clients, basic physical security was no longer the chief concern; but with population changes and greater aspirations, economic destitution or a reduction in status were greater threats, particularly since, in a transitional society, aspirations tend to outrun opportunities.[19] Thus family ties and clientage relationships, which lead to both the political and economic spheres, are exploited for reasons connected with social advantage rather than survival in a situation of scarcity.

In Greece, the content of the basic socialization process, although affected by modern geographical mobility and mass media, seems to have remained remarkably constant. The elements inculcating a sense of mistrust linger. As Tarrow suggests for southern Italy, family and local loyalties dominate because more extensive ties have been inhibited by the entire structural development of society.[20] The fact of uncertainty, regardless of its cause, brings an exaggerated belief in fortune, in both rural and urban areas. The world is in God's hands; there is nothing for the individual to do but face his existence.[21] Similar attitudes are found elsewhere, as in the Philippines: "The achievement of personal goals is in the hands of God, luck or higher authority, and the individual can only maintain good relations with these sources of help by showing respect and living up to his debts of gratitude."[22] Along with this distrust of the future comes a disregard for time. In this way, an unpredictable future can be postponed. In Greece, this is most evident in the villages, but even in the cities it is rare to find public clocks. Shopkeepers, housewives, and the government itself seem to operate with little concern for deadlines or schedules.

Greeks tend to be pessimistic about social change in part because of a sort of geographical determinism.[23] Moreover, attitudes toward politics tend to parallel the attitudes toward uncontrollable natural phenomena, such as rocky slopes, poor agricultural weather, occasional earthquakes, and even the fluctuations of the world market. In such a setting, existence is clearly seen as a struggle. From his earliest years, the Greek is plunged into a hostile world. Even in urban areas, an infant is thought to be vulnerable to evil supernatural forces, and the practice of child swaddling serves to protect the child physically and mentally. The young child is faced with similar human threats, even if they take the form of testing and teasing. Affection and permissiveness are accompanied by punishment and discipline. However, as in Banfield's Montegrano, gratification and deprivation depend on the whim of the one with power.[24] The constant use of deception on the young child soon educates him in its use, and there is no penalty attached to taking advantage of others in this manner. In essence, the Greek reaches adulthood well-grounded in the belief that he cannot trust anyone, or take any action at face value. This is not to imply that love and respect are not possible between the Greek child and his elders; but the whole pattern of socialization makes complete trust difficult.[25]

It is to the elementary family alone that the individual Greek owes his time, energy, and loyalty; any expenditure of these on outsiders would be disloyal. After subsistence, the most essential family need is to maintain a ratio between property and children; the accumulation of land and money is important, as is the ability to transmit this wealth.[26] There must be sufficient patrimony to provide for a continuation of the farm, form the daughters' dowries, and perhaps educate several children in a profession or trade. The family also feels it necessary to protect its members, even if they engage in admittedly deviant behavior. Freedom and self-dependence are family goals, not those of individuals. A Greek is always tied to his family, and this is not considered dependence; he is born into a place in the structured family, and all his associations with the outer world come through the family and its links to the outside.

The family itself may extend to second and third cousins, and sometimes relatives by marriage will be very important.* Since the family is the one stable element, questions of dowry, buying and selling of land, or providing an education for one of the sons must be discussed and decided by the entire family. The division of family fields, houses, or water rights often increases the economic interdependence of the family members.[27] However, since the family and not the individual is the basic unit, there is no effort at fair apportionment; one university education or one large dowry may be given, while the rest of the family impoverishes itself. These actions and the status they may produce will bring honor, and perhaps economic benefit, to the whole family.[28] Even within the family, however, there is distrust. Villagers take it for granted that impartiality cannot be found when personal interest is involved; therefore, when a distribution is made of family property, a Greek prefers that the decision be left to chance rather than to human decision.

In referring to Greek society in the first years of the kingdom, John Petropulos notes that "though its role varied from place to place according to custom, the family constituted not merely the basic social unit, but the fundamental economic and political unit as well."[29] This description is still valid today. Family members must join together to meet the threats from outsiders, and family cohesion is in the self-interest of every individual member. To deceive the state, strangers, or even associates is accepted, and often applauded as evidence of cleverness. Villagers do not often attempt to establish new or direct relationships with strangers, since the Greek is in a relationship of tension even with associates and neighbors. Other villages are described as inhospitable; strangers are equated with thieves. Social links between a man and his wife's relatives emerge only after the marriage contract is made final—in fact, the trickery and fear of treachery

* This differs from the situations in Andalusia and southern Italy described by Pitt-Rivers and Banfield, but is similar to that noted by Grossholtz in the Philippines. The difference may be due to the extent to which the outside world imposes itself on the local community.

that went along with betrothal and marriage in the past are only now disappearing in the most conservative areas. Nearly every rural household has a dog for protection, and even these efforts are not sufficient to guard unattended orchards and crops.[30] Village houses are so placed that events in all but a few are shielded from the eyes of the rest of the community.[31] Ernestine Friedl notes that when a rural Greek is hospitalized, relatives are in constant attendance to keep a check on the doctor and the treatment he prescribes.[32]

This state of affairs makes a genuine community loyalty difficult to achieve. The important family concerns are not bound up with the community, but lead out of the village through links with kinsmen living elsewhere. There are few instances when interests will be the same for every family; in most cases, it is almost a matter of every family against every other. There are issues that may provoke village enthusiasm or loyalty—competition with other villages for public works, for example, or community boundary problems. When community efforts are found, they can usually be attributed to an obvious congruence of public and private interest.

Although the immediate future is perceived in family terms—dowries, education, and marriage—it is recognized that a family cannot realize this future without outside assistance. There is a widespread feeling that the poor resources of Greece cannot supply enough of anything to satisfy the needs of all. The prosperity and good fortune of one family or person, therefore, threatens the continued existence and well-being of others. Under such conditions, most Greeks believe that government must ultimately distribute resources. However, family loyalty outweighs public feeling; it is commonly accepted that political office will be used to advance family or clientage interests. Public office was perhaps more blatantly exploited in earlier periods of Greek history than it is now, but family loyalties still seem to predominate. Today, a man who has a favorable position in government—or in business, for that matter—may not be expected to distribute income to his less fortunate relatives, or to find places for all his cousins and nephews. However, he will certainly give special attention to their demands on the institution of which he is a part, or will transmit their demands to those institutions with which he has personal ties.[33]

Politics in Greece, besides being a desirable occupation in a society with few opportunities, is essential for settling individual economic conflicts and for tempering administrative exactions. Public office is highly valued for the advancement of private interests. Naturally, even though favoritism and nepotism are expected, the distrust of the state as an institution is reinforced. As the traditional portion of the population diminishes, the political system is confronted with an increased volume of widely varying demands. More and more individual demands for prestige and wealth, or aspirations for power, must be directed at the political system.[34] Neither the individual nor his family can deal with the outside world alone; consequently, in Greece as in other transitional societies, some links beyond those of kinship are necessary. The most obvious patron, assuming a person is not related to someone of prominence in the community, has been the *kumbaros,* the godfather to a man's children and the best man at their weddings. When a family searches for a kumbaros, although social equals or even relatives may be selected, the usual choice is a person with wealth and position that will be a source of potential help for the parents and their children. The patron-client relationship was thus formalized to create an artificial relationship with a series of mutual obligations built on religious connotations.[35] The kumbari relationship leads from the countryside to the town, and is most often a relationship of unequals in the social as well as the economic sense. The kumbaros is not likely to be a person one would exchange labor with in the local fields; instead, he is most often consulted for advice on activities not centered at the village level, such as education, marriages, and dealings with the state. It is difficult for anyone to refuse the role of kumbaros because of its religious implications. In early modern Greece there was another relationship, called "fraternal friendship," in which two men swore to defend each other for life. This formal bond was often used in the organization of the secret revolutionary society, the Philiki Hetairia.[36]

In the history of the Greek political system, the traditional ties provided a basis for the factionalism of the Revolutionary period and the two following decades, and meshed well with the new representative institutions, which were introduced in 1844 and further developed in 1863. Local notables were able to mobilize support for their political careers on the basis of mutual obligations; and several nineteenth-century politicians were reputed to number godchildren in the thousands. Today, it is still useful, both politically and commercially, to have a large number of clients bound to your support in this manner. A family well established in politics is likely to have a traditional involvement with many neighboring villagers. Once a peasant becomes accustomed to dealing with one prominent family, it is easier to continue this relationship than to switch one's ties to another family. As the rural areas became aware of government—for example, when the state imposed taxes and drafted young men—patrons were utilized to mitigate the effect of these government demands on the individual. This relationship allowed persons with little knowledge or appreciation of the political system to become a part of the political process. For his part, a notable was forced to bargain on the national level to obtain favors for constituents and to maintain his own position and power; to do so, he formed similar reciprocal relations with those more influential than he.

The clientage relationship has roots in the Greek notion of *philotimo,* or "self-esteem." This is respect accorded the individual as a person, not because of his status or achievements. Self-esteem is the essential element in undertanding individual actions; in all probability, it is the aspect of Greek life that is often interpreted as democratic. The individual's personal being, his status within a family or village, and his very Greekness rest upon this self-esteem. In a relationship of leader and followers, there is a division of responsibility that cannot be understood solely in hierarchical terms. The essence of philotimo is inviolability and freedom, and it is damaged whenever events or people impose upon the inner emotions of the individual. If this happens, there is sure to be retaliation. Sanders suggests that Greek nationalism rests upon this base. Every Greek shares equally in the country's glorious past; to equate the low standard of living with backwardness would violate both the individual philotimo and national self-esteem.[37]

Greek behavior is limited in many ways by a fear of appearing ridiculous. Few villagers would become involved in work such as carpentry or mechanics for this reason; few who are not "professional" would dream of running for public office. Jokes are made even at the expense of people who run for minor parties that have no chance of winning. This is one result of the Greeks' intense individualism. It is not expected that one should know how to do more than one kind of work, and specialization is another way of differentiating oneself from one's neighbor.[38]

The traditional Greek value of philotimo and the Greek clientage system have meshed well with the theory and institutions of modern representative democracy; because of this, tradition is still strong in Greece. A century ago, Greece was a country with a largely unmobilized peasantry led by a small elite. There have been changes, but the attitudes and practices described by early travelers are much like those described by modern sociologists working in rural Greece. The relatively modest urbanization, the impact of the refugees, and the events of World War II and after did not dissipate these rural attitudes. For one thing, scarcity is as important a factor in the urban as in the rural setting. Large-scale urbanization is a relatively recent phenomenon in Greece, and may be just as easily thought of as a "ruralization" of the cities. These factors make the rural bias of the sociological material less crucial. Friedl notes that the rural and urban components of kinship groups are kept in constant contact because of the practice of making many decisions "family" decisions and spending considerable time in discussing them. The modern communication network makes continuous visiting between urban and rural relatives feasible, and thus maintains family ties and traditional values.[39] Calliope Moustaka notes that great numbers of guests from rural areas are found in town dwellers' apartments.[40]

Although family ties remain important now, it is possible that second- or third-generation urban dwellers may not maintain them. Patron-client relationships are most characteristic of the rural areas, but moving to the city does not entirely extinguish them, even though they are more difficult to maintain. However, a native urban dweller is less likely to know a suitable patron in the city. His demands will be greater, and more difficult to satisfy through the usual clientage structures. The decline of traditional, family-oriented patronage ties is an important cause of change in the Greek political system.

2. The Development of the Modern Greek State

Today, the Greek War of Independence is commemorated on March 25. On this day in 1821, Bishop Germanos, the Metropolitan of Patras, raised the standard of revolt at a monastery in the northern Peloponnesus. This date, however, is primarily a matter of historical convenience, for the revolution began as a scattering of largely unconnected outbursts against the Ottoman rulers. The conditions facilitating and encouraging the insurrection, its immediate motivations, and its ultimate goals—insofar as they were considered—varied with the place and the participants.[1] There had been innumerable abortive outbursts in Greece before, the last important one in 1770. In 1821, the precise catalysts for individual clashes may not have been different; but conditions in the first decades of the nineteenth century facilitated the spread of insurrections. By 1821, the once efficient Ottoman administration had suffered a marked decline.[2] Policies and appointments at all levels tended to be decided by bribes and favoritism. Administrators on the periphery of the Empire were almost independent; but since their tenure was uncertain, they tended to be rapacious and to enrich themselves as quickly as possible. C. M. Woodhouse notes that in this period, "of the two elementary functions of government, security and justice, they [the Greeks] were assured of neither."[3]

This situation was not new in itself. In fact, uneven justice had up to this point helped to prevent concerted action by the Greek people. If conditions were intolerable in one part of Greece, they were better somewhere else; moreover, they would probably improve with the next administrator. Actually, the Ottoman administration had so far been preferred to others, probably because traditional institutions were left intact: for example, the Greek population in the Peloponnesus generally applauded the Turkish reconquest from the Venetians in 1715.[4] In 1821, however the various injustices became intolerable enough to produce armed insurrection, and other factors intervened to facilitate its continuance.

For several decades before the revolution, foreign influences on Greece had been growing in diversity and intensity. The Russians, using the ties of Orthodox Christianity, had early become active agents in Greece. In fact, the insurrection of 1770 was touched off, in part, by their propaganda activities, which, if nothing else, acquainted the Greeks with an alternative to Ottoman rule.[5] Western European influence was also significant. Up to this point, the Greeks within the Empire, smarting from memories of Western actions in the crusades and the tension between Pope and Patriarch, had generally been hostile to the West.[6]

Commerce within the Ottoman Empire had been carried on by the non-Moslem groups—particularly the Greeks, who eventually obtained a near-monopoly of shipping in the eastern Mediterranean. On land, professional corps of *agoyates,* or mule drivers, led caravans between the areas of Greek settlement. The commodities they carried were significant, but the news and ideas they spread were ultimately more important.[7] Similarly, the Orthodox church hierarchy, especially the monks, were a mobile element during this period. This expansion of commerce brought contact with Western Europe during a period of intellectual ferment in the West, the Enlightenment; and trade continued to grow during the period of the French Revolution. Greeks who were successful in commerce and trade secured positions in Europe for their sons, financed European educations for other promising young men, or opened local schools with Western curricula.[8] The renewed European interest in classical literature and art, assisted by a rash of travel accounts and several archaeological discoveries, together with the growing influence of German nationalist writers such as Fichte and Herder, made the Greeks in Europe and their cousins at home more conscious of their classical heritage and cultural identity.

The French Revolution, the Empire, and the circumstances of the final French defeat all had consequences for Greece. First, the ideas and practices of the French Revolution were transmitted through both literary and political channels. The intellectual traffic alone was considerable; but for many Greeks, the experiences of their compatriots in the Ionian Islands were more important. These islands had been ruled by Venice for some time, during which a modicum of Western influence had always been transmitted to the parts of Greece under Ottoman control. They came under French control for two years following the dissolution of the Venetian Republic in 1797. From 1799 to 1807, the Russians controlled the islands, at least nominally; during the liberal period of Alexander I, the first independent Greek state of modern times, the Heptanesian Republic, was formed. After a short French restoration resulting from the peace of Tilsit, the islands became a British protectorate.[9] Throughout this period, the Ionian Islands were a place of refuge for Greeks fleeing the Turks; here they were introduced to European administrative forms, as well as to Western values and ideals.

Other factors contributed to the widespread dissatisfiaction with the status quo in Greece. There was increasing pressure on the land, especially in the Peloponnesus. Ownership had become concentrated in the hands of a relatively few Turkish and Greek landlords. Since the alienation of Turkish lands was forbidden, the Greek landlords and the land-hungry Greek tenants, despite basic differences of interest, could combine against the Turks.[10] In addition, the maritime dislocations of the Napoleonic period produced an economic crisis in Greek shipping centers. Although this initially produced cleavage along class lines, the opportunities for plunder and enrichment in a war against the Turks unified the interests of capitalists, captains, and sailors.[11] In continental Greece, there was a long-smoldering conflict between the landholding notables and bands of irregulars from the mountains as each competed for Turkish favor. Moreover, since this area was poorer, Greek tenants were pressed more severely, creating another set of tensions.[12]

Events elsewhere also contributed much to the success of the revolution. The Serbs had revolted in 1804, and had gained, initially, an independent position within the Empire. More significantly, Ali Pasha, the Lion of Yannina, had virtually turned his Ottoman province in the Epirus into an independent state. Not only was his achievement instructive, but the Imperial effort to subdue him drew Ottoman forces from the Peloponnesus and continental Greece, creating an initial advantage for Greek conspirators.[13] Furthermore, there were conflicts in other parts of the Ottoman realm. Uprisings in the Lebanon, a war with Persia, and active incursions into the Sudan and Arabia by that recalcitrant subordinate of the Sultan, Mohammed Ali of Egypt kept the Imperial government fully occupied.

The Philiki Hetairia, a secret society for the liberation of Greece, was founded in 1814 by Greeks in Odessa. The bourgeois founders, with a Western secular outlook, were hostile to things Byzantine. They looked with distaste upon the Phanariots, Greeks in the Ottoman administrative service; they also viewed the church as corrupted because of its association with the Turks. The Phanariot prince Alexander Ypsilantis, who provoked disorders

in Rumania with the hope of starting a general uprising against the Ottomans, was the formal leader of the movement, which eventually gained a
membership estimated at 200,000.[14] Its first concern was the freeing of the
Greeks from Ottoman domination, but its ultimate aims were less clear.
One vision included the creation of a modern, independent state, but appeals to many Greeks promised a reconstructed Byzantium. The goals of
the movement became so diffuse that the organization served as a vehicle
for all Greeks opposed to the Turks, whatever their reasons. The insurrec-
tionists of 1821 were all affected in some way by the Philiki Hetairia. Hetairist agents had been active in the Peloponnesus and the island shipping
centers; their influence had touched some in the more inaccessible mountain
regions of continental Greece as well. The high clergy, if not actively involved, at least knew of the organization.

Because of these changes in the intellectual, social, and economic environment, tolerance of the Ottoman rule vanished. Petropulos notes that in the
decade prior to the outbreak "virtually no one argued for Ottoman rule.
Opinions differed only on matters of timing and planning."[15] Fundamentally, there were two incompatible visions of the future Greece. One view
assumed that the Greeks would come to inherit the Ottoman Empire intact; and that Byzantium would be restored as Greeks came to occupy more
and more of the important state offices. The other favored secession and the
formation of an independent state. Moreover, the partisans of each goal
were a mixture of modern and traditional elements.[16] Initially, the incom-
patibility of these ultimate aims was not always apparent, and the contra-
dictions among the insurgents were not developed.

Two broad groups within the Greek nation owed their positions to the
Ottoman rulers: the high clergy and the Phanariot Greeks who served in
the central state administration or as governors of various provinces in European Turkey. The other groups eventually involved in the revolution—the
Peloponnesian notables, the island capitalists, and the mountain chieftains—
drew their strength from local connections. Only after the French Revolution did a rift develop between the Phanariots and the high clergy. During
the Enlightenment, both had been active importers of Enlightenment ideals,
manners, and knowledge. However, in the wake of the Russian reaction to
the Revolution changes occurred in the Orthodox hierarchy. Ultimately, a
renewed hostility to things Western and an obscurantist educational policy
developed.[17] Western influence was again viewed as a threat to the purity
of the faith and the authority of the clergy. The Phanariots, on the other
hand, maintained their Western ties and secular outlooks.

The Phanariots had parlayed their knowledge of Europe, gained from commercial ventures, into high administrative positions. They were indispensible once the Ottoman Empire began to interact with Europe on a regular basis. As they acquired more importance with the decline of the Empire, they began to aspire to ultimate control. Although they were modernists, purveyors of nationalist doctrines, they mistook Orthodoxy for a uniting force. For example, Alexander Ypsilantis, the Phanariot head of the Philiki Hetairia, was unable to rouse the Orthodox Rumanian peasantry to enthusiasm for the revolution because Greek prelates and princes were their immediate oppressors. Once the revolution began, the Phanariots, involved because the Sultan also assumed that religion was the line of division between the loyal and disloyal, were deprived of their influence.

The Ottoman Empire had used religion as an organizing principle. This assured the preservation of the Greek language and faith, but it was a bar to specifically Greek national feeling. The Orthodox clergy at this time, with few exceptions, were not nationalists. The Patriarch of Constantinople in 1821 ruled a theocratic state within the Ottoman Empire that included all Orthodox Christians, not merely the Greeks. Within the Christian community, however, the Greeks had an acknowledged supremacy. The clergy had far-reaching judicial, fiscal, and administrative powers; authority in these spheres, derived from the Ottoman Sultan, was delegated by the Patriarch to other levels of the religious hierarchy.[18] In regions of homogeneous Greek population, this meant virtual self-government. The clergy were the cultural and spiritual leaders, as well as the possessors of governing authority, and thus had enormous influence in the Greek community. But they were successful only because they were patronized by the Ottoman administration and because they advised and defended the Greek population. The higher clergy and the monastic orders from which it came were generally held in low esteem by much of the Greek population. Since the clergy was charged with carrying out the demands of the Turks, its occasional unpopularity was not surprising. The church itself was generally corrupt at the higher levels, since rank here, as elsewhere in Ottoman society, was obtained by bribery and not ability. At the lower levels the priests were as illiterate and uninformed as most of their parishioners.

The ecclesiastical interests of the Greek church were more powerful than national feeling; and for the clergy, the revolution was simply another round in the struggle of Orthodoxy and Islam. Initially the church expected deliverance by the armies of Russia, or at least Russian intervention under the guise of protecting Orthodoxy. The Patriarch of Constantinople denounced the Philiki Hetairia when it became evident that the revolution was not countenanced by the Russian government. In addition, the anti-ecclesiastical opinions and westernizing sentiments of the local hetairist leaders and some of the military chiefs made influential churchmen feel that the Sultan was more likely to protect their privileges than any new secular Greek state. The high clergy and the Sultan had a common purpose in attempting to separate Greek nationalism from the cause of the Orthodox church; however, in a system of government by hostage, the clergy paid with their lives for not preventing the spread of the nationalist virus.

The major groups intent on gaining a new Byzantium lost control of events. The revolution, after the initial outbreaks had been quelled, lingered only in parts of the Greek nation over which they had little control. The clergy, because of its dependence on the Turks, denounced the revolution and in consequence lost all authority in those areas where fighting still raged.[19] The Phanariots, having confused Orthodoxy with Greek nationalism, also suffered a crushing defeat. They were left to trickle into independent Greece as refugees. The Philiki Hetairia faded into the past, although Demetrius Ypsilantis, the brother of its former chief, became a temporary rallying point during the revolution. Despite the propagandizing successes of the Hetairia, the commercial class, concentrated as it was along the coasts of the Black Sea and Asia Minor, or in Constantinople and the other major cities of the eastern Mediterranean, was unable to exercise much control over revolutionary activities in Greece. They provided the impulse to revolution, but they were unable to lead it. In the long run, the governmental form they desired was imposed by the Great Powers. However, these same Great Powers excluded the commercial middle class, the most modern part of the Greek nation, from the territory of the new Greek state.

The Greeks who merely sought an independent state were divided between modernizers and traditionalists. On the one hand were the few middle-class elements who admired Western values and institutions: the Greek graduates of Western schools, the sons of traders, merchants and capitalists, and several representatives of the traditional notables, who looked forward to the creation of a modern state on the European model. The westernizers, who were joined by the Phanariot refugees once the revolution had commenced, favored nationalism, centralization, bureaucratic structures, and even constitutionalism.[20] However, these men were in a small minority, especially in the areas that ultimately became the nucleus of the Greek state. A second group, divided along regional lines, was primarily interested in eliminating the Turk, the cause of their inferior status and insecurity. Since many of these men enjoyed Ottoman patronage, they were at first hesitant. However, as Woodhouse notes, they were dragged into the fray by the "enthusiasm of the lower levels of the population," who were ignorant of the odds against them.[21] These indigenous leaders did not intend that the existing power relationships among Greeks should be upset. Ottoman administrative forms would remain; only the incumbents would change. They had no vision of a modern state on the European model, and were largely hostile to Western values and institutions.

The Peloponnesus, or Morea, was the most important part of insurgent Greece. It was the primary production unit, and an important source of taxation. Strictly speaking, there was no aristocracy in Greece; it had been exterminated by the original Ottoman conquest. There was an equality of status in that all Greeks and Orthodox Christians were viewed as inferior to Moslems. Beyond this, the Moslem conquest had improved the condition of the rural population in the Peloponnesus, since the serfdom inherited from the Byzantine Empire and continued by the Franks was destroyed. However, the fact that the Ottoman government employed Greeks as administrators over other Greeks did restore status distinctions. Greek traditions of local autonomy under elders and notables were continued because they fit the Ottoman system of indirect government and served the fiscal needs of the Empire. The tax contribution of each Peloponnesian province—and subsequently, of every district and commune—was fixed by the Turks. As long as it was paid, there was little contact with Ottoman authorities. The clergy and the lay leaders, ordinarily selected by acclamation or election (though only by a part of the commune), were a buffer between the Greek community and the Ottoman provincial administration, which was continually modified by policy needs and personality clashes. The village elders selected men to represent them at the district level; from this assembly, in turn, representatives were sent to the next higher administrative unit. Finally, two Greeks remained as advisers to the pasha assigned to administer the Peloponnesus and two more represented Peloponnesian interests in Istanbul.

The very nature of the positions assigned to the Greeks in the Peloponnesus limited the candidates to local notables, men of wealth and stature in the community. The patronage of the Ottoman administration further enhanced their positions. Ultimately, the major notables, or "primates," became an "aristocracy" of tax farmers. They generally adopted the style of life of their Ottoman overlords, with entourages that occasionally rivaled those of their masters. The Peloponnesian primates were self-perpetuating through intermarriage and other bonds, even though challenges at the local level sometimes caused disruptions.[22] Local primates guaranteed tax collections, and served as hostages for the good behavior of the Greek community as well. But in return for these risks they enjoyed a high status within the community, exercised considerable discretion in local government, and were well-off financially. In addition, since taxes were collected in kind, the primate class, by the end of the eighteenth century also had a considerable interest in commerce.[23]

The local Greek authorities in the Peloponnesus, then, could not agree completely with the aims of the revolution. However, once the hetairist agents had roused the peasantry against the small minority of Moslems in the area, the notables were compelled to assume the leadership of the revolt, since the Ottomans recognized only religion as a line of cleavage. Once the first blows had been struck, the primates hastened to assume the authority of the murdered Moslem officials, and to enhance their own power and position with public funds. Once mobilized, they often forced reluctant peasants to participate also. The primates in authority were faced by challenges to their continued supremacy from elements in the peasantry, from rival groups of notables, and especially from the Greek military, the captains formerly employed for personal and community security.[24] During the revolution, authority finally gravitated to those with military power rather than formal position.

The military chieftains who formed the elite group in the mountainous districts of continental Greece did not at first react to the revolution. The hetairist agents had not been as numerous or as successful in these precincts; and there was no intermediate layer of Ottoman authorities in these regions, which were under the direct control of the Imperial government. As early as the eighteenth century, these areas were described as a "hotbed of chronic insurgency."[25] There were few Moslems here; the inhabitants, largely of Albanian stock, were only imperfectly assimilated into the Greek nationality. At times, the chieftains of the numerous irregular armed groups in the area had an official role as *armatoloi*, or military commanders with control over armed communities. In this capacity, they were employed to keep order in the mountain regions. However, when not acting officially, they were generally characterized as *klephs*, or brigands, and were considered to be enemies of all established authority, Greek and Turkish alike.

The leadership in continental Greece was selected on the basis of personal qualities. Martial values were exalted, and others were depreciated. In the years prior to the revolution, the Ottoman government had declined to employ some of these groups, and instead had favored the local primates. When this happened, the armatoloi naturally returned to their traditional banditry and became a scourge to the agricultural population of the plains, Christians and Moslems alike. The revolution thus allowed the continental military chiefs to regain a formerly held position; they were accorded the status of revolutionaries once the rebellion commenced, and several chiefs eventually achieved national leadership. While some version of national consciousness eventually penetrated here, the major concerns were only tenuously connected with the form of future government or the goals of the new state. Most military chieftains were concerned primarily with extending their personal control over adjacent territories.[26]

The several islands off the Attic coast and individual islands in the Aegean, such as Psara and Kasos, also aided the independence movement. Theoretically, these islands were under the control of the Admiral of the Ottoman Fleet; in practice, they were left under the local authorities as long as taxes were paid and peace kept. The local power structures varied from the extreme oligarchy of Hydra to the democracy of Psara. However, only in Hydra and Spetsai were merchant capitalists clearly distinguishable from landed proprietors. In these islands, the outbreak of the revolution coincided with economic distress; under these conditions, the propaganda spread by the hetairist agents found fertile ground, especially among the unemployed sailors. Regardless of the local power structure, the possibility of plundering vessels and towns belonging to the Turks was enough to bring many islanders to the side of the revolution. There was no necessity to eliminate a hostile majority, since no Moslems lived on the islands. On one island after another, the wealthy oligarchs were forced into revolt, often against their will.[27] Here, the revolution tended to have a democratic character, since the wealth gained from plundering the Turks threw up a new leadership to replace the old. The last years of the conflict found plunder outweighing national feeling as a motivation, and the islanders became pirates parading as revolutionaries.

Although each region, and each of the diverse groups within it, often put self-interest first, the Turks (and later Europeans) viewed them as participants in a common enterprise. The longer the revolution lasted, the greater the sense of nationalism that developed. Even so, the Greeks were divided. The revolutionary battles were primarily a series of skirmishes under local leadership; no great national leader appeared. It was impossible to produce any central institutions with the power to lessen sectionalism; in fact, every effort was made to retain local autonomy because it was feared that any central government would merely reinstitute the taxations of the Empire. Moreover, the thought of subordination to a fellow Greek apparently was a distasteful one to all the various leaders.

THE FIRST MODERN GREEK STATE

The First Greek National Assembly met at Epidaurus in December 1821. It was composed of representatives from the regional governments, and produced a constitution providing for a central government that did not actually disturb the local basis of oligarchical power or mitigate interregional jealousy.[28] The only area in which it could operate, the Peloponnesus, was firmly in the hands of the local primates. The Second National Assembly, with a more heterogeneous membership, resolved itself into two camps, military and civilian. The ensuing feud between the legitimate government and certain military leaders was soothed by the arrival of a European loan; but it later flared again, and resulted in the invasion of the Peloponnesus by armed irregulars from continental Greece.[29] Order broke down; Greece's military incapacity and the faults of her leadership threatened the success of the independence movement. Politics and war came to revolve about regionally based factions with both civilian and military components. A further complication was the involvement of foreign powers in factional conflict. The more perceptive rebels recognized that central authority of some type was necessary to resolve these anarchic conditions, but no indigenous leader could be put in a position of overlordship. In 1827, after several years of sectional bickering, the Third National Assembly, representing a superficially unified country, appointed foreign officers to command the naval and military forces. More important, the Assembly invited an outsider, Count John Capodistrias, a native of Corfu who had served Alexander I of Russia, to accept the Presidency of the country. This appointment reflected the necessity of securing foreign confidence, which in turn required that internal factionalism be quelled.[30]

Capodistrias came to Greece as a liberal, as a man imbued with the ideals of the Enlightenment, and as a friend of Russia. He sought a bureaucratic, unitary state, "administering an enlightened law code with the concurrence of the propertied classes in the interests of all the people."[31] Capodistrias was opposed to both oligarchs and revolutions; his goals and methods seemed most appropriate to a benevolent despot. In contemporary terms, his was to be a tutelary regime. He had great faith in Western education, but he also favored adherence to the traditional religious beliefs and cultivation of the Greek language in order to preserve Greek nationality. The creation of an internal administration and the general reconstruction of the country- side required, in Capodistrias's opinion, a central authority with absolute power. However, his assessment of Greek leadership, although it justified his own assumption of power, did little to advance the cause of unity. He called the primates "Christian Turks; the military chiefs, robbers; the men of letters, fools; the Phanariots, children of Satan."[32] Capodistrias asked for and received a mandate for a constitutional dictatorship from the Third National Assembly in 1828. After this, he worked to create a centralized state: first, because it indicated a desirable level of modernity; and second, because it would undermine the positions of his regional opponents. At the same time he attempted to transfer the loyalties of the peasants from the untrustworthy local oligarchs to himself.

However, Capodistrias was unable to overcome regional animosity and factionalism without creating his own political faction, which was based on the old Russian-oriented faction of the Peloponnesus and backed by the bureaucratic machinery of the state, both civil and military. He gave re- sponsible positions to Greeks from outside the insurgent areas, who would be dependent on him alone. He encouraged local opposition in the fiefdoms of his major regional opponents. Although attempting to modernize and consolidate the state, he did not alter the usual forms of Ottoman adminis- tration (e.g., the system of land tax and the practice of tax farming) in those regions where the local leaders were personally loyal to him. Beyond this, he attempted to create some mass support; and even dedicated enemies ac- knowledged his popularity.[33] He attempted, unsuccessfully, to build a mid- dle class that would support his vision of the Greek elite. At the same time, he hoped to encourage an independent peasantry by distributing to veterans property seized during the war. The suffrage laws were revised to exclude a property qualification; universal male suffrage, operating through the filter of indirect elections, created an Assembly largely subservient to the President. Eventually Capodistrias's modernization involved little more than securing the loyalty of regional chiefs, and if this failed, attempting to secure the personal loyalty of their clients. Local and disconnected dissatis- factions eventually became a widespread opposition to centralization. This opposition, with the news of the establishment of the July Monarchy in

France, was legitimatized under a "constitutional" label. There is some evidence that prior to his assassination in October 1831 by a disaffected Peloponnesian clan leader Capodistrias may have been planning to "manage universal suffrage to elect himself sovereign of Greece."[34]

The attempts of Capodistrias to create a political system based on personal loyalty to himself failed. Despite all his efforts, most individual Greeks remained loyal to more local leaders, since there was no tradition of any more overriding loyalty. Indeed, the armed masses were not politically aware enough to take a stand on constitutional issues.[35] At this time there may have been a vague demand for some governmental system; but the options of a reconstituted Hellenic empire, a resurrected Byzantium, or a modern state were not part of the consciousness of most Greeks. Greece was defined in local terms, or in religious terms only; to be a Greek was to be distinguished from a Turk. A modern Greek nationalism had not yet developed, and personal and factional conflict remained the rule. European politics provided political labels for the contending factions in Greece, but the actual struggles remained traditional.

THE TUTELARY REGIME OF THE BAVARIANS

The demise of Capodistrias gave renewed impetus to international intrigue. A provisional settlement was reached in 1832, when the Great Powers guaranteed Greece's sovereignty, stipulated that the new state would be a monarchy, and found their own candidate for the throne. Otho, Prince of Bavaria, became the King of Greece. At this time, the kingdom could hardly be called a state, for central authority did not exist. From the first, the Bavarian regency for the young king, and later the king himself, attempted to modernize the Greek political system. They also sought to overcome regional and party jealousy through a highly centralized administration, and to substitute loyalty to the monarch for party feeling. However, their efforts, like those of Capodistrias, did not reduce Greek factionalism. The regency, and finally the monarch himself, were drawn into factional conflict.

The problems of extending central control in Greece were almost insurmountable. The factions rested on the pervasive clientage structures in Greek society, and the only way to control them was to create conditions that would make the patron-client tie unnecessary. In short, Greece needed a modern political system, with fair and impartial administration in all spheres of life, as well as a flourishing economy that could provide opportunities in other than the governmental sphere. However, a modern system of this kind could not be created as long as clientage ties existed, for such relationships would by their nature undermine the modern structures. This paradox was not widely appreciated at the beginning. The Bavarians assumed that the goals of westernization were widely accepted; they misunderstood the nature of the clientage system, underestimated its consequences, and glossed over the involvement of the Great Powers in clientage structures.

The regency brought in several regiments of highly skilled Bavarian troops, as well as administrative specialists to man the newly created institutions. At the same time measures to undermine the presumed basis of the indigenous Greek leadership were undertaken. The existing Greek military establishment was severely shaken up, and the Greek irregulars were disbanded without much attention to pensions or promised land grants. Similarly, the church was subjected to government authority, and much of its land was taken over by the state. The government instituted a system of central appointments down to the provincial and district level, and officials with no personal ties were preferred at all levels. Finally, a check-and-balance system was created as administrative authority was divided into competing jurisdictions. There were plans to change the financial system by eliminating tax farming and basing taxes on land values established by auction prices rather than productivity.[36] More direct moves were made against the factions themselves. Officially, the state took no notice of the various parties. The major party figures were removed from their strongholds by requiring them to hold honorific posts in Athens or abroad; there were further attempts to undermine the authority of party leaders by the appointment of their lieutenants to official posts. In addition, the original Bavarian plan included placating the factions by distributing appointments in proportion to the size and power of each faction. As a last resort, armed force was to be used against internal opponents.[37]

The regency's policies were not successful. First, they were not carried out; the regency itself favored first one and then another faction or foreign power. None of the measures to separate the native elite from its clients were very successful either; in fact, these measures only served to make the factions more cohesive and to undermine the centralizing policies of the state. The extension of authority and the staffing of the new administration was the focus of all political activity. Each faction, with its chain of clients, was mainly occupied with finding government office, since there were few other opportunities. Even professional training was preparatory to public office, from which livelihood, prestige, and protection from the rapaciousness of others in official position could all be acquired.[38] Staffing the government with foreigners created widespread dissatisfaction; yet only foreigners were deemed immune from factional loyalty. As centralization proceeded, pressures for office were more severe, because livelihood, prestige, and protection were even more dependent on it.

The central administration created on paper never functioned as intended: clientage groups penetrated the bureaucracy, obliterating the system of checks and balances; subordinates undermined official actions. Because it was committed to Western legal norms, the Bavarian regime was at a loss to deal with the activities deemed permissible by Greek tradition. Its opponents resorted to rioting, outbreaks of brigandage, and abusive newspaper campaigns to force the government to change personnel or policies.[39] The government was in part responsive, but the nature of these demands was not understood. The Bavarian officials could not operate in the Greek context; as they adapted their techniques and goals, their original aims of westernization and modernization were compromised. Many devices were tried: tax farming; the creation of loyal patrons and clients; the development of the Royal Phalanx, an organization to occupy dissatisfied revolutionary veterans; and the distribution of honor, position, and patronage to Greek party figures. Fundamentally, a political machine capable of ruling was not created—yet any attempts to rule through an existing Greek faction were avoided.

Otho himself, when he came of age and discarded his Bavarian advisers, attempted to rule by absolute methods. "The monarchy, rather than a constitution, would educate the people to exercise their political duties and would guarantee them, likewise, from the tyranny of their former Greek masters."[40] Otho was personally popular, and the monarchy itself was a symbol of unity and a hope for territorial expansion. But Otho, too, was faced with the problem of creating a central administration in the traditional Greek setting; and by and large, his efforts were no more successful than those of his former advisers. The regency had attempted to use the factions; Otho tried to balance the existing factions by his distribution of patronage, and to prevent common action by the factions or the foreign powers. He appointed Greeks with no local ties; but his appointees often used the opportunities of public office to create a following of their own.

By the beginning of 1841, it was painfully evident that the Crown had failed in two of its most persistent efforts over the previous eight years. It had not established an efficient and impartial administration. It had not weakened the political parties. If anything, administration had grown progressively worse and the parties even stronger.[41]

At this point, international pressure especially a sudden demand for repayment by all guarantors of loans to the Greek state, forced a disastrous curtailment of internal expenditures. The civil service was cut, much of the military demobilized, and potential sources of political support alienated. Even worse the united demands of the "protecting" powers unified the internal opposition to the government.[42]

In form, the Greek kingdom was similar to a colonial administration. Initially, only Bavarians or other foreigners held positions of authority. All appointments and revenue remained the prerogative of the king; there was no constitution or representative assembly, and the participation of Greeks in the formal decision-making structures of the kingdom was negligible. However, absolute authority in theory could not alter the fact that in practice the traditional clientage structure effectively resisted its application. Any attempt to extend administration to the rural areas, no matter how minimal or unsuccessful, upset the traditional elites. Temporary loyalty in the traditional Greek pattern might come from the royal bestowal of public office or other favors, but as yet there was little loyalty to the Greek kingdom or to the king himself. The bulk of the population was not aware of either the kingdom or the king. The state boundaries were arbitrary, and individual horizons did not extend beyond the local community. For the elite elements a king with a different religion, small knowledge of Greek, and a desire to undermine local bases of control could hardly inspire allegiance. He was necessary because his dynastic connections could be used to free additional territory from the Turks, and because his throne was guaranteed by the Great Powers. Now these advantages seemed questionable, particularly since the Great Powers had unified to extract the loan repayment.

Consequently, the old revolutionary elite engineered the bloodless revolution of 1843 for its own benefit. The rebellion was confined to Athens, and the traditional leaders and their retainers were the only participants.[43] Threatened by centralization, they wished either to save their positions or to staff the new central institutions themselves. Otho, however, was a bulwark against anarchy; and although the revolutionary elite could cooperate against him, they did not want to return to the anarchy of the revolutionary period.[44] The cooperation lasted only long enough to carry out the revolution of 1843 and to force a new constitution on Otho. Once the constitutional crisis was passed, this cooperation ceased. The new constitution itself was a patchwork; its major provisions involved patronage, appointment, and matters of secularization. Representative institutions and mechanisms characteristic of Western governments were introduced, and Otho's remaining Bavarian advisers were replaced by Greeks. Although the constitutional document had been imposed by an assembly on a recalcitrant monarch, the king retained substantial power, even in matters of appointment. However, the traditional leadership now commanded the central administration, and commenced to operate the new institutions in conformity with traditional values.

At first, Otho competed at the party level, using the constitution of 1844 for his own purposes by nominating candidates, managing elections, and using extra-parliamentary cabinets. He was able to draw some members of the revolutionary elite to his side, and others were exiled to distant legations. The extension of central authority and the operation of representative bodies created a greater awareness of the state and its institutions. The general conditions of order encouraged commerce and communications. A second rebellion, in 1862, was also carried out by a united, indigenous opposition to Otho; but unlike the earlier coup, it "reflected a nationwide popular movement."[45] Mutinies and street demonstrations in the major provincial centers culminated in an outburst in Athens, and Otho was deposed. On this occasion, not only were veteran politicians and army officers involved, but students and the provincial intelligentsia as well.[46]

A number of motives coalesced to bring about the demise of Otho's regime. Domestically, Otho's political opponents were restive under the system of manipulated elections. At the same time, the growth of central institutions, an increase in economic capabilities, and the lessons provided by Otho in manipulation and control were not lost on the most influential of his subjects. Moreover, the Greek elite and the mobilized population judged the monarchy as an institution, and the incumbent himself, in terms of their effectiveness in foreign relations. Whether the goal was a new Hellenic empire, Byzantium restored, or simply an enlarged kingdom depended on one's point of view; however, in each case, Otho and his policies were failures. Since the major task confronting the new state was the liberation of Greeks still within the Ottoman Empire, a goal far beyond the capacity of the country, international goodwill was essential. Otho's regime, failing to meet the test of domestic utility, also forfeited its foreign support because of its endeavors in behalf of the unredeemed Greeks. To a large extent, Otho was a victim of the international system of the mid-nineteenth century.

The new democratic constitution of 1863 called for universal male suffrage and a single-chamber parliament. These Western political institutions were operated by an elite most familiar with the non-national traditions of Byzantium and the Ottoman Empire. As the local notables moved into the state offices, there was a blending of two Byzantine traditions: the rural tradition of local autonomy and rule by elders; and the imperial tradition of great centralization, territorial expansion, and cultural hegemony. The notables now imposed their parochialism on the central institutions of the state. Elite status was acquired largely through office-holding, rather than through intellectual or economic channels. The chamber of deputies became an arena for the satisfaction of personal and local wants on the pattern of the clientage system. At the same time, the chamber, as a representative voice of the Greek nation, could demand the reclamation of the Greek irredenta. The Greek bureaucracy was not a counter to local elites, but was utilized by them. The modern institutions, both administrative and political, were now operated along traditional lines, and the vision of a modern system held by Capodistrias, Otho, and the Bavarians was finally lost.

Prince William of Denmark, who ascended the throne as George I, was selected as the new monarch by the Great Powers. His domestic role was severely limited by the constitution, even though his powers in foreign policy remained substantial. However, instead of being titled King of Greece, as was Otho, he was "King of the Greeks." The growing nationalist fervor for expansion had been given at least token recognition; and there was an attempt to tie loyalty to the monarchy to the Greek nation, rather than the territorial Greek state. The revolution of 1862, the subsequent constitutional revision, and the appearance of a new set of personal factions largely unrelated to the old revolutionary parties marked a new era in Greek politics.

FORCES FOR CHANGE

Since the mid-nineteenth century, nearly every generation of Greeks has been confronted with a major disruption of its normal existence. Each event triggered a sudden mobilization of additional segments of the population. In addition, there was a normal but gradual mobilization of the population occurring because of the growing penetration of the countryside by government officials, the expansion of educational facilities, the growth of the communication infrastructure, and the increasing marketization of the economy. The impulses for this social mobilization have been varied: war, foreign pressures, and even occupation, as well as the regular pressures of modernization.

The scale of military activity increased throughout modern Greek history. There were many irregular military clashes with the Turks from the middle to the end of the nineteenth century. In 1854 unsuccessful Greek raids took place in the Epirus and Thessaly. The Greeks gave assistance to the Cretans during a rebellion in 1866. There was another attempt in Thessaly in 1878, more disturbances in Crete in 1886, and finally a disastrous formal conflict with Turkey in 1896–97. These clashes appear to have been largely guerrilla activities with the exception of the last.[47] After the 1897 disaster, the regular drafting of age-classes began. The Greek forces in the Balkan Wars were made up of recruits from all over Greece, and even included Greeks who had returned from the United States. These were national wars in a way that previous disturbances were not. The confused neutrality of the 1914-17 period, with clashes between the partisans of King Constantine and former Premier Venizelos, as well as the presence of Allied forces in the Kingdom, affected much of the Greek population. Similarly, Greece's ultimate entry into the conflict on the Allied side, together with the invasion of Anatolia in 1920, exposed large numbers of Greek males to military discipline and training, and more important, acquainted them with a world beyond their own villages.

World War II and the ensuing Civil War had a great impact on the future political behavior of the Greek people. The resistance movement reached into the countryside and mobilized townsmen and peasants for action against the Nazi occupiers; these men were usually ready to respond to calls for particular political action in the future. The resistance movement filled the vacuum left by the suppression and exile of the traditional Greek political leaders; it reached the younger Greeks as no other political movement had done, and inspired them with a great sense of their own importance. Not only was the traditional authority of the father over his children questioned, but in many cases, women were called upon to perform tasks in the name of the nation that might not have been sanctioned by their husbands and fathers in the past.[48] The Nazi forces, with each hostage shot, increased the size of the mobilized opposition.

The civil struggle that erupted after the occupation also forced many unmobilized elements into the political world. Often, personal vendettas were translated into political quarrels. The excesses of the period of left-wing dominance were repeated once the extreme right wing of the country gained the advantage. Both the activities of the guerrillas and the policy of the government affected rural Greece. In areas under their control, the guerrillas forced the rural youth into military service and the rest of the population into active support. The government's evacuation of the most isolated areas of the country and the temporary resettlement of the villagers in the more secure provincial towns increased social mobilization among the more traditional groups. In many cases, two years of town life gave women and young people new ideas and new demands that the traditional peasant world and traditional politics could not satisfy.[49]

The recent institution of universal military training has also influenced those living in the rural areas. Although military service has been an obligation of Greek citizens for many decades, it is only relatively recently that the army has been a genuine educational institution. Not only have the armed forces been concerned with the inculcation of particular loyalties, but they have exposed the recruit to new technical skills and to a new set of values that contradict those prevalent in a peasant culture. When the soldiers return home after their military tour, traditional authority structures in the villages are often upset; sometimes the traditional patron-client relationships are strained as well. Further, a class of men no longer satisfied with rural life and equipped with minimal skills that are often in overabundance in Greek society congregate in the urban areas.

As territories were added to the Greek state throughout its history, the extension of the new governmental system in itself caused the social mobilization of some people in the newly acquired provinces. Government affairs had to be settled in Athens, and local demands had to go through new channels. Athens, therefore, became the center of political life for the Greeks, as Constantinople had not been under the Ottomans. However, the pace of nineteenth-century and early twentieth-century social mobilization was relatively leisurely, and at first only the top local leaders in the newly acquired areas were mobilized. They made personal demands on the political system, and transmitted the few demands of the relatively unmobilized peasantry.

The greatest shock to the political system was produced by the population exchanges that marked the end of Greece's territorial ambitions in Asia Minor.[50] The problems of minority populations in Greek territory were largely eliminated: northern Greece was hellenized, and only a few Turkish enclaves were left in Thrace. But in 1928 about one-fourth of the total Greek population was made up of refugees. Some had come from the Greek cities of the Ottoman Empire, and had experience in local self-government and far-reaching contacts with the rest of the world. Others,

who came from the more remote areas of Anatolia, had only a limited political consciousness. However, the shock of the war, the forceable expulsion
from Turkey and other areas of the Middle East, and the wretchedness of
immediate conditions in Greece created a bond between all refugees and
mobilized them for political action. Refugees were dependent on state or
international assistance for mere survival from the moment of their arrival
in Greece. Even the rural refugee, who had demands of perhaps broader
scope than his native Greek neighbor, was more likely to express these
demands in a political manner. The native Greeks were also affected by the
removal of the Moslem population and the disruptions caused by the refugees; but the settlement pattern of the refugees, and the consequent reaction
to them, varied in different parts of the country.

In more recent decades, the development of communications and transportation has had an impact upon the individual Greek. In 1951 there were
2.4 times as many roads as there were in prewar Greece.[51] Only three roads
traverse the Pindus Mountains, which form the "spine" of continental
Greece; but only one existed in the prewar period, although none of them
are really all-weather roads even now.[52] Many of these roads were built to
open remote and inaccessible parts of the country to the defense forces during the civil war; less threatened areas were less favored. Regardless of
motivation, travel and communication are now much easier than ever before. Newspapers and other printed materials, though not abundant, are
now more easily acquired in the rural areas. A network of bus lines reaches
even the most remote parts of the country, connecting the villagers with
their urban relatives. American aid, largely responsible for the roads, was
also instrumental in the development of the power lines and the new gen-
erating plants that brought electric power to many rural areas. Radios,
formerly scarce in Greece, could now be used almost everywhere, and
peasants could at last hope to use the conveniences seen in the urban centers.
All of these developments have enabled the peasant to see the outside world,
and have raised his expectations accordingly.

In prewar Greece, a relatively small sector of agriculture was devoted to
marketable cash crops. This is no longer the case; and as peasants form
new economic relationships, they find that mutual aid and kinship ties are
not sufficient. New demands must be made upon the state structure, demands of a different character from the old. Fertilizer, price supports, and
irrigation projects cannot be delivered easily because of a simple tie to some
individual politician in Athens. As agriculture becomes more dependent on

world conditions, and as mechanization becomes more common, the shortage of land, aggravated by the small size and excessive fragmentation of farms, is creating political unrest. Peasants no longer accept the situation with fatalistic resignation, but are dissatisfied with the state itself. Another effect of the decline of subsistence agriculture is a labor surplus. A study by Calliope Moustaka indicated that in Greece the search for work was the strongest factor causing villagers to leave their birthplaces.[53] The general insecurity of employment, and of city life after that in the village, plus the appearance of new demands, has produced a substantial class of mobilized urban dwellers.

To summarize, there was little impulse for change in the nineteenth century. The military conflicts, economic changes, and political reforms did not involve much of the population. Large-scale popular involvement began with the Balkan Wars and culminated in World War II and the Civil War, when the whole civilian population was made aware of the political system. In the interlude, the arrival of the Greek refugees not only provided a sizeable group of mobilized citizens but provoked similar mobilization in the native population. The marketization of the Greek economy, the networks of communication and transportation, although initiated in the nineteenth and early twentieth centuries, were not developed extensively until after World War II. While the pace of social mobilization has varied from one part of the country to the other, the comparative data assembled by Bruce Russett and his associates leaves little doubt that contemporary Greece is, with the exception of the most remote areas, largely a socially mobilized society.[54]

3. The International Factor

The international factor is often neglected in the study of internal politics in an individual state.[1] In the case of Greece, this neglect would seriously distort any analysis of the political system. True, some international pressures are not peculiar to Greece; worldwide depressions and wars affect large and small nations alike. However, Greece's geographic location, level of economic development, and unique demographic pressures make her particularly vulnerable to the pressures of external events.

Once subsistence agriculture gave way to commercial "luxury" crops for the European market, the Greek economy became increasingly dependent on foreign tastes, the vagaries of the international economic system, and specific tariff and quota pressures from other nations. Tourism, one of the major sources of foreign exchange in contemporary Greece, is also dependent on conditions largely beyond the control of the Greek government. Another major item, remittances from Greeks abroad, has been contingent on the laws of other nations. The imposition of the quota system in the United States, for example, severely slowed Greek immigration here; and as family ties have grown more tenuous, remittances have declined. More recently, funds sent by Greek workers in Western Europe, particularly Germany, have become important to the Greek economy. Here again, outside events—continued prosperity and a continuing labor shortage in Western Europe—are responsible. Greece, too, has not been insulated from significant political, social, and cultural currents elsewhere in the world. Many of the Greek revolutionaries were influenced by the Enlightenment and the French revolution.[2] The exploits of Garibaldi in Italy inspired similar attempts against the Turks in the nineteenth century; and the Young Turks themselves were models, particularly for the Military League during the crisis of 1909. The image of Mussolini in the 1920's inspired similar ambitions in several Greek military officers. Socialist and Communist ideologies in Greece were likewise inspired by events in Europe.

Beyond the influence of specific individuals and events, the Greek political system has always responded to the latest fashions in institutions and
policies. A casual observer might feel that the Greek government in the
nineteenth and twentieth centuries ingeniously combined the worst aspects
of French, American, and assorted Latin American regimes.[3] Although this
has sometimes been true, there has been a conscious effort to emulate more
acceptable models. The Greek monarchy itself was established, at least in
part, because monarchy was the prevailing institution in early nineteenth-
century Europe. The original state apparatus was modeled on the French,
with several Bavarian innovations; and successive Greek governments have
imported foreign missions or individual experts to transform various agencies into replicas of foreign equivalents. Political parties, too, have sought to
copy their Western European counterparts in organization and program.
Lately, the major emphasis has been on economic development, a goal similarly borrowed from abroad.

It is not the impact of worldwide cultural, economic, or social influences
that has made the international factor a really significant intervening variable in Greece. It is not even the fact that self-sufficiency has been impossible,
or that decision makers in every country, large and small, must be in some
degree responsive to world opinion. It is, instead, the direct involvement of
foreign states in the Greek political process. The predominant foreign influences, and thus the actual institutional or policy styles in Greece, have
varied as different nations have assumed the protector's role. In short, Greece
is and has been a penetrated political system. In the Greek system: "Nonmembers of a national society participate directly and authoritatively,
through actions taken jointly with the society's members, in either the allocation of its values or the mobilization of support in behalf of its goals."[4]

The strategic interests of the Great Powers, either in the eastern Mediterranean or globally, have long determined the direction of Greek politics.
The Greek peninsula is a borderline area with international significance out
of proportion to its size; from the beginning, international influence has
been exercised through diplomatic and military pressures, and through
financial pressure in the form of loans or outright gifts. The objects of foreign interest have been not only the foreign policy of Greece, but her form
of government, her political leadership, and her specific domestic policy.
There have been few major governmental actions or domestic crises that
were not caused by the interventions or pressures of foreign powers, or developed in response to an international crisis that allowed for no other

course. For their part, Greek politicians have never been averse to using foreign support to crush internal opponents; and the Greeks themselves have often tried to produce the regime they considered most acceptable to particular major powers.

THE REVOLUTION AND THE BAVARIAN DYNASTY

In the beginning, much revolutionary fervor in Greece was built on misplaced hopes of assistance from Orthodox Russia. After the Greeks had demonstrated their staying power the British and French were forced by strategic considerations to join the Russians in offering assistance.[5] Although many influences, such as the surge of philhellenism, the repugnance of Turkish atrocities to European opinion, and the commercial disruptions caused by the rebellion, were involved in this decision, naked balance-of-power calculations were most important. Mutual jealousy was eventually transformed into the Treaty of London, through which Britain, France, and Russia became the joint protectors of Greece. These powers determined the size of the new state, whose original truncated shape was due to British and French fears that Greece might emerge as a client state of Orthodox Russia. The protocols that gave Greece sovereignty also prescribed her form of government and dictated various features of her public law. The guaranteeing powers were given the right—and, indeed, the obligation—to establish and maintain internal order, by direct intervention, if necessary.[6] As Petropulos notes, "Britain, France and Russia established a special international status for Greece, a type of European suzerainty exercised by themselves and disguised in the more palatable phrase 'under the guarantee of the three powers.'"[7]

Although three powers together legitimized the Greek state, this did not preclude them from pursuing their separate aims. Each Great Power had a candidate for the crown of the new state and a following of local politicians. When Capodistrias, the reputed representative of the Tsar, became the provisional president, other provincial leaders bristled with armed resistance encouraged by Britain and France. The protectors eventually selected Otho of Bavaria as the ruler of their new creation, and a treaty between Bavaria and the three powers regulated his acceptance of the crown of Greece. The Greek state, largely unrecognized, and with only the shreds of a government, had no part in the negotiations or the subsequent treaty; Otho, although proclaimed "by the Grace of God, King of Greece," was clearly King by the grace of the major European powers.[8] The treaty could not be changed without the consent of the four signatories, who presumably had the authority to modify any legislation they considered unacceptable.[9] In fact, this treaty made the practice of intervention in Greek domestic affairs habitual. The first loans to the new kingdom were granted only for particular purposes: the civil list, the army, and the bureaucracy. The amounts and intervals of payment were established, as well as procedures for supervision of the Greek treasury by the resident ministers of the three powers. The continued financial dependence of Greece created the conditions for permanent penetration by the "protecting powers."

Throughout the reign of Otho, internal controversy over the eventual form of the Greek government followed the lines of international politics. In its first years, with a minor prince advised by regents who were subjects of a foreign monarch and employed imported soldiers and bureaucrats, Greece was virtually a Bavarian protectorate. In the effort to stabilize royal authority, only Bavarians were felt to be trustworthy.[10] Although the original protocols had made Greece a kingdom, no limits to royal power were included, and the diplomatic agents of the protecting powers were often the only counters to royal authority. From the first, the French and British, through their ministers and their local partisans, urged Otho to grant a constitution; the Russians, joined by the Austrians, latecomers to Greek politics, supported his refusal.[11] As Otho's Bavarian retinue disappeared, he became more dependent on foreign support, either directly or through the local factions attached to each of the major powers. Even after he reached his majority, the position of individual regents, and later, of the Greek government members, depended on the goodwill of the ministers of the Great Powers.

At first the new government was occupied with the establishment of a national administration. The frustrations and failures in this area were mounting at the same time that a new series of crises erupted in the Near East. Finally, irredentist pressures in Greece, combined with domestic frustrations, forced Otho to announce Greek territorial claims.[12] Greece was too weak to press her claims by any means other than diplomacy; and the protecting powers refused to countenance Greek demands. King Otho, faced with international failure and internal opposition, was forced to grant a constitutional regime in 1843. The revolution of 1862 removed him from the scene completely. The conspirators were successful not only because of widespread internal dissatisfactions but because the protecting powers did not see Otho as useful to them. He could not ignore the demands of domestic Greek nationalists, of whatever variety, and no Greek government could sit idly by once revolts erupted in parts of unredeemed Greece; yet the interests of the Great Powers, individually and collectively, conflicted with these aspirations. In his efforts to realize Greek territorial ambitions and keep his throne, Otho threatened the larger interests of Britain and France in the Ottoman Empire; his equivocation over his personal faith alienated the Russians. When Otho's successor, Prince William of Denmark, ascended the Greek throne as George I, he did so as the result of treaties between Denmark and the Great Powers. Among the treaty clauses was one in which the new monarch promised not to encourage insurrections against the Ottoman Empire. The religious problem was solved by George's marriage to a Russian princess.

GREECE AND THE NEAR EASTERN BALANCE OF POWER

The success of Greek foreign aspirations was contingent on the international interests of the Great Powers. In the nineteenth and twentieth centuries, Greece was only one point on the frontier between conflicting Russian and British interests. The British, when their shell of classical and Byronic memories was peeled away, were interested in Greece because of the necessities of imperial security; this interest continued regardless of the party makeup of the British government. Likewise, Russian interests, though often couched in religious terms, were part of larger Russian aims in southeastern Europe. Greece herself, because she felt more protected by sea power, and perhaps more menaced by it, was primarily dependent on British goodwill in this period. The British, for example, had expressed their disenchantment with the Bavarian regime in 1850, when British warships had blockaded Piraeus to force Greek acceptance of the relatively dubious claims of private British citizens against the Greek kingdom. After the fall of Otho, the Greeks showed their fealty to Great Britain by voting overwhelmingly for the 18-year-old Prince Alfred as monarch, even though it was understood that under the Protocols of 1830 a British prince was ineligible for the honor.[13]

Greece herself did not have many capabilities for translating her aims into reality. Her territorial aspirations, and even her program for internal development, dependent as they were on outside financial assistance, could be pursued successfully only when Greek interests agreed with the interests of her protectors, especially Great Britain. On the other hand, the Greek governments could not control the activities of guerrilla bands either outside or within the state boundaries, nor contain the periodic nationalist crusades that appeared in various sectors of the domestic political system. Greece was not treated with much respect whenever her activities clashed with the interests of the major powers. Throughout the nineteenth century Britain, and sometimes France, intervened in the Greek kingdom, not only because of continuing financial interests, but because of fears that Greek national aims would upset the carefully wrought balance of the major powers. The most constant form of pressure was financial, but military action was not unknown.

The fulfillment of Greek foreign ambitions could come only when all the powers agreed or were indifferent, or if one of the major powers favorably disposed to Greek aims exercised a paramount influence in international affairs. Time after time, Greek efforts to promote territorial ambitions independently were stillborn because of foreign pressures. During the Crimean War, the Greek government was under intense domestic pressure to assist the Russians because of the ties of religion and because Russia's enemy was the Ottoman Empire. Her disguised participation in the conflict brought British and French squadrons to the Piraeus, where they remained until 1857. In 1877, during the Russo-Turkish War, Charilaos Trikoupis, the anglophile Greek foreign minister, trusted the British government to compensate Greece, since she restrained her natural impulses and did not attack Turkey. However, this admirable restraint produced a strong public reaction in Greece; a cabinet favoring aggrandizement was soon selected, but before it could act, the war ended. In 1881, as a reward for her neutrality, Greece received Thessaly and the province of Arta in the Epirus. The Treaty of San Stefano that ended the struggle was altered under British pressure because in this case British interests against Russia coincided with Greek interests against Bulgaria.

Because of conflicting interests, the Great Powers were continually involved with Crete; but in their attempts to maintain equilibrium in the eastern Mediterranean, they merely prolonged instability. In 1867, France and Russia, for different reasons, advocated Crete's union with Greece; but Britain opposed it. Two years later, another Cretan crisis erupted, and this time general conflict was averted only through the good offices of Bismarck. In 1886, the Greek government of Theodoros Deliyannis prepared to force the issue of Crete again, this time in concert with Bulgarian activities against the Turks. However, the Great Powers presented an ultimatum, and finally blockaded Piraeus to prevent Greek ventures. At the end of the century the

internal disputes in Crete finally blossomed into armed conflict. The protecting powers were unable to deter Greece from going to war with Turkey
in 1897, in part because of divisions in British public opinion. But the war
went badly, and the Greeks were forced to appeal to the Great Powers for
a settlement. An international commission with British, French, Italian, and
Russian members was formed to administer Crete in 1898. Eventually, a
Greek prince was selected to head the island administration; and Greece
officially annexed the island during the Balkan Wars.

A political crisis in 1909 was at least partly caused by Greece's failure to
make gains in international politics. There was increasing uneasiness among
the newer professional and commercial classes in the growing cities; the old
political leaders, who were remnants of families that had come to power
during the revolution, had not understood the problems of these new groups.
The Military League, an organization of young, professionally oriented
officers, felt that the Crown and the oligarchy of semihereditary politicians
formed during the nineteenth century had mismanaged both foreign and
domestic policy and caused the defeat of Greek nationalist aspirations.[14] The
League brought Eleutherios Venizelos, a Cretan representative of the new
political classes of lawyers and petty capitalists, to Athens as Premier. The
first Venizelos government, and several other administrations, did undertake important structural changes in Greek government; but the basic economic and cultural factors that vitiated these reforms were not understood.
Foreign policy, in essence the desire to reconstitute Byzantium in the form
of the Greek kingdom, continued to occupy the primary attention of most
Greek officials.

The potential revival of Ottoman fortunes under the Young Turks
prompted the Balkan states to begin their territorial quests promptly. The
great successes of Greece and the other Balkan states against Turkey in the
First Balkan War were symptomatic of changes in the overall European
balance of power. This time the traditional restraints on Greek aggrandizement were lacking: France was concerned with Italian and Austrian power
in the Mediterranean, and Britain was increasingly occupied with Germany.
The Second Balkan War exposed the essential instability of the Balkan
power balances, a warning that was borne out by World War I.

Greece was an impoverished state, and the question of foreign debts bedeviled Greek politics throughout the nineteenth and twentieth centuries,
influencing policies of internal development, taxation, and diplomatic alignment. By manipulating their financial demands, foreign powers could force

abrupt changes in the allocation of Greek resources for domestic purposes; the resulting dissatisfactions could cause the overthrow of the Greek government.[15] Nearly every governmental upheaval in Greece, apart from those directly concerned with foreign policy, was connected with the financial problems of the state. Debts contracted at independence, as well as those secured later, had been used not for reconstruction but for many less creditable projects. Because of Greece's unpaid debts, most of her foreign efforts, whether successful or not, were mounted without sufficient financial resources. After each such adventure, there was usually an economic crisis, and both the nation and its bondholders suffered; this ordinarily resulted in further foreign intervention. Many loans had been unnecessarily contracted; most, despite safeguards of various kinds, were floated at 30 to 40 per cent discount, and even these reduced proceeds were generally not directed to any productive purposes.[16] When defaults occurred, bondholders relied on their home governments to exact payment by measures ranging from simple protest to active intervention. The Greek solution to default was to borrow additional money to meet the old debt charges and to assign customs revenue from one more port to the representatives of the creditors, or to create one more state monopoly and assign its proceeds in the same way. Between 1879 and 1893, loans of 750 million gold francs were spent, but there was no essential improvement in the Greek economy.[17]

Eventually, the Great Powers came to manage Greek finances through an international control commission, since the Greeks could not "manage their financial affairs in a manner satisfactory to western tenets of fiscal administrative efficiency."[18] In 1898 the international commission set up a Management Company of Greek State Monopoly Goods to handle the distribution and sale of monopoly goods, such as salt, matches, playing cards, and kerosene. Although this company was under the jurisdiction of the Greek state, Greece was not permitted to enact any law that encroached on its sources of revenue.[19] The international commission died during World War II. The Greek government now collects the monopoly revenue, but the Management Company continues to exist as the representative of the largely unpaid bondholders.

WORLD WAR I AND AFTER

In the periods of great international tension beginning with World War I, the major powers did not hesitate to intervene directly if the Greek government persisted in pursuing policies they considered contrary to their interests. Although King Constantine was reluctant to follow his brother-in-law, the Kaiser, because Greece was at the mercy of the British and French fleets, his antipathy to the Allied cause eventually cost him his throne. The internal conflict on constitutional matters between the King and his prime minister, Venizelos, was exploited by the Allies, and they, in turn, were used by Venizelos. After the Austro-Bulgarian invasion of Serbia, Greece was asked to intervene because of treaty obligations. Intricate negotiations between Venizelos, the King, and the Allies finally produced a plan for an Allied landing at Salonika, with the Allies supplying the troops that Serbia was obligated to produce under the treaty. The Allied divisions landed, but the agreement fell apart.

The Allied forces assisted Venizelos and several associates in secessionist moves that removed Crete, the major Aegean islands, and Macedonia from the authority of the King. In fact, the Allied governments supported the secessionist regime in Salonika and at the same time maintained relations with the government in Athens. Both Greek governments were forced to submit to Allied suggestions in details of troop placement and choice of government personnel, as well as in such major questions as elections. From the Athens government, the Allies demanded the demobilization of the Greek army and the cession of the Greek fleet; eventually, Piraeus was blockaded and occupied. The Allied commanders occupied whatever places they desired, proclaimed martial law on their own in provincial cities, and took over control of police activities in Athens.[20] The protecting powers had guaranteed the Greeks a constitutional regime in 1862; this was finally taken as sufficient reason to demand the abdication of Constantine. This was done in June 1917 by the French envoy; to enforce compliance, Thessaly was invaded and the Isthmus of Corinth occupied. The removal of Constantine reunited Greece and brought Venizelos to the helm once again; Greece then entered the war on the side of the Allies.

GREAT BRITAIN AS "PROTECTOR"

Greek foreign policy from the time of independence had been directed toward the creation of a large hellenic state that would include not only Greeks but all population groups that inhabited areas once part of Byzantium. The Greeks, though conscious of their own nationality, often assumed that Orthodox Christianity was synonymous with Greek national feeling. Although the Ottomans also began with this assumption, they eventually tried to preserve their regime by recognizing the differences. By creating separate national branches of the Orthodox Church, however, they merely increased national feeling among the subordinate nationalities; this in itself made Greek aims in these regions difficult to realize.

Greek territorial aims after World War I were shaped by the decisions of the Allies, especially Great Britain. Greek ambitions beyond Macedonia were thwarted by the decisions of the peace conference, and expansion in Cyprus, northern Epirus, and the Dodecanese was blocked because greater powers controlled those regions. The one area open for aggrandizement was Anatolia, and during the war the Allies encouraged Greek aspirations in that direction. Venizelos embarked on the venture, although faced with strong internal opposition in Greece. When his opponents came to power, however, they continued the plan, perhaps to show that not only Venizelos could be successful in foreign affairs. But Greek sovereignty in Asia Minor could only have been established with the help of major powers, and after the war new considerations entered the picture. Russia no longer counted. The British, and to a lesser degree, the French, feared for the security of their new mandates in the Near East; this lessened support for Greek moves against Turkey. Italy had interests that were opposed to a "greater" Greece. Despite initial successes, the activities and attitudes of the major powers ordained disaster for the Greek military adventure in Anatolia.[21] This failure brought ruin to King Constantine, who was again forced to abdicate, and death to the unfortunate ministers who were guiding the action.[22] Further moves in northern Epirus were blocked by Italy, who acted as the agent for the new Albanian regime. The Corfu Incident of 1923, in which the Italian fleet bombarded and occupied Corfu in retaliation for the murder of an Italian official on Greek soil, illustrated, once again, the dependence of Greece on external support. At the behest of the British and the French, the Greek government was forced to accede to most of the Italian demands.[23]

Despite British pressure over the Corfu Incident and the failure of British support in Anatolia, the keystone of Greek policy in the interwar period was the maintenance of the most friendly ties with Great Britain. This policy, on the whole, was dictated by Greece's extended position in the Mediterranean. The authoritarian Metaxas regime might have been sympathetic to Germany or Italy; but Metaxas, too, recognized strategic necessities. In World War II, after the limits of Axis expansion had been reached, the exiled government of Emmanuel Tsouderos still conducted policy "in such a way as to promote the realization of his [Tsouderos's] assumption that after the war, Britain would continue playing a preponderant role . . . a pa-

ternalistic role," in the affairs of Greece.[24] Although the legitimate government considered itself a client of the British, the Greek Communist Party
had quite faithfully followed the twistings of Soviet policy throughout the
interwar period. Later, during the resistance, it became an outright agent of
the Soviet Union. Wartime calculations again placed Greece in the British
sphere of influence; and despite the postwar attempts to break this tie by
force, Greece remained attached to the West.

The Greek government in exile, although a sovereign state according to
international law, was little more than an adjunct of the British Foreign
Office, continually concerned with British support and approval, or with
British intercession with the other major powers.[25] On the eve of the German occupation, an Anglo-Greek agreement put military units of the Greek
government, now in exile, under the British High Command. These units
were to maintain their national identity, but would be organized along
British lines and equipped by the British. The exile government was often
kept in the dark, and was generally hostile to British intelligence activity in
Greece during the war. Ultimately, the British were blamed for assisting in
the creation of an underground armed force within Greece that came to be
dominated by Communists hostile to the legitimate regime. However, the
British, operating under the prewar agreement, put down the mutiny among
various Greek units in the Middle East, and felt free to combat the uprising
of December 1944 in liberated Greece as well; for in theory the entire Greek
armed forces, whether belonging to the exiled regime or the elements
fostered by British intelligence activity, were still under the British High
Command.

During the confused period from liberation to the advent of the Truman
Doctrine, Greek governments existed on flimsy constitutional ground, and
with little popular support. British suggestions had force because the Greeks
were completely dependent on the outside for both economic and military
assistance; in fact, the governments, and in the final analysis the political
system itself, were of British making. The intricate maneuvers surrounding
the question of the monarchy reflected British interest. The British pref-
erence for a "crowned republic with all its constitutional freedoms" could
be traced to Churchill's close friendship with King George II.[26] The provisions for a plebiscite and subsequent election agreed to at Varkiza in 1944
under the paternalistic gaze of the British were subsequently reversed, in
part through the urgings of the Allied governments. This certainly had some
bearing on the election results, since by that time the question of govern-

mental form was intricately related with the Communist issue; however, the Allied commission that observed the elections reported no outstanding irregularities.

THE UNITED STATES AS "PROTECTOR"

The United States had so far remained aloof from Greek affairs. After Yalta, the American government "had indicated its willingness and determination to take part in the Allied guarantees designed to safeguard the right of smaller nations, freed from Axis domination, to choose by peaceful and democratic means the governments under which they wished to live."[27] It was generally recognized that American financial aid might be necessary, since the necessary conditions for peaceful and democratic elections were linked to economic stability. Early efforts at securing American aid for Greece had foundered, in part because of the multiplicity of claims on the American treasury—but more particularly, because of Washington's distrust of the economic policies of the Greek government.[28] In early 1947, however, the American government was informed that the United Kingdom could no longer supply assistance to Greece. Since Greece had to have outside aid for internal reconstruction and military support, the American government was forced to assume the responsibility.

The Truman Doctrine made the security of the United States contingent on a friendly Greece, and the American government supplied much more material for both military and economic purposes than the British; but it also went further in "giving advice and in insisting that it was carried out."[29] The American aid program was operated on the assumption that any Greek program receiving assistance was subject to American approval. Since nearly any activity required the use of foreign exchange, the American mission had a controlling position in Greek government. It was assumed that any suggestions offered by the United States in regard to policy or reform would be taken very seriously.[30] American advisers and supervisors were attached to the Greek ministries. Military operations were conducted by a joint Greco-American general staff, and there were American observers down to the divisional level. The Greek forces were almost completely equipped with American goods, and most decisions on weapons and organization (and, according to one commentator, promotional policy as well) were made by the United States.[31]

The United States felt obligated to intervene in Greek politics whenever political instability seemed to endanger the larger aims of economic stability and victory in the civil war. As American involvement grew more extensive, conflicts within the American establishment also affected Greek politics. Often the policies promoted by the American mission had purely economic goals in mind; to some degree these policies exacerbated political instability, apparently the major concern of the American Embassy. The Greek elections in 1950 and 1951 were partly a result of the American quest for stability; some of the personnel changes in this period could be ascribed to the same cause. When instability returned, or when American policy failed, the Embassy could grandly announce that it did not subscribe to any policy of interference in the domestic affairs of another nation.

Threats to withhold American aid were constantly advanced if the proper governmental stability was not reached, or if a suggested policy was not enacted.[32] However, political stability and particular policy suggestions were often mutually exclusive. Every drive for a particular action made a coalition shaky, and each attempt to broaden the composition of a government gave the minority politicians added leverage against the government. Various sectors of the Greek political world were attached to different parts of the American establishment. The complexity of relationships between Greece and her protectors was further increased by internal political pressures, particularly liberal pressures, in Britain and America.

Greek foreign policy in the postwar period was conditioned by the seeming insolubility of domestic problems, plus a desire to embarrass the left-wing groups. These domestic factors, as well as conditions imposed by her association with the West, led Greek governments throughout the period to embark on almost irrational and completely ethnocentric foreign policies. The Dodecanese were acquired because Italy was defeated, and because all of the powers agreed to the transfer; but advances in Thrace were precluded, not only because of Greece's own policy of friendship with Turkey, but because good Greco-Turkish relations were in the best interests of the British. Cyprus continued to be out of reach; the Greek state could do little more than keep the question open. Greek governments concentrated their territorial aims to the north, although their dependence on British or American power created a strategic limit to expansion in this direction, and although there were no compact Greek populations in the area. Since Greek claims on historic and ethnic grounds had repeatedly been disallowed for such areas as northern Epirus, the new claims were tied primarily to strategic considerations.

When Greece became more dependent on the United States, the question of Cyprus was reactivated.[33] However, the termination of British control over the island did not solve the issue; and as the ultimate resolution of the problem became more doubtful, American pressures increased. For the United States, disputes between NATO members had to be subordinated to the greater interests of the alliance; and the status quo in Cyprus was in many respects a better solution than one that would rend the southeastern flank of NATO. According to Stephen Rousseas, American penetration of the Greek military establishment was so complete, and involvement elsewhere in the Greek political system so extensive, that Greek aims in Cyprus were shelved for a long period.[34]

Rousseas even argues that American policy makers, growing increasingly restive at the seeming independence in foreign policy exhibited by the Papandreou regime after 1963, actively promoted the downfall of the Papandreou cabinet and the split in his political party.[35] Of course, if this reasoning is correct, the American government must have had foreknowledge of the coup in April 1967 as well. The evidence for direct American involvement seems circumstantial; but nonetheless, since the American government acquiesced in the military take-over, and because of its acknowledged involvement in the past, the presumption of active American support is widespread in Greece. Those involved in the coup apparently expected American commendation, and not mere acquiescence. The initial American reaction was hesitant, and some American aid was temporarily halted. This action was naturally resented. One of the Junta leaders, Brigadier Pattakos, said of the Americans: "They can do everything they want, they are very strong. They are stronger than we are. We haven't given any cause for something like this."[36]

Not only have specific foreign powers intervened in Greek affairs, but international agencies, beyond those concerned with internal Greek financial arrangements, have been able to impinge on Greek sovereignty. The refugee commission established through the League of Nations to alleviate the problems caused by the population exchanges that followed World War I largely ignored the prerogatives and sovereignty of the Greek state. For example, the laws on land reform, enacted under Venizelos, had never been completely implemented. The commission secured international loans on the basis of state-owned land, regulated the distribution of this land, and in general operated outside the jurisdiction of the Greek authorities.[37] When the United Nations Relief and Rehabilitation Administration operated in Greece after World War II, controversies arose that were finally settled in favor of the international agency. The Greek government distributed some relief supplies, mainly to its civil servants; the UNRRA considered this improper and wanted to secure the power of distribution within Greece. Eventually, the UNRRA was able to force the Greek government to submit to international inspection of its distribution practices.

SUMMARY

Greeks have been encouraged in an attitude of political irresponsibility by the tradition of external involvement in Greek affairs. Just as a rural Greek often expects government assistance to continue indefinitely after a natural disaster, so the Greek state has come to expect the international midwives of 1830 to continue their benevolent attentions. That Greece is unique and deserving of special consideration has been a constant theme in Greek foreign relations: Greece deserves special consideration because Western civilization originated there; Greece deserves special consideration because she has sacrificed herself to prevent barbarism from overwhelming the world; and so on. A typical statement of this sentiment is that of Premier Papandreou at the end of World War II: "Because of its services to the Allied cause, and its sacrifices, Greece expected to be treated as a unique case."[38] More recently, after the country gained associate status in the European Common Market, many Greeks became aware of the economic difficulties that would arise when she became a full member of the organization. However, it is hoped that the other members will recognize the special situation of Greece and make allowances and exceptions for her when the time comes.

In many cases, Greece has not been able to alleviate her most basic human problems, such as famine or job security, without the assistance of other states. Hence Greeks have a habit of assuming that all basic problems must be solved by outside forces. To be sure, the Greek government does concern itself with these same questions, but only on the level of the individual. Politics, instead of being concerned with general policy, is primarily concerned with patronage. There have been few efforts at innovative policy and little dynamic leadership; any innovations are assumed to be foreign-sponsored, and any imaginative politician is assumed to be self-seeking or under foreign influence. Greek politicians can make extravagant promises; but ultimately, all blame for any errors can be shifted to the foreign embassies. Because the pressure of international politics has been close to the Greeks, they have often magnified the real importance of Greece in world affairs.

It has been difficult for Greeks to appreciate that major powers have interests elsewhere that might dictate policy toward Greece, or that outside powers do not have to control every internal action.

Although Greeks display a tremendous interest in foreign affairs, it is the interest of spectators rather than that of activists. In a sample of 55 members of the 1964 parliament, only three (one a former diplomat) claimed expertise in international affairs; and only four put international affairs as the subject in which they were "most interested," although many more had educational and occupational backgrounds that might have favored this interest.[39] National affairs, which to a Greek include subjects like Cyprus, were the primary concerns of 34.6 per cent, while purely local affairs were most important to only 3.6 per cent. The same number, 34.6 per cent, volunteered the observation that it was impossible to disentangle local, national, and international issues because, for Greece, all were intimately connected. The question itself did not make sense to 20 per cent of the sample. When all problems are perceived as interconnected, and when it is assumed that Greece can do little about problems at the international level, it is not surprising that parliamentary deputies concentrate on nonlegislative functions.

Foreign affairs, as such, are rarely debated in parliament. The fundamental underpinnings of the Greek position in the world are rarely discussed, and the international background for her internal problems is taken as given. The left wing has associated ill fortune with the malignant influence of the United States and NATO; the other political spokesmen, ignoring these charges, bring up issues of Communist control or threats of "slavic barbarianism." There are a few deputies with Western educations who do have a personal concern with international affairs, but it is usually based on domestic political profit. By attending international conclaves and the meetings of the many European regional associations, they are able to associate with world notables. If the proper photographs appear in the Greek press, these connections can raise a deputy's prestige in his home district.[40]

A Greek cannot really come to terms with international issues, although in many cases he is passionately aware of them and poses his own solutions to them. Because he is aware of the impact of foreign policies of other nations on internal Greek concerns, the Greek tends to feel that his nation is the center of all international affairs. However, on the international front, Greece is much more a pawn than a participant. On the issue of most passionate interest, Cyprus, the Greeks can do little, even though every political figure publicly makes the correct declarations. The broad middle band of issues—social security, defense spending, and the budget—do not provoke much interest in the press, the public, or the parliament.

The international factor, then, has impinged on the Greek political system in two major ways. First, foreign penetration has hindered the creation of consensus in Greek society for both foreign and domestic goals. Second, Greek goals have conflicted with those of the major powers. Since Greek independence, the major powers have been clearly identified with particular groups in the Greek political system, and conflicts among these groups have generally reflected the divergent interests of the powers. Legitimate attempts at national development have often been thwarted by the interests of the major powers; yet aggressive foreign policies phrased in terms of territorial expansion have often been supported. Since the limits of the international system have been well known to the leaders of conflicting groups in Greek society, much of the furor of virulent nationalism has been used to establish a new equilibrium among the domestic political groups. When foreign-policy goals are expressed by competing groups in Greek society, they are usually identified with the goals of a sponsoring great power, both by domestic opponents and by other international actors. In short, to paraphrase a recent discussion of the linkage problem in foreign policy and the international system, there has been neither consensus on the means and ends of Greek policy nor compatibility with the structures and opportunities of the international system.[41]

II. The Political System

4. Consensus and Dissensus

One commentator on Greece in the mid-nineteenth century noted that "one might be tempted to look upon Greece as one of the most ideal kingdoms to govern."[1] As one reason, he cited the lack of enduring cleavage within the country. It is doubtful that any monarch or prime minister since that time would echo those sentiments. The last century has been characterized by intense political conflicts, civil war, and fundamental changes of regime —all this in addition to crises caused by external events. Basically, there has never even been consensus on the meaning of "Greece" itself. The revolutionary elites had heterogeneous backgrounds and conflicting images of the future. The major difference among them could be described as a conflict between modern and traditional values, or perhaps more accurately as a conflict between those with Western, secular views and those clearly identifying the nation with Orthodox Christianity.

Karl Deutsch notes that nationalities turn into nations when they acquire the power to back up their aspirations.[2] In Greece, the power to unite the state came from outside; there was barely sufficient common identification, much less solidarity, to create the nation-state. National identification was more a presumption of outside powers than an internal reality. It cannot be denied that Greece does seem remarkably homogeneous when judged by the usual objective criteria. With a single language, a single religion, and a common revolutionary past, the Greek kingdom in the mid-nineteenth century did seem to be an ideal state. However, this appearance was as misleading then as it is now. The Greek kingdom displayed apparent solidarity when facing external threat; but when this external stimulus was lacking, even the elements of national identification were controversial. There were cleavages in Greek society along the lines of language and culture from the beginning, and even religion has not been the unifying force it is assumed to be. Now, there is also a growing tension between the urban and rural sectors of Greek society; and even within these sectors there is little agreement on the meaning of "Greece" or the nature of the regime. One of the major requirements for a national consciousness, the existence of mutually compatible values, has not been met.[3]

The conflicts that could have erupted initially because of the incompatible visions of the Greek revolutionary leaders were postponed. First, the area successfully included in the new state clarified some alternatives. In particular, the most "modern" element among the leaders, the commercial class of the Greek cities in Asia Minor, was excluded. Further, the early leaders were prevented from pushing their views by the Great Powers. And finally, the new political institutions themselves imposed some limitations. The energies of the revolutionary elites were directed to competition for favor and office, so that their bases of support could be maintained; this, rather than the future of the state, was their fundamental concern. By the middle of the century, the children of this diverse elite, because of a common education furnished by the new national university and because of intermarriage, were relatively homogeneous in outlook. The penetration of the modern institutional framework by the traditional social structure was largely accepted. At this time, the bulk of the Greek population remained unmobilized. The rural Greek was largely unaware of the Greek state and oblivious to nationalism of any variety. Insofar as he was connected to the political system at all, it was through clientage relationships that led to the revolutionary leaders or their heirs.

From about 1880 on, increasing social mobilization in Greece increased the problem of national identification; it reinforced the existing differences instead of obliterating them, and created new lines of cleavage. In this instance, there was not merely a distinction between the traditional and the modern in Greek society, or the overlapping of the two in a "transitional" synthesis, but fragmentation along personalist and group lines. For most people, the definition of "Greece," the nature of the regime, and even obedience to authority had come to depend on the personal ties and clientage networks that connected the individual to particular political incumbents. However, as new areas were added to the state, and as new groups with different backgrounds came to prominence, the accommodations between modern and traditional elements that had characterized the transitional political system, as well as the limitations imposed by the major powers, came under increased attack. The rate of social mobilization of the traditional elements from both the old and new areas outran their rate of assimilation into the dominant value system of the old elite. New groups, particularly on the left and within the military, emerged as important but disruptive elements in the political system, further impeding the development of common national values. The outlines of a reconciliation system could be discerned.

GEOGRAPHICAL AND HISTORICAL DIFFERENCES

Karl Deutsch, in his study of nationalism and social communication, notes that the essential aspect of the unity of a people is the complementarity or relative efficiency of communications among individuals.[4] Geographical factors were largely responsible for the original diversity among the Greek revolutionary leaders; and the same factors have inhibited the development of those communications networks that might have aided in the creation of a wider national allegiance. Even more important, the clientage networks, dependent as they are upon intense localism and insecurity stemming from economic scarcity, are themselves related to geography; and their existence has meant that loyalty is rarely accorded to national institutions. The bureaucracy, the military, the parties, or the monarchy have not been genuinely national, but have instead been utilized for parochial purposes.

Until recently, a description of Greece as a collection of small, populated districts separated from each other by more or less impassable barriers of land and sea was as apt as it had been for ancient Greece.[5] The initial areas of the Greek kingdom, as well as those incorporated later, had never been treated as a single administrative unit by the Turks. Ottoman rule had favored sectionalism by "allowing communities and regions a large degree of autonomy and by never attempting to introduce any widespread uniformity of administration."[6] Each region had different customs, as exemplified in holidays, dowry requirements, and land tenure. The differences in administrative frameworks have been discussed previously.

Originally, there was little social diversification within each region, since the major occupational categories were geographically determined.[7] At the time of the revolution, agrarian pursuits were dominant in the Peloponnesus and in continental Greece. Farm tenancy was common in the Peloponnesus, but on the continent, particularly in mountainous areas, most peasants were freeholders. The Cyclades and the islands adjacent to the Peloponnesian coast, although in general contrast to the rest of the new Greek kingdom, differed among themselves. By and large, the islands had remained uninhabited during the barbarian invasions commencing in the declining years of the Roman Empire. They were gradually populated by refugees from the mainland in the next centuries; however, except for part of the island of Andros, the Cyclades were not touched by the Albanian migrations that engulfed much of the Peloponnesus and continental Greece in the several centuries before the Ottoman conquest. Differing traditions and social structures stemming from the Frankish and Venetian periods often remained intact. Some islands, originally uninhabited, had been populated by refugees from Ottoman rule elsewhere in the Aegean littoral. The islands were largely ignored by the Ottoman authorities.[8] Moreover, geography determined the contribution of each section of Greece to the revolution: native leadership and revenue from the Peloponnesus, martial skills from continental Greece, and naval and financial support from the islands.[9] Each of the separate regions, and the many communities within them, had its own ties to local heroes and battles of the revolution. Nationalism, though encompassing loyalty to a vague notion of the Greek state, could be devoted to local objects; and in the course of the revolution, the many jealousies and rivalries based on region illustrated the lack of commitment to a single, overriding national symbol.

Once independence was achieved, the Peloponnesian primates, the mountain chieftains, and the island leaders each attempted to guide the new state to their own advantage. Even after the state was organized, there was little uniformity in policy or administration. The national institutions set up by the Bavarians were soon penetrated by the separate regional elites, who operated them for parochial rather than national benefit. Moreover, special privileges in representation were given to some areas; and the application of tax laws was also far from uniform. Despite sporadic efforts to increase the number of individual peasant proprietors, the form of landholding continued to vary. By the mid-nineteenth century, individual proprietorship tended to be the rule in the Peloponnesus; but in parts of old Greece, especially Euboea and Boeotia, where conditions for agriculture were relatively good, large estates were common.[10]

The first acquisition of the new kingdom, the Ionian Islands, had been ruled by the Venetians, French, Russians, and British, though never by the Turks.[11] Throughout the Greek revolution, these islands had enjoyed a peaceful development under the British. The various feudal social structures on the Venetian model that originally existed throughout the island group were altered, although not uniformly, by Great Power occupation. Here, a tenant farmer supplied labor and contributed half the produce of his farm to the landowner. By contrast with other areas, he could not be dispossessed, and he could pass on his tenancy to his children. Institutions of representative government, an extended suffrage, and an extremely free press without parallel in Europe were developed under British supervision. Education was encouraged, and the Ionian Academy educated many future officials of the Greek state at a time when there was nothing comparable in Greece. The pattern of Ionian politics, entwined as it was with Liberal and Tory groups on the British political stage, had a vastly different tone than any existing in Greece at the time.

Thessaly and the province of Arta in the Epirus were finally acquired in 1881, after a certain amount of Greek self-denial and a greater amount of Turkish procrastination. This region also had significantly different traditions and social conditions. The Turks had been relatively secure in this area during the revolution. The Greek state acquired a region with rich agricultural resources but with a system of land tenure that differed from the rest of Greece; in fact, the kingdom acquired a "land question." The large estates here had generally been held by Turkish absentee landlords, who sold their estates to wealthy Greeks after the annexation. This transfer made the settlement of the land question more difficult. The peasants were obligated to pay a third of their crop to the owner, as well as the costs of production; given the uncertain weather conditions in this region, they were perpetually in debt.[12] There were no significant traditions of political participation, and whole villages were little more than serfs. Despite the productivity of the new region, the Greek state now had a territory and population outside the major traditions of the kingdom, as well as a chronic agrarian discontent to add to the other problems confronting the state.

Greece annexed Crete in 1913, as a result of the Balkan Wars. Of all the indisputably Greek portions of the nation, Crete had the most persistent tradition of insurgency. There had been insurrections in 1770, outbreaks at the time of the Greek revolution, and rebellions in 1866, 1889, and 1896. The Ottoman authorities had worked through many institutions without really setting up any common administration for the whole island. However, local assemblies with some competence had existed for short periods in the last part of the nineteenth century. Finally, the Great Powers stepped in, and an international administration emerged, with the Russians, French, British, and Italians applying their own administrative forms and usages to four separate districts, while a fifth was administered jointly.[13] In Crete, as in other areas, identification with the Greek nation obscured the internal differences engendered by the past.

Aside from Crete, the provinces acquired in the aftermath of the Balkan

Wars had diverse traditions of land tenure and administrative control, and different historical backgrounds. The Epirus had a long history of relative autonomy, and its citizens had traditional commercial connections with Constantinople and Europe that could not be duplicated by Greeks in other parts of the realm. Moreover, the Epirotes had played a significant role in the revolution, although Epirus was not initially included in the Greek state. Macedonia and the Aegean Islands had diverse historical traditions, and, at the time of their acquisition, sizeable minority populations as well. The variation was even more significant in some of the smaller areas; for example, Samos had been an independent principality under the suzerainty of the Porte. Finally, the acquisition of Thrace in 1919 and the influx of refugees after 1922 added to the diversity of traditions. The refugees had such a variety of backgrounds, histories, cultural traditions, and dialects that Greece was truly a foreign country for many of them. This group remained unassimilated for several decades, and a portion of it is still outside the Greek political system.

The piecemeal acquisition of new territory ensured the continuation of parochial attitudes toward the state. There was no particular identification of the present Greek kingdom with the Byzantine Empire of the past. The fervor of Greek national spirit that accompanied each annexation was not directed specifically to the kingdom. The leaders of the kingdom viewed themselves as representatives of the imperial Byzantine tradition, but the residents of the newer areas generally differentiated the Empire from the kingdom centered in Athens. For many, Constantinople remained the putative center of the Greek world. The kingdom had been created relatively rapidly; its boundaries had been marked within the living memory of many of its citizens. This newness limited the extent of feeling for the state. Associations and habits remained different; customs and preferences varied. Even today, civics textbooks do not discuss the period after the Balkan Wars with much thoroughness because at this point everything, including the form of the state, became controversial.

LANGUAGE

The term "Greek" differentiates the language spoken by inhabitants of modern Greece from the languages of the surrounding countries; but there is disagreement on what the Greek language was, is, or should be. At the time of independence, the range in local dialects was significant; substantial portions of the population spoke Albanian. The intellectuals among early Greek leaders hoped to use language reform to weld the diverse elements of the nation together. Unfortunately, the Greek language of 1821 was not rich enough in syntax or vocabulary to communicate effectively with the West. In exalting Greece as the founder of its own civilization, the West had taught Greek expatriates to love their own past. These intellectuals were convinced that by purifying the language the ancient tongue could be recovered, and perhaps the ancient glories.

In the long run, the purification of the language did not weld the population into one nationality, but widened the gulf between the educated and the illiterate. The purified language, or *katharevusa,* differed from everyday demotic and from the liturgical language of the church. Moreover, differences in the spoken language remained. This language differentiation, introduced early in the nineteenth century, still exists in a tempered form. Until 1911, katharevusa was the official language of the elite and of those striving for status; it was the language of the town, of the educated, and of government. The influx of refugees in the 1920's, with their many dialects and little acquaintance with the katharevusa form, created serious problems. Language became an important political issue from 1911 to World War II, when demotic and katharevusa vied with each other for inclusion in the school curricula as regimes changed.

Language is still an important political issue in Greece. The continued mobilization of those with minimal formal education has in a sense overwhelmed those who would make the katharevusa the language of all Greece. More literature is written in the popular language, and more newspapers are published in it. However, the katharevusa remains the language of the university, of the bureaucracy, and of editorials in all but leftist publications. Advancement is difficult without knowledge of this formal language. Two communities continue to exist; and language, originally a point of conflict between westernizer and traditionalist, is now an element in the continuing struggle of the advantaged versus the disadvantaged, of city versus countryside.

CULTURE AND RELIGION

It can be argued that many inhabitants of Greece are not pure Greeks, but cultural assimilation makes ethnic differences irrelevant. There is no large minority of those who speak a non-Greek language, although there are local dialects and a number of very small groups with different linguistic and cultural backgrounds. There are certain nomads in the Epirus,[14] and small numbers of Armenians and Jews. The nomads are being forced into a more sedentary life; the Jews, after near extinction during World War II, no longer have an autonomous cultural life. The once vigorous Slavic element has been either expelled or assimilated. The Turkish minority in Thrace, numbering perhaps 60,000, remains apart from the national life of Greece. Its community identity is based on religion, so there is also difficulty in relating to the secular Turkish state. The Turks in Thrace seem to remain a backward cultural enclave, whose main value is as a counter to those Greeks who have a similar status in Constantinople. This minority seems never to have approached the Greek political system as an ethnic bloc; instead, they have relied on the same pattern of patronage and the same clientage relationships that exist in the rest of the nation.

The relationship of Greek national feeling to Orthodox Christianity is well known. The church was the repository of language and culture during the centuries of Ottoman domination. There are a few Protestant Greeks, and a few more Roman Catholics; but these religious minorities are overwhelmed by the identification of the Greek nation with Greek Orthodoxy. But religion has not been the binding force one might expect. The Greeks of the nineteenth century, no less than those of Byzantium, assumed the complete unification of church and state. Once a political separation was made between those living within the new Greek state and those outside its boundaries, it was natural that a separate church should represent the faithful within Greek territorial limits. The Greek national church separated from the domain of the Patriarch of Constantinople in 1833; afterwards, there was a continual tension between the clergy of the kingdom and the Patriarch, increasing as each new territory was added to the Greek kingdom. Even now, Crete and various Aegean Islands are under the authority of the Patriarch, whereas the rest of Greece is organized under the Church of Greece. The Greek church is an integral part of the state structure, and is as subject to politicization as everything else in the society. The government is involved with the selection of church officials; in fact, education and religion are supervised by the same government department. Factionalism and personalized church politics are common, and splits in the church have often paralleled political cleavages.[15] Because of these characteristics, the Greek church, though a national one, has been ineffective as a source of internal unity.

As the state religion, Orthodoxy is secure enough to be tempered with secularism and indifference. Under the impact of urbanization, education, and other forces of modernity, attitudes toward the church are mixed. Everywhere in Greece there is an attitude of deference toward priests and the church; but there is also a parallel tradition of viewing priests and monks as comic figures. For the parochial population, the church is still the most important institution; and here the clergy can be more effective than government officials in promoting solutions for social and economic problems. At this level, religion is often a blend of Christian symbolism and pre-Christian traditions and superstitions,[16] in which the doctrinal content diminishes to love of religion, love of country, and the inculcation of a certain element of stoicism. The rural priest is important as an adviser for personal relations rather than as a counselor for personal faith.

As education has reached the village and as communication with the outside has increased, the priest is no longer as influential as he once was. The local teacher and others with expertise gained outside the village have become more important. Today, if a rural priest is praised, it is likely to be for virtues that make him like other men rather than for religious virtues.[17] For most Greeks, the church is influential only in the sense that a national institution is influential. Even in villages, the regular churchgoers are women; in towns, and more so in urban areas, church attendance is minimal except for special occasions. Religion is taught in the schools, but largely as one element of the national ethos rather than as a spiritual force. To many, the church seems most concerned with formal matters of liturgy and presentation. Irwin Sanders suggests that the educated Greek has adapted his Christianity to the intellectual traditions of classical Greece.[18]

The church occupies an equivocal position in modern Greece. For some persons, Orthodoxy and Greek national identity remain synonymous; for others, the church and its values are the very antithesis of a modern nation-state. For some, religion is an obstacle to change; for others, it is an instrument through which change can be effected. Some view the church as a social liability because of its political character; others view the Greek state as superior because of its religious foundations. The church is able to accommodate the traditional elements devoted to an image of Greece as a nation of autonomous communal institutions ruled by priests, teachers, and elders, as well as those who look upon the church as the one surviving element of Byzantium. Some modernists have purged their religion of its Byzantine encumbrances and look upon it as a system of ethics and morality relevant to the present. Others disregard the church completely, or view it only in political terms. For most Greeks, the contradictory norms of rationality and ritualism are held in uneasy separateness.

THE URBAN-RURAL DICHOTOMY

Social mobilization has created a gulf between the rural and urban elements of Greek society, marked by differences in religion, language, and level of education. The barrier between these two communities is related to conflicting images originally found in the revolutionary elite. Greece has no equivalent of a Jeffersonian tradition, and there has never been a movement lauding peasant virtues. On the contrary, classical Greece was an urban civilization, and the glories of Byzantium were also associated with the city. Virtually anyone, on whatever social level, would rather live in reduced circumstances in Athens or another major city than live in prosperity in the provinces. In the past the concentration of professional men in the urban areas was partly due to greater opportunities. Now professional positions in medicine, engineering, or any technical field have a salary differential designed to encourage settlement in the provinces. These incentives are largely ineffective: even the graduates of agricultural schools prefer technical positions in the Ministry of Agriculture.[19]

The peasants' attitudes toward urban areas are ambivalent. The rural Greek is sure that life in the city is more desirable than life in the country; but he is also aware of the contempt city people have for those from the country. Nevertheless, many families strive to make it possible for their son to secure an education, or for their daughter to catch the husband who will make urban life possible. One way for a village family to gain prestige is by having urban connections.[20] Villagers try to emulate the standards of living and taste they perceive as appropriate for urban dwellers. Friedl suggests that many urban goods find their way to the village not for convenience, but for the air of urban sophistication they impart.[21] On the other hand, villagers distrust Athens and urban life in general. Perhaps the seductive powers of the urban places are feared; more likely this feeling is engendered by generations of urban indifference to rural problems, and by the urban origins of authority.

Greek education has been instrumental in inducing this feeling of urban intellectual superiority. The educational system, at the lower levels, was originally designed to replace peasant outlooks conditioned by generations of foreign occupation with attitudes more appropriate to the citizens of a free nation. The 1952 constitution reflected this purpose: in Article 16, it stated that "in all elementary and intermediate schools teaching shall be aimed at the ethical and intellectual instruction and development of the national conscience of the youth on the basis of the ideological principles of the Greek-Christian civilization."[22] An education designed to make the Greek youth aware of his country's past is of necessity a literary education, relying on a curriculum heavily encumbered with ancient language and culture.[23] There has never been much concern with practical or contemporary subjects. There is practically no effort to acquaint students with the state structure, or with the rights and duties of citizens; and vocational or technical education has a low priority.

The University of Athens, because of its role as a government agent of national liberation and national integration, has generally had first call on financial resources, at the expense of education at lower levels. Because of this, two communities have developed, one a small, educated elite and the other a mass of poorly educated peasants and workers. The graduates of the University have always monopolized government employment and political life. As soon as the University was established, a complete literary education became the standard qualification for government employment. Those people who received this advanced education developed a general distaste for contact with the lower orders of society, and direct dealings with the illiterate peasantry were left to men with less status. Bureaucratic arrogance of this kind has ensured that the country at large will have little confidence in the civil service. However, as the peasant becomes politically aware, he develops greater demands on the urban community; the lower-class urban dweller reacts similarly, and to an even greater extent. The entire process of development has widened this gap.

Despite the general contempt for the peasantry and the urban disadvantaged as classes, nearly every member of the urban elite is likely to have relatives or clients in these categories. The two communities remain apart, however, because the level of economic development in Greece limits opportunity: the resources of the state are insufficient to make education available to all. The brighter young men of the lower classes, in their quest for higher status, are led by the Greek system of education into a governmental career. From the elementary grades through the universities, the standardized literary education leads only to the professions and government service

—all areas of employment that are overcrowded, temporary, and dependent on personal connections. Nevertheless, because prestige and status have traditionally been conferred chiefly by government employment, it is not surprising that successful careers in other occupations have nearly always been sacrificed for political position.

Of course, the educated elite in Greece is not entirely uniform in its attitudes or its orientation to the norms and goals of the society, even though its marked separation from the rest of Greek society sometimes produces that impression. There have always been small minorities with sympathy for the rural Greek as the "true Greek"; and there have been some urban intellectuals who have retreated into religious obscurantism. However, most members of the urban privileged classes do form a community separated from the rest of Greek society by differences in values, language, culture, and ease of access to the political system. They see Greece as a modern liberal state, and their own group as an integral part of Western civilization. For them, the contrast between the operation of Greek institutions and the operation of those in "Western" states is caused by the existence of the "other community." If pressed, they may offer further reasons—the problem of scarcity in Greek society, or the long history of foreign intervention. This part of the elite has accepted the nineteenth-century concept of modernity, which defined progress in terms of political institutions. There is another group of urban intellectuals who possess most characteristics of the elite but reject the dominant symbol system. These people, who generally look at modernization in economic or social terms, form the leadership of the "combative" parties that seek adherents among the underprivileged parts of society.

There is no consensus among the underprivileged in Greek society, either. In fact, increasing social mobilization has contributed to a growing dissensus among these elements. Generally, the peasantry is able to exist without concern for the dominant symbol system in Greek culture, although some rural Greeks have always been able to acquire it through the educational process. Others have been acquainted with some variant of the symbol system through the clientage networks. The new urban proletarians, as well as some rural refugees, though sharing the linguistic, cultural, and educational disabilities of the peasantry, have not yet accepted the dominant values of the community; since they have little access to the dominant elite, they are ready to identify with some new set of symbols.

THE POLITICAL FORMULA

Given the disparate visions of the Greek nation and the disagreement on the underlying norms and goals of Greek society, it is not surprising to find conflict over the political formula appropriate for the society.[24] Generally, certain institutional forms were implicit in each image of Greece. Those imbued with Western values looked to a modern state characterized by constitutionalism, rational-legal bureaucratic forms, and representative institutions. For others, centralized bureaucratic forms reminiscent of the Byzantine tradition were the ideal political system. Some preferred a continuation of the traditions of local autonomy that had been observed under Ottoman rule. But none of these institutional preferences were actually realized.

The modern institutions imposed by the Bavarians did not at first conform to the expectations of the "Westerners"; although they were eventually altered to conform outwardly to the prevailing liberal constitutional norms of Western Europe, they were soon adapted to the traditions of Greek society. This has meant that in Greece, perhaps more than elsewhere, there is a discrepancy between the formal allocation of control and responsibility according to the contract principle and the effective appropriation of control according to status. This disparity has been kept somewhat under control by the pattern of clientage relations, through which the peasantry and the underprivileged in Greek society have always been connected to the political system. Today, clientage relationships are found in even the modern sectors of Greek society, and wherever they exist they have modified Greek attitudes toward the political formula. This emphasis on human relationships has hindered the development of loyalty to any impersonal institution, and there are few positive feelings toward institutions without corresponding feelings toward the incumbents in those institutions. A politician's support depends on his satisfactory performance of obligations—specifically, on his distribution of public resources through the clientage networks that extend from the national level down to the individual Greek. Greeks who are not connected by these relationships to political incumbents can hardly be expected to feel any loyalty to the state institutions.

The Greek monarchy has been evaluated in clientage terms. The Greek people's commitment to the Bavarian dynasty, and to monarchy as an institution, lapsed when Otho was unable to deliver patronage because of external circumstances and personal defects. The Danish House of Gluecks-burg, promoted by the Great Powers, has not been the object of universal admiration. King George I was not loved early in his reign, during years of Greek defeats on the diplomatic and military fronts. The controversy be-tween Constantine I and Venizelos, the alternation of monarchy and re-public in the interwar years, and the referendum on the constitutional ques-tion in 1946 are all indicators of disagreement over the proper political formulas for Greece. These conflicts stem primarily from the intrusion of personal loyalty as the major factor in the judgment of institutional arrange-ments. The concern of an officeholder, whether royal or not, has been for particular sets of clients rather than for the population at large.

As each new territory was attached to the Greek state, Athens became the center of its world. Politics in the kingdom had long been confined to the capital; and the new territories joined the rest of rural Greece outside the political system. In most Greek provinces a variety of loyalty eventually de-veloped as bureaucratic positions were filled with provincial notables and a network of patronage was extended outward from the capital. But the new territories found themselves at a disadvantage compared to the older regions of Greece. The Greeks of the new regions were confronted with a legal sys-tem and political institutions whose form and operation were unfamiliar, as well as with a dynasty as foreign to them as the one from which they had escaped. Moreover, the representatives of the centralized administration who dealt with these provinces assumed the air of colonial administrators. The politicians from the older regions controlled the bureaucracy, which was staffed by men who owed their positions to political and personal ties with the established elite. The bureaucracy functioned haphazardly or not at all; if action was to be obtained, it had to be through personal connection or political pressure. However, success in these terms was generally impos-sible for Greeks residing in the new areas.

The disadvantage, and in a sense the inferiority, of the new provinces was recognized, and each new territory had a governor-general or a deputy governor to look after its interests in the period of transition. This arrange-ment lasted until just after World War II in all regions except northern Greece, where a special minister is still assigned. At first, a native of an older region was generally appointed governor, and often did less for the new territory than he did for his friends and relatives at the expense of that ter-ritory. The new areas had material disadvantages in that improvements such as roads and schools were few. The priorities of the capital left little money for these matters in the rest of the country, and the distribution of patronage continued to slight the new provinces.

The loyalties of each new region remained with the particular individuals who had helped to free them from the Turks or other foreign princes. For example, the areas annexed after the Balkan Wars were loyal to Prime Minister Venizelos as a person rather than to the Greek state and King Constantine. The refugees in 1922 were loyal to Venizelos and to several of his lieutenants but profoundly hostile to the King and the politicians, whom they deemed responsible for their plight. These patterns of loyalty are related to the patterns of support given to the major political factions in the postwar period.

Since political loyalty is given to the person rather than to the institution, there can be no unchanging political formula and no standard description of individual obligation in Greece. The constitutional documents in modern Greek history have failed to spell out crucial details of authority: there was no precise description of the obligations and responsibilities of the monarch with respect to the premier; and even a thing as fundamental as the electoral system has never been part of the constitutional provisions. Governmental procedure has never been taken seriously, and the constitutional documents have been ignored or overruled on many occasions. Usually, the formal constitution and its political institutions have merely been utilized by competing constellations of clientage networks for their own purposes. This is the effective and expected mode of operation among the dominant elite and the bulk of the peasantry; however, social mobilization and urbanization have created an urban proletariat without the necessary clientage relationships. New "combative" elites in both the left-wing groups and the military have responded to this by proclaiming a desire to change the existing system by eliminating clientage relationships, for which modern political institutions operated along rational, impersonal, and bureaucratic lines would be substituted.

WESTERN POLITICAL STYLE

The tradition of accepting ideas and leadership from above as well as from outside has long prevailed among the modern Greeks. There has never been much concern with political initiation of action or policy; in fact, many Greeks were not aware that this was even a political option. The relationship of the individual to his government was passive, and exhibited many features of a subject political culture as outlined by Gabriel Almond and

Sidney Verba.[25] The rural Greek, even under democratic conditions, has had little knowledge of the government. Until recently, with developments in communications and transportation, issues did not reach him, and politicians seldom appeared in his neighborhood. The indifference of the capital, despite debate and promise, was broken only by occasional campaigns and minimal legislation. The most apparent connection between the countryside and the capital was the burden of indirect taxation; and the tax revenues were most often expended only in Athens. C. A. Munkman reports that even now there is a feeling that any funds sent to Athens will disappear "without any benefit to Greece."[26] However, the political system today is manifested in rural areas by education, military recruitment, and agricultural supervision, as well as by taxation.

The pattern of traditional clientage relationships has always been oriented to the output side of the Greek political system. Although Western parliamentary institutions were adopted early, there is still more emphasis on easing the effects of government activity than on initiating alternatives. The deputy is viewed as someone who will intercede in administrative matters rather than someone who processes political demands. Demands are phrased in personal terms, they are transmitted through personal relationships, and the obligation to satisfy them devolves upon particular persons. The villager expects the government to be unfair in awarding jobs and in distributing benefits. For most, the possibility of changing the system is inconceivable; the best that can be hoped for is a newly forged personal tie that might provide a new set of privileges for the individual and his family at the expense of the rest of society. Those with clientage ties know that they stand to benefit from the formalism engendered by the gap between authority and control; those without ties hope to secure them.

Laws in general are not looked upon as relevant for the villager, whether they are based upon resurrected Byzantine codes or imitated from the West. Often, these laws are not very relevant for even the modern sector of society. Disobedience is not a crime, and it is expected that a law will be violated or circumvented if this action might benefit the individual Greek or his family. This trait of irresponsibility has historical weight. In the earliest years, the Phanariot leaders continued to elude laws just as they had during the Ottoman administration; the primates and bandit chiefs were hardly better as examples. The prevailing behavior through these centuries was the avoidance, not the challenging, of authority.

The cleavage in Greek society as a whole follows the line of privileged and underprivileged, although neither community is completely homogeneous. The primary criteria differentiating one community from the other are language, occupational status, and education. For most of the population vertical clientage structures have connected one level of society with the other. The rest of the population, primarily composed of urban labor and refugee groups, is without clientage ties and therefore largely outside the political system. In the following chapters, we will examine the clientage structures and political system in greater detail, keeping in mind this background of dissensus and fragmentation.

5. Interest Groups

A glance at the telephone book or a close inspection of a building directory in downtown Athens will reveal the extent and variety of formal organizations in Greece. Any comprehensive listing would include equivalents for almost every major association found in the United States or Western Europe: business organizations, a labor confederation, a broadly inclusive agricultural organization, a myriad of occupational associations, and interest groups to promote every conceivable economic, social, intellectual, or humanitarian cause. In addition, as the foregoing chapters have shown, family influence and clientage networks also abound. Moreover, the bureaucracy and the military seem to fit easily into the places assigned to them as institutional interest groups. In other words, if one approaches the Greek political system armed with the interest-group typology most commonly utilized—that is, associational, nonassociational, institutional, and anomic—examples of each type are sure to be found.

According to Almond and Powell, an interest group can be broadly defined as "a group of individuals who are linked by particular bonds of concern or advantage, and who have some awareness of these bonds."[1] The specific typology offered by these authors, however, is only tangentially relevant to the Greek political system. Basically, their formulation, although noting that all types may be found in any system, assumes that the associational type is congruent with a high degree of economic and social differentiation. Conversely, nonassociational groups are assumed to be more usual in less "developed" settings. Myron Weiner's admonition that it is misleading to make too many assumptions about differences between modern and traditional groups is appropriate here.[2] The usual criteria of differentiation—the degree of organization, the continuity of activity, and the kind or style of demands—are not very effective in differentiating types of interest groups in the Greek political system. The most common categories, the associational and the nonassociational, will be the focus of this chapter. The category of anomic interest groups does not lend itself to examination in the Greek context. Institutional interest groups like the church or the bureaucracy do not operate as independent actors in Greece. The church and the bureaucracy are both penetrated by clientage networks originating in the political world. The military does operate as an independent group, but in a noninstitutional context rather than at the normal parliamentary level. And even the two major types of interest groups, regardless of their form or style of operation, do not conform to the pattern alleged to be common in Western Europe or the United States.

As we have seen, chronic insecurity has sustained the attitudes of distrust prevalent in Greek society. Association for mutual advantage is difficult. "Social conflict does not shake down into relatively orderly class or group conflict, but remains festering in the narrow interstices of personal relationships."[3] This, in turn, reinforces and perpetuates the traditional social unit, the family, and its extension, clientage structures based on mutual obligation. Under the pressure of an increasingly mobilized and complex society these structures simply expand to include a wider range of people.

Scarcity has other consequences for Greek interest-group activity. The political system is called upon to allocate a much broader range of values than it might in a more affluent setting. In Greece, political resources are often largely composed of intangibles such as exemptions and exceptions, personal favors, or special treatment, rather than resources more amenable to distribution on a group basis. "Modern" associational groups are difficult to create and sustain in such a setting, and they have little utility. On the other hand, clientage structures, with a limited and essentially noncompetitive membership that presents individual demands, seem to work fairly well. Genuine associational ties are possible only when the governmental concerns of individuals and firms are not likely to be solved through personal connections.

The same conditions have limited the development of political organizations that could qualify as modern political parties; this, combined with early independence, has been another factor differentiating Greece from many other underdeveloped states, in which major mass organizations grew out of nationalist movements, particularly in the interwar or postwar periods. In Greece, although the resistance and the civil war produced extensive social mobilization, the groups organized during that period did not develop because they were tagged as subversive after the civil war. Since modern parties do not exist, with the exception of the left-wing groups, party-inspired occupational or social organizations of a mass character have not touched many Greeks.

The associational interest groups found in Greece, despite their apparent similarity to those in the West, are in fact different in both structure and function. This is especially the case if one defines associational groups as specialized structures that explicitly represent the interests of a particular group, possessing a full-time professional staff and following orderly procedures in the formulation of programs and demands.[4] The associational interest groups in Greece are largely "official" in character, with nonvoluntary membership, a leadership responsive primarily to the state, and explicit governmental functions, particularly in the realm of regulatory activity. It is only their official character that makes for continuity or gives them a professional staff. They are examples of a category suggested, but less emphasized, by Almond and Powell: associational groups that do not articulate the needs felt and perceived by their members but serve to mobilize support for the existing political system or social institutions.[5]

Just as governmental institutions and legal forms were borrowed from the West in the early period of modern Greek history, the associational form initially developed in the West was also borrowed, before an industrial infrastructure existed to support it. Although some groups did develop spontaneously, the Western model, if not followed initially, was imposed on the fledgling organizations. Foreign pressures forced this course of action to some extent. Since Greece was forever a debtor nation, the government had to use all possible techniques for controlling her economy in order to placate the international financial community. The state machinery alone could not deal with problems of foreign exchange, import controls, labor relations, or the tariff. The associational form was a "modern" and convenient method. The corporate character of these economic and occupational interests was so well established by 1929 that the revived Greek Senate could include representatives from the major associations and professional organizations.* In the 1930's the government of Ioannis Metaxas reinforced these corporate associations and extended them to nearly every occupational group. Governments since 1946 have continued the practice.

Because of their "official" status, Greek associations and their leaders are

---

* There were corporate groups in the Senate to represent shipowners, the University and Academy of Athens, the commercial and industrial divisions of the Chamber of Commerce, the Technical Chamber of Commerce, the General Confederation of Labor, the Agricultural Chamber, and a craftsmen's and handicraftsmen's organization.

regarded with the same distrust as the rest of the state apparatus. There is little loyalty to the organization, and its regulations are violated as readily as government prescriptions are. The leadership of a group must inform the membership of government requests and requirements, and it must advise political leaders of the sentiments of group members. This last activity is not so much the articulation of group demands as it is the passing of political information; the leadership reflects the prevailing political winds, rather than internal group sentiments. In some cases, the leadership is formally selected by the state, and high organizational office often brings ex-officio status on state committees and boards. The desires of group members for security and for individual attention generally run counter to government aims, and both members and leaders often take part in unsanctioned demonstrations.

In Greece, there is also a tendency to endow essentially family-oriented and nonassociational groups with associational structures. Lawyers, for example, are active founders of associations; in this way they obtain a form of permanent patronage and increased political influence. Access to government officials and ministers is easier with an organizational title, spurious or not. Many government officials suspect the validity of organizational labels but seldom have the time or the resources to investigate them. Most organizations of this kind come to life sporadically, when the personal plans of the leadership require activity, or when a particular client demands intervention on his behalf. In several cases, the founders of these organizations have been able to use them for personal electoral success.

Regardless of organizational form, continuity, or type of demands, there is a common thread running through most Greek organizational life: the tie of mutual obligations that connects each member with the leader. Even in formal associations, Greek demands on government are channeled through informal patron-client groups that can include both organization members and public officials. If clientage ties to the political level are unavailable, the membership must resort to unsanctioned strikes and demonstrations. Although the formal organization may appear to be interested in group demands, the clientage networks within the organization are primarily oriented to individual concerns. They want changes in administrative regulations, or personal exceptions and favors. To gain these ends, they must deal with the premier or with the minister concerned; in some cases, the lower-level bureaucrats might be included in the bargaining process. The strategy of action differs from one general area to another partly because Greek government is so constructed that responsibility is hard to establish. The Greek acts as an individual, through personal or clientage ties; he does not recognize the existence of a common interest, or the necessity for organization.[6] Whenever modern structures do exist, they are penetrated by the clientage networks.

Most Greek groups fall most easily into the nonassociational pattern, with intermittent patterns of articulation, no organized procedures, and little continuity in structure.[7] The same is true elsewhere. Sidney Tarrow notes that in southern Italy the system of clientage is "shifting and informal, and has no institutional recognition in concrete institutions."[8] Binder, describing Iranian politics, notes that "the extended family stands at the center of Iranian social organization, and it remains the single most important political fact."[9] The emphasis on clientage ties in these countries, as in Greece, means that general interests are rarely enunciated; and legislation is rarely used as an instrument of social change. By their very nature, individual demands processed by clientage networks are best satisfied with a minimum of institutional disruption.

Political phenomena in large-scale political systems, such as those in the West, are frequently compared with phenomena in small-scale systems, and formulations useful on one level are transferred to another. In most instances, fruitful insights and increased understanding result. However, size alone may sometimes limit the utility of comparisons. For example, even in the most advanced sectors of Greek society there are so few individuals and firms that organizational activity may not be crucial, or even practical. Even in large-scale systems, especially large firms may often ignore existing associational groups and intervene directly in the administrative or legislative processes.[10]

The pattern of interest-group activity at subnational levels in other large nations, particularly in federal states, provides one possible comparison with the Greek case. In these settings, regardless of a country's level of development, the potential membership for most groups is not as large; and there are likely to be more connections among the leaders in the various social and economic sectors. Moreover, the limitations imposed on a small state by the international system may function in a way very similar to the limitations imposed by a national government on its constituent elements. For example, Weiner's discussion of interest-group activity (or rather the lack of it) at the state level in India closely parallels the Greek situation. According to him, organizational activity in the Indian states is inhibited because local ties and traditions impede cooperative activity; instead, each individual acts to protect or serve himself, even if it damages someone with a similar status or occupation. As in Greece, the focus is on the modification of governmental action rather than on the formulation of demands for legislative processing. This pattern of action is successful at the state level because the local administrators and deputies, unlike the top echelons of Indian government, are amenable to personal influence.[11]

THE INSTITUTIONAL FRAMEWORK

It is axiomatic that regardless of organizational form or representation formulas, interest groups in any society seek those points in the governmental structure where demands are likely to be satisfied.[12] Whether these points lie in the bureaucracy, a political party, or some point in the formal representational institutions depends upon the pattern of power in the political system. In India, few demands are directed to the members of the national parliament or the higher bureaucrats: the representatives have little power to satisfy demands, and the bureaucrats are either hostile or unresponsive. As a result, interest demands are channeled largely to the leaders of the Congress Party.[13] Below the national level, however, bureaucrats and deputies may be approached as easily as party leaders. In Italy, according to LaPalombara, interest groups intervene primarily at the bureaucratic level, although certain legislative institutions, such as standing committees, can be important.[14] Grossholtz notes that, in the Philippines, "demands have been handled not by bureaucratic planners, as in other developing countries, but by politicians with a democratic bargaining spirit."[15] Interest-group literature for Western Europe and the United States is equally concerned with problems of access. Even in these modern settings, the kinds of demands made may make a difference, since individual and "group" demands may be handled through different institutional channels. Almond and Powell suggest that personal channels may be utilized in any system, regardless of its level of social and economic differentiation.[16]

In Greece, demands have tended to remain "individual" in character for reasons suggested earlier. Modern associational activity is of minor importance in the Greek political system. However, individual demands, or even interest-group demands, are not viewed by most sectors as a threat to the public interest. Political institutions existed before more complex economic and social structures developed; and partly because of this, demands of all kinds tend to go to the political level. Since, with the exception of an occasional individual, the Greek political parties and bureaucracy are not committed to any long-range goals (e.g., modernization), the whole basis of Greek political organization has been office-holding; in this context, the satisfaction of individual demands is the normal mode of operation. Weiner suggests that "only when politics becomes increasingly legislative in character, and when elections and universal suffrage are introduced, do numbers, and consequently organizational numbers, begin to count."[17] However, the Greek experience suggests that under certain conditions, if universal suffrage is introduced before social and economic differentiation is far advanced, organization and numbers may still not be crucial. In Greece, the existing clientage structures simply accommodated universal suffrage; this, in turn, inhibited large-scale interest politics, at least until recently. Moreover, although the bureaucracy in many countries follows rational-legal norms and is relatively immune to personal demands, the Greek bureaucracy has been penetrated by political clientage groups from the beginning.

Most political demands in Greece are not "group" demands, and the points of access in the political process are most amenable to individual pressure. So much is evident in the responses of the 55 Greek deputies interviewed in 1964 for this study. They were generally unencumbered with organizational memberships other than those required by their particular professional backgrounds. There were some exceptions, particularly on the Left, but in these cases the organizations were of a literary, international, or front-organization type. Several deputies said that they tried not to get mixed up with outside organizations. Most of those interviewed could not recall representatives of organized groups coming to see them. Others, although they remembered such visits, seemed to regard them as inevitable but unproductive; these men came mainly from the urban areas. Two of those queried had made their reputations as representatives of specific interest groups: one was a former officer of a civil servants' union, and the other was close to various sports organizations in Athens. This kind of identification has been possible only in areas where adherents of the particular organizations were concentrated, and may have depended on an electoral system that allowed voters' second and third choices to become effective. The problem of linkage between society and the state apparatus in Greece, therefore, is not as severe as it is in countries like India, inasmuch as the peasantry, the bureaucracy, and the political organizations all operate by a system of obligations.

POLITICAL RESOURCES AND POLITICAL DEMANDS

There is a substantial gap between the ostensible and real functions of political institutions in contemporary Greece. The basic public law is the starting point for any discussion of this phenomenon. The contemporary legal system, with a civil law based on conflicting Byzantine sources, a nineteenth-century French commercial code ill-adapted to its new environment, and adaptations of more recent foreign codes masquerading as legal reforms, is characterized by complexity and intense conflict.[18] The codes may have originally been prescriptive in character; but decades of training in jurisprudence have produced a bureaucracy that judges all activity by its conformity to regulations, even contradictory ones. There is a constant need for new legislative enactments, ministerial decrees, and administrative rulings to fill in gaps or adjust conflicts in the existing laws. Thorough legislative reform in any area is discouraged; instead, minor adjustment or alteration is the rule. These conditions encourage particularistic bureaucratic treatment and constant political interference in the administrative world. Enforcement officials are left with many personalized choices because of this legal tangle. Access to the political leaders, particularistic riders to legislation, and interference in bureaucratic procedures are all useful as inducements to "sway the specific choices or the strategies of another individual."[19] It is for these things that a voter casts his ballot for a deputy; and it is for these things that individual firms form connections with particular political groupings. Although politicians may decry formalism and the poorly functioning state machinery, these circumstances are the main source of political capital in Greece.

Formalism, at the same time that it creates political resources for politicians and bureaucrats, impedes the formation of genuine interest groups. Common interests are difficult to detect because the emphasis is always on the amelioration of individual grievances. Each member of a group or social category has a better chance to gain an advantage through personal connections than through legislation of a general character. For example, the nature of Greek tax policy diminishes the common interests of the business sector.[20] Ordinarily, a new government activity is financed by a specific new levy rather than by general funds; the service and those benefited by it are determined on political grounds, and may have no relation to the part of the community that must pay the new tax. Specific business elements constantly suffer from the almost random imposition of these taxes. In general, the tax position of any individual industry depends on its political influence, which is determined by family connections or clientage ties to political leaders. Anyone with a substantial financial interest cannot afford to be unprotected; if he eschews clientage relationships, his wealth will diminish.

The Greek tax system is not an instrument of general government policy, but a political resource available for the satisfaction of individual demands. The various taxes on consumption are levied on such a variety of items and at such varying rates that no total assessment is possible. There are numerous exemptions for specific individuals and firms. In general, the taxes fall hardest on that portion of the population that can least afford to pay them. The income-tax system has also developed numerous advantages for specific individuals. The income tax set up in 1950 already has 423 exceptions that benefit the royal family, members of parliament, shipping companies, merchant seamen, journalists, artists, and certain agricultural enterprises.[21] Only one-twelfth of the working population pays the income tax;[22] and even for those who cannot get exemptions, the rates are hardly confiscatory.

In the 1920's tariffs were imposed, partly for protection and partly for balance-of-payments purposes. They, too, have particularistic aspects. Certain favored industries, developed in this protected atmosphere, have had little incentive to improve operational efficiency or to undertake additional commitments for industrialization; yet they are the beneficiaries of action supposedly taken in the national interest. As effective as the protective tariff in eliminating competition has been the postwar government practice of declaring certain industries "satiated": this means that no new firms can be established in a given industry. The first price-fixing laws were established in 1834; they are still in effect, though with many changes. Laws of unequal competition have long been a part of the Greek business scene. These measures, too, because they can be applied for the benefit of individuals or single firms, hardly promote collective action. All of these government regulations and policies have been particularly amenable to personal connections and family influence; hence they have not affected the business community uniformly.

MAJOR INTEREST GROUPS

There are three major organizations in Greece, each with connections to the state and each concerned with specific sectors of the business world: the Chamber of Commerce and Industry, the Chamber of Craftsmen, and the Technical Chamber. These organizations advise their membership of government actions and report the feelings of their membership to official agencies. They also have some governmental and regulating functions. For example, the Chamber of Commerce and Industry is an arm of the Ministry of Commerce. It acts officially in approving applications for import licenses and in disciplining price-control violators. Various official revenue-collecting duties are carried on by each of the business organizations.

These business organizations were either created by the Greek state or were formed with official encouragement. Since the commercial sector of the Greek nation had been left outside the boundaries of the new state, the state itself initiated some economic activity and the corresponding associational activity. Local Chambers of Commerce were set up in the nineteenth century;[28] in the early part of the present century, the major business organizations in existence today were formed. In theory, these groups are structures for relating views to policy makers; in practice, they have operated more as adjuncts to the state administration, without articulating the interests of their members. From this perspective, such associations can only hinder Greek political development. However, the precarious character of the Greek economy, the necessity for government allocation of most resources, and the deficiencies of Greek public administration have all encouraged the state to use these groups as levers to control certain economic sectors.

The compulsory character and diverse membership of the business associations makes them ineffective as a link between their membership and the state. As parts of the state apparatus, they are distrusted. The all-inclusive nature of their membership creates conflict in the Chambers and is a basic cause of disloyalty in the component organizations. Naturally, there is little common interest between large and small firms, between importers and domestic producers, and between the different sectors of commerce and industry; there is even a regional conflict between concerns located in the Athens-Piraeus area and those in the outlying provinces. Yet these diverse units must all operate under the umbrella of the same business organizations. There is no real alternative, since the small total number of firms means that there are rarely enough in any single business to create a viable organization.

Collective action is difficult for these organizations because their advantage to the individual is not always apparent; and support, either financial or moral, for organizations with long-term aims or deferred prospects is difficult to obtain. The family nature of most Greek firms and industries has meant that family values predominate, which also weakens the impetus for formal associational activity. Moreover, ownership and employment in Greek business are both highly concentrated, and the two are very often synonymous. In 1963, of the 189,209 persons employed in Greek commercial establishments, 49.9 per cent were proprietors, and another 13.3 per cent were unpaid family members.[24] At the same time, 70 per cent of all corporations had fewer than nine shareholders, and 22 per cent fewer than five.[25] The prominence of cottage industry, the small market area, and the emphasis on service occupations further diminish organizational activity: in such cases, the family is the economic unit; and it, like the individual, looks upon those in a similar position as competitors for scarce resources rather than as potential collaborators. Alec Alexander found that the fathers of most present-day industrialists either had the same status as their sons or came from the ranks of craftsmen and large merchants; the step to the industrial category involved expansion of the original activity.[26] This development pattern has produced a large number of relatively inefficient small firms, running more in response to family values than on principles of economic efficiency. The focus remains on gaining individual exceptions rather than on presenting group demands.

The owner of a small business, of course, does not have access to the highest points in the administration. However, if he has a moderate class position, monetary resources, or the ability to provide reciprocal favors, he can work directly with the civil servants. In return for assistance in circumventing government regulations or acquiring wealth, he can furnish a poorly paid bureaucrat with bribes and gratuities. If this fails, or if the administrative channels are clogged, the small businessman can receive a prompt hearing from his deputy. In any case, he is likely to be concerned with information, favorable rulings, or relief from specific enactments; there is no need for collective action to realize such demands.

There are a great number of occupational interest groups in Greece whose chief concern is the formation and administration of pension and insurance funds. These funds were established gradually for individual occupations, beginning in the nineteenth century; they now number over 150, each with fiscal and administrative autonomy, and each authorized by the state to compel contributions.[27] Of the total number, about six cover almost all economically active Greeks. Any change in a fund's structure of contributions, sources of outside revenue, or scale of benefits must be approved by the government. Although all the funds are legally and organizationally separate from the occupational groups they cover, many occupational groups were in fact organized solely as sources of revenue for their funds. And in most cases the organizational officers play a part in the administration of the welfare fund.

An all-inclusive welfare fund was established in 1937 to provide old-age pensions and medical insurance; it also administers unemployment and housing benefits. It covers most nonagricultural workers, and is financed by contributions from both workers and employers. A social insurance scheme for agriculture was established in 1961; besides providing medical and old-age benefits, it includes crop insurance. Revenue for this fund comes from a surcharge on the income tax, a stamp duty, a specific tax on tobacco, and extra taxes on items such as coffee, cocoa, whiskey, and malt. Another revenue source is two-thirds of the yield of a 3 per cent tax on the wholesale traffic in agricultural products. These two are general funds that do not reflect particular occupational organizations. However, the remaining insurance funds are closely related to organized interest groups; and they also obtain revenue from sources beyond actual beneficiary contributions. The fund covering shopkeepers and self-employed craftsmen has revenue from several stamp duties and surcharges accruing to it. The fund for civil-service pensions is aided by taxes on the sale of office supplies and the rental of buildings to the government. The fund for the Seamen's Union receives part of a payroll tax, 3 per cent of the gross turnover in marine passenger transport, and a share in the basic tariff. The medical workers' fund gets tax revenue on prescriptions, reports, and examinations of several varieties. The bakers' fund levies a tax on each kilo of wheat ground domestically and a similar impost on imported flour. The social insurance fund for legal personnel has 21 different sources of contributions and revenue.

Other less important formal organizations exist in the cities, but they are badly fragmented. Cooperation for common demands is resisted, and each group pursues its individual purposes in competition with other groups. Defects in leadership and in membership, characteristic of the larger formal organizations, are also found here. The excessive fragmentation to be found even within groups simply illustrates the personalist character of these organizations. Veterans' associations provide an instructive example. There are separate groups formed along political lines—some stemming from particular units and particular wars, and others organized for specific categories of the disabled. Moreover, there are additional organizations for dependents of veterans. Potential demands of veterans as a group are passed up in favor of more specific demands that favor only one small category of veterans. Perhaps it is recognized that since nearly all Greeks are veterans, only relatively specific demands are likely to be satisfied. Whatever effect these fragmented organizations have comes from the ties of leaders or individual veterans to political leaders or bureaucratic officials.

In the larger cities of Greece, there are "origin" associations for those who come from specific parts of the country. In some respects these organizations are modern; in other ways they seem to be variants of the traditional clientage structures. They attract people who would normally be competing with each other in the rural setting, and create regional or provincial loyalties; they communicate with their members by weekly or monthly newsletters; they tend to promote general group concerns; and they are permanent organizations that emphasize formal meetings, social activities, and celebrations. On occasion, they are useful to recent arrivals from the countryside, since they can work through traditional channels to provide assistance in finding employment and housing.

The older origin associations in the Athens area have become mainly social and cultural in nature, although they may sometimes still assist new arrivals. However, they have largely eschewed a political function, and their usefulness to the recent migrant is less than it used to be. There are similar origin associations in Thessaloniki. Since this is a newer city, and because the origins of newcomers are not so diverse, the major provincial origin associations still have significant political influence. Not only do they satisfy demands from individual members through clientage channels, but they act as a group to influence local elections and the selection of deputies to the national parliament. When origin associations are oriented toward politics in this way, they also prove useful in the home provinces, through influence on the members' relatives who have remained at home.

THE ADVANTAGED

Greeks who are successful in any sector of society usually have personal connections with individual members of the major political groupings. For them, the Greek system works well, as long as equilibrium is maintained between the parliamentary level and the other major groups, such as the military and the left wing. These men are better able to secure satisfaction of their personal requirements than those less highly placed. Because Greece is small, and because Athens is the foremost commercial, financial, and intellectual center, as well as the capital city, there is constant communication between one sector and another—between politicians, state officials, leading professors, bankers, publishers, and shipowners. There are few "leading figures," and the number of members in any single sector is small. None of these men need association support. Since they have resources useful in the political arena, they can press personal demands through the normal channels of mutual obligation. A government minister—the source of favors, special legislation, or support for the status quo—provides the key to success. The minister needs political support; those around him need governmental favors. Even the most highly placed business or professional men find it difficult to maintain reciprocity with all important sectors of society, and a politician can act as a broker for those with insufficient influence in one sector and a surplus in another.[28]

Even though corporate power is concentrated in the hands of a relatively few families, it is clear that the major business interests are far from united.[29] The Commercial Bank of Greece, together with its subsidiaries, is controlled by Stratis Andreadis.[30] Although he was closely identified with much of the economic activity under the Karamanlis regime, Andreadis seemed eager to express his friendship for the Papandreou government as well. The National Bank of Greece is more closely tied to the prevailing political group, since its governor is selected by the Prime Minister. The deputy governor of the bank in recent years has played a role in nonpolitical, caretaker governments and in negotiations between the political world and the royal family. Most of the financial aspects of Greek economic development programs have involved both banking groups; conversely, each banking group has members active in both major political groupings.

The directors of the banks, insurance companies, and other major financial interests are often selected from the ranks of retired generals and politicians. Moreover, each of the major banking and insurance groups has ties with particular banking houses abroad, and each has its own stable of industries in Greece. For example, some 70 per cent of the insurance assets are controlled by six companies, of which the two largest, Ethniki and Astir, are closely affiliated with the two largest banks.[31] Aside from the Bank of Greece, which is the central bank of issue for banknotes and serves the government in the realm of monetary policy, these two commercial banking groups control 96.3 per cent of all assets.[32] Other key figures in business and finance have ties to different banking groups and access to different politicians; some are also leading political figures, and so have no need for access to government through interest-group organization.

Certain other sectors of society are also crucial to the political level. The press, because of its importance in the political struggle, has always been subjected to a good deal of government interference, in the form of both punishments and rewards. In Otho's day, newspapers were required to deposit funds to be forfeited in case of libel; but one newspaper was enabled to exist with only sixteen paying customers because of government subsidies during the same period.[33] A provision in the penal code concerning "insults against authority" has traditionally been used to discourage journalistic criticism of those in power; its wording is vague enough that a minister can press for its application whenever he wishes, depending upon his personal whims and the political situation. In the immediate postwar period, many newspapers were reestablished by government financial assistance. Naturally, these funds were allotted on political priorities; however, political loyalties have in some cases changed, even though the loans are outstanding. The loans are now so old as to be politically uncollectable, but the threat of enforcing them is still a weapon available to any unduly harassed government. Governments have also manipulated labor legislation to penalize certain publishers. Nevertheless, publishers have benefited individually and as a group from their political connections. The state undertook to import and distribute newsprint because of the foreign exchange problem immediately after World War II. This practice continues, but now it is a form of financial subsidy to the newspaper owners. Newspaper owners are exempted from regular income taxes.[34] But these financial benefits also give the government still another lever to control dissident journals. Even though all Greek publishers have privileges and liabilities of a similar kind, they are not united because the privileges and liabilities can be invoked in a particularistic manner.

The Union of Journalists, one of the most prestigious and privileged organizations in Greece, is composed of about 500 older journalists. The members of this group have received substantial privileges from the state because of their crucial role in the political process. An individual deputy cannot become known without some assistance from the press; except for major figures given space because of their position, every politician must forge ties to senior journalists if his name and activities are to be mentioned in the newspaper columns. Since no Greek newspaper is large enough for extensive coverage, the journalist has discretion of great political importance. Ordinary citizens know of the Union of Journalists through its annual lottery, a closely guarded prerogative. From this source of revenue, journalists receive a handsome pension and a large financial settlement upon retirement; in fact, the journalists' lottery, before the 1967 coup, ranked with those established for such past worthy causes as archeological excavations and battleships. Journalists (who are defined solely in terms of membership in the Union), like members of parliament, are allowed to bring autos into the country without paying the usual surcharge to Their Majesties' Fund, which accounts for about half the cost of an imported car.

The Union of Journalists, because of its privileges, has become an exclusive organization; but journalism is a popular profession in Greece, and there are many younger journalists who must remain outside the Union. A rival journalists' organization has developed; but since it has acquired no privileges, it is an organization with no membership solidarity, without purpose or prospects. Journalists as an occupational category have not benefited from special privilege, only those with useful ties to the political world. The senior journalists have made gains not because of their organization, but because of their crucial role in the political process and their individual ties to the various political groups.

Shipping interests have won many special considerations in Greece, regardless of the government in power. Each major political faction on the parliamentary level has its own shipowners in attendance; of the most well-known, Stavros Niarchos flourished during the Karamanlis regime, and Aristotle Onassis had close ties with Sophocles Venizelos, one of the leaders of the Center Union. Personal connection and friendship, not organizational politics, keep the shipowners in the various political camps. Shipping has received special consideration because it is crucial to Greek politics. A politician from the islands, for instance, must have connections with a major shipowner not only for personal use, but to transport voters from the mainland to their home constituencies. It is not accidental either that members of parliament and journalists receive free transportation on domestic lines. In return, shipping has received substantial tax benefits. The lagging development of other kinds of internal transport in Greece may be related to this state of affairs.

A Greek doctor or dentist is automatically a member of his professional association. However, these associations are far from united; each contains all the cleavages prevalent in Greek society, and additional points of conflict as well. In proportion to the whole population, these fields are not overcrowded. However, the high concentration of doctors and dentists in the Athens-Piraeus area and in several other urban places does make for intense competition. The province of Attica, with some 37 per cent of the population, has 64 per cent of all general practitioners and 85 per cent of the specialists.[35] The fact that state-sponsored welfare schemes and the urban unions are major employers accounts in some measure for this concentration. However, the state has been unable to encourage settlement in the provinces, in spite of government salary incentives and other privileges. Basically, the professional man is reluctant to leave the metropolitan area.

In addition to efforts to encourage the relocation of medical men, there are also attempts to limit entry into the field, both by tightening qualifications and by putting restrictions on the practice of those with medical degrees earned abroad. Practices often pass from father to son, making it difficult for a newcomer to become established. The beginning doctor may be forced to barter his services (an appendectomy, for example) for future favors from others. Most doctors and dentists must have both private patients and several government connections in order to survive. The state, as usual, is viewed as the major opponent of physicians; and the Ministry of Health is an adversary rather than a sponsor. In dentistry and medicine, as in other occupations, competition is so intense that survival and advancement depend not on the activities of a professional association but on personal connection and political friendship. Nevertheless, these professions, perhaps because of the insecurity of their membership, do not have the political importance of their Western counterparts.

THE DISADVANTAGED

The sectors of Greek society without clientage ties are at an enormous disadvantage; and it is in these sectors that the development of modern associational activity has gone the furthest, especially in the urban areas. Those without clientage ties have many of the same attitudes of distrust toward the state, organizations, leaders, and their fellows as other Greeks do, but the fact that they cannot operate through the traditional relationships forces them to organize. The groups that have difficulty uniting are precisely the ones that ultimately pay for the privileges given to more influential members of the community. Unfortunately, the mere creation of associations based on mutual interest and the subsequent formulation of group demands do not mean that either individual or associational grievances are likely to be acted on. The major elements in the traditional parties depend largely on constructing networks of clients, not on the cultivation of the group vote; in fact, there is no national executive office filled by popular vote. Moreover, given the scarcity of resources, sweeping group demands are difficult to satisfy; political resources are distributed on an individual basis not only because they have a greater effect but because there are not enough to go around.

The Refugees

The population exchanges in the Balkans after 1922 brought more than a million refugees into Greece. These people, although sharing a common plight, were originally differentiated by origin, cultural level, education, and occupation. They had neither the status to work at the highest levels of politics nor the clientage ties necessary to improve their conditions; at the same time, they were largely lacking in the mutual trust and hierarchical authority necessary for cooperation and collective action. Today, the largest refugee association in Greece is the Pan-Refugee Congress, which primarily represents refugees who were not permanently resettled or properly housed prior to World War II.[36] The agreements on population exchanges had left Moslem property in Greece in the hands of the Greek state, just as Greek property in Anatolia was left to the Turkish state; the Greek government was to use this property or its income for refugee resettlement. In 1955 about half of this "exchangeable" property still remained in the hands of the government. The cost of its administration was nearly equal to the income from it, since liquidation, when carried out, had provided far less than the property's appraised value. By and large, refugee demands for increased scholarship aid, assistance in paying fees demanded in order to obtain clear titles to refugee homes, and public assistance in general, have been contingent on the supposed resources of the refugees, the exchangeable property. Eventually an independent authority for the administration of this property was set up, but it is unlikely that the demands of the refugees will ever be fulfilled.

The major problem for the unsettled refugees in 1956 was still housing. The Karamanlis regime had tried to meet this need by state construction of housing, and also by providing urban refugees with land and with money to build their own dwellings. But progress was too slow: already, three generations of refugees had appealed for the housing due them; and events since the mid-thirties had merely intensified their hardships. Since traditional political avenues were closed, and since organized group action has little impact on Greek parliamentary politics, the refugees have turned to other political forms, particularly to the radical politics of the Left. This renders a settlement of the refugee problem more difficult than ever: in a world of scarcity, no political regime is likely to gamble by placating its enemies at the expense of its supporters. In addition to this older bloc of refugees, there are newer groups who were expelled from various Middle Eastern nations, especially Egypt, after World War II. By and large, these groups have eschewed connections with any political party. Since these particular refugees often had wealth, education, and skills, they are better able to operate within the transitional political milieu. Nevertheless, their problems in regard to employment, discrimination, taxation, and pensions have not been completely solved either.

The Worker

For Greeks who are low on the social scale, overcoming the disturbing effects of formalism is difficult. The recently mobilized urban laborer cannot influence a bureaucrat except through an intermediary. He has little more than one vote among thousands; he, his family, and his associates cannot be significant in an urban electoral district. Even a labor organization has little impact on the parliamentary level of Greek politics. True, some of the worker's needs are recognized. On the surface, Greek labor legislation appears to be comprehensive and progressive; there is a complete system of social insurance and a great deal of legislation on working conditions. However, the simple fact that the state administers the system means that in order to benefit the individual has to have access to the bureaucracy. There is little effort to inform the worker of his rights, and still less attention is paid to channeling complaints to the proper authority. Violations on the part of employees and malpractices by union leaders are common. The Greek worker's major concern is job security, and he is likely to accept abuses of the labor legislation passively, since the channels for correcting them are full of obstructions. Moreover, the Greek state is interested chiefly in economic stability, and has many weapons to enforce it. A legacy of restrictive labor regulations from the Metaxas period is available for any government. Since the government is so involved in the economy, strikes and disruptions of any kind can be interpreted adversely. Threats of military call-up or dismissals are constant when strikes threaten to curtail essential services, either public or private. The army has been used to replace striking workers on several occasions. The police are not very careful when dealing with labor disturbances. Under these conditions, strikes rarely last long; one or two days is the usual term, since neither the workers nor their unions have the financial resources to continue.

To the extent that formal labor demands are made, they seem to be channeled primarily through the political spokesmen of the Left, and almost always concern economic benefits or adjustments in job security. These demands are rarely satisfied; in fact, statistics from the Ministry of Labor indicate that the most common result of a strike is a "no result." Most strikes begin with little notice and end without mediation or negotiations.[37] Given its limited access to the political level through personal ties and its minimal solidarity, it is not surprising that the Greek working class is at a great disadvantage in the struggle for political favors.

The first labor unions were organized in areas of "unredeemed" Greece at the beginning of the century, and workers in the tobacco industries were the first to be involved in union activity. The early unions seem to have had a personalist rather than an ideological orientation; in fact, they seem to have been a variety of the traditional Greek social unit. Personal quarrels among leaders, as well as extreme differentiation of unions by region and function, inhibited any general organization. The unions first became involved in politics in the 1920's, during the controversy over the future of the regime. The leaders of individual unions, with their membership in tow, rallied to diverse camps. For example, coastal sailors, drawn mainly from the Peloponnesus, were intensely royalist, whereas sailors from many of the islands were republicans.

Large-scale labor organization has had little success in Greece. In 1929 the tenuous General Confederation of Greek Labor split into two parts. A separate Communist labor group, the United General Confederation of Labor, was formed, and existed until the Comintern's united-front period, when the two confederations were finally reunited. At this point, the advent of the Metaxas regime brought complete government control of all labor organizations. After World War II, the General Confederation was reconstituted, and a Communist was elected as the new secretary-general. However, the government stepped in to annul the election; consequently, a provisional secretary-general was appointed. This appointee, whose position was later ratified by election, remained the spokesman for the labor movement until 1964, when he was removed by the new Papandreou government. Throughout this time, the official labor leadership cooperated willingly with government and industry; it was an arm of the state rather than an independent political actor. Although the Papandreou government apparently wished to free the labor movement from explicit government control, efforts to remodel the General Confederation were delayed. Labor remained fragmented, with separate union groups tied to individual politicians and diverse sectors of Greek political life. Basically, the dispute was not only over formulas for representation, but over the ultimate relation of this labor organization to the state itself. The military coup of April 1967 postponed any solution of the problem.

The dominance of agriculture in Greece (it involves over 53 per cent of the economically active population) and the multitude of occupations in which self-employment has been the rule have fatally limited the scope of union organization.[38] The proportion of the Greek labor force employed in manufacturing actually dropped between 1929 and 1961, from 14.1 to 13.1 per cent.[39] In 1961 there were only 188,877 persons working in manufacturing industries employing more than ten persons.[40] Most of these are employed in traditional manufacturing operations, such as food processing, rather than in heavy industry. The small scale of commercial and industrial activity tends to perpetuate the clientage structures inherited from the countryside. Nearly 80 per cent of all Greek commercial establishments, even wholesalers, employ only one or two persons, usually the proprietor or his family.[41] In 1966, only 1,353 commercial establishments in all of Greece (1.6 per cent of the total) employed ten or more persons.[42] A businessman or entrepreneur can easily assume the patron's role in this context, further inhibiting organizational activity. Moreover, union membership remains unattractive for some Greeks because of the heavy Communist influence in the labor movement in its early years.[43] Finally, an occupation involving manual labor is not popular, since labor seems to be synonymous with servitude. In fact, a Greek workingman often changes into a suit and tie before leaving his place of employment, transforming himself into a white-collar worker for the bus ride home.

The fundamental dilemma for trade unions in Greece is simply that there are more laborers than jobs; underemployment and unemployment are chronic. Another bar to organizational activity, in labor and elsewhere, is the tendency for a person to be involved in several different occupations. In such a context, and considering the basic mistrust of those unconnected by mutual obligations, it is not surprising that labor organization is impeded, or that there is little class or occupational solidarity. In the postwar period, labor organizations were not able to force wage gains, even to equal productivity increases.[44] As in other countries, the pressure of unemployment or lack of opportunities in rural Greece drives people to the cities. However, Greece's modern industries cannot accommodate these new arrivals, and most other establishments can absorb only a small fraction. The migrants eventually enter the already crowded service sector, where the proliferation of individual occupations and the intense competition further inhibit any organizational activity.[45]

The Rural Greek

If the Greek peasant is in a better condition than the lower-class urban dweller, it is because government does not affect him as directly, and because his clientage ties remain intact. In the lore of modern Greece one often encounters the proposition that the peasant is and always has been intensely aware of national politics. On the other hand, Irwin Sanders has suggested that the Greek peasantry would be indifferent to politics if allowed to pursue its own affairs. He found that most peasants are chiefly concerned with community affairs, crops, and personalities.[46] There is concern with politics but it is a concern similar to that for earthquakes or bad weather. Beyond that, political discussion is confined to personal relations and mutual obligations.

Throughout Greece, but particularly in the rural areas, there is a feeling that correct party affiliation is crucial for the receipt of government benefits.[47] It is also assumed that improvements beneficial to a whole community are distributed with an eye to how the village as a whole voted in the last election. Even within the village, although party affiliation is not as crucial as it is assumed to be in the outside world, there is evidence that political factions do arise and persist. It is not a matter of the rural notables opposing the rest of the population; rather, as Myron Weiner notes for rural India, "conflicts between persons, families, factions, and castes virtually preclude joint enterprises by those who have wealth."[48] The network of friendships among the village officials becomes a de facto party because it operates as a patronage system.[49] Party labels may not be used in local campaigns, but the network of personal ties that forms behind each competing candidate may reach out of the village to patrons at the provincial level, and ultimately to Athens.

The rural Greek feels that he is related to the state as a subject rather than as a citizen. The ordinary villager may be able to deal with local officials, but he must also cope with the laws and regulations emanating from the central government. He is not self-sufficient: money is required for goods not produced at home, for tax purposes, and for status. The peasant relies on government credit, and is increasingly involved in politics because of government agricultural policy. The government, although legally offering many benefits and services to the individual Greek, does little to publicize them; and the average citizen has difficulty in determining which governmental agency should be approached with any given problem.[50] The administrative structure is further bedeviled by various "legal entities of public law," which are ostensibly private concerns but carry on state-financed activities. These agencies are more mysterious to the peasant than the government itself; and when he confronts them, he needs the intercession of a politician.

Even if the proper channel can be determined, the rural Greek has a difficult time approaching civil servants, even minor officials, because of his low status.[51] In nearly every government office, including those at the provincial level, the ushers at the door are haughty enough to keep all but the most persistent lower-class petitioners away. Bribes, often in the guise of gifts, are the accepted practice in dealing with officials; they may be cash gifts to minor officials, or some gift such as produce offered to a higher bureaucratic official out of "goodwill" rather than as payment for a specific request. Since very little discretion is allowed to lower members of the civil service, it is often crucial for the petitioner to bring his case to the attention of the higher officials; however, the differences in status and the bureaucratic system itself discourage this.

Some leftist groups attempt to gain government attention by strikes or riots. But the ordinary petitioner has only a few alternatives. He can write to the Prime Minister, whose personal office has a staff of about 50 political appointees to handle communications addressed to him. The office takes note of questions and complaints and sends a copy of the petitioner's letter to the appropriate minister, together with a form letter from the Prime Minister. However, the letters sent by this office are standardized, and the recipient can tell from the form of the letter whether or not he should respond with action. The citizen hears nothing about his request unless he comes to Athens or has someone check for him. Another channel for complaint is the Council of State, which supposedly protects the citizen from arbitrary acts of the state; but it cannot help the average Greek in his dealings with the bureaucracy. In fact, during the Karamanlis period, advice from this agency was consistently rejected or ignored. The courts are equally unsatisfactory. There is an insufficient judicial staff and by and large it is of poor quality. The court system cannot be more effective than the laws it has to enforce; if laws are largely formalistic, responsibility for state action or inaction is difficult to place. The courts, in the Greek system, are part of the political bargaining network and the bureaucracy, with all the usual liabilities. The existence of an independent judiciary is largely illusory, as is any expectation of redress for individual grievances.

The only solution for the ordinary villager is to turn to a patron, to someone with influence in the community who also has connections outside it. This patron is usually a deputy, and the kind of assistance he can provide is geared to the individual client—a job, the adjustment of a particular wrong committed by the state, or intervention in the bureaucratic process. Any patron is assumed to be able to do more material favors for a client than the client can possibly return in kind. Eventually, this can create a political obligation. The Greek peasant is likely to have a closer tie to the deputy in his district either personally, or through local notables, than a city dweller does. The rural deputy is more likely to respond to demands because electoral districts are small, and consistent slights may lose votes. This system is not unlike Weiner's description of rural Indian politics. In Indian cities the disadvantaged person is likely to become involved in group activity; in the country, his interests can be served by attachment to a particular politician. The same attachment that makes rural India a bulwark of the Congress Party makes rural Greece the stronghold of traditional clientage-based political organizations.[52]

The pattern of organization in Greek agriculture parallels that of labor. "Cooperatives" existed in several localities in the nineteenth century; but they were actually variants of the indigenous clientage systems, despite their label. The lines of loyalty went only from the peasant to the leader; there was no particular bond connecting one member with the next. As in other transitional societies, the leader was responsible for organization and direction.[53] Although the original impetus for cooperative activity had been to some degree local, the state eventually became involved. First, the Western pattern of agricultural cooperatives was superimposed on the local groups, beginning in 1915.[54] Shortly afterward, during the upheavals caused by the refugee resettlement, membership in the cooperatives was made compulsory.[55] Ostensibly, this action had two aims: first, the cooperative movement would be strengthened by its increased membership; second, since compulsion required government assistance, the state could use the cooperative movement to exert some degree of economic control over the agricultural system. This remains the pattern today; and cooperatives throughout the country are tied together in the Pan-Hellenic Confederation of Agricultural Cooperatives.

The basic impetus for individual membership in a cooperative must be a person's belief in common interest and mutual advantage. This is as lacking in rural Greece as it is elsewhere in Greek society. Some traditional variants of mutual aid are found in the country districts; but exchanging labor or animals, for example, and that only with neighbors or relatives, is hardly an indication of fundamental trust.[56] Perhaps the Greek peasantry ought to see the mutual advantage of cooperative organizations; but in this setting of insecurity, each man's interests seem at variance with the interests of all others. Cooperatives require the peasant to think in terms of mutual advantage, future benefits, and distant markets—modern economic values, rather than traditional family values. In short, cooperatives are designed for farmers, not peasants. A Greek peasant feels that he is better served by his own clientage ties to specific people above him. This attitude creates numerous factions, with membership drawn from all levels of the rural community. Cooperation among rural Greeks of similar status is inhibited, as is the development of loyalty to institutions rather than persons.

The cooperative movement, sponsored and regulated by the state, performs several valuable functions for the rural Greek: cooperatives are naturally concerned with marketing orders and price control, as well as with measures to increase productivity; a further important service is the administration of rural credit through cooperation with the Agricultural Bank. The reaction of the peasantry to this official atmosphere is predictable. The organization and its officers are distrusted, and are viewed as state officials rather than servants of the cooperative membership. They are assumed to be as partisan and politically motivated as other elements of the state apparatus. To the rural Greek, these officials must be approached as are others: through personal connections and clientage. And he will circumvent decisions of the cooperatives in the same manner he would any government decree. If possible, he will sell his own produce outside the marketing organization, and he must often be persuaded not to destroy the implements or physical plant of the cooperative organization. He will seek as large a loan as possible from the Agricultural Bank, hoping to postpone or evade payment indefinitely. Even considering the inadequacies of the Greek cooperative system, one must admit that the rural Greek, like his Indian counterpart as described by Weiner, has "developed an almost incredible capacity to resist and to negate" efforts to change rural life.[57]

There is some regional variation in rural attitudes toward cooperatives. In most areas the cooperative movement is viewed as a governmental instrument, but where catastrophe and economic development have combined to transform the peasant into a farmer, the movement seems to have more vitality. Especially in the tobacco-growing areas of northern Greece, cooperatives seem to operate less as state institutions and more as pressure groups. This is one of the few areas where cooperative leaders have had sufficient popular support to enter elective politics.

SUMMARY

The Greek political system does not fit the developmental patterns generally suggested, and questions about its ultimate form are impossible to answer. Implicit in our discussion of interest groups is the notion that certain types, particularly the associational form, are most appropriate in a highly differentiated society. Moreover, it is assumed that nonassociational groups will take on an associational form and behavior as society becomes increasingly differentiated. This formulation suggests that the clientage-based Greek interest groups will be transitional. However, such a prognostication —apart from the question of future Greek development—ignores factors like the size of the system, the problem of individual trust, and the existence of particular institutional patterns, all of which seem crucial in the Greek case.

LaPalombara notes that the proliferation of strong, autonomous associational interest groups is vital to the establishment and maintenance of a liberal democratic society in Italy.[58] Weiner feels that even voluntary groups organized along traditional lines can ultimately contribute to the consensus necessary to maintain an orderly and democratic government in India; he argues that the "community" groups there have a role to play, and should not be viewed as a threat to the Indian state.[59] And Grossholtz finds that although individual demands predominate in the Philippines, traditional loyalties are gathered into apparently modern groups.[60] It is tempting to suggest that developments in Greece will follow this general pattern, but some caution is necessary. First, the narrow clientage organizations found in Greece are not completely analogous to those in India. The Madisonian world of multiple interest groups may indeed come to exist in the Indian context, creating a necessity for compromising and bargaining.[61] However, it seems doubtful, even from Weiner's analysis, that a similar pattern will emerge at the state level. Likewise, in Greece, the small size of the polity makes the development of the type and number of groups and the pattern of activity that Weiner suggests questionable. When the Philippine situation is examined closely, it seems possible that the groups appear more modern than they are. However, in that setting the constitutional pattern and the national election of the president may affect interest-group development.

In countries other than Greece traditional interest-group patterns may contribute to progress. The traditional bargaining culture in the Philippines seems to aid the development of a democratic political system.[62] On the local level in India there is a similar bargaining system between patron and client. Weiner views the development of a bargaining culture on a higher level as important to a democratic system, and thinks that such a culture will develop as the traditional groups take on modern associational forms and practices. However, in Italy, although bargaining on an individual basis is found, modern interest groups tend to operate as if "the state was something to be conquered by some group to the disadvantage of others."[63] Binder notes that in Iran bargaining is the standard process for resolving political problems, or indeed any problems at any level; but he does not suggest that it must result in the development of a democratic system.[64] Obviously, the several types of bargaining must be differentiated. The patron-client relationship based on mutual obligation can be characterized as a bargaining relationship. However, implicit in this relationship is the satisfaction of an individual demand; implicit also is a status distinction. The transformation of this bargaining to a higher level is not automatic. There is no assurance that even with economic and social differentiation, trust will be strong enough to make associational cohesion possible; loyalty to one's fellow does not necessarily replace commitment to a leader. There is likewise no assurance that if groups do develop they will act as interest articulators. It would seem that the institutional framework, the character of the bureaucracy, the legislative institutions, and the parties in a political system may all be intervening variables of great importance. Similarly, the size, resources, and internal diversity of the society must all be considered. The existence of a bargaining culture, by itself, is certainly not a sufficient condition, and perhaps not even a necessary one, for the development of an interest-group infrastructure on the Western pattern.

6. Political Parties

Political parties seem to perform certain common functions in all systems—for example, political recruitment and the communication of demands to political decision makers. In addition, parties seem related to particular levels of modernization, as defined in terms of economic and social differentiation.[1] Initially, the parties found in the major European states were used as models in the study of political organization, and non-European elites adopted similar structures as indicators of "modern" status. However, studies of politics in different settings have suggested that party structures and functions may vary considerably from those found in the European context. Moreover, if all European political systems are examined, it is apparent that there is not only a great diversity of party systems, but a considerable variation in parties within each system in terms of organization, electoral or legislative behavior, and general goals.

Joseph LaPalombara and Myron Weiner, in suggesting criteria to identify "modern" political organization, focus on the continuity and permanence of an organization, its relationship to the mass electorate, and the aims of its leadership (specifically, whether or not leaders seek decision-making positions within the system).[2] In the Greek case, it is clear that the major political groups at the parliamentary level cannot meet the requirements of modernity; indeed, they are now and have remained for decades, at the "antecedent" stage of development, composed of "cliques, clubs, and small groups of notables."[3] If this categorization is correct (setting aside for the present the matter of the left-wing political groups), we must ask why these groups failed to develop into "modern" political parties, as did their Western European counterparts. In the mid-nineteenth century Greek political organizations and processes were much like those in Western Europe or the United States. According to LaPalombara and Weiner, most explanations for party development fall into three general categories: institutional, historical-situational, and developmental.[4] Examining these explanations in the light of the intervening variables suggested previously as particularly important for understanding the Greek political system may explain the failure of the antecedent political organizations in Greece to evolve into modern political parties.

The institutional explanation for party development is offered by Max Weber and Maurice Duverger, among others, and centers on the expansion of suffrage.[5] The notables occupying the representative institutions are compelled to organize the masses of new voters at the local level in order to maintain their personal positions. In consequence, political organization extends from the representative institutions into the new mass electorate. In Greece, of course, suffrage was extended at the same time that representative institutions were established, and the Greek elite was never threatened by a sudden rush of new voters. The new voters were affiliated to individual political leaders not through modern associational ties but through ties of mutual obligation. The political forms and practices found in contemporary Greece, then, are in part merely extensions of the localized patron-client relationships prevalent at the time representative institutions were inaugurated. The institution of universal male suffrage did not break up the traditional clientage structures, but instead reinforced them, since votes could be exchanged for personal favors. Greek political organizations throughout the nineteenth century and well into the twentieth were in reality only clientage groups tied to a regional leader. Until the mid-nineteenth century the Greek "parties" were labeled French, British, or Russian, depending on their sources of foreign support.[6] Each major political figure had a regional base that was secured through ties of mutual obligations running to the local level. In parliamentary politics after 1862, the parties were simply factions named after their leaders and founders; there was little cohesion, no continuity, and in consequence, governmental instability.[7] Under these circumstances, it does not seem strange that Greece failed to develop modern political organizations.

Party development in Greece can also be explained in terms of historical situations, especially the crises occasioned by problems of legitimacy, political integration, and political participation.[8] As we have seen, universal male suffrage came with the initial development of representative institutions; thus there was never any crisis of participation. Integration did not initially provoke a major crisis either, since for most individuals loyalty was to the incumbents of political offices rather than to the institutions. Individuals were automatically integrated into the political system by virtue of their ties to political leaders. The most common political crisis in Western Europe involved the legitimacy of representative institutions. If "the legitimacy crisis is adequately resolved . . . where parliaments are established and the power of the monarchy diminished, . . . then the 'parties' formed may not involve a broader public and may be more appropriately conceived of as incipient parties."[9] The prevailing notion of modernity in the mid-nineteenth century centered on the development of representative institutions. Since this goal was relatively easy to achieve, and was compatible with traditional Greek patron-client structures, there was no need to disturb existing authority relationships in the society; consequently, there was no crisis of legitimacy. The legitimacy crisis was solved for other reasons in Greece, but the consequences were the same.

The Greeks did face some problems of legitimacy that did not have European counterparts. The representative institutions and bureaucracy were dominated by the hereditary politicians. True, loyalty to individual political figures could sometimes be transferred to political institutions. However, any conflicts between individual leaders and client groups, under certain conditions, could provoke conflict throughout the society and ultimately create doubts about the legitimacy of Greek political institutions. In fact, a major crisis of this kind did occur in the early twentieth century. At this time there were two major political constellations, much alike in structure: one centered on King Constantine; the other was tied to Eleutherios Venizelos, the prime minister. This conflict—in part personal, in part constitutional, and in part over Greek foreign policy in World War I —became a struggle over the form of the regime itself. The issue was fought out through coups and countercoups during the 20's and 30's, and was eventually settled in the postwar period. A more current crisis of legitimacy is related to a recent change in the prevailing conception of modernity. When economic criteria came to replace political institutions as the measure of modernity, the existing political system lost legitimacy in the eyes of some Greeks. The existing parties maintained themselves through patronage politics; the behavior of politicians, the expectations of the electorate, and the operation of the bureaucracy all seemed to preclude economic development. Only a regime that could make decisions largely on economic grounds, create a bureaucracy imbued with legal-rational norms, and impose a measure of discipline on an unruly and favor-seeking electorate could be viewed as legitimate. This vision was responsible for the creation of several minor parties devoted to total reform. It has motivated some Greeks to look to left-wing political organizations and others to welcome military intervention.

Perhaps the most crucial factor in understanding Greek political party development is the process of integration—the manner in which people are moved to active participation in the political system. In Western Europe class differences or religious deviance have been the chief causes of integration crises, but this has not been the case in Greece. Instead, the problems of integration center on those who are not bound to the political system by ties of mutual obligation to political leaders. Throughout much of the nineteenth century most Greeks met their political requirements by ties of this kind. By the end of the century certain elements, particularly the urban and provincial professional classes, had come to feel that they were excluded from the highest reaches of the political system. The "revolution" of 1909 brought these elements into politics. However, they did not create a modern political structure, but instead established new clientage networks of the traditional type. Politics continued to be characterized by fluid attachments to factional groups. The "new" politicians intermingled with the "old" politicians, and the traditional political patterns were preserved.

Between the World Wars, gradual social mobilization loosened traditional clientage ties to some extent, and many Greeks were left without patrons. These people, together with the newly arrived refugees, could enter the more modern types of political organization.[10] The activities of the Communist organizations in Greece began at this time. More important, the major political groups began to exhibit a certain dualism. Many voters were now tied to their party leaders not through bonds of mutual obligation or through intermediaries, but for other reasons. Sometimes their support was given for policy reasons, sometimes because of the personal qualities of the leader himself. The refugees, especially, were loyal to Venizelos personally but did not have individual patronage arrangements. They found the indigenous population hostile, they were totally unfamiliar with the institutions of the kingdom, and they did not have previous ties to the system. After Venizelos left the political arena, some followed his associates; but many transferred their allegiance to the various parties of the Left. Ever since, there has been intense conflict between politicians with support based on clientage networks and party leaders bent on acquiring mass support. Thus in Greece the crisis of integration has stimulated the development of more modern political structures.

The unevenness of the developmental process in any country is evident in its political organization. It is misleading to assume that political organizations must be either modern or nonmodern. In Greece, the major political groups at the parliamentary level have some components that can be viewed as modern and others that are traditional. In order to describe such organizations, Fred Riggs has adapted a party typology suggested by David Apter.[11] Apter's system uses two dimensions: a party can have either a bureaucratic or a personal control structure, and its organization is either durable or fragile. Riggs revises this typology by adding "polyarchic" as a control structure between bureaucratic and personal and "persistent" as a compromise between durable and fragile. A polyarchic party has a form of collective personal leadership resting on consensus or on some voting procedures; a persistent party's life is measured in decades, whereas a fragile party lasts for years and a durable party for generations. The basic components of Greek political organization, as we have seen, are the personal clientage structures built up by local politicians; these may be described as "polyarchic and persistent" organizations. However, most of the major parties also contain a "personal and fragile" component, made up of those attracted by the demagogic qualities of particular leaders and unconnected to the more traditional clientage structures. The Greek parliamentary arena also contains a wide variety of other, less important groups. Some parties have been "personal and durable," no more than families with political labels; others such as the Left are "bureaucratic and durable."

FORMAL PARTY ORGANIZATION

The formal organization of contemporary Greek parties of the traditional type has been influenced by several factors. First, the leaders of these parties have some knowledge of political organization in more developed countries, and often imitate these foreign institutions. Second, the effectiveness of the Greek Left is popularly attributed to its formal organization. At least in the urban areas, the major parties must appeal to the same segment of the population as the Left does; therefore some attention must be given to influencing and organizing voters with instruments similar to those used by the Left. Third, the political leaders have become sensitive to charges of autocratic personal control of the parties. Formally democratic party organizations are an answer to this problem.

The organizational charts of the two major political groupings, the National Radical Union (Ethniki Rizospastiki Enosis, ERE) and the Center Union (Enosis Kendrou, EK), were similar in the winter and spring of 1965.[12] Both were created out of existing parties; incumbent deputies merely changed party labels. In the case of the ERE, most adherents had been members of the Greek Rally (led by Field Marshal Alexander Papagos until his death). The EK was formed by George Papandreou from the parliamentary remnants of several Center party groups; its statutes were approved by a parliamentary group that attached itself to the new label. The paramount influence of the founder and leader is indirectly evident in each formal party organization. The ERE has many agencies with specified functions and a detailed set of statutes, but it has no formal means of electing a party leader. When the party was founded, ultimate authority was lodged in a general assembly, which was to meet every two years to establish party rules and policies. The assembly was to be a representative body, including the members of the party actually in parliament, the defeated party candidates, and delegates from the various party agencies and local organizations. The party statutes left the agenda for the general assembly in the hands of the parliamentary group, and most authority was officially in the hands of the leader. However, the whole matter is academic, since the general assembly has never been called in the history of the party. Likewise, the original statutes of the Center Union included a provision for a congress whose representation was similar to that in the Radical Union. Here again, although the Congress was to be the final authority in matters of policy and party organization, it has never functioned. The ERE provided for a general council of ten members elected from the general assembly to determine party policy between meetings of the assembly. There was also an executive committee that included the leader of the party, the secretary general, and three party members. The blueprint for the EK included a ten-man executive committee, as well as a ten-man organizational committee presided over by the party leader. Both parties also planned to establish disciplinary councils, but neither appears to have done so.*

Both the ERE and the EK have been chronically short of funds, and party finance committees are as formalistic as the rest of the party organizations. In the past there have been few wealthy party leaders. Panayotis Kanellopoulos and George Papandreou, the respective leaders of the EK and the ERE, are men of moderate means, although each has some followers with substantial wealth. The party in power is financially better able to campaign. During the Karamanlis period the ERE received large-scale campaign contributions from the business community; it was charged that state funds were also used. After the party's defeat in the 1964 elections,

---

* Papandreou, the leader of the Center Union, did not use any formal party procedures in 1963 when he unilaterally expelled and reinstated Sophocles Venizelos, the leader of the largest party faction, for supporting the Pipinellis caretaker government in that year. After becoming prime minister, Papandreou expelled two influential members of the party's left wing for declining to go along with his choice for president of parliament.

however, Kanellopoulos noted its precarious financial position.[13] Likewise, some of the earlier Papandreou defeats might be partially attributed to a lack of funds. In a system that runs on favoritism and patronage, most funds naturally go where favors can be returned. The parties do collect a small percentage of their deputies' salaries, but this sum barely covers the rent on party headquarters.

A special place is given to the parliamentary group in the formal organizations of both major parties; but in practice, these groups have no unity. Deputies' efforts in their home provinces are directed to personal rather than party interests, and the party leader provides the rank-and-file deputies with little information. On broad issues, a statement of the party leader may provide some guide; however, the average deputy must rely on the daily newspaper for information about his party's stand. Few deputies are concerned with policy matters anyway; if a deputy feels required to speak on a particular issue because of interests in his constituency or because publicity of some kind would be desirable, he can go to the party leadership for advice and permission. Few meetings of the parliamentary delegation of the ERE have been held, and deputies have rarely been consulted on policy or strategy. In the EK, Papandreou, although acknowledging the parliamentary party when forced to, operated without regard to it when he could. Until the crisis of 1965 the parliamentary membership was occasionally informed but rarely consulted. After 1965 Papandreou appointed a series of policy committees from the parliamentary party. Whether these committees actually operated is not known.

Before their suppression by the military in 1967, both parties had central secretariats with offices for the party leader and his chief associates. In the ERE the secretariat included formal sections responsible for organization, policy, propaganda, and finance. During the author's period of investigation (1964–65), the ERE was out of power. Its formal organs had atrophied, and Kanellopoulos and his associates were obviously operating without regard to party formalities. The permanent party workers were really the personal retainers of the leader. Other personnel gravitated to the newspapers and enterprises closely identified with the top party leadership, and some party functions were carried out by these organizations. When a party is in power, the personnel and functions of its various sections are intermingled with the government itself, particularly with the personal political bureau of the premier. This was the case with the EK in 1964–65. In either case, the party secretariat actually functions only at election time.

In theory, both parties had nationwide organizations, with units at the

communal, provincial, and regional levels. However, permanent party centers existed only in the major cities, where they were less party centers than
the headquarters of leading party figures. There were also formal national
organizations for various professions. Women, as a special group, were organized only in the cosmopolitan setting of Athens and its suburbs. These
organizations come alive only at election time. Each party also has a youth
group centered around the universities in Athens and Thessaloniki, and
these appear to have some vitality throughout the year. Some criticisms directed at the "undemocratic" aspects of party organization have been stilled
by the existence of these organizations, but they have not been uniformly
effective in appealing to the modern sector of the population. Greek parties
still gain support and transact business mainly through their informal, personal institutions.

SIGNIFICANT POLITICAL STRUCTURES

Within the significant Greek party structures, there is constant conflict
between the polyarchic-persistent and personal-fragile aspects of the party.
The chief conflict is at the level of the party leader, although the consequences of this tension are evident throughout the party. The paths to party
leadership are diverse. Since there is little continuity in party organization,
there are many opportunities for individual politicians to establish their own
parties. Between 1946 and 1964 no less than 95 parties and coalitions appeared on the electoral lists.[14] This figure does not include splinter groups
that did not survive long enough to contest an election or minor parties
that did not actually enter the lists at the election. The major political parties that we have considered so far are both of recent origin. The prewar
Populists became the Greek Rally, and ultimately the National Radical
Union; the prewar Liberals splintered and reformed, eventually producing
the Center Union. These organizations are termed parties here only for the
sake of convenience. Despite some appearances to the contrary, they are primarily the followings of individual leaders. Moreover, their genealogies are
much more complex than this rendering indicates.

Some politicians in the Greek parliament create their own parties, usually
by enlisting sitting deputies or political friends, either for purely personal
motives or because of pressures from clients. They may seriously aim at
capturing the premiership, or may simply use a personal party to give leverage when coalitions are formed or ministerial portfolios awarded. In other
instances, parties are established by men with personal followings outside

the parliamentary arena. For example, the minor personal parties formed by Kanellopoulos in 1936 and 1950 included many of his former students and associates at the University of Athens. Papandreou also had a following outside the parliament, which included those recruited in his early political career and others attracted to him during his premiership in 1944. In both cases, his personal following was not the usual regionally based clientage network. Field Marshal Papagos, the founder of the Greek Rally, used the prominence he had gained outside of politics to create a party drawing on both deputies and those not connected to existing political groups.

Since Greek parties have a polyarchical component, there is ample opportunity for the monarch to intervene in parliamentary politics by naming as prime minister someone other than the obvious leader of the winning party. However, the premiership can propel a man to party leadership. Karamanlis was appointed prime minister by the king at the death of Papagos; this allowed him to refashion the Greek Rally into his own instrument, the National Radical Union. But taking control of a party in this way is difficult, and a new leader must form the same personal ties as his predecessor. In the Populist and Liberal parties between the wars, the political enterprise was inherited by a close relative of the former leader, who could attempt to continue the personal relationships that tied the parties together. In both cases the heirs had problems; and eventually both parties splintered badly and were absorbed by new political groups. The same problem was evident in 1963, when Karamanlis left politics after the defeat of his party and appointed his wife's uncle, Panayotis Kanellopoulos, as his successor.

The character of the Greek political system makes the premiership and the ministerial offices crucial to a man's—or a party's—success. These prizes in the political system, the commanding heights of the state machinery, are sought by many politicians. The premiership is a prize because the governmental resources that it controls can be bartered for political support. Since a leader must cement a coalition of factions to his cause, he must rely upon patronage and favors; and unless a politician can at least secure a ministerial position, his personal power will diminish as his supporters desert for more accommodating patrons. For the traditional component in Greek politics, appeals to principle have little effect. However, the leader seeking the highest position must also express some interest in reform in order to pacify that portion of the population described as "modern" yet still attracted to the traditional political arena.

When asked about the qualifications necessary in a minister, a sample of

Table 6.1. Deputies' Perceptions of Qualifications for Ministerial Office

| Qualification | Number citing this qualification | | |
	Total (55)	Party in power (32)	Out parties (23)
Support for government	4	2	2
Political strength	11	6	5
Favoritism	11	7	4
"Operators"	3	1	2
Administrative ability	6	5	1
Intelligence	12	10	2
Moral qualities	12	8	4
Specialization	18	11	7
Leadership	3	1	2
No answer	8	3	5

Note: Some gave more than one response. Five of the eight "no answers" are from former or present ministers.

55 deputies mentioned two broad categories: personal attributes and political backing (see Table 6.1). Although common wisdom suggests that any cabinet is selected on the basis of political calculation, the responses of the deputies most often listed desirable personal characteristics. However, political considerations carried equal weight for both EK deputies and those from out parties. In fact, EK deputies mentioned favoritism by the chief more often than others did. The number in this sample is not large; perhaps the most one can say is that all deputies, irrespective of party, tend to have the same perceptions of ministerial qualifications.

Although the cabinet ministers cannot be examined for most of these qualities, the importance of a minister's degree of specialization does seem to be exaggerated. The Papandreou cabinets seem to have been formed with little thought to subject specialization. In fact, it probably makes little difference whether a minister has expertise in the field over which he is to preside, since few ministers see themselves as anything more than patronage dispensers. It would seem that expertise and specialization develop after appointment to the ministerial chair, rather than before. Political considerations, not expertise, are probably the major reasons for the initial appointment.

For the most part, Greek party structures still do not reach the local level. If political organizations are found here, they are usually the clientage groups of local notables or individual deputies. A voter's electoral decision is largely based on personal ties to a local leader, and he may not even be aware of the parliamentary faction that his vote will ultimately support. The membership of all major party groupings is calculated by the number of voters who supported each at the last election. There are very few actual members of the national political parties. For example, in the spring of 1965 the total printing of the sporadic ERE party bulletin was 800 copies, including those that went to the 100 ERE deputies in parliament.

The provincial notables are the essential components of a deputy's following. They may be local politicians and lawyers, heads of families, or merchants with influence among the villagers.[15] Lower in the scale, the village notables act as buffers between the rural inhabitants and the outside world. This local leadership reflects qualities admired in rural culture, and may also have, at least to a limited degree, urban values of education and culture. However, an uneducated man who is a good farmer, with a good family and good judgment, may attain prominence. Any professional person in the area is a potential leader. Commission merchants, bus drivers, or, in fact, anyone who can provide a link between the village and the outside world, may also have political influence. But the influence of most of these people is not as durable as the patron-client tie found in the kumbaros relationship or in the other connections based on some kind of mutual obligation.

Local government officials can be a link between the community and the higher political level. A priest or teacher may also act in this capacity;[16] however, the prestige of the church and the teachers has steadily declined. Local politicians are able to protect their neighbors from the vagaries of the central government, but this is not their primary function. Tax farming continues to provide certain local revenues; and the preparation of the tax rolls is itself an operation that entails compromise and negotiation between the village authorities and the peasant. The signature of the village president is needed on most government forms and certificates; he is also likely to have influence with the agricultural police, the branch of authority that the rural Greek most often deals with.[17] All of these functions provide opportunities to build a political following at the local level, which can be used to extract favors at the next.

The provincial notables are tied to their deputy or to a provincial politician in much the same way that the villagers are tied to them. It is only through these relationships that the patronage and favors necessary to preserve the local clientage structure can be secured. There may be some shifting of allegiance at the local level if a deputy cannot satisfy local demands. However, most deputies have a broad enough base so that they do not have to worry about shifts of small-scale leadership. The influence of a local leader is based chiefly on his access to party or governmental leaders, which will be useful in favor seeking. Hence those party leaders who are out of power may find their followers deserting because local influentials cannot wait for the pendulum to return their patrons to power. The problem of access and the need for assistance are always present.

The ties that bind an individual deputy to a larger group or party parallel the relationships at the lower levels. A deputy's main concern is maintaining his personal position. In return for parliamentary support, he has access to favors and patronage that can fulfill the demands of local clients. When the defeat of their party blocks this access, some deputies begin switching to the dominant political coalition. Since every break is in reality a personal one, it often brings on vitriolic debate and extreme methods of discreditation.

Despite the limited opportunities for a political career in Greece, many men are eager to obtain the positions that do exist. However, there are no elective offices at the provincial level, and municipal offices have only sporadically been filled by election. The only level that a beginner can reasonably aspire to is the parliamentary one; but the attractiveness of a public career outweighs the hopelessness of the aspiration. Between 1926 and 1964 over 10,000 different men appeared as candidates in the 14 parliamentary elections (see Table 6.2).[18] The opportunity for advancing in a personal profession, the possibility of adding to personal political resources, and the desire to gain the status and income of a "political man" seem to be motives powerful enough to overcome harsh reality.

There is an inherent tension between the party chief and the other leading figures in the major Greek political groups: the party leader is constantly seeking to make the party into his own instrument; his associates try to retain its polyarchic aspects. The major parties have all originated in the parliament, and the most important figures in them are deputies secure in their own constituencies, perhaps the bosses of regions. These men have their own networks of support, which include constituents, fellow deputies, and prominent figures in national society. For these deputies, patronage and party-hopping are a way of life; they are attracted to a given party by the hope of ministerial portfolios and the opportunities for patronage that these offer. Naturally enough, they are less concerned with policy

Table 6.2. Parliamentary Seats and Candidates

Year	Seats open	Number of candidates	Candidates per seat
1926	279	2,025	7.3
1928	250	1,354	5.4
1932	250	1,496	6.0
1933	248	825	3.3
1935	300	808	2.7
1936	300	1,665	5.5
1946	354	1,540	4.3
1950	250	3,042	12.0
1951	258	1,881	7.0
1952	300	1,045	3.5
1956	300	976	3.0
1958	300	1,483	4.9
1961	300	990	3.3
1963	300	1,263	4.2
1964	300	909	3.0

or with social change than with the maneuvering that solidifies their own positions. Other coalitions will often pay a price for defection; and the connections of any major parliamentary figure in the bureaucratic and social worlds are extensive enough so that a momentary loss of access and patronage will not immediately damage his position.

The ties that bind the leading figures to the party chief are primarily personal, and depend on the satisfactory performance of mutual obligations. When the party is in power, these are the individuals who must be accorded cabinet places, which they generally use to bestow individual and group favors, building up a national support that will hopefully lead to the premiership itself. The ministers determine candidatures and are the arbiters of party affairs in their own provinces. Since they are both the necessary supporters and the chief rivals of the premier, he tends to keep major political questions in his personal grasp. Cabinet discussions and planning did not seem to be very common in either the Karamanlis or Papandreou governments.

A second group in the party is more properly the possession of the party leader himself; this is the personal-fragile aspect of party organization. In this group one finds the clientage network of the chief: the new deputies who have not had time to consolidate their positions; the party stalwarts from the marginal districts (elected more because of the influence of the party leader than through personal connections in the district); and those individual voters who have been clients of the leader in the past. Deputies from the large urban districts will also be likely to follow the leader of the party, since voters in these areas are less likely to have clientage ties to particular politicians. Candidates in these competitive districts are selected by the party leader, even though some pretense at local control is kept. Since the supply of potential candidates always outstrips the number of places on the ticket, confusion results; and the leader, as the only source of favors, is able to keep control in his own hands.

Those who occupy the political offices can buy votes with their patronage, and even have the opportunity to create political resources by instituting new programs and by promoting restrictive legislation. Despite these advantages, no party chief or premier can ever hope to satisfy everyone, or even a majority of those with demands. Immediately upon victory, a winning party tends to draw deputies and influentials to its side, all of them anxious to share in the new distribution of resources. Each deputy, particularly in the governing party, is confronted with an almost unlimited number of requests, which are channeled to the ministers and often to the premier himself. When political resources run short, as always happens, some ministers and some deputies are inevitably favored or appear to be favored over others; this results in disappointments and defections. Such lapses from party discipline may call forth policy statements from the party leaders; however, the rhetoric merely hides the feeling that obligations have not been fulfilled.

Eventually, a government party is faced with defeat: the number of demands outstrips the government's resources; voters become tired and frustrated; and the parliamentary support of the leadership grows weaker. Basically, the seeds of disintegration are the same for all parties. In defeat, only the chief party figures are likely to secure parliamentary seats. That part of the party properly belonging to the party leader is swept away; and unless he has built up ties and clientage relationships throughout the society, so that he can survive a long period without cabinet office, he will continue to lose parliamentary clients. In most cases, the party leader in the out party is merely a coequal part of the polyarchic leadership.

KARAMANLIS AND PAPANDREOU

Until 1956 Greek politics did not diverge from this pattern. The long tenure of Constantine Karamanlis is exceptional. However, Karamanlis had several advantages in combating the centrifugal tendencies of his parliamentary party. For one thing, his accession to the premiership was a surprise. Although he had substantial ministerial experience, he was not counted as a possible successor to Field Marshal Papagos. Since his tenure was expected to be short, some of the leading members of the Greek Rally returned to other parties. Hence Karamanlis could use the government machinery to build a personal following at the same time that his leading opponents were opting out of his organization. The ERE candidates in 1956 included not only new faces recruited by the premier, but also many Center deputies who had been enticed into the new political organization. The ERE changed the electoral system to its advantage, as is customary in Greek politics. This resulted in a massive failure of the opposition parties; and many of the new ERE deputies elected by this maneuvering had no real constituency support and had to rely on Karamanlis himself.

Karamanlis was faced with several mass defections from his parliamentary party. Ordinarily these larger departures would have brought about the disintegration of the ERE. But Karamanlis was fortunate in that his premiership coincided with an expansion of political resources, as indicated by a dramatic increase in public revenue and expenditure.[19] Although American aid was coming in less rapidly, Karamanlis was in fact reaping the political benefit of past aid.[20] The public services were undergoing a rapid expansion, providing opportunities for politically advantageous appointments in both the government departments and the public corporations. The economic boom itself, particularly in the realm of public works and urban real estate, also provided many useful political opportunities. For the first time, a Greek premier had vast sums to distribute; and the personal and fragile components of the party overshadowed the polyarchic and persistent, at least for a time.

These conditions existed until just before the elections of 1961. In those elections, the Karamanlis government fell back on the military and security forces, as well as private organizations of the extreme Right, to stay in power.[21] The general outlines of the operation were widely known shortly after the elections; the specific details were exposed by the EK after its assumption of power in 1963. "Operation Pericles," as it was known, involved the chief of the armed services, as well as special agencies, e.g., the Greek Central Intelligence Agency. Ultimately, these electoral methods, a slight economic turndown, and an eventual diminution of political resources alienated too many voters and politicians. The government attitude toward the Left and toward moderate elements of the Center encouraged police irresponsibility and also served to encourage pressures and intimidation on the part of other right-wing groups. The Battalions of National Security (TEA), home-guard units based in the countryside, used every opportunity to harass their opponents. The celebrated Lambrakis affair (the murder of Gregory Lambrakis, a leftist deputy, by a member of a right-wing organization) and the subsequent inactivity of the police and the Ministry of Justice were typical of the internal situation in Greece.

The ERE's opposition, composed primarily of politicians with independent power bases, was particularly subject to internal dissensions. The major opposition group was George Papandreou's EK; and from this party's formation in 1961 to its eventual victory in 1963 there was constant conflict between the traditional leaders, who comprised the polyarchic and persistent part of the party, and Papandreou, who represented a personal-fragile type of party leadership. Papandreou, although a long-time parliamentary figure, preferred not to operate in a parliamentary milieu. He had great faith in his own ability and vision, and was gifted with a dynamic oratorical style that made him particularly effective in mass rallies. Papandreou intended to be in command, and he sought to achieve this by forcing a total confrontation with the government. This would make it unnecessary to compromise with moderate elements from the ERE, and it would pull into parliament many deputies personally dependent on him.

The modern aspect of Papandreou's appeal was evident in his campaign techniques. In 1956, for example, he included the United Democratic Left (Eniaia Demokratiki Aristera, EDA) in his center coalition in an effort to secure an electoral majority. Traditional politicians had been conscious of the personal political advantages to be gained from the patronage implicit in the development of a communications and transportation infrastructure, but had not capitalized on the existence of this structure for larger political purposes. After 1961, Papandreou and his associates traveled throughout the provinces on the newly built roads, reaching areas where politicians had seldom been seen even at election time. These rural tours were accompanied by rallies in the major cities. A "back to the people" mood captivated a large segment of the urban youth, and was impressive to the rural population as well. The style and extent of this campaigning actually did contribute to the EK's eventual victory.

Whatever the reasons, the EK was successful in 1963 and 1964. Once in power, it soon displayed the tensions inherent in Greek political organization. In 1965 the party split, and a Center-Right coalition government was formed, mostly because of the conflict between the traditional polyarchic and persistent elements with secure power bases and the new men loyal to Papandreou alone. The majority of those defecting to the new Liberal Democratic Center (Philelefthron Demokratikon Kendrou, PDK) had secure parliamentary seats and were not dependent on personal ties with the premier for their election. Although the basic causes for this and other political crises lie in the extraparliamentary level of politics, the failure of Papandreou meant the temporary resurgence of the traditional mode of Greek parliamentary life.

CHARACTERISTICS OF POLYARCHIC-PERSISTENT ORGANIZATIONS

In the Greek context, polyarchic-persistent political organizations are characterized by a diverse and fluid membership, uncoordinated electoral activity, and a tendency to avoid facing any concrete issue. They are difficult to describe if one is limited to the usual labels applied to political groups in Greece—republican, royalist, Right, Center, or Left. For example, the republican and royalist labels were somewhat descriptive in the interwar period because they signified personal attachments to political leaders. By the end of the war, though, this cleavage was disappearing, at least between candidates of the two major political groupings. Tables 6.3 and 6.4 illustrate the political backgrounds of parliamentary candidates in the eight elections from 1946 to 1963, including, for each year only those who had run before.*

The elections of 1946 and 1950 were replays of the 1936 election. In both cases, a proportional representation system was used. The seats were divided among the competing parties on the basis of the proportion of votes each received. There were three allocations of seats: the first in 38 electoral districts, the second in nine regional districts, and the third for the country as a whole. The relatively small percentage of candidates moving from the Center and from minor parties to the Right and the minimal group moving from the Right and minor parties to the Center, illustrate the extent of the old monarchist-republican cleavage in the postwar period. However, the major party categories, even in the 1946 election, really included a variety of factional groups, which banded together to compete in the election but split once they entered parliament. Moreover, the election of 1946 was held under abnormal circumstances: some potential parties offered no candidates; and those that did had difficulty filling all their lists. The Commu-

---

* The data for these and other tables analyzing election results were obtained from the returns published by the Greek government after each election.

Table 6.3. Political Backgrounds of Candidates
from "Mainstream" Right Parties, 1946–63

		Parties of previous candidatures				
Year	Number of candidates	Right	Minor Right	Center	Left	Minor
1946	211	68.3%	9.6%	17.8%	–	4.3%
1950	183	80.2	4.4	7.1	–	8.2
1951	448	32.9	24.4	36.9	–	10.2
1952	273	45.7	7.1	43.1	–	4.1
1956	241	33.0	19.4	43.4	.4%	2.5
1958	328	38.3	22.2	37.0	–	2.5
1961	251	41.4	19.9	35.8	.4	2.4
1963	242	46.1	21.0	33.0	–	–

nists did not contest the elections, instead claiming that all who abstained favored them.

In the elections of 1950 candidates were distributed among many more parties; as would be expected, each party had a large number of men running for the first time. The extreme fragmentation meant that there was little party switching. In the 1951 election, and later, many more candidates switched parties. This was in part due to the changed electoral system. The proportional representation system was still used, but only parties polling at least 17 per cent of the total votes cast in the country could take part in the second allocation of seats. There were other refinements, all designed to reduce the number of competing political groups. In 1951 the major Right

Table 6.4. Political Backgrounds of Candidates
from "Mainstream" Center Parties, 1946–63

		Parties of previous candidatures				
Year	Number of candidates	Center	Minor Center	Right	Left	Minor
1946	297	64.9%	12.9%	13.7%	–	8.5%
1950	259	62.2	13.9	12.5	1.1%	10.3
1951	565	70.0	11.0	8.9	1.9	8.2
1952	252	73.8	8.7	9.1	4.0	4.4
1956	271	54.4	23.3	11.5	7.8	3.0
1958	432	46.1	12.5	19.2	2.8	19.4
1961	246	45.7	21.0	20.3	4.0	9.3
1963	231	47.7	6.0	17.6	10.7	18.0

party had candidates with consistent Right backgrounds, with mixed Right and minor party backgrounds, and with Center backgrounds in almost equal strength. In 1952 the Greek Rally had almost equal numbers of candidates from the Right, minor Right, and Center categories. Although an analysis of the 1964 election is not included here, impressionistic evidence leads one to believe that party membership was still fluid.

The candidates for Center parties have had less diversified political backgrounds, partly because of excessive fragmentation in the Center. Most often, the fragments have combined in electoral coalitions. In such instances there are usually enough candidates from among coalition partners to occupy all the places on the consolidated list, and there is little room for outsiders. More important, from 1952 until 1963 the right-wing government was in power, and there was little incentive for right-wingers to join the Center. Those who did switch were mostly unsuccessful rightist candidates.

We must conclude that assigning conventional labels to Greek political groups is not particularly meaningful.[22] Such a typology seems to be a correct description of parliamentary seating arrangements and little else. The shifting membership of the major political groups indicates a discontinuous and issueless political process. Deputies, ministers, and candidates wander from one group to the next in search of patronage and favors or because of personality clashes with factional leaders; the only common link between members in any party is the personal tie to the party chief or one of the other key figures. Political parties are much like other Greek secondary associations in this regard.

The political manipulation of the electoral laws is an important part of Greek party politics. In particular, the long postwar period of Right governments produced electoral legislation that discriminated against the Center and the Left. We have already mentioned the various proportional systems used from 1946 to 1951. In 1952 the system of proportional representation was abandoned. Greece was divided into 99 electoral districts, with a varying number of seats allotted to each; the party getting a plurality in any single district received all of the seats. Ostensibly, this system was adopted to encourage the development of a two-party system and to provide one party with the necessary majority in parliament to form a stable government. Naturally, the constituencies were drawn to give the utmost advantage to candidates joining the Greek Rally. Since 1952, electoral legislation has become much more complex. The electoral law prepared for the 1956 elections, for example, set up three types of constituencies, each with a different electoral system. In constituencies returning up to three members (usually the rural districts dominated by political notables), all deputies came from the party winning an absolute majority. In constituencies with 4–10 delegates (most often the larger provinces, where there was some party competition), the party with the most votes got 70 per cent of the seats, and the second party 30 per cent. Finally, in constituencies with more than 10 members (the metropolitan areas where the Left was strong), a straight proportional system applied. In 1958, the proportional system used in 1951 was again adopted, although with revisions. To share in the second allocation of seats, individual parties had to receive 25 per cent of the votes cast nationally, coalitions of two parties had to secure 35 per cent, and coalitions of more than two parties had to receive 40 per cent. The provisions concerning coalitions severely penalized the Center, and in effect made it possible for the Left to become the second largest party in parliament. The same system was used in 1961 although the minimum proportion of votes needed to qualify for the second distribution of seats was reduced to 15 per cent for single parties, 25 per cent for two-party coalitions, and 30 per cent for coalitions with more than two parties. The elections of 1963 and 1964 were held under similar systems of reinforced proportional representation.

Even if he belongs to one of the major parties, each Greek deputy must rely on his own resources in campaigning. The party really does not exist as a unit, at least as far as assistance to individual candidates is concerned. The party leader may sometimes tour the country and greet the voters together with the local candidates on his list, much as an American presidential aspirant travels from state to state and sponsors local and national candidates. The party may also supply a local candidate with pictures of the chief and general party literature; however, he must finance personalized materials himself. In exceptional cases the party may supply funds for local campaigns; but the recipient is expected to repay the loan if he is elected. Usually, each candidate must use his personal fortune or seek funds from his clients and friends in the community. In most electoral situations, the voter has only one choice; he is not called upon to support a party list. In a district that usually elects a number of men from one party and few from another, the candidates of a given party may do some campaigning together. But in general a united effort is rare, since each candidate knows that he is running not only against other party lists but also against the other candidates of his own party. This being the case, he is most likely to campaign

Table 6.5. Success Ratios and Party Affiliation

Party and year	Candidates by success ratio		
	.100 to .400	.401 to .700	.701 to 1.00
ERE: 1958	15.0%	45.0%	39.9%
1964	5.0	31.0	64.0
PK, 1958	8.3	38.8	52.7
EK, 1964	30.5	33.6	35.9
PADE, 1958	30.0	50.0	20.0
ELK, 1958	25.0	–	75.0
KP, 1964	20.0	40.0	40.0
EDA: 1958	34.5	38.2	27.2
1964	18.2	40.9	40.9

Note: This table does not include deputies who won the first time they were candidates.

by stressing his personal ties with the party leader, which would allow him to offer patronage if he is elected.

Affiliation with particular political groups is related to long-term political success in Greece, but it is not a party's organization or program that aids its members. The deputies coming from an area that gives substantial support to a particular political group have longer tenures or greater "success ratios" when they run than those coming from the less secure party areas. This means that the governing party will have more deputies with modest success ratios than will the minority political grouping, since the latter will return deputies only from its strongest areas. The percentage of ERE deputies in 1958 falling into each of the three success ratio categories in Table 6.5 is instructive when compared with the 1964 distribution. The Liberals and their descendant, the EK, also show a change, but in the opposite direction. The steadier EDA figures indicate that the party leadership does keep a core group in parliament, often by shifting promising deputies from the more marginal districts to the large urban districts.

Electoral success and long parliamentary tenure is also associated with geographic area. Table 6.6 indicates that deputies from areas such as the Cyclades, Crete, Old Greece, the Ionian Islands, and the Epirus do have greater success ratios than those from elsewhere. The most important factor is the nature of political competition in the particular region. Most of the areas with high ratios have long-standing affiliations with one of the major political groups—or rather, long-standing affiliations with individuals or families prominent in the group. The relationship between success and party area must be modified by the observation that in some areas of one-

Table 6.6. Success Ratios of Candidates, by Regions

Area	Candidates by success ratio		
	.101 to .400	.401 to .700	.701 to 1.00
Athens–Piraeus			
1958	18.7%	34.9%	43.0%
1964	15.7	45.2	39.1
Old Greece			
1958	9.9	43.3	46.6
1964	20.6	23.5	55.8
Peloponnesus			
1958	21.7	39.1	39.1
1964	23.2	37.1	39.4
Thessaly			
1958	43.6	26.1	30.4
1964	18.5	40.7	40.7
Crete			
1958	13.4	46.7	40.0
1964	31.6	10.6	57.9
Epirus			
1958	18.2	36.3	45.3
1964	7.1	42.9	50.0
Macedonia			
1958	21.7	53.3	23.4
1964	22.7	33.3	43.9
Aegean Islands			
1958	–	59.9	40.0
1964	18.6	24.9	56.1
Ionian Islands			
1958	14.3	28.6	57.2
1964	33.3	22.2	44.4
Cyclades			
1958	–	20.0	80.0
1964	20.0	–	80.0
Thrace			
1958	–	30.8	40.0
1964	30.8	30.8	38.5

Note: Table does not include those elected on first candidature.

party dominance (Crete and parts of the Peloponnesus, for example), the dominance itself makes for a factionalism that may displace an incumbent.

The pattern of political recruitment in the traditional sector of Greek politics depends on the fluctuation of party fortunes. Parties with a history of success generally have few places for new candidates (see Table 6.7). If places are available, those offering a chance of victory are most likely to go to relatives and clients of the party leaders, although some may go to aspirants who have already run unsuccessfully with some minor party but have made a creditable showing. The new recruits to the major parties do not have a spectacular record of success, mostly because they usually run in areas where the party fortunes are lowest. The percentage of new entrants in an election is a good indicator of a party's status: major political groups have only a few new faces; minor parties offer a high percentage of new candidates at each election.

The Populists (LK), the Liberals (PK), and the GLRE led by General Georgios Kondylis were major political forces in 1936. The Free Opinion Party of General Ioannis Metaxas (EF), the Democratic Alliance of Alexander Papanastassiou and George Papandreou (DS), and the Populist offshoot led by Sotirios Cotzamanis (MK) were parties with a regional complexion. The National Union Party of Panayotis Kanellopoulos (EE) was a true minor party, a political group founded outside the existing political structure; the Greek Communist Party (KKE) and the Agrarian Party (Agrot) fit into this category also. The 1946 election was abnormal because it followed a long interruption in normal political life. As might be expected, all political groups had significant percentages of new recruits. The new National Party (Ethnikon Komma Ellados, EKE), was largely a regional party, with many members who had been active in one of the guerrilla organizations. It was made up primarily of new candidates.

The pattern in 1950 was more normal. The older parties, the Populists and the Liberals, had the lowest percentage of new people. The new national parties—such as George Papandreou's Party (KGP), the EPEK of Nicholas Plastiras and Emmanuel Tsouderos, and the expanded EKE of Napoleon Zervas—had more than 60 per cent new entrants among their candidates, as did several other minor parties. More ephemeral organizations, such as the EPEL and the "X" party of General George Grivas, had more than 70 per cent new candidates. The Left also emerged in 1950, as the Democratic Front (DP); it had 71 per cent new entrants, indicating that the cadres of the prewar period had been largely replaced.

Table 6.7. Percentage of New Candidates by Party

Year	Mainstream Right	Mainstream Center	Left	Minor Right	Minor Center	Minor
1936	LK 24.1 GLRE 29.0	PK 30.5 DS 37.9	KKE 54.2	MK 41.8 EF 37.9	EE 86.0	Agrot 59.0
1946	HPE 40.4	EPE 64.0 PK 60.0 EKE 72.5			Other 76.1	Agrot 70.6
1950	LK 26.8	PK 28.0 EPEK 62.2 KGP 65.5	DP 71.0	PAP 60.5 NK 55.9 EPEL 72.5 "X" 80.0	MEA 51.7	
1951	ES 26.4 LK 29.7	PK 24.1 EPEK 32.6 KGP 39.8	EDA 14.4		Other 24.8	Agrot 49.5
1952	ES 9.0	EPEK-PK 7.7	EDA 58.7	LK 0.0	Other 39.4	Agrot 30.5
1956	ERE 19.4		DE 9.7	KP 54.3	Other 46.1	
1958	ERE 20.0	PK 22.6 PADE 31.4	EDA 59.0		Other 82.8	
1961	ERE 16.3	EK 18.0	PAME 41.0			
1963	ERE 19.3	EK 22.7	EDA 45.0	KP 54.1		

In 1951 the Greek Rally (ES), led by Field Marshal Papagos, made its appearance. Strictly speaking, it was not a very new party since it was peopled largely with old, established political figures. In 1952 and 1956, with the electoral system prejudiced against smaller parties, the older political groups had even fewer places for new candidates. Only the minor parties and the category of independents continued to be relatively open. In 1958, the two major party organizations, the ERE and the PK, continued to offer few openings. The pattern since 1958 has generally been that of few openings in the major parties, except in areas of continued party weakness; the Left and the minor parties, by contrast, continue to have a considerable turnover. For the Left, at least, this seems to be a party policy designed to make the party appear as democratic as possible.

A candidate with political experience has a definite electoral advantage. As Table 6.8 indicates, only once in the period 1936–63 did the new entrants for any party do better than the experienced candidates. In the major parties, newcomers are particularly unsuccessful; the vacancies that exist are at the bottom of the electoral list or in areas where the party leadership does not expect to win. In a minor party nearly everyone, with the exception of specific leaders, has an equal chance of losing, and the difference between the success of the two groups is not as great. Even powerful family connections will not enable a young man to succeed on most minor party tickets. Of course, anyone with connections is more likely to find a place on a more promising electoral list. The major party groups have few openings and the chance of victory for a new entrant is less than that for the party as a whole. However, the open positions are eagerly sought. First, the chance for success, though small, is greater than that for similar places on minor party lists. Second, even a defeated candidate acquires political resources that can be used to obtain patronage from the national leaders. He may even acquire the rudiments of a personal clientage organization that can assist him in the next election.

According to V. O. Key, one feature of a factional political system is the relative absence of meaningful issues in the electoral struggle. He argues that issues cause the formation of competing groups, and that competing groups raise new issues.[23] In the Greek case, the absence of issues other than office-holding at the beginning has largely continued, and an issueless politics prevails at the parliamentary level. The unstable coalitions, characteristic of factional systems, are held together by patronage and favors. The

Table 6.8. *Relative Success of New Entrants and*
Politically Experienced Candidates

Party and year	New candidates elected	Experienced candidates elected	Difference	Party and year	New candidates elected	Experienced candidates elected	Difference
1936				**(1951, cont.)**			
LK	5.7%	30.8%	25.1%	PK	0.0%	43.1%	43.1%
GLRE	3.6	27.7	23.1	EDA	9.7	3.8	−5.9
PK	26.6	49.7	23.1	LK	1.3	4.9	3.6
DS	1.7	6.3	4.6	Other	0.0	3.8	3.8
KKE	0.9	14.8	13.9	**1952**			
EF	0.0	6.8	6.8	ES	74.1	83.0	8.9
MK	0.0	16.0	16.0	EPEK–PK	4.8	19.9	15.1
Agrot	0.0	16.7	16.7	Other	0.0	5.7	5.7
Other	0.0	12.0	12.0	**1956**			
1946				ERE	38.0	59.3	21.3
HPE	49.6	64.0	14.4	DE	27.6	45.7	18.1
EPE	16.5	25.1	6.6	Other	0.0	10.3	10.3
PK	34.8	36.5	1.7	**1958**			
EKE	6.5	21.2	14.7	ERE	35.0	50.0	15.0
Other	2.6	19.1	16.5	PK	0.0	15.5	15.5
1950				PADE	0.0	5.0	5.0
LK	19.6	40.5	20.9	EDA	15.8	41.5	25.7
PK	10.0	27.2	17.2	ELK	0.0	4.8	4.8
EPEK	12.9	26.6	13.7	**1961**			
KGP	0.6	40.0	39.4	ERE	38.9	62.5	23.6
DP	7.0	26.8	19.8	EK	12.9	37.8	14.7
PAP	4.1	9.5	5.4	PAME	4.1	10.7	6.6
MEA	0.9	6.1	5.2	**1963**			
EKE	0.0	9.1	9.1	ERE	17.2	50.4	33.2
1951				EK	17.6	54.5	36.9
ES	18.4	40.5	22.1	EDA	0.7	16.5	15.8
EPEK	10.4	29.7	19.3	KP	0.7	0.8	0.1

leadership, even if it is concerned about programs and policies, is forced by the pressures of maintaining power to be primarily concerned with the distribution of existing resources. Since a politician is tied to specific individuals, he cannot combine interests into any single universal policy. In Greece, major policies have always been suggested and implemented outside the parliament. And in most cases, there has been little debate and little thought given to the consequences of legislative activity. The matter of differences in party attitudes on issues was explored in my interviews with

Table 6.9. *Perceptions of Party Difference, by Party Background*

Difference	KP (2)	EDA (4)	EK (32)			ERE (17)		
			New	Old	Former Right	New	Old	Former Center
Historical and leadership	–	–	1	–	–	–	1	–
EK more progressive and democratic	–	–	11	11	1	–	–	–
EK soft on national security	–	–	–	–	–	–	4	4
No difference	2	1	–	–	–	1	3	2
Unclassified	–	1	–	1	1	–	2	–
No answer	–	2	1	5	–	–	–	–

55 of the 300 Greek deputies serving in 1964–65 (see Table 6.9). The small size of the sample does not allow one to make definitive statements, but the general atmosphere of issueless politics is sustained.

The two deputies from the Progressive Party (Komma Proodeftikon, KP), a minor faction made up of the small nationwide following of its leader, Spyros Markezinis, could see no real difference between the major parties. In fact, they could not see any difference between themselves and the major parties—except, as one said, that the two major parties had governed, and "we hope to govern." The Progressive Party has formed a wide variety of campaign alliances, without respect to the formal programs of its allies. Successful Progressive candidates are often enticed into other parties after election; conversely, dissatisfied deputies of the major parties sometimes find a place in the KP for a time. Although the deputies themselves often mentioned their personal ties to Markezinis, their actual election seemed to result from personal ties at the local level, or from other special local conditions. Four EDA deputies were also interviewed: one suggested that there was no difference between parties, one evaded the question, and two declined to answer at all.

The EK deputies who were interviewed fell into three groups: those newly elected, those with a consistent Center background, and those with political experience in both the Right and the Center. The first category had the closest ties to the leader, since most of them represented marginal districts; they depended on his personal influence, as well as his demagogic appeals to the voters. The other two categories had some independent political strength. They had their own clientage organizations, and could use their own lateral ties to the bureaucracy to satisfy local demands, without working through the party leader. In the group with Right-Center backgrounds, the ability to switch from one party to another denoted firm local ties. When interviewed, the newly elected deputies repeated the major statements of the last political campaign—namely, that the Center Union was more internally democratic, and that it supported civil liberties. Deputies with consistent EK backgrounds gave the same general response. However, several of these, although declining to answer the question specifically, made other comments implying that there was little real difference between parties. Only two EK deputies in the third category were included in the sample, and one of these also felt that most parties were essentially similar.

The 17 ERE deputies in the sample fell into two categories: those with consistent Right backgrounds and those with mixed backgrounds. The group of the party directly tied to the party chief was minimal, since the party had been defeated, and since its founder and leader was in voluntary exile. The ERE, for practical purposes, was reduced to those deputies with strong local followings. The single newly elected deputy could see no difference in policy between the major parties; three of the ten old-line Right deputies and two of the six deputies with mixed backgrounds felt the same. The other major sentiment expressed was that the EK was soft on the issue of national security; four of the consistent ERE group and four in the group of deputies with mixed political backgrounds volunteered this response.

It is significant that the political issues mentioned most often by the deputies of the major parties—national security by the ERE and democracy or civil liberties by the EK—were the obverse of one another. Moreover, these issues were current electoral slogans; they were almost automatic responses. When pressed, few deputies could add content to the slogan. Perhaps even more indicative of the artificial character of the issues was the fact that by the time of the interviews it was quite apparent that the EK was no more "democratic" internally than the ERE. It was similarly apparent that despite the eased atmosphere and new attitudes toward the Left, the Papandreou government had not taken any important steps to change the legal status of the Communist Party or the many political prisoners. Since this was the basic problem that both slogans referred to, the responses of most deputies actually showed little concern with real issues.

Only two deputies suggested that there were historical reasons for party differences. It would seem that the bitter cleavage of the interwar period has largely disappeared, and that Greek politics are once again "normal." The major concerns of the postwar period have been reconstruction and social reform, although the nature of the latter has not been explicitly spelled out by any major party. By and large, the major difference between the Right and the Center, especially in the last few years, has been in their divergent attitudes toward the Left and its place in the Greek political arena. This difference stems from factors outside the traditional political level.

POLICY ORIENTATIONS, 1955–65

Cyprus has been the chief policy problem for Greece since 1955, regardless of the party in power.[24] The responses of both Karamanlis and Papandreou to the West, represented by the NATO alliance, and to other nations, especially to Greece's Balkan neighbors, were largely contingent on the status of the Cyprus controversy. It is misleading to assume that Karamanlis consistently sacrificed national aims to placate the NATO allies, or that the fall of the Papandreou government occurred because of its willingness to sacrifice the Western alliance for settlement of the Cyprus question along lines desired by Greece. After 1952, the Greek Rally, which included many of the leading figures in the later Karamanlis administration, had worked to smooth relations with other Balkan states, including the traditional enemy, Turkey. Papagos, as premier, had also tried to find a way out of the Cyprus imbroglio. However, relations with Turkey and Britain deteriorated steadily, culminating in the Istanbul riots against the Greeks in September 1954, a month before the death of Papagos and the accession of Karamanlis. The United States remained neutral, and relations with her became tense after this episode. Events on Cyprus prevented any reconciliation, regardless of the feeling in Athens or elsewhere.

Karamanlis barely won the elections of 1956, in which the opposition concentrated on foreign-policy issues. For the next three years, since settling the dispute "within the family" seemed unlikely, Greece sought "friendships increasingly outside the circle of the Western alliance."[25] This expansion of contacts, characterized by a cultivation of many of the new postwar states in the Middle East, was an effort to get the Cyprus issue settled favorably to Greece within the United Nations. On several occasions the Greek government was not responsive to minor American requests; moreover, Greece signed new trade agreements with the Soviet Union and Poland. Cyprus was again a major issue in the 1958 election, and again Karamanlis won. After this election Karamanlis and the Greek Cypriots bowed to the inevitable. The independence of Cyprus was assured by the Zurich Agreements of 1959. Relations with the Western powers improved, and ties with other states began to weaken. Karamanlis's opposition, of course, claimed that needless concessions had been made to foreign pressures, at the expense of national aspirations.

The elections of 1963 and 1964 did not involve the Cyprus question, and the reasons for the Papandreou victory lie elsewhere. However, the constitutional structure agreed upon in 1959 proved unworkable; and in February 1964 Cyprus erupted once again. The reaction of the Papandreou government was a familiar one. A policy of good relations with Balkan neighbors was initiated. An accord was signed with Bulgaria, and Papandreou paid a state visit to Belgrade. Once again, official relations with the major Western powers became cooler, and minor indications of dissatisfaction were evident.

The actual policies of both administrations were not dissimilar. The opposition, whether EK or ERE, could always decry the handling of foreign policy issues; but once in power, it made no major changes. Foreign-policy options were limited externally by the major allies; moreover, the Greek government was never able to control the actions of Greeks on Cyprus. The specific events culminating in the crisis of 1965 and the downfall of the Papandreou cabinet were also related in part to the Cyprus question. They will be discussed in the chapter to follow.

Economic Development and Social Reform

Since Greece's reconstruction after World War II, economic development and social reform have been acknowledged goals for every government. One must look at specific programs to determine party differences. The task is difficult, for seven years of ERE rule must be compared with scarcely eighteen months of EK administration. It is primarily a matter of contrasting results with intentions. In terms of domestic policy, the climate and atmosphere, rather than the results, were profoundly different. There was substantial economic growth under both regimes.[26]

The ERE economic program was largely a continuation of the policy inspired by Spyros Markezinis during the administration of the Greek Rally. Each of these governments used state resources and pressures to benefit those portions of the population most sympathetic to themselves. Although there was some attempt at long-range planning, those plans that did emerge were poorly conceived and coordinated, and certainly did not indicate any logical system of priorities for solving Greece's most fundamental economic and social problems. The keystone of ERE policy was continued monetary stability; this was accomplished, in large measure, by rigorously controlling wages, often in an apparently haphazard manner. The German ideal of a "market economy" also caught the fancy of the ERE rhetoricians, as though free competition, together with state capital investment, would be sufficient to recreate the German "miracle" in Greece. The ERE encouraged the investment of foreign capital by extravagant legislation and favorable contracts, but success was limited. The state itself provided the funds for public works and particular capital investments, and private firms made the profits.

The EK was faced with the same problems as the ERE, and to some extent it propounded the same solutions. In urging the restoration of democratic politics in Greece, the EK generally assumed that "democracy" would be applied to economic and social problems; but specific programs were completely lacking or intentionally vague. Certainly, economic development, particularly industrialization and increased agricultural productivity, was a key part of the Papandreou formulation. It was recognized that state, foreign, and private investment would be required. However, much of this program seemed fanciful. Foreign capital was no more likely to appear under Papandreou than under Karamanlis, particularly since the incentives for its investment were diminished. The expectation of increased domestic investment in industry or agriculture seemed to discount the realities of Greek culture: the very rich regard conspicuous consumption as a way of life; and the middle class puts its savings into economically static investments, such as urban real estate and cash dowries. The EK's specific proposals, such as that for regional industrial zones, seemed to be based on political, rather than economic, realities. On the positive side, the EK did make serious efforts to promote long-range economic planning; the privately operated Center for Economic Research, for example, was envisaged as the core of a refurbished Ministry of Coordination. But Papandreou's tenure was too short for the success or failure of this endeavor to be evident. The battles between the new and the traditional elements in the Greek economic bureaucracy were still raging when the regime fell.

A major difference between the ERE and the EK appeared in their attitudes toward the use of state resources. The ERE distributed favors to individuals and to certain groups (businessmen, some agricultural interests, and the military). The government tried to maintain the status quo in salaries, and tried to discourage labor unrest by putting severe restrictions on the labor movement. There was some increase in social-service benefits, particularly to agriculture, and there were halting attempts at an improvement of the educational system. By and large, however, the ERE used subsidies, tax privileges, and foreign credits to buy support from people with extensive influence networks and from specific population groups.

The EK, by contrast, tried to use public finances in another way. Papandreou announced salary benefits for various groups—civil servants, the military, the lower clergy, and urban labor—almost immediately after coming to power. Agriculture also received increased subsidies and social-service benefits. To some extent, this was the usual campaign for public support; but it was also designed to lift support from the purely personal, clientage-oriented level. However, none of these programs were carried out completely. Financial benefits were announced for classes and groups, but certain individuals also benefited. It was extremely questionable whether the public finances could sustain this largesse. Policies of union reform remained incomplete; every action provoked criticism from either the Right or the Left. In education, plans for a longer period of compulsory education and the expansion of free education to the university level were not fully realized.

Administrative Reform

The ERE was satisfied with the traditional structure of Greek politics and made no attempt to change it. Under the EK, however, many proposals for administrative reform were advanced. Some were novel, such as the creation of a School of Public Service to provide qualified personnel for the bureaucracy. Others were more typical of newly elected governments, such as the proposals to reduce the size of the bureaucracy and to decentralize the administration. In addition there were programs to reform the assessment and collection of taxes. In practice, only those aspects of administrative reform that would assist the governing party were seriously undertaken. Decentralization was not seriously promoted. Bureaucratic employees were reclassified, and those with more than 35 years of service were retired. The "temporary" employees of the Karamanlis years were replaced by new "temporary" employees. Promotions and appointments continued to be at least partly dependent on political affiliation.

A concern with unearthing the sins of the previous administration, characteristic of an issueless political setting, was a prominent feature of the EK government. But Papandreou, although embarking on a thorough investigation of the preceding regime, did not go far enough to satisfy the extreme Left and went too far to please many of the more moderate and traditional elements in his own party. Court action was initiated against some former ministers and against Karamanlis (although he had left the country). A new law obligated all political figures to file statements of their net financial assets with the secretary of the Parliament. In theory, this would have prevented some of the abuses that had been common under the Karamanlis regime; but most deputies, and certainly the majority of the people, greeted this legislation with skepticism.

National Security

The question of national security provoked much discussion throughout both the Karamanlis and Papandreou administrations. During the ERE period the Left and much of the Center campaigned vigorously for a "normalization" of Greek political life. Although this call was interpreted differently by different groups, it essentially implied a reinstatement of the Greek Left in active politics. Several measures were involved: legalization of the Communist Party of Greece, the KKE; permission for the return of political exiles; the release of political prisoners; a restriction on the use of certificates of social conformity, which limited the access of the Left to employment and education; and a general relaxation of the "emergency measures" that curbed the political activity of the Left. This issue, more than any other, caused dissension in the EK and made good relations with the monarch difficult.

After gaining power, Papandreou hesitated to enact his complete program. Although associating with the Left for political purposes, he remained an anti-Communist. The status of the KKE was never changed, and certificates of social conformity were still required. A few refugees were permitted to enter the nation—although fewer than during the Karamanlis years—and only a few political prisoners were released. The Papandreou government maintained, as its predecessor had, that the political prisoners were in fact imprisoned for specific criminal activities; and it used devices such as administrative deportation to handle individual cases, just as the ERE had. However, there was some improvement in the general realm of civil liberties: police brutality and harassment became less common; newspapers circulated more freely; and court action against editors for specific newspaper stories diminished.

There is some evidence that party policy under both the EK and the ERE was partly intended to aid specific groups in the population, rather than individuals embedded in particular clientage networks. Unquestionably, some "groups," particularly in the business sector, were so small that benefits were actually given to individuals. However, agricultural subsidies or broad social-welfare measures did affect a great many Greeks. These can be viewed as efforts of the premier and his personal-fragile party following to transform the Greek political system into one that we could call "modern." Unfortunately, these "group" benefits often increased the importance of membership in a clientage network. For a benefit that must come through the state bureaucracy, the average Greek needs assistance—which must be sought, as before, from the polyarchic and persistent elements of the party.

The slight differences in party policies that we have examined do not conflict with Key's suggestion that "politics generally comes down, over the long run, to a conflict between those who have and those who have less."[27] Those with clientage ties to the parliamentary level have the advantage; those without ties are disadvantaged. It should be noted that not all "haves" are treated alike, given the general conditions of scarcity. Each political leader can use the state to discriminate against particular individuals and to favor others. As long as the center of gravity in traditional political groups is with the polyarchic and persistent component, this remains the standard pattern of Greek politics.

THE ROLE OF THE MASS MEDIA

To an uninformed observer, the mass communications media in Greece might appear to have great possibilities as instruments of socialization and reform. However, the Greek press does not contribute much to opinion change; primarily, it reinforces views already held by its readers. The political inclination of the reader is more or less apparent when he picks out his newspaper at the corner kiosk. He knows the nature of the political views he is going to find, since the majority of Greek newspapers are journals of opinion and little else. Observers of modern Greece have often concluded from newspaper content that all Greeks are intensely political. However, these papers have a circulation of 125 copies per thousand population, one of the lowest in Europe.[28] Moreover, the nonpolitical journals, such as the sporting newspaper and the "romantic" magazines, have increased in circulation, whereas most of the newspapers have gained no readers. In fact, before the confused events of 1967 the major journals started to run serials and other materials of historical interest on their front pages, apparently attempting to draw readers for other than political reasons. Since the newspapers are owned either by individual politicians or by their close associates, the strong political flavor and the tendency to sensationalism is accepted by most readers as inevitable. Newspapers, as a channel for communication, tend to be distrusted by most Greeks for these reasons. Instead, they are a source of conversational material, a window through which the political world is merely observed.

It would seem that radio could be an alternative channel of communication. To a large extent, it does compete with the press. This is particularly true in rural areas, where newspapers are scarce and where political pressures often prevent the circulation of papers with extremist views. However, radio receivers are no more common than newspapers in remote rural areas. A United States Department of State survey in 1951 found that Greeks looked upon radio as "more truthful" because it was controlled directly by the state. In reality, the state radio networks have not always been neutral,[29] since all appointments to their staffs are political in inspiration. In the 1950's the radio was openly conservative. By 1964, there was a degree of fairness during the political campaign, and all three major parties received equal time for political broadcasts. By and large, the political content of the radio programming is not great; most programs are for entertainment rather than for information.

ELECTORAL ANALYSIS

Political behavior in Greece does not seem explicable in terms of cash crops, labor force, size of agricultural holding, or any of the usual variables of aggregate analysis. Instead, the major explanatory variable is traditional political attachment.* Seventy of the 146 eparchies in Greece can be said to have strong traditional attachments, which fall into three categories: some eparchies consistently give lopsided majorities to the candidates and political organizations of the Right; others are similarly attached to the Center; and a few areas have followed the meanderings of a particular family or set of candidates across the political boundaries. As we have seen, this ideological labeling is for convenience only; there is little real difference between "Right" and "Center" candidates. In these eparchies, the individual candidates are likely to have personal clientage networks. The leading regional politicians are usually prominent in one of the major national parties.

* For a classification of eparchies by recent voting behavior, see Appendix B.

The specific political affiliation of these leaders seems to be related to historical factors, especially to the circumstances under which their region became part of the Greek state.

There are 20 eparchies in which the Right has almost always received a majority. Between 1946 and 1963, the collective right-wing vote in these areas was usually 70 or 80 per cent, and the Left seldom made much of an inroad. All of these eparchies were in the original Greek kingdom, in either the Peloponnesus or the Cyclades, except for Corfu and Paxi, both annexed in 1864. In the nineteenth century, and even in much of the twentieth, these areas supported individual families or local notables; the families, although originally factionalized, were forced to combine into some type of political grouping after 1910 to combat the Liberal Party of Venizelos. The representatives from the solidly traditional areas are still the major figures in the right-wing parties. In this case, the loyalty of the voters to families and notables has been transferred to whatever broader political organization these leaders happen to represent. There is little temptation to switch to the other side; at most, there may be an occasional tendency to form splinter parties.

The major Center grouping has a similar stronghold although the stratification of eparchies is more complex. There are eleven eparchies that have consistently given the center grouping majorities, usually from 75 to 90 per cent of the vote. All but one of these eparchies are on Crete—the home island of Eleutherios Venizelos, who brought the island into the Greek kingdom and also founded the first Center coalition. The lone exception is the eparchy of Kalimnos in the Dodecanese; although the Dodecanese was the last region to become part of Greece, its annexation was presided over by the son of Venizelos. The memory of Venizelos is sufficient to hold the political allegiance of all these areas. Where there is competition, it is within the same political grouping.

To these eleven eparchies must be added an additional seven, all on Crete. These have almost always voted for the Center, but each has switched sides in one of the eight elections since 1946. The year of exception to the rule has varied, but in nearly every case there has been a split in the ranks of the Center. In the eparchy of Temenos, which includes the city of Iraklion, the Left was able to capitalize on this split to pick up a small plurality. In Lassithi, the Right received a majority because the representative of a traditional political family ran on their slate. The electoral geography of Crete is very complex, although the island as a whole can be counted upon to support the organizations that have descended from the Venizelist party. Many of the twenty eparchies are extremely small and isolated. Allegiance to certain families remains the rule. In some of these the traditional loyalty may be to a family descended from those who were at odds with the Venizelist faction in the internal politics of Crete prior to her absorption into the Greek state. These quarrels occasionally surface today, when the Center splits over the formulation of electoral lists, or when other types of personal antagonism produce minor parties.

Another group of eparchies, some nineteen in all, has voted for the Right in all but one election. Most of these are in the old portions of the kingdom —five in the Peloponnesus, four in the Cyclades, six in Old Greece, and two in the Ionian Islands. Two, Kastoria and Grevena, are in Macedonia. Kastoria, on the northern frontier, has been extensively resettled with peasants from the crowded areas of the Peloponnesus to replace citizens who died or defected to the adjacent Communist countries during the civil war. Grevena is a different case: a popular local leader joined the lists of the Right in 1950 and has managed reelection since that time. The reason for the one off year in all these eparchies is not clear. There is, to be sure, always some shifting of deputies and candidates from Right to Center lists. However, most of the exceptions came in 1950 and seem largely due to the proliferation of candidates that the new proportional representation system encouraged in that election.

There is a final category of traditional eparchy, in which the vote shifted abruptly from one political grouping to another and continued to favor the second. Usually, this happened in 1951 or 1952, and the switch can be associated with the formation of the Greek Rally, led by Field Marshal Papagos. In 10 of the 13 areas in this category, the leading political figures changed parties, and the district followed suit; these areas were primarily in the Epirus and Thrace. The switches in the other three eparchies occurred because local notables wanted a new patron, or because a popular new entrant appeared on the list of the minority party.

The remaining 76 eparchies and the various urban electoral districts are not as strongly traditional in outlook, and their electoral behavior cannot be explained so easily. Most of Macedonia, Thrace, Thessaly, the Aegean Islands, the Epirus, and Old Greece fall into this category. The attachments of Macedonia, Thrace, the Aegean Islands, and even the Epirus had been to Venizelos as an individual; this loyalty was not transferred as completely to the Center political groups as it was in Crete. Thessaly is somewhat different: an area devoted to commercial agriculture, with a tradition of agricultural dissent, it has tended to fluctuate or to take an independent course in most elections. The major cities of Greece are also located in the eparchies in this large category; in these cases, too, the traditional attachments have become more tenuous.

In studying these areas, I assumed that the fluctuation in support for either major political group would be contingent upon something other than traditional attachments, which were lacking or severely eroded. An index of fluctuation was constructed for each eparchy, and was then correlated with the acreage of various cash crops and with urbanization.* Nothing of significance emerged; in fact, there was a negative correlation between political fluctuation and the amount of land devoted to cash crops. (In retrospect, it might be argued that cash crops are so subsidized that political fluctuation is not likely to occur because of farm prices.) One must conclude either that the political shift in each constituency is dependent on the peculiar set of economic determinants found there, or that Greek politics is simply not explicable in nonpolitical terms. Although economic influences, urbanization, and the like are felt in these eparchies more than in other areas of Greece, their influence is not specifically on party affiliation but on an individual voters relationship with a particular deputy or candidate of any political grouping. Thus the personal political relationship remains the most crucial factor in Greek electoral politics.

* The index figures were obtained by dividing the standard deviation of the right-wing vote in each eparchy (1946–63) by the mean right-wing vote for that eparchy. Only the right-wing vote was used, since the Center was badly fragmented during this period, and since the Right held office. Different socioeconomic variables were then correlated with each index figure, using the Pearson product-moment formulation. In retrospect, this seems to have been an inappropriate technique; a more detailed and accurate electoral analysis is now in progress.

7. Politics at the Parliamentary Level

The chamber of deputies and the government selected from it are important sectors of the Greek political system. Elections create parliamentary majorities, which invest certain leaders with ministerial office; in return, the political resources at the disposal of the ministers flow through clientage networks to the deputies, and eventually to individual Greeks. However, parliament is the context for bargaining only among the more traditional elements of the Greek political system. Bargaining between parliamentary leaders and the other major political groups does not take place in an institutional framework. Certainly, the chamber of deputies is not crucial in determining public policy, either for the traditional sector or for the whole system. However, the modest importance of the Greek legislature in policy making cannot be ascribed to the general causes of similar decline elsewhere.[1]

Basically, the decline of legislatures in the West has been attributed to the complexities of the modern industrial setting. The subject matter for legislation is considered too complex for legislative understanding; and the pace of the modern world requires more rapid decisions than the legislative process allows. Given this complexity, the devices for control of the executive by the legislature have also been inadequate. Sometimes the shortcomings of representative bodies have been traced to the party system: party discipline prevents initiative and makes a mockery of executive control.[2] Refinements of this argument suggest that ideological conflict has subsided, and that the leaders of parties formulate policy without consulting the rank and file; or, conversely, they suggest that ideological conflict is extremely severe and must be settled by elite negotiation outside of the parliamentary setting.[3] Nevertheless, in each of these cases leaders with their roots in the parliamentary setting are involved in bargaining and negotiation, and making decisions for the whole political system. The major portions of society view the parliament and its derivative institutions as the legitimate arena for conflict resolution. The concern with micropolitics and patronage so characteristic of the Greek parliamentary system, though not completely absent, is far less important in Western governments. Certainly, part of the difference can be traced to differing levels of economic development, which influence the type and number of demands and the level of political organization. Family influence, for example, is likely to be much more pervasive in the less industrial settings. The existence of particular political institutions can also have a significant influence on the style and focus of political activity.

In other transitional societies, the nature of parliamentary politics resembles the Greek pattern. The concerns and the channels for action of the rural Mexican are not unlike those of the rural Greek, and the village *cacique* is still an important figure. However, political bargaining and negotiation takes place within and between the sectors that make up the dominant party (PRI, Partido Revolucionaria Institucional) rather than at the level of the Mexican Congress.[4] In Iran, the political system is essentially a traditional one, according to Binder, and "its principle mode of operation is through bargaining."[5] There are a number of independent power centers: the shah, the military, the separate ministries and councils, the great families and tribes, and some others. Bargaining takes place between these groups, outside any formal institutional setting. Clientage structures are the fundamental Iranian social units; and they are concerned with appointments, administrative favors, special legislation, and the like, rather than with broad demands. The bureaucracy is heavily penetrated by these clientage groups. The government is characterized by lack of coordination, and generally cannot deal competently with the major problems of modernization.[6] As in Greece, the parliament (*Majlis*) seems to be unconcerned with high policy making; however, the parliamentary representatives are not the major channels for individual demands, as they are in Greece. The relationship between voter and deputy does not rest on the use of the vote as a bargaining tool. In part this can be ascribed to the late development of parliamentary institutions in Iran: other channels predated the representative body; and clientage networks do not culminate in the Majlis because the powerholders in the Iranian political system are not ordinarily found there.

As earlier references have suggested, the pattern of Philippine politics (as presented by Jean Grossholtz) has many parallels with the pattern of Greek parliamentary politics.[7] The political culture and the style of bargaining ("the use of the vote as the *quid pro quo* for quite personal services") are much the same in both countries.[8] Philippine congressmen are concerned not with appropriations, budgets, or policy as such, but with the acquisition of the "necessities of electoral success"—in other words, with public works, patronage, and bureaucratic intervention. However, in the Philippines the major decisions for the whole society seem to be made entirely within the political sphere. The president and his associates do not have to bargain with a monolithic bureaucracy, a military, or other "veto" groups that do not participate in parliamentary politics. In the Philippines, as in Greece, the traditional clientage structures were congruent with representative institutions; in both settings, the bureaucracy developed in the same way, and was penetrated by clientage networks. But in the Philippines the colonial experience (and perhaps a peculiar combination of international factors as well) has produced a military that accepts civilian control.

In all of these "transitional" systems the characteristic social structures have been patron-client relationships based on reciprocal obligations. Few Mexicans, Iranians, Filipinos, or Greeks are concerned with legislation in the sense of broad policy decisions; instead they pursue the satisfaction of individual demands. The method of satisfying these demands has varied in each context, depending on the institutional channels available. In addition, the role of the constitutional institutions in settling those major policy questions that do exist or in maintaining a balance between the major political sectors has varied, depending on the groups involved and on whether they view the representative institutions as legitimate or not.

In Greece, the revolutionary elites and their heirs took command of the representative institutions before a bureaucratic apparatus had time to develop. The parliament was never an instrument of the bureaucratic elite, as it was in some systems described by Riggs.[9] The early politicians simply operated as patrons, interceding in administration for the benefit of their rural clients. The bureaucracy was not a mechanism for control of the political sector; it was an instrument for the use of the parliamentary elites, who occupied the ministerial chairs. Wealth, status, education, and political resources in the form of votes were all in the hands of the same political elite. This orientation toward government output continued throughout the nineteenth century, and is the prevailing attitude of parliamentarians and the general population today. In modern Greece the top echelons of the bureaucracy and the parliament are interchangeable. The minister who heads a government department is of necessity a prominent politician. In general, he is the master of his bureaucratic house, although his personal connections and the expected length of his tenure may sometimes affect the situation. The future of any government department is largely dependent on the political influence of the minister who heads it. It is his task to innovate programs, and to find ways to finance them. The assignments and promotions of the ministerial employees are largely dependent upon him. Finally, a minister may be able to build a parliamentary following because of his control over departmental patronage.

The Greek bureaucracy, then, is hardly a monolithic structure; it is penetrated by the political world. Patronage, seniority, tenure, and part-time employment are all individual concerns. As in other sectors of Greek society, it is still largely a matter of each individual bureaucrat against every other. Administrators are more concerned with protecting existing relationships or with acquiring new status than with organizational output. Scarcity contributes as much to insecurity in the bureaucratic world as in other parts of Greek society. The traditional political groups, as represented by the ERE, have stressed national security in large part because it gave them protection against new socially mobile elements in the society, who might well have family or friendship ties that could get them into government service. There is a formal merit system for hiring and promotion in the Greek civil service; but it is undermined because the pinnacle of the system is political, and nearly every politician can intervene at the lower levels. A bureaucrat with personal aspirations cannot afford to alienate the political leadership. He is likely to have less loyalty to higher authority in his own department than he has to influential politicians outside it. All of this forces a bureaucrat to concentrate on playing politics, rather than on doing his job.

The assumption that policy making ought to be the central concern of the political system underlies all formal constitutional relationships in Greece, as it does in most Western countries. However, neither parliament nor the cabinet pays much attention to policy. In a society characterized by ties of personal loyalty, there are few general interests and demands to be articulated and answered; there is only the reality of each personal demand. The ministerial level has little knowledge of available resources and general public demands. The bureaucracy cannot supply this knowledge, since it is also concerned with personal matters; besides, it may not have any adequate sources of information either. As a result, policy making becomes a rather formal exercise. Theodore Couloumbis notes that the most momentous policies in postwar Greece were presented to parliament by ministers with little knowledge of their content or consequences. The parliament passed them with very little debate. For example, the NATO alliance was approved in 1949 in an atmosphere of complete unconcern.[10] The association with the European Common Market seems to have been made in a similar way.[11]

The Greek government sometimes tries to use legislation as an instrument of social change, almost always with unintended results. Few government leaders have an accurate picture of the real situation in any sector of Greek society; hence there is no way to plan changes, or to integrate programs of change in one sector with those in another. The habit of looking upon legislation as a way of increasing political resources further limits the possibility that a given policy or action will produce the desired result. Since the major concern of the parliamentary level is the satisfaction of individual demands on the government, politically motivated exceptions to any policy always appear, and contradictory legislation is often forthcoming. The political world, then, is an unreal world, a world of micropolitics, personality, and patronage.

The consequences of Greek legislation for the promotion of economic development are worth examining in detail. Adam Pepelasis has outlined the role of legal factors in Greek economic development.[12] One theme that constantly recurs is the wide range of government interest. But here, as elsewhere, government action promotes the interests of particular individuals rather than those of the nation as a whole. The twin requirements of economic advancement and political necessity rarely coincide. The legal system, the primacy of family considerations, and the general mistrust in Greek society have worked to keep the forms of enterprise primitive and industrial activity retarded.

The behavior of Greeks involved in the economic sector has differed from that of entrepreneurs in the West simply because the environment in which they operate is different. The corporate form of management has always been distrusted because it is assumed that corporations will invariably bilk the public and the government by their extraordinary skill in finding tax loopholes, and will rob minority stockholders because of family control of the corporation. The corporate form seems to have been discouraged by the government as a public service. For these and other reasons manufacturing between 1911 and 1930 did not contribute more than 10 per cent of the gross national income in Greece;[13] in 1960, the figure was only 19.7 per cent.[14] There is still no real protection for minority interests when they do exist; and devices like accounting standards, audits, and honest publicity, which might make corporations more responsible, are all lacking. Even foreign consultants have difficulty in acquiring the trust that enables them to see the second set of books. In the past, corporate charters had to come from the Ministry of National Economy or from the cabinet itself. Only after 1955 did legislation allow a true limited liability company to be formed; and even this legislation was faulty in several respects. Until recently, corporate litigation could be appealed to the highest court as a matter of course. These delays were compounded by judicial moratoria that prolonged settlements for generations.

Several cultural factors have also impeded the development of a substantial manufacturing sector in Greece. The middle class, often nonexistent in other underdeveloped countries, has a high propensity to save for items such as dowries and education. Funds for these purposes are usually invested in real estate or left in liquid form, rather than being put to more productive uses. Greek business has tended to invest in commercial ventures (i.e., in trading rather than manufacturing), since these can usually be financed by family funds and can respond quickly to changed economic and social circumstances.[15] The same bias is found among other agencies with investment capital; pension and welfare funds, for instance, do not invest in corporate securities either. The traditional Greek pursuits of commerce and shipping have remained more lucrative and prestigious. The upper class, often with fortunes derived from speculation in real estate, has not acted to advance economic development, but is noted for its conspicuous consumption. Basically, any industrialization efforts have to face these attitudes, which make capital difficult to secure; they have also been hampered by the widespread feeling that a Greek product could not possibly be as good as a foreign one. One might expect that foreign concerns would take advantage of this demand for capital; but there was little foreign investment in Greece before World War II, and postwar efforts to attract foreign investment (especially a law that allowed favorable terms for the repatriation of capital and profit) were unsuccessful. Internal stability has been more important in creating capital inflow than anything else.[16]

The Greek government has tried to use tax subsidies to encourage economic development. However, taxes are particularly liable to favor certain individuals and firms at the expense of competitors. Political resources are created, but economic development is only incidentally encouraged; and the tax structure becomes more warped than before. For example, the Greek turnover tax is not applied to construction firms, service and retail industries, and newspapers; yet these are precisely the enterprises that should not be encouraged if economic development is to result.[17] The lack of a capital gains tax also encourages speculation in the less vital sectors. The use of standards of consumption to assess income taxes does promote saving among the upper classes. However, only the fact that the method for checking on commodity tax payments is so intricate and cumbersome removes one's suspicion that these taxes have been specifically designed to penalize the most modern and efficient firms, and to allow the least progressive, such as small urban craftsmen and retail traders, to escape.

The governments since 1952 have attempted to encourage economic reconstruction and development by granting loans to private enterprise at favorable rates and by building state industrial plants. In the second case, inefficiency, nepotism, and other features of the Greek bureaucracy are merely transferred to the public enterprise.[18] Public corporations merely create additional fields for political intervention. The government's willingness to enter any particular sector of the economy is a political weapon that can be used against existing firms. Given the small number of firms in Greece, any government economic program is bound to benefit a few easily identifiable firms or individuals. This is true whether state funds are used to upgrade old production units or to create new ones. It is especially true when the state locates plants and picks the managers and workers itself. In recent years, there have been numerous programs to encourage the relocation of industry into underdeveloped regions in Greece, which is intended to speed up regional development by creating provincial industrial zones. The concentration of industry in the Athens-Piraeus area can easily be explained in economic terms: this is simply the optimum location in all of Greece.[19] Despite this, subsidies and other enticements are offered to industries that locate in the more remote provincial areas, even when their placement is inherently inefficient. Here, too, the administration of the programs is motivated primarily by political requirements.

The same patterns can be noted in Greek policies toward agriculture. Legislation designed to improve agricultural output or better the position of the peasants has often had the opposite effect. The limitations and failures of the cooperative movement have been noted in Chapter 5. The government's approach to the problem of farm fragmentation is similarly instructive.[20] State land distribution schemes have been primarily responsible for fragmentation, although the topography of Greece has contributed to the problem. Inheritance laws (which encourage equal division of land) and the Greek dowry system have kept holdings small. Excessive fragmentation results in a waste of land and manpower, and limits the possibilities of mechanization and modernization. However, given the peasants' distrust of any government agency, schemes for voluntary consolidation are not likely to be successful. Until recently, in fact, the government pursued contradictory policies of distribution and consolidation with equal vigor. Other efforts at agrarian development—the development of irrigation works, the encouragement of the use of fertilizers or mechanization, and state efforts to develop markets by special agreements with other nations—seldom benefit the peasant in practice. For example, the government operates one fertilizer plant itself, and has supplied capital to a private group for another; but government policy throughout has favored the manufacturer of fertilizer, at the expense of the consumer. Trade agreements have often meant that a farmer pays higher prices for the imported goods he must use. Although the rural Greek's position is improving, he has not benefited from the recent economic gains to the same extent as the urban dweller.

Regardless of its purpose, legislation in Greece is almost exclusively the province of the government in power. Ministers submit proposals to parliament, and these are forwarded to the proper committees. The rank and file of the government party are rarely called upon for advice; in fact, they generally receive no advance notice of impending government legislation. Even those deputies with backgrounds in the relevant subject are allowed to do little more than react. The chief legislative officer, the president of parliament, is part of the inner circle of the majority party group. The content and scheduling of legislative business is a matter for him and the premier to decide.

Although the Greek parliament has a complete panoply of committees, which correspond to the ministerial portfolios, they are not crucial to the legislative process. A given committee's membership, generally from 10 to 15, reflects the relative party strengths in the entire parliament. Although formal assignments are made by the president of parliament, there is a fair amount of cooperation among the various factions on these matters. In most cases, the individual deputy has little control over his committee assignment. Since committees are relatively inconsequential in the legislative process, and since a deputy may have little interest in the particular legislative committee to which he is assigned, it is not surprising that the average deputy gives committee work a low priority, and that attendance at committee meetings is poor. Most deputies would prefer to spend their time in satisfying the patronage requests of their constituents, a far more productive and necessary activity.

When committees do function, they rarely hear anyone other than the minister directly concerned with the legislation. Committee proceedings are ostensibly closed, but in most cases individual deputies, bent on publicity for the home folks, make arrangements with the press gallery for leaks. The committee has no option but to report the proposed bill to the full chamber, giving its recommendation. The report of the committee is appended as an introduction to the bill, together with the minister's introduction. Any deputy may then propose amendments, even if he is not a member of the committee that has considered the legislation. These amendments are submitted to the president of parliament, who directs their printing and their submission to the committee and to the rest of the deputies. The minister who originated the bill controls committee proceedings and the final hearing in the chamber, and announces which amendments he will accept and which he will not.

Even the full parliamentary sessions are not important to most deputies. The premier and the ministers rarely appear; when they do, their main purpose seems to be receiving applause. Individual ministers appear whenever they are scheduled for questioning on legislation or on the activities of their ministries. Policy statements are given to the press, rather than to party or parliamentary gatherings. Debate between party leaders often takes place in the newspapers rather than in parliament. Although parliamentary rules require attendance, they are rarely enforced; however, a large number of relatively mute deputies do attend because of them. During my interviews with the sample of 55 deputies, it was rare to find anyone engaged in legislative work. For the most part, no trace of proposed bills, committee reports, or even a record of the previous day's legislative events could be found in their offices.

The major function of legislation at the traditional level of Greek politics is the creation of "artificial" political resources. Here, formalism becomes functional. Legislative enactments can ignore reality because there is little expectation that they will be enforced or implemented. The ministers, either by legislative initiation or by administrative ruling, have many opportunities to create resources useful for the satisfaction of political demands. Tax rates can be raised or lowered for specific groups. Fees and tariffs can be varied, and can be collected or not. Concessions can be given, and competition restricted. The general controls over imports and foreign exchange, as well as the controls on both commercial and rural credit, can also be used for political purposes. Foreign loans and grants are also distributed by the ministers. Since most economic sectors are small, there is always the possibility that a general policy can be directed to specific ends. Since demands for favors, access, and all the goods and services subject to government control are always greater than the supply, some noneconomic criterion for distribution is necessary; and political obligation becomes the standard, rather than fairness or equality. In short, the highest level of traditional politicians has a control over most groups in Greek society that can be used to maintain political power. As the formalism in the society increases, citizens increase their demands for the mitigation of its effects. These personal demands can be satisfied by the traditional political system; more general demands for material benefits cannot be so easily satisfied.

The description of prismatic finance offered by Fred Riggs, since it is predicated on a scarcity of resources, seems appropriate for Greece.[21] The tax base in Greece is too narrow to support the tasks of government, even if the country had an efficient bureaucracy and higher levels of taxation. Reliance upon grants or loans from abroad, the Greek practice since independence, is one solution to this problem. The territorial expansion of Greece and the attraction of material and human resources from the provinces to the capital have also been useful. The gap between the wealthy and the poor is widened by widespread tax avoidance and by the government's reliance on regressive indirect taxation, compounded by unfair exemptions. Bribery and bargaining between payee and collector are common practices. Duplex bookkeeping, part of the Riggs model, is also the normal procedure. The formal apparatus of governmental accounting and auditing, although it involves innumerable cross-checks and much red tape, does not reflect actual practices. Kickbacks and bribes are a concomitant part of the administrative process.

Other aspects of Riggs's prismatic model are evident in the Greek case. Both state and private monopolies of the control and sale of particular goods and services are common, and they invariably provide the government with funds. Revenue collected from a particular source is permanently diverted to finance specific activities. This is not in itself "prismatic." For example, gasoline-tax revenue in the United States is often devoted to road construction. The difference is that in Greece the source of taxation and the ultimate recipient of the tax revenue have little connection. As a result, some activities are over-financed and others poorly supported.[22] Revenues earmarked for specific purposes are really the result of ministerial attempts to innovate or to create personal political resources. In general, a minister cannot call upon the ordinary revenues of the state to finance new activity. The state revenues are insufficient; moreover, other major political figures are unlikely to gratuitously increase the political resources of a competitor. By separating the new source of revenue from the service it is to finance—essentially, by hunting for a new source of uncommitted funds rather than trying to justify the diversion of already existing funds—a minister avoids the political costs of assigning revenue on the basis of program priorities.

The actual priority of Greek financial programs depends on the needs of the political circle to which the top officials and ministers belong. The government must also make concessions to political groups that are not formally represented in parliamentary politics. Riggs suggests that in a prismatic society officials must place the demands of the military, the interior departments, and the education departments above those of housing, labor, agriculture, or cultural activities;[23] this is certainly true in Greece. The most influential politicians gravitate to the ministries with the greatest political resources. Under these conditions, and in the absence of annual financial legislation, resource allocations tend to be initiated and perpetuated without regard to program priorities. Greek finances are further strained by a fluctuating balance of payments, which makes financial planning difficult.

Two classical sources of legislative authority, control of the purse strings and rule-making, do not have much importance in the Greek system. First, both have been limited by the environment. Subsistence agriculture, the paucity of natural resources, and the small commercial and industrial sector have all caused Greeks to rely on outside sources for financial solvency. Because of the fluctuations of the world economy and the vagaries of foreign loans and grants, the governmental purse has never really been subject to complete parliamentary control. Policy making is similarly limited by financial deficiencies and the concerns of foreign powers. Second, even though the fiscal powers of the government have increased, particularly after 1952, most legislators do not regard this as a threat. Instead, both they and the ministers view budgeting and rule-making simply as ways to increase personal political resources.[24] If legislative control is attempted at all, it will be by minor "combative" parties or by the out-of-power traditional groups. In the latter case, control is used to embarrass the government in the hope that it will fall, or sometimes to provide a lever for the extraction of favors.[25]

The chamber does come to life when the legislation before it can be applied to the specific patronage or constituency interests of the various deputies. For example, in general sessions devoted to legislation that sets subsidies for various agricultural products deputies from nearly all constituencies feel called upon to speak; considerations of retirement laws, tariff revision, or tax legislation are also occasions for an individual deputy to seek specific favors for his own clients. This kind of legislation is as predetermined as any other, but its character is such that loopholes can be inserted by amendment. In order to keep his own support within the parliament, a minister must accept a certain number of "photographs," as these riders are called in Greece. The deputies, of course, are far more concerned with the "photographs" than they are with the total bill. In some cases a minister may be able to promote a measure that is something more than a collection of special pleas, but this is unusual. All deputies except those of the leftist EDA engage in this behavior. The leftists are most concerned with general demands based on class or group interests. They discourage any concern with personal favors on the part of EDA members, and they barely tolerate personal demands from their few supporters outside the party. This practice helps to maintain the feeling of solidarity essential to left-wing political operation, which would disappear if every individual had a chance of receiving special treatment. The party is able to continue its intellectual and moral disapproval of patronage chiefly because most other deputies would probably not go along with EDA efforts to secure "photographs."

Normally, the chamber of deputies convenes several times a week at about 7 P.M., with a question hour at each session. One minister is questioned each time, according to a regular rotation. There will be a number of prepared questions, followed by one general criticism expressed as a motion to conclude the proceeding. Except for certain topics that have priority, such as Cyprus, the matters questioned will not be current, but will have been placed on file months earlier. Regardless of the government, the great majority of the questions will have been submitted by the deputies of the Left, who often combine their relevant remarks with a general criticism of the government. The rest of the deputies rarely have policy questions; most of their queries are concerned with specific state injustices against individual constituents. The ordinary deputy uses his public questioning privilege mostly as a threat. He will usually go to the minister privately; only if the results are unsatisfactory will he be likely to ask open questions in the chamber. Although the deputy is sacrificing publicity by acting informally, he may be able to get results for his constituent by doing so, and he may build up a reserve of goodwill with the minister. It is a bargaining relationship, pure and simple.

In short, the Greek legislative process does not involve the parliamentary deputy very heavily, and he is not especially concerned about it. Functions shaped by the clientage structures characteristic in Greek society are more important to him. Most legislation is developed by ministers and their staffs outside the parliamentary arena, and the legislature is not viewed as a place for framing solutions or alternatives. The public regards the deputy as a counter to the state rather than as a part of authority itself, and he is not expected to translate demands into legislation. Moreover, most Greeks recognize that solutions and alternatives are limited by forces external to Greece. Neither the public nor the deputies view the legislature in connection with processes that involve the "institutionalization, crystallization, and resolution of social and political conflict."[26]

LEGISLATIVE ROLES

A useful method for studying the parliamentary level of Greek politics is the technique of role analysis suggested by John Wahlke and his associates. "Role orientations are probably not unrelated to the legislator's perception of the power pattern of the political system and the kinds of functions which the legislature is called upon to perform."[27] These authors distinguish several types of role orientations: purposive, emphasizing legislative decision making; representational, emphasizing the style of representation; areal, emphasizing the relationship between the legislator and his district; and pressure-group or party orientations. In Greece only the first two categories, purposive and representational, can be said to exist. For the most part, a Greek deputy is not bedeviled by overlapping role orientations. If there is any conflict, it is between his idealized concept of what a legislator should do and Greek reality.

The 55 deputies interviewed for the present study were questioned on their own perceptions of the legislative role: "How would you describe the job of being a deputy? What are the most important things you should do? Are there any differences between what you think this job is and the way your constituents see it?" The responses to these questions fell into the purposive and representational categories. Those in the purposive category were the most numerous; and we will examine them in detail before considering representational role orientations.

The purposive responses could be divided into four classes. The first, or "ritualist," group included deputies who were oriented to the job of law-making in terms of parliamentary rules and routines. They tended to ignore legislative functions that might be influenced by the goals of parliamentary groups or the power situation in the total system. The complexity of the legislative process was their biggest concern, and legislative maneuvering became an end in itself. The "tribune" category included legislators who looked upon themselves as the advocates of popular demands or the de-fenders of the public against the state. The term "inventor" was applied to those who felt responsible for discovering solutions and exploring alterna-tives to public issues. Finally, the "broker" orientation indicated a concern for the conflicting demands of pressure groups; deputies in this category felt that the proper role of the legislative body is the integration of national economic and social life by the negotiation and bargaining of group claims.[28] Many deputies responded in more than one category. Among the total pur-posive responses, there were 34 ritualists, 45 tribunes, 15 inventors, and only one broker.

The two major purposive role orientations, the ritualist and the tribune, are related to the pattern of development of the Greek representative insti-tutions. The tribune orientation, which sees legislators as advocates of the people, is congruent with the basic clientage relationships found in Greek political life; however, the Greek deputy is less concerned with the demands and interests of all the people than with those of individual persons. The ritualist orientation looks at parliamentary life in terms of lawmaking or legislative control.[29] Sophisticated deputies know that parliaments elsewhere are concerned with these things, and their idea of the ritualist role becomes a standard against which they measure Greek performance. These two orientations are often found together: a Greek deputy thinks that he should act as a ritualist, but he actually functions as a tribune. The inventor and broker orientations are not highly developed in the Greek context.

The 34 deputies who indicated a ritualist outlook, a concern for the par-liamentary process itself, were expressing sentiments at odds with the reality of Greek parliamentary institutions. A concern for the etiquettes, privileges, and procedures of the parliamentary process is the chief characteristic of a ritualist orientation, and Greek parliamentary history is primarily an exer-cise in the disregard of these matters.[30] Although the parliament has been in existence for over a century, there is still little force of tradition behind it; few Greek deputies have any "feel" for the parliament as an institution.[31] There is no conscious effort to train new deputies in the procedures and habits of the chamber, and there is little emphasis on seniority. The intricacies of the legislative process are of little concern to most members.

Several responses that I placed in the ritualist category were quite unambiguous; they seem completely congruent with the Western ideal of legislative life: "The job of the deputy is to legislate, both by helping to prepare bills and by giving them thoughtful consideration in committee. The major role is parliamentary control of the government, although this is done mainly by the opposition deputies." Other responses showed a more realistic view of Greek parliamentary life, but they still emphasized parliamentary activity. One recognized the dominating role of the government in legislation: "The most important job of the deputy is to work in the Parliament by debating and improving laws submitted by the government. It is theoretically part of the deputy's job to introduce legislation, but in fact, that aspect is rather impractical." Others adopted a much more passive role:

The job of the deputy is to watch continuously the work of parliament.

A deputy must watch the work of making laws and try to improve them, and must watch and control the ministers for the sake of justice and the advancement of the standard of living.

The primary emphasis in these responses was on parliament as an institution. The functions deemed important were lawmaking and control of the government. It was not always clear whether "government" was perceived as the executive alone or as the executive and the parliament.

In most cases, a deputy's ritualist response was primarily conditioned by his knowledge of what parliaments were supposed to do. Generally, a ritualist response was qualified by a statement about the real situation in parliament.

Your work in parliament, bills and speeches, is the most important, although, of course, you must think about the matter of reelection. . . . [The constituents] expect their deputy to do things for them.

To legislate is a deputy's main function, but the people do not understand that the deputy is for legislation; they want him as a tool for their own purposes.

The main job of the deputy should be to work in parliament, but unfortunately, the deputy today must deal with everything but parliament. . . . The voters of the countryside think the deputy's only job and responsibility is to promote their personal affairs.

A deputy's job is to make the right laws, and to ensure real parliamentary control of the government . . . to make sure the right questions are put to the government and the correct answers returned. ... Most voters see the deputy as the instrument for the promotion of their personal affairs, right or wrong.

The most important job of the deputy is legislation—discussing and amending legislation proposed by the government. However, in Greece, outside the EDA, no deputy has the time to look at legislation because of the necessity of doing favors for his constituents.

In my opinion, the deputy's job is to legislate, and to judge and criticize the government if necessary. ... The voters are interested only in personal favors.

It would seem that these deputies experience a conflict of roles, the magnitude of the conflict depending on how seriously they take the Western notion of parliamentary purpose. The deputies who qualified their statements with remarks about Greek reality were more likely to have had educational experience outside of Greece. For them, the socialization gained from their education and experience in Greece was in conflict with knowledge gained elsewhere.

In many responses the ritualist perception merged into the tribune perception. The first might be concerned with control of government as a proper function of the legislature; the second felt that the deputy should be able to influence the state machinery in order to protect his constituents. In a society characterized by popular distrust of authority it is not surprising that most Greek deputies consider themselves "tribunes." Those who do appear to have less role conflict, precisely because they do not think of lawmaking as a distinguishing feature of the deputy's job; their attitudes and specific activities involve the advocacy and defense of particular constituent demands. These demands are not likely to be phrased in terms of constitutional or property rights, but in micropolitical terms.

Parliamentary ability is required in order to support the rights of the voter.

The deputy's main task is to survey the legislative work, and to defend the needs of the people and prevent injustices that are caused by the faults of the bureaucracy. I think that there are no basic differences between the deputy's opinion and the constituents' opinion, because, apart from favors, they want their man to do well as deputy.

The job of the deputy is to help the people of his area; there is no difference between this view and the constituents' view.

The deputy must be devoted to the interests of the people and the nation. ... He must help his district through legislative action. There are no differences between his conception and that of constituents.

The deputy should study people's interests and take care of them and defend them in the *Vouli*. Unfortunately, most of the voters see the deputy's role in a different way. People's needs are great, and the resources to meet them are few; people need the state services, which do not work well, so the voter needs his deputy to help him.

This orientation was voiced for the most part by deputies from the rural constituencies. It conforms to the patron-client relationships that have characterized traditional Greek politics. However, there is no relationship between a deputy's orientation and his visits to his constituency or the number of constituents who visit his Athens office. The number of callers at the political offices of the deputies interviewed ranged from six to 900 per week (one deputy claimed to see 2,500 per week), depending on a deputy's position in his party and the proximity of his constituency to Athens. The number of times the deputy visited his constituency was more dependent on his tenure in the parliament and the state of his personal finances than on anything else.

The tension between ideal and reality was also evident in those deputies whose primary interest was in problem solving, a response that placed them in the inventor category. Here, a role calling for general solutions to general problems conflicted with the demands of individual constituents. The inventor is interested in political input, whereas his constituents are concerned with government output.

The main job is to help the government, if that helps the nation and the people. The deputies can help the government in the problems it is dealing with. . . . The demand for personal favors is the exception, met with only in case of absolute necessity; unfortunately, the necessity of my constituents is great.

The work of the deputy is national foreign policy and internal reconstruction. The voters are occupied, for the most part, with their personal problems.

The work of the deputy is to find, both in parliament and the party, measures and policies which serve the general interests of the country. . . . The deputy's tasks, unfortunately, cannot be done well by the Greek deputy, especially the government deputy.

He must support the right demands and stand up for his ideology in parliament, mainly by voting on laws. He must avoid personal interests and promote only the general interest.

In one case, although the deputy offered specific solutions for particular economic and social problems, he still felt that his constituents were of a different mind.

The deputy's job is to form better laws, which should be mainly concerned with a better distribution of public income. This could be done by some laws that would stop what happens today.... A few strong people are squeezing blood from the rest.... One should stop this even if some corporations have to be nationalized. The constituents have a different view.... If their party or deputy does favors, they will have constant demands.

In this category it was rare to find a deputy who did not include a statement deploring the difference between his own perception of duty and his constituents' view of his role. However, representatives of the Left noted that the views of their constituents did not differ from their own.

My task, after the maintenance of democracy, is the independence of our country, liberation of Cyprus from the imperialism of NATO, the improvement of the standard of living of the Greek people, disarmament, and the stabilization of Greece and the world. My voters have the same opinion.

The job of the deputy involves the deepest study of economic and social policies, to solve the problems of the people and also the international problem. There is no difference between these views and the views of the constituent.

The deputy must know the problems and their solutions. He should try to promote these solutions and to inform parliament about them.... The conscious, not the transient, voters of the EDA ... have the same point of view as their deputies. The rest think that the deputy's job is to solve their personal problems.

An inventor orientation marks the Left off from traditional parliamentary politics, and three of the four EDA deputies perceived their function in this way. Wahlke *et al.* have noted that the inventor orientation "comes at a later stage of political development than the foregoing orientations."[32] The EDA stands out as the one modern political organization operating in the Greek parliament.

Only one deputy saw his role as that of a "broker" who balances diverse pressures and conflicting group interests. As previous chapters have suggested, interest groups of the Western associational type are not well developed in Greece. Even if clientage organizations are viewed as competing groups, the focus remains at bargaining on a personal level. Moreover, such bargaining would be unlikely to involve the average deputy and would not occur in the parliamentary context. In my sample of 55 deputies, 27 mentioned group memberships, but these memberships appeared to have political significance in only a few cases. All but two deputies said that groups came to see them, but most deputies gave no indication of paying attention to group demands. If attention was given to a group spokesman, it was given to him as an individual rather than as an organizational representative.

It is difficult to distinguish some aspects of the representational role orientation from the tribune category of the purposive role orientation. The representational role implies a more sophisticated view of the political system than that required for purposive perceptions, in which the deputy is merely "representing the demands" of his constituents. The representational role orientation is concerned with who is represented—a group, individuals, or an area. It is also concerned with determining which factors weigh most heavily in legislative decision making. The Greek deputies who do see themselves as representatives are oriented toward the district or province. According to the Greek constitution, each deputy represents the entire nation; in practice, each deputy is concerned chiefly with his constituency, and especially with specific clientage groups. A deputy may have obligations to specific party leaders, but he has none to the party as a whole. The lack of interest articulation means that few deputies view themselves as the representatives of special groups. Since only a few deputies are personally involved in shaping legislation, constituents seldom judge their representatives by legislative voting record; thus a deputy rarely has to choose between his conscience and instructions from his constituency.

The responses to the general question on legislative role that fell into the representational category were coded into three groups: trustee (18), delegate (5), and politico (2). The third role orientation combines the roles of trustee and delegate. These roles may be held simultaneously (making role conflict likely) or one at a time, depending upon the legislative context. The politico in the American legislative context is more aware of conflict, more flexible in posing alternatives, and in general less dogmatic in his orientations than the other two. To some extent, the politico orientation seems to result from the multiplicity of group demands that conflict with each other and with the public interest.[33] It is not surprising that so few Greek deputies are found in this category, since few demands are phrased in group terms and there is little concept of a "public interest."

The trustee sees himself as "a free agent in that, as a premise of his decision-making behavior, he claims to follow what he considers right or just, his convictions and principles, the dictates of his conscience."[34] He may feel that his principles or objectives are in harmony with those he represents; he may act on his own because he does not trust those from whom he might take advice; and if his opinion differs from the opinions of his constituents, he feels obliged to convince them that his position is correct. Few of those with responses in the trustee category felt that their principles and objectives were in harmony with those of their constituents; moreover, many felt that the deputy himself should try to change opinions in his constituency.

The main job of the deputy is the transformation of the people. The deputy should not only be the servant of the people; he should not have to act for them in personal matters, but only in general matters.

The deputy's main task is to deal with legislation in the parliament for the country, his district, and the Greek people. Quite often people are confused about the deputy's job; but the state machinery is responsible for this, not the people themselves.

In my opinion the deputy must be mainly interested in the promotion of his district's interests, and then in leading the people and his voters as a shepherd does. I don't think there are many differences, except that voters try to use the deputy as their employee and to ask for impossible things.

He must work for the general interests of his people, and he must persuade his constituents and voters that this is the right path, and not the favor-making one.

The deputy must work for the elevation of the educational, cultural, and technological standards of his district.... You know what the constituents think.

Several mentioned difference and said nothing more: "I have a basic difference with my voters because they want me to carry on their personal cases and only that." One deputy evaded the issue by posing the confrontation in different terms: "In the case of a difference between party policy and that held by myself and constituents, I would publicly state my objections to party policy."

Regardless of this conflict in perceptions of the legislative role, the demands of the clientage system prevent much actual variation in legislative behavior. Little policy is set by the parliament, and even that policy is of little relevance to most voters; the average deputy is probably free to vote or not to vote, as he wishes. The major determinant of voting behavior would seem to be the demands of political leaders to whom the individual deputy is tied through a high-level clientage network, since a deputy must provide parliamentary support for the leaders of his political group if he is to receive the political resources necessary to maintain his personal position.

The "delegate" category of representational roles is somewhat misleading in the Greek context. A delegate is presumed to make legislative decisions on the basis of instructions from his constituents, his party, or interest groups. However, it is unlikely that many Greek constituents have views on particular legislative proposals; they are simply not oriented to the input side of the political system. The pervasiveness of personal demands retards associational development, and this precludes instructions to the deputy from interest groups. Although conjecture would give the political party primary importance in legislative decision-making, no deputy mentioned his party as the determiner of his vote. Presumably, deputies whose responses put them in the delegate role are really perceiving themselves as representatives not in the legislative arena but in the state machinery itself. If they are delegates, they represent traditional clientage networks; they do not seek policy, but patronage. Almost every deputy deplores the errand-boy function so pervasive in Greek politics; but in the final analysis, only those with substantial staff assistance or strong support in their districts can afford not to pander to the wishes of the voters.

The deputy must keep in close touch with the voters and listen to their demands. He must be on call 24 hours a day and listen to their fantastic demands. The constituents don't care how well the deputy is educated or what he does in the parliament as long as he serves them.

The deputy, in his work, should try to help his people solve their problems and should report to the parliament the problems, desires, and needs of the people he represents. He must study the problems of people by coming in contact with them. He must also take part in the meetings of the parliament. . . . In Greece and in some other countries, the deputy's job is not what it should be. He is the servant of the people; the voters expect their deputy to solve their private problems and to do favors for them.

Very few deputies looked upon themselves as representatives of particular segments of the population, as did this deputy: "My passion is to serve the poor working-class people . . . but perhaps from habit, or need, quite a few voters, when they vote, see their deputy as the executor of their personal affairs."

Ordinarily, a representative is expected to be the spokesman for district interests, since there is little else to represent. But Greek deputies do not feel any need to discover the interests of their districts. In any case, the districts are small enough so that interests are usually not very diverse. Although some deputies mentioned their concern for national problems, most focused on the district level.

A deputy must deal with the general problems of his district, and also with the personal problems of his constituents, which are many and various.

I know that the deputy must be sincere and honest, and one who knows the general problems of the district and stays away from micropolitics. Voters are interested in national problems, but if the deputy doesn't fulfill a personal favor he is lost.

The deputy's job is intense and continuous activity on behalf of his country, religion, family, and people. To bring about a renaissance of the Cyclades and Syros, every party must have the same purpose.

The job of the deputy is difficult and complex. The mission of the deputy is national representation. He has an obligation, theoretically, to deal with the country and society's welfare. But in reality, there are so many demands from his voters that his need for reelection forces him to overlook moral rules, and even obligations toward society, in order to become useful to their demands.

The district interest, in fact, merges with the personal interests of those to whom a deputy has obligations in his constituency. The patronage and favors that the deputy can provide cannot be distributed to the whole district; a minister might be able to provide public works or a plan of regional development, but a deputy has only the means to satisfy individual demands.

SUMMARY

The Greek deputy is confronted with two general models for political behavior. On the one hand, there is the Western pattern, in which legislators are presumed to be concerned with lawmaking, the representation of general interests, and the balancing of conflicting social interests. The structure and the rules of the Greek parliament are congruent with this model. On the other hand, there is the traditional Greek pattern, with its clientage networks that extend from the village to the parliamentary level and require the satisfaction of individual demands. These personal demands are directed at governmental output; they arise because of the basic distrust present in Greek society, because of the malfunctioning of the state machinery, or because of formalistic legislation. They are not the kind of demands that can be absorbed in more generalized concerns. Each request must be satisfied largely by intervention with the top political leaders or in the bureaucracy, rather than through legislative activity.

As long as the Greek population remained rural and relatively unmobilized, and as long as the basic social organization depended on clientage, the traditional political pattern was functional. The individual Greek recognized that the satisfaction of his demands rested on the mutual performance of obligations, and did not expect to have access to patronage if the clientage network to which he was connected was not in office. However, with urbanization and with the decreasing isolation of the peasant, both economically and intellectually, traditional legislative roles are subject to increasing strain. First, social mobilization has produced more demands. Despite increasing governmental resources (as measured by expenditures since 1954), scarcity has never really been overcome. Second, many new problems cannot be settled simply by the amelioration of individual dissatisfactions; they are actually group needs, even if the individual does not perceive them as such. Third, even Greeks in the more remote parts of the country demand equal treatment, and they are less willing to accept the political consequences of supporting the wrong man. And finally, there are increasing numbers of Greeks involved in the clientage networks.

The Greek parliament, then, because of limitations imposed by its environment, cannot operate as its Western counterparts do. Lawmaking in the sense of providing solutions to broad problems or balancing conflicting group interests does not occur at this level. However, the penetration of the modern representative institutions by the traditional clientage structures has given the parliamentary representative definite roles. The deputy representing the least modern sectors of Greek society does function as a "tribune"; he does represent his constituents in the battle with the state. As long as these traditional roles are maintained—that is, as long as the satisfaction of individual demands remains the major focus—the stability of the larger system is maintained. However, if a political group in the parliamentary milieu should change its style, either because of new interest pressures in the society or because of ideological reasons, the parliament would begin to operate more on the Western model. Policy would be decided, and new resource allocations would be made. Political blocs unrepresented at this level and elements refusing to recognize parliamentary institutions as the authoritative decision-making agency would find this situation intolerable.

8. Politics at the Extraparliamentary Level

The level of Greek politics lying outside parliament can be termed the crisis level. This is the arena where rival ideologies clash. During and after World War I, the conflict over the nature of the regime and the direction of Greece's international allegiance was fought out between King Constantine and Venizelos at this level. In this instance, and during the crises caused by the rule of General Ioannis Metaxas and by the civil war, the traditional political level vanished or remained quiescent, only to reassert itself once "normality" had been restored. Normality was usually restored because international society expected a return to a democratic parliamentary structure, and because prolonged rule by an extraparliamentary element soon fell into the traditional political pattern. In the past, political crises that had to be resolved at the extraparliamentary level were caused by disruptions within the parliamentary world, and the chief participants were also involved in parliamentary politics. Today, an extraparliamentary level exists alongside the traditional level; its forces, though standing apart from parliamentary politics, continually intervene in parliament informally, usually because of conflict at the extraparliamentary level itself.

The traditional patterns of personal politics in Greece were well suited to the slow transition from an unmobilized society to a mobilized one. The more modern forms of political organization found at the extraparliamentary level have only become important with the appearance of a large mobilized population and the increasing complexity of the international scene. The events of the world wars, the influx of refugees, and the growing marketization and urbanization of Greek society have produced a population that cannot always be accommodated in the traditional parliamentary system. Some mobilized elements are no longer a part of traditional clientage networks, and have demands that cannot be satisfied on an individual basis. Because the traditional political organizations have monopolized the parliamentary level, these new elements have operated outside of the parliamentary arena, where clientage ties are largely absent.

The extraparliamentary structures are characterized by hierarchic author-ity, impersonal bureaucratic organization, and ideological coherence. They have been heavily influenced by foreign models. Two major components of the consociational system are in this category: the military establishment and the left-wing political organization, the EDA. Both are hostile to the traditional parliamentary level, although both will cooperate with that level in certain situations. They either actively oppose the traditions of patronage and favoritism or grudgingly accept these practices as part of present-day Greek reality. Both the Left and the military are concerned with policy, and especially with modernization and economic development. However, the ideologies and the policies they espouse are opposed on almost every sub-stantive point. The EDA would like to forge stronger ties with the neutral-ist and Communist countries, and to modify those with the West. The mili-tary views this as a treasonable policy. The Left advocates thoroughgoing reforms within the traditional society. This would require an assessment of governmental programs in terms of basic priorities, which would bring sig-nificant reductions in military spending. The military not only feels its own position threatened, but looks upon the segments of the population who sup-port the EDA as unreliable citizens. The military tends to view itself as a model for government operation; it feels that governmental policies them-selves are correct, but that they are administered incorrectly.

Any change in the relative position of the two extraparliamentary forces creates a threat to the precarious balance of the consociational system. If the Left seems likely to gain because of specific operations by traditional parties or because of increasing frustrations among the modern, mobilized sector of the population, the military must intervene. If the military gains because of parliamentary policies or foreign assistance, the Left feels challenged. The dynamics of the Greek political system hinge on the interplay between the left wing and the military, and on their relations to the traditional level of Greek politics.

THE MILITARY

In the nineteenth century, the Greek military took part in the factional struggles of the parliamentary world. However, the military men of that period were virtually indistinguishable from any other members of the political elite. Throughout the period of the revolution, and well into inde-pendence, political and military leadership tended to coincide. The military did not have a monopoly of higher education, as in Turkey. Although a separate military school was created, it coexisted with the University of Athens. In general, the Greek military was under civilian political control because there was little differentiation between civilian and military leaders.

A competent professional army became necessary as Greek territorial aspirations increased and as the armed forces of adjacent states, particularly the Ottoman Empire, improved. The military academy was reformed, and foreign military missions trained junior officers and noncoms. The new professionals, largely drawn from the growing middle class, imbued with modern training, and formally separated from the political world, were no longer willing to let dilettantes lose battles or monopolize the higher command positions. Therefore, they constantly attacked the traditional military establishment represented by the crown prince and his brothers, particularly after the Greek defeat by the Turks in 1897.

The professionalism of the new military establishment could only be preserved and developed by intervention in civilian politics. For this reason, professional officers formed the Military League, which promoted the revolution of 1909. At this point, Greek civil-military relations appear to fall into the democratic-competitive category suggested by Morris Janowitz, in which the military offers important political support to a civilian group.[1] The older governing groups were replaced, and the officers retired from the arena of active politics after their demands had been met by the new political men. The professional military was given social status, more independence, and a greater role in Greek society. Unlike the military in many new states, the Greek armed forces did have an immediate function. Greece was at war almost continuously from 1912 to 1923 and from 1940 to 1949. A large part of the national income went to the military; and a military career, like any with security and bureaucratic status, was quite attractive to the average Greek.

In spite of its new importance, the Greek military was not a completely "modern" organization for some time after 1909. The crisis over foreign alignment during World War I split the military establishment, as it did the rest of Greek society, into rival camps supporting either Venizelos or King Constantine. Each of these strong figures had a personal following in the military, as well as a traditional clientage structure with military components, and each was backed by foreign powers. The Balkan wars permitted many men to rise from the ranks; many of these new officers were devoted to Venizelos. Constantine, too, had attempted to create personal ties in the army by expanding royal use of the traditional kumbaros relationship. From this time until the end of World War II and the civil war, there were really two military blocs: Venizelist and republican, and anti-Venizelist and monarchist.[2]

In 1922, younger officers staged a coup and executed the politicians and the general deemed responsible for the Greek military failure in Asia Minor. This was the capstone to military involvement in the political arena. By this time, many younger officers were committed to the idea of a republican regime, and other military elements were clearly monarchists. Each of these groups intervened whenever it appeared that the traditional parliamentary groups with which they were identified might compromise on the regime and return to normal parliamentary pursuits. As the political parties alternated in power, by either elections or coups, the officer corps of the Greek military establishment also alternated in command positions. Each of the political and military groups had its own formula of legitimacy and its own ideal of state institutions.

This pattern was upset when General Metaxas seized power in 1936. The republican officers were removed from the Greek armed forces, just as royalist forces had been demobilized during periods of republican power. The left wing had gained strength as refugee and other urban elements, increasingly alienated from the traditional political forum, voted for the Communist Party in 1936. The Metaxas regime, which represented the older, more conservative, and highly professional military elements, attempted to eliminate all politics, Right, Center, and Left. The politicians of the Populist Party were formally royalist; this did not prevent their detention and exile. It would be a mistake to characterize the regime as merely super-royalist; rather, it was antipolitical.

The military dictatorship of Metaxas, a variant of the traditional military oligarchy, succeeded in removing parliamentary politics. Since they no longer had access to government resources, the traditional politicians lost their political ties and were forced into retirement. Only the Communists, who had the necessary underground organization, retained their identity. Metaxas made only half-hearted and unsuccessful efforts to create a mass base. His nonpolitical, authoritarian regime lasted as long as it did because of outside threats that gave it temporary legitimacy. Metaxas died at the beginning of World War II, and his successor committed suicide; the king then called upon a politician to lead Greece.

The armed forces that met the initial Italian invasion of Greece in 1940 were largely commanded by professional officers with royalist tendencies. These "establishment" officers were far better trained, because of Metaxas's efforts, than the republicans whom they had replaced. In fact, the former republican officers, demobilized in 1935, served as enlisted men if they served at all. After the Nazi occupation some of the regular officers collaborated with the occupation regime; others escaped from Greece to form the nucleus of the Greek forces in exile. The republican officers, who mostly remained in Greece, could contribute to Allied victory only by service with the resistance forces. Although these forces were aided by the British, they were eventually dominated by Communist elements.

During the war the guerrilla movements in occupied Greece and the Greek forces elsewhere in the Middle East were under British command. In fact, by the end of the war the British had created two Greek armies: the exile army was chiefly staffed by professional officers from the old army; the resistance included republicans and new recruits. At the end of the war, once the Communist direction of the resistance army was apparent, the exile forces and the military men who had remained quiescent during the Nazi occupation combined to form the new Greek military establishment. When the civil war broke out, some republican officers remained in the guerrilla forces; but nearly all officers and men ever involved in the major resistance groups were considered Communists, if only by association.

Under the confused conditions at the end of the occupation and during the early stages of the civil war, the military was unavoidably involved in the traditional political world. Army units could not pursue guerrilla bands because influential politicians demanded that provincial cities not be left undefended. The system of staff control was impossible; orders came to be consensual instead of being issued through hierarchical command.[3] The inability of the political leaders to manage domestic crises caused instability; this increased the uneasiness of the military, since the degree of foreign military and economic aid often depended on government stability. After the United States announced the Truman Doctrine in 1947, the direction of the war was taken from the politicians and placed in the hands of the general staff alone. The establishment of a joint United States–Greek command further removed the conduct of the war from purely political considerations. The United States supplied virtually all military equipment and much of the direction.[4] Officers and noncoms were sent to the United States for professional training.

The defeat of all armed opposition in the last months of 1949 marked the beginning of a new era for the Greek military—a period in which it emerged as a major power bloc quite independent of the traditional parliamentary level. The armed forces became a symbol of national unity; they had saved the nation from the barbarians. The new Greek army, created by the fight against the guerrillas, can be compared to armies formed by national liberation movements elsewhere. It had an ideological commitment, a cohesion formed by common experiences, and a heightened sense of self-esteem.[5] Once the old regime was reestablished, and once the monarchy was secure as the national symbol, the military could assume a "nonpolitical" stance while retaining an interest in politics. The army felt that its main purpose was to protect the nation from Communists, both foreign and native. Its external mission complete, it now proposed to maintain internal security. All young Greek men are liable for military service, and those with higher education serve as reserve officers. The armed forces, especially the army, set up a thorough indoctrination program to evoke anti-Communist sentiments and to imbue recruits with loyalty to the nation, as represented by the armed forces and the monarch as commander in chief. The military maintained ties throughout the country by a network of military stations and a system of reserve units, the TEA (Battalions of National Security). The split in the military establishment that had been evident before the war no longer existed. From the outside, at least, the Greek armed forces appeared to be united and above politics.

The basic ideological position of the military, based on postwar experiences, was a hard-line anti-Communism. There was little awareness of the contemporary Communist world, and little understanding of the Left's changing character in Greece itself. The goals of the military were shaped to some degree by its dependence on the Americans, but the only common theme was anti-Communism. Unlike other armies in developing countries, the Greek military establishment had a limited view of its contribution to modernization. It did not, for example, push for industrialization, even when this would have improved military preparedness or national security. Because of its self-imposed isolation and its dependence on the United States, the military became more and more divorced from the other sectors of Greek society. Association with the Americans and, later with the armed forces of other NATO members, led the Greek military to operate closer to the bureaucratic ideal than did most Greek institutions. Moreover, as the military became technologically oriented, it became more dependent on the outside world. The new norms of efficiency and incorruptibility increased its hostility to the traditional political world.

The military remained the one group with a total institutional life for its members. It had an exclusive means of communication through special radio stations and other mass media. Subsidized commissaries, low-cost housing, and other privileges removed the military, at least partially, from the civilian world of scarcity and clientage. Of all the elements in Greek society, the military is, as Janowitz observes in another connection, "more likely than other professional groups to have its members' kinship ties loosened and their sociometic ties more rooted within the organization."[6] The military can assume modern organizational forms and can decry traditional politics because insecurity derived from scarcity is largely lacking among its members.

Although essentially antipolitical, the military has used its resources to gain friends at the micropolitical level of parliament. With universal military service, there are always civilian demands for military reassignments or deferments, which are channeled through political leaders; similarly, there is always pressure for commissions, and for promotions that can be used to placate the politically powerful. The engineering branch of the Greek Army not only has planning responsibilities in the field of public works, but has mechanized units stationed throughout Greece to make plans into reality; moreover, it has financial resources even greater than those of military units. The military is able to favor its friends and ignore its enemies when planning and executing public works. However, the formal head of the defense establishment, until the 1967 coup, was a civilian, and the military budget had to be formally approved by the parliament. Thus, despite the military's reluctance to deal with the traditional political level, it could not entirely avoid involvement.

The Greek military establishment views itself as a threatened group existing in a society mismanaged by corrupt politicians who are bent only on personal power. From its perspective, the concerns of the parliamentary level seem either trivial or dangerous. Generally, the career of an officer does not equip him to understand the problems of economic scarcity; this lack of understanding, combined with his ideological indoctrination, prevents him from realizing the basic reasons for the strength of his major adversary, the EDA.

THE MONARCHY

It is difficult to assess the place of the monarchy in the Greek political system. At times the monarch has actually held political power; at other times he has merely been a pawn of others. The actual ruler, rather than the monarchy itself, has always been the focus of loyalty or hostility. On occasion the monarch, instead of promoting national unity, has caused fundamental cleavage in the society; and he has often been the victim of conflicts originating elsewhere in the society, beyond his control. Although the monarchies of Western Europe have symbolized continuity in societies undergoing economic, political, and social change, the Greek monarch has seldom been above the political milieu. He has usually been visibly for or against the major changes occurring in the society, and has either supported or opposed the major factions in the society.

The monarchical form of government was originally selected for Greece because it was the most respectable in nineteenth-century Europe. Beyond this, since the monarch himself was selected from outside the country and was above the warring internal factions, both the institution and the incumbent were considered a force for stability. However, this aloofness also meant that the monarchy as an institution and the monarch as a person did not have strong roots in the country. The efforts of the first king, Otho, to foster widespread support for himself and the monarchy were resisted by the indigenous leaders, and ultimately caused his downfall. In practice, the Greek monarchy has seldom been an apolitical unifying symbol. The king has been forced to descend to the level of mutual obligation and patronage whenever he has sought to inspire loyalty. Consequently, loyalty and commitment to the monarchy or the king himself have been as fragile as loyalty to any ordinary political leader.

Although it is not a legitimate symbol of national unity, the Greek monarchy does have an independent position in some minor areas. Their Majesties' Fund, formerly the Queen's Fund, has approximately $10 million per year to distribute, and it is not under government supervision.[7] The Fund is financed by surcharges on the import duties of luxury items such as automobiles; it also contracts for the manufacture of handicrafts and sells them in its own shops. Primarily a welfare agency, it has the allegiance of those who administer it, as well as those who benefit from its charitable activities. In the Greek political culture, this allegiance can be translated into vigorous political support. Apart form this, at least some Greeks do admire the monarchy as an institution and the monarch as a person. For some, this is a clientage relationship; for others it is a sort of traditional deference. Finally, socialization through the school and the church and political education in the armed forces—although of questionable effectiveness, considering the strength of primary group loyalties—have equated loyalty to the monarchy with national loyalty.

The precarious position of the Greek state gave the monarch some importance in the nineteenth century. He could use his dynastic connections to lobby for Greek interests, particularly territorial acquisitions and financial assistance, among his cousins and uncles on the other thrones of Europe. "The conception of the crown as a court of last appeal in the conduct of foreign policy had come to be recognized as one of the conventions of the constitution";[8] and it remained unchallenged until World War I. Foreign policy, because it included problems of foreign debt, franchises for foreign investment in internal development, and trade agreements, could affect almost every facet of domestic policy. Most Greeks expected the monarch to use foreign policy to strengthen his own position by manipulations in the domestic sector. Because of this, he was almost invariably drawn into domestic political questions. It was, in fact, customary that there could be no change of government without some formal complaint against the conduct of the crown.

The first king, Otho, was a compromise selection, but he did have satisfactory dynastic credentials. He was finally overthrown, but not because of his unconstitutional actions and his efforts to undermine the position of the indigenous leadership. Instead, he had identified himself with virulent Greek nationalism and alienated the Great Powers, from whom future benefit had to come. He was jettisoned because he had failed to advance Greek territorial ambitions and had become a national liability in the process. The British contribution of the Ionian Islands at George I's accession enhanced the new king's political stature; the eventual acquisition of Thessaly and part of the Epirus was also helpful. However, the recurring problem of Crete and the disastrous war with Turkey in 1897 put a cloud over the monarchy. The revolution of 1909, though mainly directed against the established political elite, was also a protest against alleged royal failures in military matters. Credit for the great successes of Greece in the Balkan wars was given to Premier Venizelos as much as to the king or royal princes. In nineteenth-century Europe it was usual for the crown to be a major force in the conduct of foreign policy; it was not so usual for the monarch to suffer personally becauses of his foreign policy mistakes.

After the struggle between Venizelos and King Constantine before World War I, the Greek monarchy had little to do with foreign policy, which formally became a matter for the political level. Since that time, the Greek monarchs have been more the pawns of domestic political figures than the actual manipulators of power. Republican military officers and outraged radicals easily forced George II to sign the death warrants for the leading politicians of the right after the Anatolian debacle in 1922. When the crown returned in 1935 after a republican interregnum, it was controlled by rightist politicians. King George may have facilitated Metaxas's takeover in 1936, but he was in large measure unable to do more than acquiesce. A plebiscite restored the monarchy in 1946, probably because estimations of the kind of regime the Greeks needed at home were modified by estimations of the kind she needed in order to get on with the Allies. Since the royal role in foreign affairs has diminished, many voices have been ready to question the wisdom of an annual expenditure of $650,000 to support the royal establishment.[9] There is constant criticism of specific special expenditures on royalty, such as the dowry voted to Princess Sofia and the expenses for the wedding of the king himself.

The character of Greek political groups gives the monarchy a natural place in the traditional political system, and the king has always been involved in parliamentary politics. A recent premier argued that the monarch was necessary because he was the one stable element in a nation given to political volatility.[10] Presumably, he was implying that the selection of a head of state by normal electoral processes would be more than the political system could bear, and that parliamentary politics needed a "nonpartisan" referee. Moreover, the king does have some formal power, in that he appoints the premier. During the first decades of the Glueksburg dynasty there was no actual limit on the king's power to appoint or dismiss ministers and to dissolve the parliament, and George I frequently worked with minority or extraparliamentary governments.[11] This practice later receded, but not because of any constitutional prohibitions. The monarch could still act arbitrarily when it suited him: for example, Venizelos was both the beneficiary and the victim of royal authority to remove ministers and premiers, even those enjoying the confidence of the parliament. The provisions of the 1952 constitution were relatively vague concerning the relationship of the king to his ministers. The king could not issue any order unsigned by a responsible minister; however, there was no collective cabinet responsibility, and a single minister could cooperate with the king without the premier's permission. Likewise, if one government refused to cosign a royal order for its own dissolution, the next government could.

The main reason for the king's role at the parliamentary level is the factional political structure itself, which gives him great freedom in issuing invitations to form governments. This was obvious during the immediate postwar period, when no party had a majority, and in 1955, when Karamanlis was selected as premier after the death of Papagos. The system began to break down in 1965–66, when George Papandreau protested that his dismissal by King Constantine was unconstitutional; his supporters in parliament and in the streets nearly blocked the king's appointment of a new premier. The vagueness of the constitution and the factional character of Papandreou's Center Union party allowed Constantine to have his way.[12] The coup of April 1967 and the later flight of the king to Italy revealed the precarious position of the monarch as an actor in the consociational Greek system. The involvement of the king at the parliamentary level had conflicted with his position toward the military at the extraparliamentary one.

THE LEFT

The National Liberation Movement (EAM) and its military arm (ELAS) had functioned as the virtual government for much of Greece during the later years of the Nazi occupation. Since the occupying forces were stationed only in the few large cities, the EAM was almost completely in control of the country. It had an operating government that held elections and congresses, and even a functioning school system using specially printed texts.[13] The prime movers of the resistance were the Communists, though other leftist groups and some Center politicians were involved.

Dimitrios Kousoulas argues that the situation in 1946 strongly favored a Communist takeover. The party was legitimate; it had cadres and influence because of its role in the resistance.[14] The older generation of political leaders was occupied with personal quarrels or the question of the monarchy. The disorganized economy, the breakdown of administration, and the fact that most of the country was occupied by Communist-led resistance groups seemed to give the Communist Party of Greece (KKE) an undisputed advantage. But the advantage was dissipated by Communist brutality toward domestic opponents, and ultimately lost when the party could not retain the loyalty of the population under its control. The visible Left was smashed by the civil war. The KKE and its associated parties were eventually proscribed, and the climate of opinion made it difficult for left-wing public sentiment to reassert itself for some time. The Greek resistance movement and its later transformation to Communist insurgence closely resembled resistance movements and rebellions elsewhere, particularly in former colonial areas; however, the ultimate collapse of the Greek movement prevented the social revolution that tended to accompany other liberation movements.

In 1950 several socialist splinter parties, together with various trade-union elements, formed the Democratic Front (Demokratiki Parataksis, DP) in order to compete in the elections. The following year these same groups founded the United Democratic Left (Eniaia Demokratiki Aristera, EDA). The announced aims of the new organization were "peace, democracy, and amnesty." The EDA, unlike other groups operating under party labels in Greece, does meet the requirements of a political party as suggested by La-Palombara and Weiner: continuity of organization; permanent organization at the local level, with firm ties between local and national units; determination of leaders at every level to capture and hold decision-making power in the society; and a concern with seeking popular support. Beyond this, the EDA in many ways conforms to Riggs's description of a "combative" party, and to Giovanni Sartori's model of an "anti-system" party.

The EDA represents those with no ties or access to the government through the traditional parties, and its supporters are largely those who oppose the existing political system. Naturally, the electoral system has invariably been manipulated to discriminate against it. The EDA parliamentary group has little influence in politics at that level, and is not viewed as a possible coalition partner or a potential government. It is not recognized as the equal of the other parties by either the crown or the state apparatus. The demands formulated by the EDA cannot be met through the existing state machinery, since even the minimal social changes that the party promotes drastically alter the society and the status quo.

Organization

The other major parties in Greece are highly organized in theory, but not in reality. The theory and practice of EDA organization tend to coincide. In fact, the EDA's success has stimulated the development of formal organization in the traditional parties. The current organizational structure of the EDA is based on party statutes adopted in 1955, and resembles that of other left-wing parties in Western Europe.[15] The family loyalties and clientage ties normal in other Greek parties are discouraged. The involvement of a man's family in politics, though useful in evoking early interest and awareness, is not crucial to the initiation of a parliamentary career under EDA auspices. The party is most successful in urban settings, where family ties are tenuous or lacking, even among candidates from the major political constellations.

The EDA discourages the formation of personal or clientage ties between its deputies and their constituents, and deputies appear to be rotated from one area to another. The deputies do not handle requests for patronage or favors, and the party asks its members not to make them. The requests that do arise, whatever their source, are handled directly by the party secretariat. Requests for government assistance—and especially complaints of bureaucratic intimidation—are forwarded to the EDA deputy from the province nearest to their origin. Ordinary complaints will rate separate telegrams to the ministry concerned, the president of parliament, and the press. A more serious complaint might call for a question in parliament.

The EDA has functioning organizations in most parts of the country. During much of the Karamanlis administration, however, the activities of the party were severely curtailed, especially at the lowest levels. The circulation of the party press was virtually restricted to Athens and Thessaloniki and their environs. Only in areas with great concentrations of EDA strength such as Mytilini, could the local committees operate openly.

The lowest EDA units are in individual villages, and at the neighborhood level in the larger cities; occasionally, they are based on place of employment. These primary party organs must have at least three members. Depending upon size, they are directed by a single secretary or by a committee of three to seven members. The EK or ERE units at this level, when there is any organization whatsoever, are composed of local men who "own" a certain number of votes, but even here the EDA has a more or less professional staff. The next level of organization is in eparchies and cities of over 100,000 population. Finally, there are organizations at the *nomoi* (departmental) level, and regional organizations for Macedonia and the Peloponnesus. The departmental and city organizations send representatives to the Party Congress, which is supposed to meet at three-year intervals. The entire EDA parliamentary delegation also attends. The congress sets the general party line and elects the governing committee of the party, which is responsible for affairs between congresses. In 1965, the governing committee had 95 members; it met about five times, although it is specifically charged with meeting only twice during a calendar year. The presiding officer elected by the governing committee becomes the president of the party.

The governing committee determines the size of the executive committee, and selects the membership from its own ranks. This smaller committee (it had 15 members in 1965) generally meets weekly and handles day-to-day policy. Its members include the president of the party, a number of parliamentary deputies, and some officials drawn from the party secretariat.

The Secretariat consists of special commissions set up by the governing committee; in general, these are assigned to party organization, trade unions, women, and cooperatives. A separate supervisory committee to handle problems of discipline and party finance is elected by the party congress from those not on the governing committee. Other supplemental party organizations are permitted by the party constitution. The governing committee can convene a "panhellenic" congress between sessions of the party congress to modify the party lines; a similar conference, with more limited powers, can be called more easily for the same purpose. There is also provision for a national council to study newly raised issues and advise the other party organizations.

The EDA in the period under study was committed to a parliamentary role, and the parliamentary delegation seemed to take the lead in the formulation of day-to-day party policy. The chairman of the party himself was a member of parliament; in 1965, the executive committee included six deputies. In case of a controversy between the deputies and the rest of the executive committee, the dispute would be taken to the governing committee. There is no evidence that this ever occurred.

Although EDA literature emphasizes the democratic nature of party organization, democratic centralism is the operative principle of the party, operating in Greece much as it does elsewhere. Discussions are held at the lower party levels, and resolutions do advance up the hierarchy; but real direction and initiative come mainly from the summit of the organizational network. Even in formal terms, the powers of the governing committee and the executive committee seem to limit the real authority of the supposedly supreme party congress. The governing committee determines the agenda of the congress and provides the chairman. The executive committee can replace old members of any party organization or appoint additional members; any action along these lines by the lesser party organs must be ratified by the executive committee. Nevertheless, the EDA's lower party agencies do have at least as much influence as those of the other Greek parties. The EDA is relatively unified when compared with its competitors, and does not have major problems of internal conflict between the party leader and the parliamentary deputies. This does not mean, however, that personal conflict reminiscent of that in the traditional political groups is unknown— in the EDA it is simply obscured by ideological bickering.

Like other parties, the EDA includes some people who actively seek nomination; but more often, particularly since EDA nomination means automatic defeat in some areas, the party does the recruiting. Formally, the local committees propose candidates, and the governing committee merely ratifies their choices; but in actuality, most choices are made by the smaller executive committee. There seems to be a conscious effort to select candidates with the proper proletarian background. There is no internal struggle among the candidates because everyone knows who has a chance of getting elected and who has not. Certain party figures are always renominated and reelected, but the majority of the parliamentary delegation changes at each election. Major electoral decisions—for example, the decision to join Papandreou's Democratic Union for electoral purposes in 1956—are made by the governing committee.

The financial aspects of the EDA are actually more visible than those of other Greek parties, although it is difficult to come to any definitive conclusions about them. Other parties look with skepticism on EDA claims of financial self-sufficiency; however, this may be because of their own dependence on foreign and governmental funds. The EDA, unlike the other parties, does have a formal membership requirement, with minimum dues of ten drachmae per year (about 33 cents); but apparently there is a sliding scale of payment for members with more ample financial resources. In addition, the party collects the parliamentary salary of each of its deputies, amounting to 13,500 drachmae per month, and remits to the deputy a flat 4,000 per month. A substantial amount of EDA revenue comes from "friends of the party," both in Greece and abroad, and from certain trade unions. Financial assessments are made upon local party organizations, and these must be raised through dues or special contributions. The party also conducts house-to-house fund-raising drives in some areas in Athens and Piraeus where EDA membership is concentrated, and these can be quite successful: the financial campaign of 1965, necessary because two national elections and one local election were held in one 12-month period, set a goal of 7 million drachmae and collected over 9 million.[16] The EDA also maintains several shops in Athens that sell goods made in Communist nations.

Notwithstanding, the EDA's ability to meet current expenses out of the limited financial resources of its supporters might be questioned. However, the intense activity in party headquarters, the constant stream of literature, and the endless demonstrations and meetings do not cost the EDA as much as they might cost another party. The commitment and solidarity of EDA members mean that the personnel at party headquarters work for less than do those associated with the other Greek parties. The EK and the ERE must hire men to hold their placards during election campaigns. The EDA has willing volunteers, and its rallies are far superior to those of the other political groups: artists and craftsmen decorate the platform, and poets and musicians perform prior to the speeches, all without cost. There are EDA members in business who are willing to provide services and supplies at less than the market rate because of party loyalty. The party also uses the special privileges of its deputies, such as free postage and telephone service, for its own purposes; in other parties, individual deputies are allowed to take advantage of these exemptions to advance their personal interests. Meynaud suggests that outside assistance, essentially meaning that coming from the Communist nations, is limited to occasional special contributions.[17] In any case, the EDA's strenuous efforts at domestic fund raising would indicate that foreign sources are not a primary source of support.

Program

The EDA has a coherent program, based on its application of marxist ideology to Greek society.[18] Unfortunately the marxist phraseology of its pronouncements is by itself enough to discredit the party in the view of many Greeks. The efforts of the EDA to secure the legalization of the Communist Party also make it suspect. Finally, the stand of the EDA on foreign-policy issues differs from the general Greek outlook. It is the party stand in these areas rather than its program of social reform, that alarms the military and some elements in the parliament.

One of the major items in EDA programs has always been the restoration of "democracy"—which includes, first and foremost, the legalization of the Communist Party. All administrative rulings and legislation directed against the KKE must be revised, especially Article 100 of the constitution, which states that "ideologies advocating change of the existing constitutional or social regime by force and violence are absolutely unacceptable for those holding public office."[19] The precise effect of this stand on the EDA's success is difficult to determine. In a sense, the constancy of the demand alienates some potential supporters, since it makes the EDA appear as the handmaiden of the KKE. The party states publicly that the "KKE never ceased to play a considerable role in Greek public life";[20] there is no other place for this role to be played than in the EDA. However, the cohesiveness and solidarity of the EDA may well depend on the harrassment directed at it because of this association.

Even though most Greeks regard the EDA as only a stand-in for the Communists, it has received 10–20 per cent of the popular vote in recent elections. The proportion of the vote that is actually Communist is impossible to determine: the last election in which the Communists legally participated was that of 1936, in which they received 6 per cent of the vote. Even then, the dedicated Communists and the mere protestors cannot be separated. The KKE in exile claims to have accepted evolutionary and parliamentary tactics. Even so, if the party were reinstated, the EDA could no longer be considered the "extreme left." Once the most militant element in the EDA leadership was removed, the party would not differ significantly from left-wing socialist parties elsewhere in Europe. Moreover, it would still not fall into the persistent-polyarchic mold of other Greek parties.

Some Greeks feel that EDA pronouncements on foreign affairs are sufficient evidence of the party's Communist character; and the EDA does echo Soviet policies. Occasionally, Russian activities, particularly Russian support of Turkey in the Cyprus controversy, have put the EDA in a difficult political position. The party's efforts to establish good relations with the other Eastern bloc nations, e.g., its advocacy of a demilitarized zone in Eastern Europe, also alienate many Greeks. The EDA has consistently denounced Greece's membership in NATO and association with the Common Market as infringements on Greek independence. Both organizations are blamed for the country's submission to Western views on the Cyprus question under both the Karamanlis and Papandreou governments. Full membership in the Common Market would supposedly bring in more foreign monopoly capital, keeping Greece industrially backward; and Greek industry would not be able to compete with industry in other member nations. The EDA was the first group to voice these sentiments, but it is certainly not the only one. It is, however, alone in regarding the Soviet Union as an honest broker for the settlement of all outstanding world problems, as well as matters specifically affecting Greece.

The EDA's domestic program and its analysis of the Greek social system are set forth in *For a National Democratic Change*, a document adopted in 1956. Greece is described as an almost classic "colonial" country, controlled by foreign imperialists and their local representatives. The ERE is attached to the United States and NATO; it is the party of the large capitalists. The EK, in the eyes of the EDA theoreticians, is largely representative of the petty bourgeoisie; it is deficient because it has no consistent policy of promoting Greek "independence." Basically, Greece is "an underdeveloped country, industrially backward, without a heavy industry, with a weak light industry and certain semi-feudal elements."[21] An "independent Greece," that is, independent of the West, must be created before these conditions can be overcome. The EDA charges that the paucity of Greek heavy industry is caused by foreign capitalists, who manipulate national financial markets to keep Greece a consumer of foreign industrial goods and a source of raw material. American aid policy is blamed for the lack of agricultural improvement. The enormous proportion of the budget devoted to military expenditure precludes adequate state assistance to industry or agriculture. The description of objective economic conditions is not dissimilar from that offered by respected non-marxist economists;[22] however, the EDA analysis places the blame on dubious causes and suggests uncertain remedies. Regardless, the EDA program does, in both domestic and foreign proposals, suggest a new national identity and a new basis for political integration in Greece.

The EDA, besides advocating a new national independence, has tried to assume the role of successor to the revolutionaries of 1821. The literature of the EDA maintains that the German occupation and the resistance constituted a second revolution, which temporarily eliminated foreign interference and changed the Greek social structure. These advances were swept away by the Truman Doctrine and American intervention, which reestablished a non-democratic foreign-serving (and by implication illegitimate) regime. The EDA is the contemporary extension of the wartime resistance, and a continuing symbol of legitimacy. Unfortunately, this position is tenuous because the linking of the national resistance movement and the EDA is not as complete as the literature implies. The analysis concludes that all patriotic forces must unite before true national independence can be secured. The working class must join with the peasantry as the nucleus for a wider movement that will finally include the middle strata of the towns, and even the national bourgeoisie.

The specific goals mentioned in *National Democratic Change* seem irrelevant to the foregoing analysis. The program is certainly not socialist; in many respects it does not differ from that proposed by the Center Union. The EDA goals envision a Greece that is "free, well-fed, gay, and civilized," and worthy of its great traditions.[23] Revolution and the class struggle are not mentioned. The EDA, like the other Greek parties, hopes to gain support by appealing to specific sectors of Greek society, and its program seems designed for electoral purposes. The party assumes that parliament will be the major arena for political and social change. The EDA appeal for a return to the simple proportional representation system is one part of this parliamentary orientation.

The EDA program vows to raise the standard of living in Greece. Although it is assumed that economic development will eventually do this, the specifics of the program seem to depend on immediate public financing. It does not seem likely that the EDA would be as successful as the EK in balancing these two requirements. Industrialization is to be financed through a revision of priorities. Military expenditures are to be reduced, imports restricted, and exports, especially to eastern bloc nations, increased. These proposals rest, of course, on the assumption of a Greek withdrawal from NATO and the Common Market. Even if this occurred, the reliance upon the eastern bloc and the complexities of the Greek economic picture make the task easier to suggest than to accomplish. Revenues are to be increased by promoting tourism and expanding the merchant marine. Additional funds for industrialization, however, are supposed to come from abroad without any terms or political strings. Moreover, the EDA program seems quite unrealistic in its estimate of energy resources and mineral deposits. A significant heavy industry may actually be an impossibility, given Greek resources. All in all, the concrete proposals of the EDA are much like those of the EK.

The rest of the EDA's program seems less attuned to internal economic development than to providing benefits for the entire range of EDA supporters and penalizing those who benefit from the existing regime. The only social class scheduled for complete transformation is the group of wealthy families most involved with foreign monopolies. These families monopolize the two major banking groups, large-scale industry, trade, and the merchant marine. Banking is to be nationalized, but joint state-private ventures are to be encouraged in other fields, particularly in chemicals, agricultural processing, and the metals industries. Land reform is to be applied to the estates of the few remaining large landowners, such as the church and the royal family. New subsidies to agriculture and relief from existing debts to the Agricultural Bank are part of the platform, which also suggests a renewal of agricultural cooperatives in order to encourage technical improvements and the raising of more profitable crops. The worker is promised higher wages and pensions, together with improved social insurance schemes. The trade-union movement is to be reformed, and labor legislation improved. Even the lower clergy is to receive greater financial benefits. The small businessmen and craftsmen will obtain easier credit and improved social insurance benefits. The national bourgeoisie, unlike those Greeks with international connections, would be assisted by protective legislation. The EDA also advocates a drastic curtailment of indirect taxation and an increased use of direct taxation; in this case, the personal exemption would be raised, and increased tax rates would be applied to those with greater income. The non-economic sectors of society are not forgotten. Women, as a group, are to benefit by the lifting of all legal, social, and economic distinctions between the sexes.

The educational program of the state would be completely reworked with the EDA in power. First, educational opportunity would be expanded by extending the compulsory educational system and opening university places to all Greeks, regardless of their political beliefs. The EDA also makes an explicit demand for a better quality of education. The existing system is viewed as anachronistic; it is devoted to foreign cultures rather than to the promotion of patriotism and democracy at home. One major reform would be the introduction of demotic as the official language of the state and higher education.

All these proposals, according to the EDA, will be feasible only when Greek ties to the West have been revised. The difficulties of the Greek economy—unemployment, emigration, deficit financing, and the poverty of the countryside—all come from the absence of industrialization, and this lack is perpetuated by Greece's "colonial" status. The party never considers the realities of the international world, the cultural impediments to industry in Greece itself, and the paucity of Greek resources. It does recognize one major obstacle, the traditional distrust of government authority. However, it is argued that once authority is not in the hands of the local oligarchs and subject to foreign influence, this distrust will disappear. Moreover, the party would make every effort to increase the people's active participation in government at every level. Traditional favoritism by the legal and administrative systems would be eliminated; but how this would be done is not clear. This analysis fails to consider all of the cultural and environmental factors that have promoted the negative attitude toward authority. Since the EDA does not seem to envisage a total revolution, it is difficult to see how these influences would disappear.

Membership

The ERE and some segments of the EK view the EDA as nothing more than a manifestation of the illegal KKE. Some Center elements, however, look upon the EDA as merely the left wing of the Greek republican tradi-

Table 8.1. Political Backgrounds of Left Candidates, 1950–63

Year	Candidates	Parties of previous candidatures			
		Left	Minor	Center	Right
1950	41	85.8%	8.7%	5.5%	—
1951	184	83.1	8.2	6.7	2.0%
1952	78	87.8	4.2	7.9	—
1958	123	82.7	9.7	5.6	1.7
1961	177	80.0	9.7	8.0	2.3
1963	163	91.9	3.7	3.7	0.7

Note: This table does not include new entrants.

tion. For its part, the EDA explicitly claims to have Communists, socialists, and all other progressive democrats among its members. It is obvious that some Communists are attracted to the party because they have no other legal avenue for political action. Several EDA deputies had prewar affiliations with the KKE; other party figures had roles in the resistance or the civil war. Moreover, the party prefers to select its officers and candidates from men who were imprisoned for political activities or ostensible criminal activity during the civil war. One non-EDA deputy suggested that perhaps a third of the EDA parliamentary membership was Communist. In any case, the party has few elements that are not drawn from the Left (see Table 8.1).

Dissension in the EDA tends to concern policy, not party organization or ministerial positions. However, personality clashes are often masked by ideological disputes. The question of national security is the chief difference of opinion between the Right and Center parties as groups, but in the EDA it causes internal friction. Even worse is the problem of whether to pursue a moderate course or to press for unlimited change, which is reflected in internal compromises over program and tactics. Certainly, the KKE would not settle for the social and economic program of the EDA as a final goal; at most, it would be a tactical maneuver.

Although the EDA claims to have accepted the evolutionary and parliamentary course, it still mobilizes the population for extraparliamentary activities that challenge the legitimacy of traditional politics and of the consociational system itself. Any distrust or dissatisfaction with government on the part of labor, agriculture, the professions, or the students, is exploited for party purposes. Street demonstrations have been a part of the Greek scene for much longer than the EDA has existed, and those in Athens have been responsible for the fall of several regimes and many governments.

However, EDA militants now take leading roles in most extraparliamentary disturbances. In fact, the party claims to organize or support, morally and materially, all such activities, even when its role has been minimal. It attempts to turn them not only against the government in power but against the basic political system. The major cities—particularly the Athens-Piraeus complex, since it is the seat of government and has the largest concentration of EDA supporters—are under almost constant siege by one organization or another.

Electoral Analysis

R. V. Burks argues that Communism in Eastern Europe attracts two broad categories of supporters: those who originate in a "badly disturbed social order," and those who reflect the impact of Western civilization on the more backward East European provinces.[24] In the first category he places refugees and farmers with cash crops; in the second, he puts youth and women. Surprisingly, he finds little relationship between Left affiliation and class position, and suggests that personal insecurity, whatever its cause, provides the most common motive. This hypothesis also fits the Greek situation. Between the world wars, refugees were the major group unable to solve problems of personal insecurity. Since that time, the Left has appealed to the lower classes in the urban areas, who are similarly unable to utilize traditional clientage ties.

The most obvious change in the position of the Left over the last several decades has been the increase in the vote given to it (see Table 8.2).[25] The groups who supported the KKE in 1936 still support the Left under the EDA label. However, the EDA has extended its appeal to other elements in

Table 8.2. Vote for the Greek Left since 1936

Year	Percentage of total vote	Year	Percentage of total vote
1936	5.76%	1956	—
1946	—	1958	24.42%
1950	9.70	1961	14.62
1951	10.57	1963	14.34
1952	9.55	1964	11.80

Note: No Left parties ran in 1946; the EDA-EK coalition in 1956 precludes a separate percentage for the Left.

the Greek population, despite the constant harassment of those who persist in left-wing political beliefs.

Nineteen scattered eparchies in Greece can be classed as generally competitive.* In these areas any one of the three major political groups might receive a plurality of votes; in other words, the Left has enough electoral strength to compete. Votes for the Left are relatively sparse in the great majority of rural constituencies; however, rural support increases in the provinces added to the Greek state in the twentieth century. These are districts with a more modern agricultural sector, more refugees, and fewer clientage ties to bureaucrats and politicians in Athens. There are some exceptions to the general pattern of EDA rural weakness. The island of Lefkas supports the EDA because a local notable, a doctor, runs on the EDA electoral list. The eparchy of Palis on the island of Kefallinis is harder to explain; the high percentage of men from the island employed in the merchant marine may have some relationship to EDA strength there. The island of Thasos off the Thracian coast and Ikaria, the small island adjacent to Samos, are also included in the competitive category; the reasons for left-wing strength in these areas seem obscure. The only competitive rural district in continental Greece is the eparchy of Tirnavos in Thessaly. The long tradition of agrarian discontent in this region could possibly account for this radicalism; if so, one cannot explain the relative quiescence of adjacent eparchies with a similar past. EDA strength in rural Greece does not seem to be related to agricultural difficulties. Correlation analysis using rural population per square kilometer and EDA vote in 1958 resulted in a modest Pearson r value of .266. Analysis using particular cash crops did not produce anything better.[26]

The strength of the Left in Greece today is directly related to the status of the refugees who arrived in the early 1920's. They comprised about a quarter of the population at that time, and had a great impact upon the political, social, and economic aspects of Greek life. The refugees themselves were of diverse backgrounds: those from central Anatolia, the Anatolian littoral, Constantinople, the Caucasus, and eastern Thrace, as well as the smaller groups from other Balkan states, all differed in dialect and culture.[27] Regardless of their background, most refugees were not immediately accepted by the native Greeks. There had long been a minority in Greece who expressed resentment against Greeks from abroad, and the large infusion of refugees introduced a discordant note into the political system.

* For a complete classification of eparchies, see Appendix B, pp. 324–27.

The settlement of many agricultural refugees meant that there was less land for the indigenous Greeks to divide. In the towns, the refugee businessmen, entrepreneurs, and craftsmen had greater skills and more worldwide contacts than the more provincial Greeks of the kingdom. The entrepreneur from outside the kingdom was more likely to have a Western education, experience with Western techniques and knowledge of Western tastes. A 1961 survey showed that one out of five Greek industrialists had been born in Turkey.[28] Native Greeks often disguised their awareness of these economic considerations by a hostility based on the premise that people with such different customs and such peculiar dialects could not be truly Greek. Although the origins and cultural levels of the refugees varied, it was not difficult for the native Greek to assume that the cultural level of all refugees was equal to that of the least cultured.

Politically, the refugees supported Venizelos almost to a man. King Constantine and the politicians of the Populist Party were viewed as responsible for the defeat in Asia Minor. Venizelos, they thought, would have piloted the Greeks to victory, and the native Greeks had removed him from the helm of state at the most critical juncture. In any event, the loyalty of the refugees went to Venizelos as a person, and not to the Greek state or the king. They continued to support him and the Liberal Party until his death. Urban refugees, resettled in the new communities near Athens, were levers available for Liberal and republican politicians to use against their Populist and monarchist opponents. Very shortly, the refugee vote became crucial for political control. Both General Pangalos and General Kondylis achieved power in the twenties with refugee assistance.[29]

The Communists were more successful in recruiting voters and sympathy among the refugees than among the indigenous Greeks from the very beginning, but it was not until the romance with Venizelos began to fade that they made great strides. The Liberal's support began to shift to the Left after the abandonment of refugee claims against Turkey in the 1930's, when Venizelos sacrificed domestic support to get a rapprochement with Turkey. A substantial shift from the Liberal Party occurred in 1936; the political loyalty of many refugees has been to the parties of the Left since that time.[30]

The government's promises of housing and land for all refugees remained unfulfilled throughout the interwar period and well into the present. Those refugees who were resettled in rural areas often had grievances also. To some extent, the national aim of hellenizing Macedonia was given priority over the economic well-being of the refugees. Many were settled in the inhospitable borderland, rather than on more desirable land in less strategic places. Under the system of land distribution, the native Greek tenant farmer was given a larger and better landholding than the incoming refugee. Many refugees, who had never known land scarcity, were annoyed at the small size of their farms and the different technical requirements for cultivation.

The most nontraditional of the Greek parties, the Communists, were able to capitalize on refugee dissatisfactions. Burks found high coefficients of correlation between refugee settlement and Communist vote: the coefficient was .62 in 1926, .57 in 1933, and .67 in 1936.[31] Communist ideology was sharpened to appeal to those frustrated with a new and often more difficult life. Perhaps the fact that many of the refugees came from the Soviet Union made them more susceptible to this appeal. More important, the traditional Greek political structures, built on personal political relationships running from the small community to the national level, simply did not admit the refugee to membership. The refugee was an outsider in most communities, and there were very few places in which refugees were the majority of the voting population.

The refugee groups created a refugee press and began to organize for political purposes very early, although their diversity and their dispersion throughout the nation tended to hinder these efforts. This organization was built on the one thing that all refugees had in common: their separateness from the rest of the Greek people. The attempt to build a bond of "refugee-ness" that would equal the tie of the ordinary Greek to his political patron was not completely successful. Electoral districts were gerrymandered to minimize the possibility of refugee majorities; and many of the refugees were women and children, who could not vote. After 1926, the independent refugee parties began to die out.

All political groupings eventually put refugees on their political lists, but they were most successful in the Liberal Party, led by Venizelos. However, refugees provided a larger percentage of the vote for the KKE than they did for any other party.[32] Refugee deputies sometimes received cabinet posts, although only the lesser positions usually came their way. One of the vice-presidencies of parliament was also reserved for a refugee deputy. Leading refugee politicians could be assured of at least a minimal political career in the older political groupings. But the very fact that certain positions were considered "refugee posts" tended to perpetuate the refugee's separation from other Greeks. In addition, the refugees never had a parliamentary rep-

Table 8.3. *Refugee Deputies in Parliament*

Year	Number	Percentage of parliament
1923	43	10.8%
1926	36	12.5
1928	34	13.6
1932	39	15.2
1933	30	12.0
1946	35	10.1
1958	36	12.0
1964	32	10.8

resentation that matched their real strength in the population (see Table 8.3).[33]

As Table 8.4 indicates, the correlation between the left-wing vote and refugee settlement has declined since the war. To some degree this would be expected, given the dislocations caused by conditions since 1936. The refugee census of 1928 has not been repeated, and can hardly produce much of a correlation with current electoral data. Individual refugees, particularly those who have risen in social status, are probably voting for other parties; those who have not been so successful seem to have remained with the Left. Successful refugees are more likely to be accepted into traditional clientage networks, since they have something to offer a patron besides a single vote. Readily identifiable refugee enclaves in the Athens-Piraeus area, which are characterized by poverty and general insecurity, continue to support the Left. In rural areas, villages whose support for the extreme Left dates back to the 1930's have continued to vote for the EDA. However, there is no uniform voting pattern among all refugee villages. Only nine of the nineteen competitive eparchies have substantial refugee populations.

The urban and suburban districts of Athens, Piraeus, and Thessaloniki fall into the competitive category, as do provincial centers such as Volos, Larisa, Naoussa, and Kavalla. These areas, besides having large refugee populations, are industrialized; and the usual association of industrial employment with radical politics would seem to explain the EDA strength. Correlation of urban population data from the 1961 census with EDA vote in 1963 revealed a coefficient of determination of .2228;[34] but when the relationship between EDA vote and the percentage of the active population employed in industrial activity was examined, the coefficient of correlation

Table 8.4. Refugees and Postwar Left Vote

Year	Coefficient of correlation
1950	.1338
1951	.1867
1952	.2099
1958	.2179
1961	.1242
1963	.1412

Note: In no year was the correlation significant at the .05 level.

was a mere .0103.[35] By contrast, Burks found correlations of .40, .70, and .59 between the KKE and industrial workers in 1926, 1933, and 1936.[36] He concluded that the Communists were most successful in capturing the trade-union movement when there was only a small industrial labor force, and notes Comintern figures for 1921 in which 50% of the total union membership in Greece was in Communist unions. Even today, this is not a very large figure in actual numbers. Particular unions, e.g., those in the building trades, still contribute a large bloc of supporters to the EDA; but in general, the party draws support from a much wider segment of the population than in the prewar period.

The reservoir of potential supporters for the EDA has increased with social mobilization and urbanization. Villagers who go off to the city in search of work or an education often find the experience disappointing. Jobs are scarce, and a former peasant usually has to join the surplus industrial labor force or eke out a living in some overcrowded service occupation. Although a recent arrival can sometimes fall back on relatives and friends, there is no real substitute for the family unit found at the village level. In many cases, one must rely on the state for welfare benefits or subsidized housing. In a recent study, 88.7 per cent of the former villagers interviewed felt that their decision to leave for the city had been correct, but nearly a third were unhappy in their new environment.[37] Since there are no patrons of the traditional sort to satisfy the demands of these people, they are attracted to political activities of a more modern kind. The temporary emigration of Greek workers to the industrial countries of Western Europe builds still more support for the Left. The inadequacies of the Greek public services and the lack of economic opportunity are likely to seem particularly severe to man who can compare them with the conditions elsewhere. Moreover, this man has seen that left-wing groups are generally respectable in Western Europe, and may be more inclined to join Greek groups having similar labels and programs.

A significant part of the left-wing support in the urban areas comes from university and gymnasium students. In the 1930's the Communists and other left-wing groups were exceedingly prominent in university precincts; and today, the EDA youth groups seem to dominate student politics. However, it is questionable whether this activity produces long-term left-wing affiliation. It is more likely that the radical phase ends for many students when they leave the university setting and seek a career through the traditional patronage networks.

Although EDA strength is largely an urban phenomenon, the increase in the EDA vote does not seem related to the rate of population growth in the major urban centers (see Table 8.5). The relationship is undoubtedly more complex than the techniques used here could reveal. It seems possible that support for the Left lags behind population increase because the insecurity stemming from urban residence and the diminution of older clientage ties only gradually becomes apparent. Regardless, the major metropolitan centers, Athens, Piraeus, and Thessaloniki, with their suburbs, account for a large part of the left-wing vote in any election. The percentage has remained fairly constant since 1950, ranging from 49 per cent in that year to 36 per cent in 1951 and 1958; in 1963 the proportion of the total EDA vote provided by these three cities and their suburbs was 40 per cent.[38]

The leaders of the EDA, like those of the Italian Communist Party in similar circumstances, "have been good sociologists, and have provided these displaced, insecure, and economically and socially frustrated masses with their first meaningful associations."[39] However, their success has increased

Table 8.5. *Urban Growth and EDA Vote Increase, 1951–61*

Urban growth category	Number of cities	Mean population change	Mean change in EDA vote
Over 30% increase	4	37.79%	4.73%
20–30% increase	14	24.20	9.59
10–20% increase	13	15.25	9.64
0–10% increase	17	4.96	8.94
Decrease	7	−8.32	5.84

Modified from Kayser and Thompson, p. 206.

the instability of the already precarious consociational system. One major stimulus for the coup of 1967 was military uneasiness at the Left's growing strength.

STRAINS IN THE CONSOCIATIONAL SYSTEM

The history of postwar Greece is mainly one of the interplay between the monarchy, the armed forces, and the Left, and of the relations of each to the traditional level of Greek politics. For some time the equilibrium of the consociational system was maintained because most of the leaders in these groups had an interest in preserving the existing system. The patriotic character of the war against the Communist guerrillas overrode some differences; and Greece's dependence on foreign powers kept quarrels in check.

The Greek monarch has had the unenviable task of placating both the traditional political level and the armed forces. The military establishment has viewed the Left as its major opponent; and any actions by the monarch or the parliamentary politicians that might be interpreted as concessions to the Left have been met with some type of intervention. This has been a matter of reactive militarism: the military perceives civilian weakness as a threat to its own position.[40] The left wing has viewed the monarch and the armed forces, because of their contacts abroad, as the main compromisers of Greek independence. The traditional parliamentary political groups are viewed as willing accomplices of the military, or as indifferent to the major problems of Greek life. The traditional politicians conceive of both the military and the extreme Left as actively or potentially hostile to Greek democracy as it is currently practiced. However, any of these groups may help the others in particular situations. Demands for change in the Greek political system have come either from the personal-fragile component of the traditional parties or from the left-wing party. The military establishment and the polyarchic-persistent portions of the traditional political organizations have usually done no more than react to the activities of the other elements in the system.

There are two main sources of contention among the various groups: the position of the Left in national political life, and the priority of military expenditure. These two questions are bound up with the problems of internal security and foreign alignment. The significant aspects of the controversy stem from the resistance and the civil war. The cleavage between the Left and the rest of the political system was fairly complete at that time. The crown, the armed forces, and the traditional political level were all considered "national" political forces by most Greeks. The Left, involved in treasonable acts, was not. The EDA has never been accepted as a legitimate element by many Greeks. The statements of the Left on major political issues and in reference to the other actors in the consociational system have done nothing to dissipate these notions.

The crown was useful as a rallying point for all nationalists in the early postwar period. In fact, the monarchy was genuinely popular from 1946 to at least 1956. Loyalty to the monarch was frequently equated with anti-Communism and patriotism, especially in the armed forces. Throughout this period the monarchy was profoundly hostile to the left wing, and rarely accorded the EDA the recognition given other political parties—although the fact that the EDA is closely associated in terms of policy with the Soviet Union does not make it any less a "national" party than the ERE or the EK, who are similarly linked with the West. In 1964, at the death of King Paul, the EDA leadership attempted to come to better terms with the monarch, with little success. If the monarch did recognize that lessened world tensions call for a change in internal policy, and if he responded to the EDA's protestations of friendship, his usefulness as a symbol to the military might be at an end. The attempts of King Paul to encourage a coalition of Center and Right politicians in 1963 would have strengthened the traditional elements in Greek politics. The similar role played by Constantine II from 1965 to 1967 might be interpreted in the same vein. The EDA remains outside the system, and the nontraditional components of the parliamentary political organizations have not been encouraged. By appearing to favor the status quo, the monarch has reaped censure for political interference; but any concessions to the modern elements are viewed with suspicion by the military. The monarch seems to be a prisoner of his position, with no enduring support from the most significant parts of the population.

The military establishment has never accepted the left wing as a legitimate part of the political system. During and immediately after the civil war, draftees with left-wing backgrounds were separated from the others and sent to a small island off the tip of Attica for military training and indoctrination. Later, they were put in special training units known for their severity. In service, these men were assigned to the most unpleasant jobs in the army, such as mule driving in the Rhodope Mountains. In the rural areas, the harassment of leftists by members of the TEA (Battalions of National Security) was common. Until the victory of Papandreou in 1963, it was rare to find either of the left-wing newspapers in the rural areas.

Even after 1963, certificates of social conformity from the local police chief or a priest were needed in order to qualify for a wide range of public employment. It is still assumed by many soldiers and some civilians that no person with political ties to the Left could possibly be loyal to the state.

For its part, the Left has continually accused the military of fascist tendencies. Military indoctrination and the backgrounds of high officers have been so criticized. Left-wing proposals for the normalization of political life have included a general amnesty for the veterans of the civil war on the guerrilla side. The military, and even the more moderate elements in Greek society, view these men as criminals and traitors; but the EDA lauds them as the real exponents of Greek nationalism and independence. The EDA has opposed the NATO alliance and all other ties to the West. It has advocated decreasing the military expenditures—since the neighbors of Greece, with the exception of Turkey, are peace-loving socialist states—and diverting the funds to social welfare and reform. These measures and attitudes threaten the very existence of the professional military establishment.

Both the military and the Left are opposed to the traditional parliamentary practices. More important, each views the other as a hostile force, a force dedicated to the elimination of democratic forms as it defines them. Each needs the other to justify itself. The military's importance diminishes if Communism ceases to be the internal and external enemy. And if the Western alliance were changed and the military forces were reduced, left-wing policy would not diverge greatly from the policy of the modern components of the more traditional political organizations; some new villains would have to be found to explain Greek underdevelopment.

Even before the coup of 1967, some members of the military were willing to intervene in traditional politics if governmental instability threatened the internal status or foreign connections of the military. The first postwar instance came in 1951, when a number of militant junior officers involved in an organization known as IDEA (Sacred Link of Greek Officers) attempted a coup.[41] The later candidature of Field Marshal Papagos could also be viewed at least in part, as a military revulsion against traditional politics. Any political organization on the traditional level that has approached the Left for electoral support has been viewed with distrust by the military. In fact, the armed forces have always intervened on the opposite side in these cases. This, in turn, has provoked the Left to more and violent rhetoric, punctuated with foreign appeals and public disturbances.

The armed forces have generally been hostile to the traditional Center parties. The Center is viewed as the most fragmented part of traditional politics; and the instability caused by fragmentation alarms both the military and its foreign supporters. Further, the leaders of the Center, in their efforts to regain power, did not inspire confidence. Papandreou's inclusion of the EDA in his electoral coalition of 1956 caused grave distrust; the military felt that he was willing to undermine the regime in order to gain personal political power. The massive failure of the Center in the elections of 1958 meant that the EDA became the official opposition party for a time; this also reduced confidence in the Center and in parliamentary politics. The possibility of a Center victory in 1961 provoked the military and certain portions of the ERE to intervene in the normal electoral processes. Some members of the military undoubtedly distrust the Center because it is viewed as the modern heir of the interwar republican tradition. Certainly, several of the leading Center figures were allies of the republican officers who alternated with the royalist military establishment during those years. Papandreou, in his campaigns of 1961 and 1963, and in his statements as premier, seemed to threaten the old order. His exposure of "Operation Pericles," the plan initiated by the military for the manipulation of the 1961 elections was especially outrageous. EK plans for the normalization of political life also annoyed the armed forces.

Conservatives had occasionally questioned the scale of Greek support for NATO. Military expenditures ran to almost half of the Greek budget in the early postwar period.[42] However, in the years from 1954 to 1965, the military share of the current-expense budget dropped from over 30 per cent to 16.3 per cent.[43] The Papandreou government suggested that even that scale of military preparedness was incompatible with economic development. It seemed likely that basic military priorities would be not only questioned but readjusted. The armed forces could not tolerate any thought of regional disarmament or of withdrawal from the NATO alliance; their professional pride and material support were dependent on this association. Officers and noncoms might lose the special privileges that set them apart from the rest of Greek society, and be thrown into an already swollen labor market. In 1964 a former general speaking as an ERE deputy opened the question of military loyalty to the Papandreou regime: "Is the government prepared to reach that point [i.e., to further reduce the military forces]? Will she find a military leadership that will accept it?"[44] Finally, the revelations of the "Aspida" affair (supposedly a contemplated coup by Papandreou and his followers) indicated that some portion of the professional military itself might share the views of those desiring a new international position for Greece and the modernization of Greek political life. Some younger officers were identified as tied to Center or Left politicians.

There has not always been harmony between the crown, the army, and the Right in Greek politics, either. Field Marshal Papagos, the leader of the most successful postwar political movement, was not on good terms with the monarch. Later, the intervention of the army on behalf of Karamanlis in 1961 rebounded to the discomfiture of the king. Whether or not he knew of the intervention in advance is problematical; but by declining to repudiate those responsible, he was identified as an accomplice. The army, Western statesmen, and part of the Greek bureaucracy had pressed Karamanlis to accept an American offer to station medium-range ballistic missiles in Greece, but he had refused. In fact, Karamanlis, though speaking for the right wing, never completely acceded to military budget requests. The percentage of the budget devoted to the military fell in every year from 1957 to 1963, with the exception of 1959. Ultimately, Karamanlis himself resigned in 1963 because of a conflict with the crown. The public issue was a projected visit of the monarch to London against the wishes of the government, but it was rumored that Karamanlis actually entertained antidynastic thoughts that made him suspect among some members of his own entourage and among the leaders of the armed forces. The details of this event remain obscure.

When the traditional political organizations seem to threaten the military, there has been little hesitation in using the armed forces for political purposes. One method has been the use of the army vote. In any election the placement of military units in marginal areas can have a substantial effect on the outcome. This is recognized by parliamentary politicians, and the electoral laws enacted before each election regularly include provisions concerning the military vote. Similar provisions are included in regard to civil servants. Table 8.6 indicates the military and civil service have voted differently than the rest of the population: the right-wing parties have received more and the Left party considerably less than the corresponding averages of the total popular vote in each election. As the military has become more professional, in the sense that draftees and short-term volunteers make up a smaller percentage of its strength, it has become more right-wing in political support. In some cases, especially 1956 and 1961, soldiers were apparently encouraged to select ERE ballots by the higher leadership.

When the Greek military intervenes to stem radical politics, the Left be-

Table 8.6. The Military and Civil-Service Vote, 1950–64

Year and vote	Military-civil share of total vote	Right	Center	Left	KP	Other
1950						
Military and civil	10.8%	40.8%	53.2%	3.2%	—	2.1%
National total		30.9	53.3	9.7	—	5.2
1951						
Military and civil	9.5	60.4	36.5	3.1	—	—
National total		43.2	46.2	10.8	—	—
1956						
Military and civil	4.7	76.7	19.2	—	2.7%	1.4
National total		47.4	48.2	—	2.2	2.2
1961						
Military and civil	4.4	78.9	18.1	2.6	—	0.3
National total		50.8	33.6	14.6	—	0.9
1963						
Military and civil	1.8	60.2	34.9	1.9	2.8	0.1
National total		39.4	42.0	14.3	3.7	0.9
1964						
Military and civil	1.9	48.3	50.2	1.5	—	—
National total		35.3	52.7	11.8	—	0.2

Note: In 1950–51 the military vote was isolated. In 1956–64 civil servants are included; they probably comprise about one-half of the total. In 1946, 1952, and 1958 military and civil-service totals could not be separated from the general totals. The KP was in an electoral coalition with the Center in 1961, and with the Right in 1964; the same was true of the EDA in 1956. No separate party totals are available for those years.

comes more willing to embark upon an extraparliamentary course. The left-wing youth group, the Lambrakists, were to some degree a product of the tensions of the later years of the Karamanlis regime. This group, in particular, has been extremely active in demonstrations and other antigovernmental activity. The Left has come to express complete intolerance for both the armed forces and the traditional right wing.

It is not to the advantage of either the military establishment or the left wing to allow a transformation of traditional Greek politics by the other—or by parliamentary politicians. Any attempt by a parliamentary political leader to respond to nascent interests in the society would require a genuine reassessment of program priorities. The personal-fragile political movement that such a man would rely on would have to break the hold of the polyarchic and persistent elements in its own party by overwhelming patron-client relationships with a broad appeal to the unattached elements in the political system. In such a situation, the supporters of the Left would have to be admitted to the political arena, and the recognition of these elements as legitimate would limit the function of the armed forces. An appeal by a parliamentary leader on program or issue terms might undercut some of this specifically leftist support, but it would also attack the traditional system. Nevertheless, it can be argued that only vigorous social reforms and political parties that perform the aggregative function can decrease the appeal of the Left to the mobilized urban sectors of the population.

It is in the interest of the Greek military that traditional, issueless politics prevail. Under these conditions, the Left, because it represents the more modern elements, is easily recognized as a threat to the status quo. The Left itself seems to prefer working both inside and outside parliament. The rapid changes now taking place in Greek society, combined with the inability of the traditional political structures to accommodate increased demands, are likely to increase the strength of the Left in electoral politics whenever it can legitimately compete. The stability of the earlier postwar period has already been shattered by the events since 1965. The military oligarchy that seized power in 1967 has temporarily frozen the process of change, and the direction of Greek politics in the immediate future depends largely on the junta's decisions.

9. Military Oligarchy: The Coup of 1967

The fragile relationships between the major components of the Greek political system have been noted in the foregoing chapter. The equilibrium of the consociational system was finally upset when the military reacted to the efforts at modernization pushed by Andreas Papandreou and the threat posed by the left wing. Although the threat of a transformation initiated by the traditional political world was important, the additional possibility that the extreme Left would be the ultimate beneficiary of any change was even more upsetting. The result of the military's reaction in April 1967 was a military oligarchy, whose form and operation fit the general pattern of military oligarchies elsewhere in the world.[1]

The Greek military was not happy with the outcome of the election held in November 1963. By themselves, however, the victories of the EK then and in the following February should not have been viewed as immediate threats. George Papandreou, the party's leader, was clearly a traditional Greek politician, who used words as substitutes for action. He had allied with and repudiated nearly every politician or political faction in Greece: he had been republican and royalist; he had been an anti-Communist leader, and later an occasional ally of the EDA. Papandreou's political affiliations were largely dependent on his perception of how best to gain political office; and the core of his Center Union was composed of notables who followed much the same principles and were little different from the leading figures in the other major parliamentary group. The members of the Papandreou cabinets, for the most part, had secured their positions largely because of their individual political strength and their associations with their chief; it is difficult to find much in the way of a policy or issue orientation among them. Likewise, most of the EK deputies were occupied with maintaining their personal political positions by dispensing patronage.

Despite the rhetoric of the new government, its policies were not particularly startling. The EK's suggested reforms in education, the bureaucracy, and economic policy had in most cases been suggested earlier. The Greek tradition of statism and government intervention in all aspects of life could accommodate even the most "extreme" views of the new ministers on government activity. Papandreou had made a number of promises to specific sectors of the population, but their fulfillment was contingent on a modernization of the Greek political system. The major difference between the Papandreou administration and the previous one was that some of those in important political positions, primarily the small group of modernizers associated with Andreas Papandreou, really intended to reform the system. Andreas, the premier's son, may have entered politics for traditional family reasons, but he brought with him a concept of the political party that was unlike that of his father and the other parliamentary political leaders. To him, "party" meant organization, discipline, and program. These modern views could only dislocate traditional parliamentary politics, and an upheaval here was bound to have repercussions at the extraparliamentary level. The military was particularly alarmed at two specific elements in the younger Papandreou's program: the matter of budgetary priorities, and the treatment and position of the Left in the Greek political system, especially in regard to the future of the rural gendarmerie and the National Security Battalions. In addition, there was a certain fear that Andreas would attempt to influence military actions by manipulating personnel.

The military could maintain a nonpolitical stance only as long as the traditional political level continued to play the role assigned to it, preoccupation with factional, issueless politics. Any politician who wished to change this pattern faced a hostile military establishment. The military, because they used the monarch as the focus of loyalty, considered themselves outside the parliamentary purview. There was little civilian control over military personnel, the defense budget could not be seriously altered, and foreign-policy questions that might alter the relationship of Greece and the military to the NATO alliance could not be broached. These and other questions, which are considered political in most countries, were stipulated to be nonpolitical in the Greek context. Any modern politician who intended to be involved in issues rather than personalist politics was bound to be charged with political interference, precisely because these untouchable policy areas had to be breached in order to modernize Greek society.

Although the military was generally unhappy with the Center Union administration, there was no intervention until the "Aspida" affair of 1965 brought tensions to the breaking point. The army, as the largest and most influential component in the military establishment, was directly involved.

The air force and navy remained quiescent at this time and were not accomplices in the ultimate coup either. Basically, it was charged that "Aspida was a secret organization of army officers conspiring, under the political leadership of Andreas [Papandreou], to take over the Greek army, throw out the King, and impose a Nasser-type dictatorship on the Greek people."[2] But the affair was considerably more than a simple confrontation between civilians and military; in fact, the web of relationships between the various contending groups was almost Byzantine in its complexity. The personal rivalries of leading figures in the EK with each other and with Andreas Papandreou provided one part of the drama. In addition, there was a rivalry in Cyprus between Archbishop Makarios (the president of Cyprus) and General Grivas, the commander of the Cypriot National Guard and the contingent of the Greek Army stationed there. The mere rumor of the plot itself suggested that the military establishment was not as monolithic as outside appearances and nationalist rhetoric proclaimed it to be. Toward the end of the affair, fundamental constitutional questions arose concerning the role of the monarch in the Greek political system.

Archbishop Makarios, who differed with General Grivas over the future course of Cyprus toward union with Greece, found that control of the Cypriot armed forces rested not with his government, but with Grivas. In an effort to counter this, Makarios was attempting to build up the gendarmerie as an alternative force. Supposedly, the Aspida plot, at first intended only to undermine Grivas, began with a visit of Andreas Papandreou to Makarios. The military saw a connection between this and the concurrent attempts of the Papandreou government to find sympathetic officers in the military establishment, which produced transfers and shifts at the higher levels. Eventually, Grivas blew the whistle. His allegations provoked demands by the king (as commander in chief of the armed forces) and by competing groups in parliament for an investigation. The Minister of Defense, Petros Garofilias, one of the old-line EK notables, was perhaps afraid of the personal and fragile modernizing leadership of the younger Papandreou, and supported the monarch. George Papandreou, viewing Garofilias as more loyal to the monarch than to himself, wanted to assume the defense portfolio. Although he apparently had other reasons for this course of action, he would have been in the position of presiding over an investigation of his own son's activities.[3] Constitutional vagueness allowed the king to disallow this course of action. Premier Papandreou then threatened to resign, and the king took the threat as fact.

The stage was set for the usual game of parliamentary musical chairs.

The king sent for President of Parliament George Athanasiadis-Novas, a leading EK notable, and asked him to form a new government based on the existing Center Union majority. For three tumultuous weeks he tried to find support; but in the end, the parliament failed to approve the appointment. The king then asked Stephanos Stephanopoulos, another leading figure from the polyarchic and persistent segment of the EK, to form a government. Stephanopoulos declined the offer, bowing to the decision of a party caucus. Then Stephanopoulos and Elias Tsirimokos, an EK veteran who had at times been affiliated with the Left, resigned from the Center Union. The king gave Tsirimokos the opportunity to form a broadly based government, but he was also unsuccessful. Eventually, Stephanopoulos was able to form a government that lasted until December 1966.

Throughout the period, there were massive demonstrations and strikes in Athens and the provincial cities; the Left was prominent, but the bulk of the participants were EK supporters. Violence erupted in the streets, with many injuries and at least one death; in the parliamentary chamber itself, all civility disappeared, and at least one fistfight occurred. The bulk of the EK membership in the parliament and the EK supporters among the people supported the elder Papandreou, who demanded reinstatement as prime minister or new elections. In fact, only 49 of the 171 EK deputies were induced to break the bonds of personal loyalty or party affiliation to support the defecting notables. All but four of the 49 eventually formed a new party, the Liberal Democratic Center; however, it existed as the governing party only with the support of the ERE and the KP. Incipient party loyalty and personal loyalty to both George Papandreou and his son prevented further attrition. Beyond that, given the extent of social mobilization, and the penetration of the mass media, Papandreou became something of a national hero. Deputies wishing a political future found it convenient to remain tied to him, even though he was out of office.[4]

The Stephanopoulos government fell in December 1966, when Kanellopoulos, the ERE leader, declined to support it any longer. The Governor of the National Bank of Greece, Ioannis Paraskevopoulos, was named head of a caretaker government, to prepare for new elections in spring 1967. It seems likely that the traditional political world was attempting to restore equilibrium. Compromises and agreements at that level might not have favored either the modernizing elements in the parties or the extraparliamentary interests.

During the interregnum between the "resignation" of Papandreou and the coup in April 1967, the army officers alleged to be involved in the Aspida plot were investigated and tried by a military court. The prosecution alleged that the elder Papandreou had succeeded in destroying incriminating evidence in the last days of his administration. There was considerable unhappiness that parliamentary immunity kept Andreas Papandreou out of court, at least temporarily. The trial was delayed and prolonged, possibly so that the charges against the Papandreous and the EK could influence the ensuing elections. However, the trial produced questionable evidence, some forced "confessions," and a torrent of countercharges; the government and the army received unflattering publicity instead.[5] Ultimately, 13 of the 28 officers accused were acquitted. The alleged military leader of the plot received an 18-year sentence. However, the outcome of the trial only incensed the military against the traditional political level.

Tensions had increased since the crisis of July 1965. The worsening economic situation and the serious political polarization were turning the long-delayed election into a plebiscite that would decide between Papandreou on the one hand and the monarch, as a representative of the military establishment, on the other. The extreme Left, with its talent for organized agitation, was attempting to build up the election as a referendum on the existing political system. Its actions and announcements, which demanded substantial changes in state policy toward the left wing, provoked many of the traditional parties, as well as the military. Athens was in almost constant turmoil. Throughout the first weeks of April 1967 there were increased strikes, particularly in the EDA-dominated building trades, as well as frequent clashes between demonstrators and the police.

The leaders at the traditional level were also active. Kanellopoulos, the leader of the ERE, clashed with George Papandreou over a provision in the proposed electoral law; this in turn brought down the caretaker government of Paraskevopoulos. The king selected Kanellopoulos as premier, but he failed to get a parliamentary vote of confidence. Kanellopoulos then called upon the monarch to dissolve the parliament and prepare for elections on May 28, 1967. Despite the closing of parliament and the termination of parliamentary immunity, the Kanellopoulos government decided not to prosecute Andreas Papandreou for his alleged role in Aspida. This decision, in the face of the trial and conviction of the army officers, suggested that the whole plot had been fabricated.

Perhaps most alarming to those who favored the current political system was the very real threat of an EK victory. Despite the delay in calling elec-

tions after the initial crisis in 1965, the EK and the Papandreous still retained great popularity. Given the elder Papandreou's age and general
health, it was likely that Andreas would emerge as the party leader, particularly since several logical contenders had defected to form the Liberal Democratic Center. Despite conflicts with his father over policy and organization,
he had already secured the right to nominate candidates in constituencies
not already held by EK deputies.[6] If the EK were to win some of these
marginal seats and add them to the 40 or so EK deputies who had favored
Andreas Papandreou in the recently dissolved parliament, the presumed
EK victory would create a parliamentary bloc that was largely the personal
instrument of a reformist politician. Some portions of the military apparently viewed this outcome as nearly equivalent to a Communist victory.
Official explanations for the subsequent coup stressed that "the real danger
was that we were sliding down the road to Communism." The Greek Communists, "acting within the framework of international Communism," were
the main antagonists.[7] The views of Andreas Papandreou on military expenditures, the NATO Alliance, and Cyprus, in military eyes, posed as
large a threat as did the Left itself.

All of these factors no doubt contributed to the feeling that the initial EK
campaign rally, to be held in Thessaloniki, was a crucial occasion. Thessaloniki, the second city in Greece and the major center of the North, had
strong affiliations with the EK and with Papandreou personally; moreover,
it was a stronghold of the EDA. According to the junta, the regional army
commander was informed by local authorities that the rally could not be
contained by local police forces. That officer, however, felt that military intervention would result in great bloodshed.[8] The conspirators later argued
that this was why they acted.

THE COUP

A triumvirate of middle-ranking army officers—Colonels George Papadopoulos and Nikolas Makarezos and Brigadier Stylianos Patakos—planned
the coup. Nine additional officers were told of the scheme some 20 hours in
advance, and 21 others 14 hours beforehand. The army chief of staff, under
whose signature the orders were transmitted to army units outside Athens,
was brought in only at the last moment. The navy and air force were uninvolved. The coup itself was carried out efficiently and swiftly, according
to a NATO contingency plan.[9] In the early hours of April 21, armored
units surrounded the royal palace, the parliament building, the major min-

istries, the chief post offices, and the telegraph offices. Transportation and communications to the outside were closed. The vast majority of leading left-wing politicians and left-wing sympathizers, together with the leading parliamentary figures from the other political groups, were arrested. Apparently over 6,500 people were arrested, and a large proportion of those with left-wing views were detained on an island in the Aegean.[10] Most of these were gradually released in the months to follow.

The first news of the coup came from the armed forces radio network, which announced that portions of the constitution had been suspended. Martial law and curfews were put into effect; schools, universities, and banks were closed; public and private meetings of more than five people were banned; and a strict press censorship was imposed. There was virtually no armed opposition to the coup, and only on Crete was there any initial protest. The EDA was taken by surprise; and the traditional political world, with the exception of Kanellopoulos and some parliamentary deputies who were abroad, remained quiet. Although the military intervention was well planned and executed, the very ease with which the coup occurred suggests that the supposed Communist takeover was less than imminent.

Apologists for the coup leaders argued that military intervention occurred only because the political situation was abnormal. Moreover, it came only after politics, in the form of the Aspida affair, had penetrated the military establishment itself.[11] The ideological predispositions of the officers who acted had convinced them that an EK victory would benefit the Communists. The military intervened to save itself and, as it believed, to save the nation. The first statement by the new premier, Constantine Kollias (a civilian with a history of involvement in extreme right-wing activities), justified the coup in these terms and set the tone for future policies.*

We have long been witnessing a crime committed against our people and our nation. Unscrupulous and base party compromises, shameful recklessness of a great part of the press, methodical attack on and undermining of all institutions, complete debasement of Parliament, all-around slander, paralysis of the state machinery, complete lack of understanding of the burning problems of our youth, moral decline, secret and open collaboration with subversion, and finally, constant inflammatory slogans of unscrupulous demagogues, have destroyed the country's peace, created an atmosphere of anarchy, chaos, hatred and discord, and led us to the brink of national catastrophe.[12]

---

* It was argued that the king's influence was illustrated by the appointment of a civilian as premier. However, authority remained in the hands of the junta leaders. Moreover, Kollias, since he had been heavily involved in extreme right-wing activity, particularly in regard to the celebrated Lambrakis affair, was hardly a symbol of conciliation.

In short, the officers intervened to stop political bickering and to restore "responsible" politics to the nation. According to their spokesmen, they were merely following the illustrious pattern of the revolutionaries of 1909, who had intervened in the midst of political confusion, brought order out of chaos, and returned to their barracks.[13] The 1909 revolutionaries are viewed as early Greek modernizers by some portions of the population. However, the parallels with 1909 begin and end with the rank of the conspirators and the fact that the forerunner of the armored unit commanded by one of the coup leaders was also used by the earlier conspirators. The present junta has far more in common, in terms of ideology, policy, organization, and attitude toward politics, with the Metaxas regime of the late 1930's. Colonel Makarezos, an intelligence officer, and Colonel Papadopoulos, a special political warfare officer, both had an ideological background lacking among officers in 1909. Moreover, all three coup leaders, and presumably some of the other officers involved, came to maturity during the Metaxas period and graduated from the Greek military academy during the last years of the Metaxas dictatorship. They, like Metaxas, came to power without a program that could be applied to concrete situations; their major innovations were taken from the programs of the previous regime. The initial reaction of both was to clear away the traditional political forces so that problems could be easily and quickly solved. In each case, the complexities of rule became apparent only later.

THE INTERNATIONAL FACTOR

There was great uneasiness over the Greek coup in the NATO countries because democracy and constitutional government had been extinguished in a Western country close to home. Many private individuals and organizations, as well as political parties, protested the actions of the junta and pressured their governments for expressions of disapproval. However, there were few sanctions that could be applied. The Common Market voted to suspend the financial credits that were going to Greece in her status as an associate member. The Council of Europe at least considered a complaint from four member governments who asked for the expulsion of Greece unless human rights were restored. The Danes wanted to bring up the matter in a NATO Council meeting, and only great pressure kept them from doing so.[14] In the long run, the hostility of the Western European states could seriously affect Greek plans for economic development.

The leaders of the coup placed a high priority on remaining in NATO, and particularly on maintaining good relations with the United States. The Greek military attitudes on foreign relations, paralleling those outlined by Irving Horowitz for the Latin American military, are "geared both to national redemption and to the international expectancies of the big foreign powers."[15] The coup leaders apparently assumed that any measures taken in the name of anti-Communism would be acceptable to the United States, and her generally unfavorable reaction seems to have surprised them. Some members of the junta had felt that America would increase her military aid, and perhaps even her economic aid, since Greece was now more firmly in the NATO alliance than before. According to Makarezos, "It was a mathematical certainty that the Communists would have taken over without a coup."[16] If more aid was not forthcoming, a Communist takeover was still a very real future possibility.

The United States did little more than protest, since the coup did not threaten the larger balance of forces in the eastern Mediterranean. No decision on diplomatic recognition had to be made, since ambassadors were accredited to the monarch, who was still the nominal head of government. The State Department announced a selective embargo on military equipment, which was later dropped. Secretary of Defense McNamara took the occasion of a NATO defense ministers' meeting to warn his Greek counterpart that American aid might be cut off unless Greece returned to constitutional government.[17]

It can be argued that American policy toward the junta gave the appearance of approval.[18] It has always been assumed in Greece that internal politics are subject to foreign approval. This was true when the main protector was Great Britain, and it remains true now that Greece is in the American sphere of influence. Greeks of all classes believe that little of major importance can happen in Greece that is not the result of American action, pressure, or at least acquiescence. It has been considered axiomatic that no military coup could occur without American complicity, particularly because of the close ties between the Greek and American military establishments. Thus America's failure to oppose the coup with strenuous measures, and her eventual acceptance of it, lent credence to the allegations of foreknowledge and involvement that were rampant in Greece and in some circles in the United States.[19]

One early report suggested that the new leadership was "more nationalistic," and that it would press for the annexation of Cyprus more vigorously. However, this is not likely to happen. The new emphasis on anti-Communism makes the Western alliance more important to Greece than any other consideration. Indeed, the junta's announced policy of "friendly relations with all nations" was soon belied when an eight-year-old frontier agreement with Yugoslavia was terminated.[20] This kind of action, anachronistic in the context of recent Balkan relations, is bound to rekindle old hostilities with Greece's northern neighbors, as is the renewed praise of Greek Christian civilization as a barrier against the unenlightened barbarians. The efforts of recent Greek regimes to curry the favor of the "third world" for support on the Cyprus question were accompanied by coolness toward the Western allies, few of whom supported the Greek position. Conversely, the renewed dependence on NATO can only have a deleterious effect on friendships in Africa and Asia. On the other hand—again in the context of anti-Communism—good relations with Turkey are essential. The recent meetings between the leaders of the two nations on the Thracian frontier, as well as the softening of statements on Cyprus, would seem to confirm this.

The military junta is even more dependent on American goodwill than previous Greek regimes. The Greek army has received its supplies and much of its training from the United States for some time, and now American acquiescence is necessary if the army is to maintain its political position. The Cyprus issue has low priority, since it would sour relations. The military distrusts Archbishop Makarios because of his neutralist tendencies, and because he has built up a police force to counterbalance the Greek-controlled military forces.[21] Moreover, the Cypriot Communist Party is one of the most active and influential of those outside the Communist states. For both Greece and the United States, the status quo is probably the most comfortable solution to the Cyprus question.

THE MILITARY AND THE MONARCH

The sudden action of the coup leaders, though also suggesting cleavage in the military establishment, clearly revealed that the armed forces were not simply a tool of the monarch. The fact that civilian governments did not control the military did not automatically mean that the king did. Constantine was not informed of the impending coup; his personal advisers were arrested, and eventually slid into diplomatic exile. Although the junta initially maintained that Constantine had signed the decree dissolving the Kanellopoulos caretaker government, it is now apparent that he did not. Several weeks elapsed before he was photographed with the new cabinet, and he did not address the Greek people until one month after the coup. It seems clear in retrospect that the king had no alternative but to acquiesce once the coup had taken place.* He had been deluded, as had many other observers, into believing that the military was loyal to him as the symbol of the nation; instead, he was only a symbol used to give legitimacy to the non-political status of the armed forces.

Some commentators suggested that the king had retained private sources of power that could be used to counter the military leadership.[22] Initial support for this interpretation was drawn from the fact that a civilian had been appointed as premier. However, it was soon apparent that real control remained in the hands of the army triumvirate. Moreover, when the king's countercoup failed in December 1967, Premier Kollias went into exile along with Constantine. The posture of disguised hostility adopted by Constantine toward the junta was perhaps aimed at restoring his lost popularity. However, he was an unlikely nucleus for opposition. The EK, for instance, still retained memories of past grievances against the throne. After all, the years of turmoil since July 1965 were at least partly Constantine's responsibility. And whatever the king's personal attitudes toward the junta, "The few overt acts he performed have all helped to cloak the revolutionary regime with an aura of legitimacy."[23]

Although he hardly had support from the traditional political world— or indeed, from any group—Constantine toured the countryside on his own, constantly referring to "the government" while conspicuously refraining from calling it "my government."[24] These activities caused evident dissatisfaction among the junta leaders. The initial coolness of the monarch was an embarrassment; as it continued, his position became increasingly untenable. The king himself willingly subscribed to the anti-Communist ideology that pervaded the military establishment, and the monarchy, as the pinnacle of the armed forces, was the institutional focus of this anti-Communist stand. However, Constantine refused to recognize that the "nonpolitical" stance of the military was in essence political: "Any endeavor, as long as it will respect the purely national mission of the army and will avert the penetration of political ambitions in the armed forces, will have my full support."[25] Unfortunately, these hopes could not be realized. The possibility of Constantine's reversing or directing the trend

---

* The statement of General Spandidakis, the new Minister of Defense, was instructive: "Of course the King speaks very little ... but I am sure that in the end he will understand it was the only solution." (*New York Times*, May 5, 1967, p. 13.)

of military activities diminished as time passed. The junta gradually removed officers who might give their first loyalty to the monarch. The attempted royalist countercoup in December 1967 had practically no support,
either among the military or among the general population. When it failed,
the king had little choice but to leave the country. The junta retained the
monarchical institutions, installing a regent in place of the king, and it
seemed clear that the removal of Constantine was not unwelcome. Iron-
ically, the new constitution, proposed by the new military regime and
adopted by referendum in September 1968, placed limits on the power of
any future monarch, in effect making him a figurehead, that the traditional
political world would probably not have been able to put into effect. Moreover, the constitution placed the corporations and institutions formerly under royal authority, from which the monarch had drawn some independent
power, under the direct control of the government.

THE MILITARY AND THE TRADITIONAL POLITICAL WORLD

The junta destroyed the visible Left. The EDA and its youth affiliate
were formally proscribed. The leaders of all left-wing organizations were
imprisoned or detained, fled the country, or went underground. Within
months, however, only the hard core who refused to renounce their political ties and to abstain from future political activity remained in custody.
The EDA archives were combed for evidence of Communist direction and
affiliation, and any information that could be so interpreted was highly pub-
licized. Beyond this, the ease with which the coup was executed and the
EDA's failure to mobilize its cadres into any form of opposition discredited
the Left among parts of the population. An underground organization
apparently remains, but there is little evidence of organized opposition to
the junta.

The major antagonist of the armed forces was the EDA, but the coup
leaders also took swift action against the traditional political world. Both of
the major political groups at this level, the EK and the ERE, contained
men drawn from the major sectors of Greek life—banking, shipping, industry, the professions, and the press—as well as the actual political figures.
These people and the social groups from which they came were all accused
of contributing to the political confusion of the past months. According to
the leader of the junta, Colonel Papadopoulos, "The political parties brought
Greece into chaos by following their own selfish designs. This created anarchy and raised the specter of a Communist coup."[26] They were respon-

sible for allowing a reformist like Andreas Papandreou to assume political leadership, and for dragging the position of the military and nature of Greece's alliance structure into discussions at the political level.

It is necessary to repeat that political labels have little relevance in the Greek context. The coup can best be described as antipolitical. It was supposedly a right-wing government that was overthrown, and the military leaders have spoken and acted strongly against all the groups involved in parliamentary politics. The youth auxiliaries of the EK and the ERE were abolished soon after the coup. The parent parties were not themselves outlawed, but major figures from both were arrested initially, along with the entire EDA leadership. Most of these men were released after the junta was firmly in power, although Kanellopoulos and the elder Papandreou remained under house arrest. Eventually, even Andreas Papandreou was released and sent into exile. By this time, the state institutions were staffed by the military; the traditional political leaders had been publicly discredited and eliminated from public life, and the bonds of personal connection that had substituted for party organization were destroyed. In essence, the military had eliminated the traditional parties, as well as the left wing, as a political force. At present, all politicians are "on a strict form of parole."[27]

The social elements closely connected with the leading parliamentary politicians were also detained, harassed, and stripped of privileges. For example, the Union of Journalists, composed of particularly influential journalists with political connections, had been allowed to conduct a lucrative annual lottery, which supplied the bulk of its pension funds.* The junta not only terminated this privilege, but detained some of the Union's leading members and exiled them to the provinces. The major newspapers closely identified with leading politicians also suffered: most were shut down for some time; and some failed to reopen at all. The circulation of the remaining papers diminished, at least initially, because of the strict censorship imposed by the junta. Eventually, publishers who would not reopen their newspapers and operate under state supervision were faced with virtual confiscation of property.[28]

The more influential business figures were arrested at the beginning of the coup; others sought asylum outside the country. The privileges enjoyed by professionals and businessmen—in fact, by anyone with the necessary

* See pp. 112–13.

connections to operate in the labyrinth of traditional parliamentary politics
—were threatened. Licenses for trade and commercial activities were made
freely available; this removed the monopolies that already existed, and encouraged greater competition. The new government ordered the payment
of the usual Easter bonus the first month after its takeover, even by companies without the financial means. All dismissals of private employees
were initially forbidden. Finally, the junta decreed that no salary in the
nation, whatever its source, could top the $1,500 a month paid to the pre-
mier.[29] The administrative leverage of traditional governments had always
been sufficient to harass hostile or unfavored elements in the business world.
Now, however, business suffered not only because of formal decrees, but
because the traditional influence networks used to ameliorate government
action were disrupted.

The military oligarchy is somewhat contradictory in its attitude toward
the business world. Because of military isolation, or perhaps because of
businessmen's involvement in traditional politics, the motivations and activities of businessmen are suspect. One of the first aims of the regime was the
reconstitution of the state "as an instrument of all the people, and not just
businessmen exploiting workers."[30] Moreover, the new Minister of Coordination, Makarezos, stated that a major task of the regime was "to raise the
standard of living by the redistribution of income."[31] These threats, however, were qualified by the statement that private initiative was to remain
the chief medium for economic growth. Basically, the business world is
distrusted by the junta; yet the development of the country still depends
on private enterprise.

Other structures connected with the traditional political level were also
attacked and destroyed. Those trade unions not members of the government controlled confederation, many of which had been dominated by the
Left, were abolished. There was a purge of cooperative leadership and a
reform of cooperative organization. All representative institutions at the
lower levels of the state were eliminated. Intermediate organizations, such
as the Union of Communes and Municipalities, were disbanded. Local
officials suspected of disloyalty to the regime were suspended, and new appointments were made. Henceforth, there would be no elections. The government intended to avoid a political role; local officials and those in secondary associations were to be merely administrators.

These actions, while more extreme and thoroughgoing than traditional
Greek practice, were not unprecedented. Leadership in associational life

and local office had always been selected on the basis of political ties, or had been manipulated by the government. The junta merely replaced leaders tied to the traditional political world with those more amenable to military direction. However, regardless of military desires, administration does involve politics. The new "nonpolitical" official must participate in the allocation of scarce resources, just as his political predecessor did, and any allocation will have political overtones.

THE MILITARY AND LEGITIMACY

The Greek military, once in power, had only a tenuous claim to legitimacy. The initial goal of preventing the presumed EK victory and the consequent success of the Communists was quickly realized, but the next steps were unclear. The militant left had been destroyed. Since the army's existence, and its claim to power, could at first be justified only on the grounds of a Communist threat, the junta's first reaction was to deny the disappearance of the threat. It was argued that Communists would reappear if the military relinquished power; in addition, the hostile international environment was stressed. Papadopoulos called for a "guided liberalism," which was to include central executive power, morality, and patriotism.[32] Beyond this, the government has relied on slogans such as "unity, work, peace, and progress," or "The life of the nation is the death of Communism." The Ministry of Public Order announced that "all Greeks would be required to stand at attention whenever they heard the national anthem or watched the raising or lowering of the flag."[33]

The military leaders, partly because of their training but perhaps also because of their actual military function in the Western alliance, have not attempted to legitimize their regime by concentrating on economic development. Instead, the junta has attempted to fill the ideological void by manufacturing a new nationalism out of Greek Orthodoxy and the classical heritage. The school and the church are the central institutions in this effort. However, before even this program could be inaugurated, the educational establishment and the church hierarchy had to be sifted to eliminate those hostile to the new regime.

The Minister of Education announced: "The first and chief objective of the school is to stimulate the national conscience. To achieve this you need high spirit and exaltation that will make the school atmosphere vibrate, and give that particularly Greek color which is the firm foundation of the survival and the great deeds of our race."[34] In fact, this task required a reassessment of the role of education in national life. If the school was to become a major instrument for inculcating loyalty to the new regime, the influence of the family would have to be lessened. School instructors were given the responsibility of directing student conduct during after-class hours. The task of socialization, to "form Greek citizens inspired by Greek Christian civilization,"[35] became paramount. This program, according to the military leaders, required an even greater concentration on the classics, religion, and other nontechnical subjects than before. For example, the new regime restored the practice of teaching only Katharevusa after the first three years of school. This purist language, with little relation to everyday life, serves mainly as a vehicle for entrance into the civil service. Altogether, the new methods of education and the exclusion of most technical and vocational subjects from the curriculum are serious obstacles to Greece's economic development.

The Orthodox church had been as politicized as any other sector of Greek society. Moreover, notable lapses of morality on all levels of the church hierarchy, as well as the sketchy educational attainments of the lower clergy, had undermined respect for the church. To counter this trend, the junta purged the church hierarchy. Archmandrite Kotsonis, the former Chaplain to the King, was made Archbishop of Athens and Primate of the Greek Church. The government appropriated the right to choose the governing synod of the church, which had previously been done by a 67-member assembly of bishops, and announced that it would select bishops for vacant sees from nominees supplied by the synod.[36] To ensure that the church could play an effective role, the junta demanded that the population take religion more seriously. Church attendance was "ordered," and a stricter public morality was demanded—and enforced by countless new blue laws and regulations.

THE MILITARY AND THE BUREAUCRACY

The new regime, properly viewing the bureaucracy as one pillar of the old regime, has made strenuous efforts to change it. Brigadier Patakos said that one major government goal was the "synchronization of the government apparatus."[37] The contrast between the military's own bureaucracy and the operation of the Greek public service, as well as the connection of the bureaucracy with the traditional political level, prompted this policy. First, military edicts ostensibly eliminated the need for political influence and favors. The coup leaders decreed that all pending business was to be cleared up in two weeks, and that future questions from citizens were to be dealt with in three days. Complaint bureaus were to be established in each ministry, and each civil servant was made personally responsible for decisions rendered by him. Finally, "influence peddling" itself was made illegal.[38] The inefficiency, favoritism, and cumbersome bureaucratic procedures that had provided political resources for politicians in the past were, in theory at any rate, eliminated. The tenure of civil servants was suspended for six months while the inefficient and corrupt were dismissed; the major political appointees and all possible opponents of the military at the lower bureaucratic levels were replaced. The diplomatic service and the judiciary were also "purified." Moreover, the independence of the judiciary was eliminated because the Minister of Justice was made a vice-president of the high court.

The coup leaders, rather than encouraging technical skills, have seemingly discriminated against them. In fact, when the new regime has "found any [specialists] in official positions, it has gotten rid of them."[39] It was estimated in March 1968 that about 5,000 officials and government employees had been dismissed after investigations of their loyalty and competence.[40] The government, however, admitted that the major factor in these personnel shifts had been connection with the old political regime.

Despite these efforts, the fundamental social causes of Greek bureaucratic corruption and inefficiency remain untouched. In many ways, the military edicts have made the bureaucracy less responsive and less accessible than before. The junta soon had to rescind some decrees because they were "paralyzing the state machinery" by inhibiting bureaucratic action.[41] The military has found that it cannot rule without the assistance of the civil service.

POLICIES

The military junta found it easiest to conduct reforms in small but relatively obvious matters. The puritanical flavor of Greek military life and thought was apparent in the multitude of early decrees; the assumption that announcement of a new rule would bring automatic compliance also stemmed from the rulers' military background. Many of these edicts made the regime look ridiculous to both Greeks and foreigners. For example, the traditional breaking of glassware at celebrations or in the tavernas was made illegal. There was to be an immediate end to price gouging, short weights, and unsealed garbage cans. The colorful street pretzel vendors and sidewalk kebab shops were given new orders regarding sanitation and display. Civil servants were ordered to pay more attention to their dress. The police were instructed to prevent the display of indecent pictures outside motion-picture houses. Motorcycles were to be checked for mufflers. In the first days after the coup, the playing of music by Russian composers, even pre-soviet ones, was stopped. Later, the ban was extended to "songs of the Communist Mikis Theodorakis, former chief of the disbanded Communist youth organization Lambrakis, which among other things are a means of liaison between Communists."[42] The government announced that young people would be required to give up seats in public conveyances to pregnant women, priests, and invalids. Throughout the early days of the regime, petty edicts of this kind were announced along with significant measures, with little attempt to distinguish between the two.

Civil liberties of all kinds were severely curtailed. The dissemination of statements "likely to arouse anxiety among citizens or lessen their sense of security and order" was forbidden;[43] during the first weeks of the regime there were many arrests on this charge. Political inscriptions or badges were prohibited. At first, all newspapers were prepared in the government offices. After two months, the junta announced that it would "tolerate some criticism in the press";[44] newspapers were ordered to resume their former policies. A month later, explicit censorship was abandoned, but punitive laws remained to deter criticism. It must be noted that there has always been sufficient power in Greek press legislation to muzzle journalists offensive to the regime, military or not.

The new government resurrected legislation inherited from the Nazi occupation to deal with the theater. Censorship was deemed necessary to protect the "moral, spiritual, artistic, and cultural standards of the people."[45] The laws banned any production that would tend to destroy public order, promote subversive theories, discredit the nation or tourism, offend the Christian faith, the king, or the government, undermine the people's healthy social traditions, or damage the aesthetic sense of the populace. The military oligarchy was primarily interested in curbing dissent; positive efforts to direct behavior were left to other institutions.

In their initial clarification of aims, the coup leaders announced that economic development within the framework of the Common Market was a major goal of their group.[46] However, considering the contradictory nature of other government policies, it is highly doubtful that the ruling junta knows anything at all about the nature and necessities of economic development. The only elements in Greek politics with explicit programs for economic development, the younger Papandreou and the EDA, were eliminated, partly because their visions of development clashed with the existing position of the military. Any program of economic development would be crippled unless military expenditure were reduced; and under present circumstances, the military budget is likely to increase rather than decrease. Moreover, the uniformly unfavorable reaction of the Common Market members to the coup produced a suspension of Greece's economic credit. Although the political instability existing before the coup was not conducive to economic improvement, the military regime does not inspire confidence among foreigners. This can be particularly crucial, since tourism and remittances from Greeks abroad are a significant portion of Greek national income.

The junta, perhaps because of its uncertainty and lack of experience, hastened to sign a contract with Litton Industries for the development of the western Peloponnesus and Crete. The previous government had delayed ratification of the agreement because of a general feeling that the terms were too favorable to Litton, and that such a contract might be the opening wedge for a new kind of colonialism.* Litton and its subsidiaries were to serve as management consultants on a fee basis, and were to act as brokers in finding capital for the proposed development projects. In essence, the junta used Litton Industries to bypass traditional Greek bureaucratic roadblocks to development, and to provide needed expertise for solving Greek economic problems in general. The oligarchy took steps to encourage private Greek investment also, particularly in building construction, by reducing the bank rate and authorizing new loans. However, as most analysts of the Greek economy have pointed out, building construction is the least desirable type of investment from the standpoint of economic development.[47]

Basically, the military leaders seem to have hopes that foreign private investment and economic aid will solve the development dilemma. However, the laws relating to foreign investment were very favorable under previous regimes, and did not attract much foreign capital then. Moreover, the United States, the chief supplier of foreign economic assistance in the past, is increasingly interested in cutting back on its aid. Finally, the natural economic deficiencies of Greece—a limited market, poor transportation,

---

* Litton was to receive a fee of 11 per cent over all costs, plus a commission of 1.90 to 2.25 per cent on all the capital that it raised. (*New York Times*, Apr. 29, 1967, p. 18.)

scarce energy resources, and a shortage of skilled labor—as well as the possibility of political upheaval, are likely to limit the success of any plans for economic development that depend on foreign assistance.

The initial announcement of the military leaders stated, "We do not belong to the economic oligarchy."[48] Moreover, since the leading figures in the economy had close ties to the traditional political world, it is not surprising that the triumvirate identified with the less fortunate in Greek society, at least verbally. Some of the measures directed against the business sector benefited the urban laboring classes. However, by and large, the regime has directed most of its efforts elsewhere. Rather than woo an urban proletariat that may be contaminated by leftist influences, the regime has concentrated on an agrarian policy that is obviously an attempt to build support in the rural areas. However, this policy is incompatible with the requirements of economic development, and is itself based on questionable assumptions. A present campaign to stop migration to the cities by promising to bring urban conveniences to the rural areas may actually increase migration to the urban areas. For example, the premier's public "demand" that the Ministry of the Interior extend the water supply, electric power, roads, and telephones to all villages in Greece only commits the regime to promises it cannot keep.[49] The attempts to rationalize the bureaucracy are unlikely to benefit the average peasant because he still needs assistance in deciding what government agency to take his problem to. There is no helpful patron in this new setting. The peasant may even be more neglected than before, since now he does not even have a vote to compel attention.

The Ministry of Agriculture, apparently convinced that landholding problems were of first concern in the rural areas, announced several measures to deal with the alleged problem. The government ordered villages to distribute their public land among landless farmers. In reality, there are few landless farmers, and most unowned land is controlled not by the municipalities but by the state itself. The problem of farm fragmentation is acute, and has been aggravated by government agricultural policies in the past and by the tradition of the dowry. To deal with this, the Ministry proposed that the state buy out the smaller landowners and distribute the land to those who held the larger parcels. Supposedly, this would create a large class of well-to-do farmers disposed to support the regime. How this operation would be carried out financially or administratively is not explained; and the proposal ignores the social and moral value that a Greek peasant attaches to owning his own land. According to the Ministry, the surplus labor created by this program would be absorbed by "rural industry."[50] Since there is almost no existing rural industry, in spite of past government efforts to encourage its development, it seems unlikely that this would solve the problem. Reforms of the kind advocated would almost certainly cause great dislocations in the rural areas and force thousands of unskilled workers to migrate to the cities—one of the very things that the government is trying to stop.

The government, in its effort to garner rural support and at the same time destroy political structures, announced plans to reorganize the co-operative movement.[51] But the general rural distrust of the state and state organizations is unlikely to disappear, no matter what form the organizations take. Another measure was a decree that old-age pensions for rural workers were to be raised by 70 per cent within the year; they were to be financed by an increase in the turnover tax, which would hit the urban consumer.[52] However, the subsidy on wheat, which was the contribution of the old political world to the rural dweller, was removed at the same time. In sum, the agrarian policies of the military oligarchy are internally inconsistent, and they conflict with policies in other sectors as well.

THE FUTURE OF THE MILITARY OLIGARCHY

The fundamental dilemma of the Greek military is summed up by Edward Shils:

the military oligarchy is not a complete regime. It has neither a comprehensive program nor a perspective into the future. Like all non-hereditary oligarchies, it has no provision for succession. It is what some of the military oligarchs themselves call a "caretaker regime." But its ideas about what it takes care of are rather scant and, even where well-intentioned, unimaginative.[53]

However, since the military oligarchy already exists, and since stability has been restored to the Greek political world, the present regime has some support. It is quite likely that many Greeks who are dissatisfied with traditional politics and suspicious of the Left strongly support the new rulers. Certainly, a portion of the middle classes prefers even short-term stability under military rule to upheaval. Moreover, since the first concern of most Greek citizens is for their clientage ties, it is not difficult for them to abandon party government.[54] Patron-client ties can still be used to penetrate the bureaucracy—and over the long run, the military leadership itself. Since an essential point in patron-client relations is the minimization of personal risk, it is unlikely that these ties would be used to organize opposition to the regime. With the traditional political groups scattered and discredited, the modern sector of the parliamentary political constellations exiled or underground, and the EDA destroyed, there is no focus of opposition. The relative lack of organized opposition, or even sporadic protests against the regime, indicates that the majority of the Greek population is simply waiting. The regime itself has not yet faced up to the problem of developing a viable mass political apparatus; instead, it views the quiescence of the population as evidence of support.

At this point, it is difficult to forsee any threat to the military oligarchy from within the political system. If the military steps down, it is likely to do so for its own reasons. The cohesiveness of the military establishment is unclear. The junta leaders resigned from the army at an early date; however, this seems to have been more formality than anything else, for army officers still dominate the government institutions. There are several possible lines of cleavage. First, there is some rivalry among the three services. Second, sectors of the army officer corps itself may have divergent interests. Finally, there may be friction between the professional soldiers and the temporary officers and draftees.

The army gets most of the state resources that are allocated to the armed forces. The coup itself was purely an army undertaking. Before his lines of communication were cut on the morning of the coup, the king contacted units of the air force and navy. Several days passed before these services gave public indications of support for the new regime. After the junta assumed power, some leaders in the air force, the navy, and the gendarmerie were replaced. The formal subordination of these services to the army—and to lower-ranking officers, at that—is not likely to be met with favor by high-ranking naval or air-force officers. Further, the air force and navy have had more privileges and higher status than the army in the past; this is likely to be reversed. Finally, both of these services are even more dependent on foreign support than the army, especially for equipment. They are more likely to be sensitive to international opinion. The army itself would appear to be less than monolithic. Some higher officers, even though they might be in sympathy with the aims of the coup, are bound to resent being commanded by colonels; some may feel slighted at not being brought into the initial coup planning. Younger officers may feel that normal progression up the ranks will be hindered by the abnormality of junta rule, although others will be satisfied as they fill the places opened up by compulsory retirements. In the first days of the coup, eight major generals, fourteen brigadiers, and hundreds of other officers were retired,[55] including five members of the Supreme Military Council. The junta, at the outset, represented at the most only 2,000 of the 8,000 army officers.[56] Although the widespread assumption that the military was simply a tool of the monarchy and the Greek Right has proved to be incorrect, there are still elements in the military who are personally loyal to the crown. Since the coup, the junta has retired many pro-royalist officers, but there is every likelihood that this purge will not be completely successful. Moreover, these mass retirements have created a sizeable pool of disgruntled officers from which any dissident military group could draw support. Finally, there is continual speculation about the relationship of the three junta leaders to each other.

The composition of the Greek armed forces would also seem to preclude singleness of purpose. Because Greece employs universal conscription, the ranks are composed of men with all kinds of political affiliation, including leftists. The reserve officers are drawn from university graduates, and might constitute a potential weak spot. Although Greek recruits are traditionally amenable to higher directives, dissident officers leading recruits drawn from an unsympathetic population could dislocate the military organization.

Friction within the military is likely to increase if the privileged position of the military as a whole is threatened. Of course, the privileges of the entire military establishment would be curtailed if the coup leaders decided to divert resources from the military to the cultivation of support from society at large. More likely, mismanagement of the economy, combined with external pressures, could end the military's affluence by causing an internal economic crisis or the diminution of foreign military assistance. Under these conditions, quarrels over a division of available resources would threaten the existing junta; but they would probably result only in its replacement by another military group.

The longer the junta stays in control, the greater the likelihood that traditional political vices will penetrate the military itself. In fact, the traditional vices of the parliamentary level, such as nepotism and favoritism, are already evident in the appointments of the new regime. For example, the Minister of Agriculture, a former director of classical studies in a small Boeotian town, has turned out to be the brother-in-law of one of the triumvirate.[57] As stability returns, and as new influence networks are built from the population to the state apparatus, clientage may reappear in its traditional form. To the extent that the military is involved in administration, loyalties may shift from a bureaucratic organization—i.e. the armed forces as the representative of the nation—to particular individuals. The require-ments of personal security will demand a return to the system of personal ties and obligations, even though these relationships must exist in a formally nonpolitical framework. In an effort to inhibit these developments, the office of Ombudsman, directly responsible to the prime minister, was created in November 1968. Citizen complaints against the bureaucracy were to be investigated and resolved by this office. When the army intervenes in politics, it, too, becomes political, and is subject to the same strains as any other political group.

The military's renunciation of a political role does not mean the death of politics. No regime, particularly this one, is likely to have the resources to meet all the demands made of it. The fact that allocations and preferences will have to be made will alienate some citizens and make loyal partisans of others. The purge of the bureaucracy and other organizational leadership serves the same function for the military as it has for the traditional parties in the past. It, too, will create a reservoir of support. Whether the military establishment will be completely penetrated by the traditional clientage system remains to be seen. The fact that the Greek armed forces retain their purely military function and remain closely tied to the NATO alliance would seem to favor their efforts to prevent such penetration. However, whether the military leadership will decide on a "Burmese" solution, a with-drawal from the political sphere to protect its own integrity, is problemat-ical.[58]

The increased social mobilization of Greek society, with the resulting decline in patron-client ties, created demands that could not be accommo-dated by the traditional parties. In many ways these problems are even less amenable to solution by the junta. Eventually, particularly disadvantaged groups may resort to strikes, demonstrations, and other forms of direct action. The usual military response to these measures is repression. As early as May 1968, new decrees aimed at strengthening the hand of the govern-ment in case of civil disturbances were announced. A state of civil mobiliza-tion could be declared "in case of external threat to the nation's security, in case of internal trouble that may disturb the economic or social life of the country, and in any other case in which such a measure is justified as deter-mined by the cabinet."[59] These measures would subject all Greeks to war-time discipline, which would allow confiscation of property, suspension of all labor legislation, and compulsory enlistment of the population in military or educational programs. A regiment of marines, the first such troops in

Greek military history, was created and given the insignia of "21 April," the day of the coup; its job was to maintain internal security. Clearly, the regime is aware of potential threats and is prepared to meet them. However, the measures selected so far seem likely to create a "cycle of distrust," with unpredictable consequences.

Perhaps the greatest problem facing the military in charting its future course is the fact that the limited initial goals of the coup and the difficulty of selecting future ones make a return to civilian rule difficult. The coup leaders have been contradictory and vague in speaking of their future plans. After much procrastination, a new constitution was finally produced, and eventual elections are promised. The coup leaders have approved a constitutional framework that includes a provision for limiting parliamentary authority, greater executive power, a permanent electoral system, and a means "to prevent politicians from making mistakes."[60] The new constitution was approved by 92.11 per cent of the voters in a referendum of September 29, 1968. It went into effect, with "temporary suspension" of a number of articles relating to civil liberties, on November 15.[61]

Now the way is cleared for the military establishment as a whole to "return to the barracks." However, the precedent for its future involvement in politics has been set. Moreover, the present coup leaders, relying on the political support they have secured during the months of military rule, might decide to enter traditional politics. The restoration of traditional politics and the consociational system in Greece will depend on the actions of the military. However, the events of the past several years are almost certain to make the shape of this consociational system different from that existing in the past.

III. Political Recruitment

10. Socialization and the Family

This chapter and the one to follow present empirical data on the mode of recruitment to political roles in Greece. This concern serves two purposes. First, recruitment patterns can be viewed as an index of the modernization process. Ascriptive standards of eligibility and selection for political roles are especially common in systems that have not yet attained high levels of role differentiation and organization. In these systems, recruitment to the sector representing traditional powerholders—in Greece, to the parliamentary level—is especially likely to exhibit this orientation. Second, as suggested in my Introduction, the pattern of recruitment to political roles affects the maintenance and operation of the entire political system.

Political recruitment is commonly viewed as an extension of the socialization process. Lucian Pye, for example, distinguishes basic socialization, the process by which a child is inducted into the culture and introduced to social roles, from political socialization, "in which the individual becomes aware of the political world and thereby gains appreciation, judgment, and understanding of political events."[1] The process of political recruitment, in his formulation, begins when a man sheds the passive role of citizen and observer of the political process and assumes that of an active participant. The focus here is on how individuals become oriented toward political roles. However, individual orientations are only one dimension; another involves questions of eligibility and selection. Analytically, the socialization and recruitment stages in the process are distinct; but in practice, the separation of these stages is difficult, particularly in systems where the family overshadows other socializing agents and is an important factor in eligibility and selection for political roles.

SOCIALIZATION

The term "political socialization" is used to describe the process of integration into the political system. From childhood on, the socializing influences of primary and secondary groups on the individual perpetuate the culture and the structures of the political system.[2] The family (and its extension, the kinship group), the church, the school, individual occupations, the mass media, and various political institutions are all recognized as agencies of socialization. In Greece, latent socialization, primarily family influence, is most critical; manifest socialization, as exemplified by civic education in the schools, would appear to be far less important. Secondary associations, whether political or otherwise, have generally not been effective agents of socialization. National institutions, such as the schools, the military, and the mass media, have most often only confirmed or reinforced particularistic family attitudes. However, as Greek culture changes in response to the modern world, the pattern of socialization may change. Until now, however, the only constant element in modern Greek history has been the primacy of family influence.

In the lifetime of the present generation, few institutions have even competed with the family in importance. The church and the schools have had varying influence, depending on the social class and regional location of the family. However, these institutions have contributed little to forming a consensus in Greek society: the question "What is a Greek?" has been answered in conflicting terms by each. As the previous chapters illustrate, the fragmented character of Greek society both reflects and contributes to dissensus. There is a gulf between the language of the educated and that of the villager. There is a gulf between the Christianity of the villager and the faith of the urban intellectual. The civic educational content of the school system has been based on conflicting heritages, the classical and the Byzantine; and different areas of the curriculum have been argued over and changed by political factions. Since the boundaries of the Greek state have been changed repeatedly, the mental picture of what Greece should be is not the same for everyone. Every adult Greek has witnessed several varieties of parliamentary system, and also several instances of extraparliamentary rule.

For most Greeks, membership in a family is superior to that in any other group. Of those Greeks with disturbed family connections, namely, the refugees and the urban workers, only the first group has had time to produce a second generation of political age. The specific impact of public events—the struggle between the Venizelists and the royalists, World War I, the population exchanges, the Metaxas dictatorship, World War II, and the civil war—has differed among all Greek citizens, and among the deputies in our sample. The individual reaction to these public events has usually been influenced by the way they affected the family.

Political socialization implies a growing awareness and understanding of political events. A related aspect of political recruitment involves the development of individual orientations to political roles. Analytically, these two processes are distinct. Empirically, as in the data gathered for this book, they are hard to distinguish. The imprecise nature of the interview schedule is partly to blame in this particular instance; the very nature of "transitional" systems also contributed to the problem. In the transitional setting, it is simply difficult for either the respondent or the interviewer to separate the political from other roles, and to separate political interest from orientation to political roles. Roles tend to merge, and each has a political aspect. The Greek emphasis on clientage structures means that individual roles in the economic, social, and political spheres coincide. Status in one area is transferable to another. Patronage roles originating in an economic setting may be easily transferred to the political sphere. Membership in a clientage structure is itself evidence of political interest; and both patron or client inevitably direct their attention toward political roles. In the traditional setting, the patron seeks to formalize his position by acquiring the legal status of deputy.

Part of the interview schedule used with our sample of 55 Greek deputies was designed to elicit information about political socialization experiences. Deputies were asked, "How did you become interested in politics?" Table 10.1 contrasts their responses with data drawn from interviews with American state legislators.[3] In both cases, respondents usually gave more than one answer.

Of the 55 deputies in the Greek sample, 31, or 56.4 per cent, came from families with relatives active in politics. For the parliament as a whole, 40 per cent had relatives who had been active politically. Those deputies with

Table 10.1. Major Sources of Interest in Politics

Source of interest	Percentage of sample responding	
	Greece	United States (N474)
Family influence	45.5%	41.1%
Political or civic participation	30.9	54.2
Current events or conditions	54.4	26.0
Personal predispositions	63.6	47.5
Socioeconomic beliefs	5.4	8.4

active political families had responses that fell into a common pattern. Typical comments were: "All my relatives for five or six generations have been politicians." "Before me, my brother was involved in politics, and I succeeded him." "When very young, I helped my father, who was a politician; while helping him, I myself became involved and interested." "I belong to a political family." For some, family involvement with particular public events was more explicit:

My earliest recollection comes from the 1920's, when my father and uncle were exiled for their royalist political sympathies.

My family took part in the 1916 Venizelist movement in Salonika.

My father was important in local politics as one of the leading Liberals; I listened to the great Venizelos and followed the foreign policies of all the Powers. In a high school essay on "What do you want to be?" I said I wanted to be a foreign minister; the professor gave me a good grade anyway.

The importance of family as an agent of political socialization cannot be overestimated; furthermore, there is substantial evidence that this is true in more modern settings as well. The Wahlke survey found that the percentage of American lawyers with relatives in politics ranged from 41 to 59 per cent in the four states studied.[4] James Barber, in his study of Connecticut legislators, found that approximately 65 per cent had relatives interested or active in politics.[5]

These figures suggest that family influence is equally important for evoking interest in political events in both transitional and modern systems. Of the Greek deputies, only twelve mentioned a single source of political interest; of these, eight mentioned only the family. However, most deputies were also influenced by personal predispositions, events, and opportunities for participation. In both systems, socioeconomic beliefs had affected very few representatives; undoubtedly, the reasons for this are different. In the United States, the low score is probably due to the presumed consensus on these matters; in Greece, the concern with personal ties and patronage obliterates class and interest politics. The contrast in responses for the other categories seems to reflect differing social and cultural environments. In the sample of American legislators, the category of "political or civic participation" received more responses than any other; among Greek deputies, this category ranked low as a source of political interest. Undoubtedly, the low Greek response merely confirms the paucity of associational life that we have noted earlier (see Table 10.2). Similarly, many more responses from Greek

Table 10.2. Political and Nonpolitical Participation
as a Source of Political Interest

| | Percentage of sample responding | |
Type of participation	United States (N256)	Greece (N17)
Study of politics	24.2%	5.9%
Activity in school politics	9.4	—
General political work	23.4	—
Party work	24.6	—
Civic or community work	14.4	11.8
Occupational or professional activities	9.0	23.5
Ethnic and religious activities	1.2	—
Legislative lobbying	2.3	—
Politically related job	9.8	64.7

deputies fell into the classification of "events or conditions" than did those from American state legislators. Moreover, when this category is subdivided, the kinds of events and conditions stimulating the two groups turn out to be very different (see Table 10.3). There is also a substantial difference in the proportion of legislators in each system whose responses fall into the "personal predisposition" category. This category also exhibits such great differences in its subclassifications that comparison is difficult (see Table 10.4).

The fact that so few Greek deputies viewed political or civic participation as a major source of political interest is evidence of the relative underdevelopment of the Greek political infrastructure. Over half of the American legislators queried gave responses that fell into this category; moreover, these responses tended to emphasize the "organizational" categories, and that of formal study. In contrast, Greek deputies most frequently mentioned activities related to occupation. This simply reflects, once again, the transitional character of the Greek political system. There are few civic organizations in Greece. Most of the existing ones have been initiated for political ends; however, membership in these organizations tends to come after political involvement, and joining them is an explicit recognition of a political goal.

Occupation is relevant to political awareness, but few deputies mentioned it specifically as instrumental in evoking their own political interest. A journalist elected in the 1964 election said, "My profession took me in constant contact with politicians." Several men educated in the law but employed as civil servants made similar responses, as did former secretaries to

Table 10.3. Events or Conditions That Helped Develop Political Interest

United States (N123)		Greece (N30)	
Event	Percentage	Event	Percentage
Political campaigns		Civil war	33.3%
or administrations	61.8%	Local conditions	30.0
Local conditions or issues	21.1	War and occupation	20.0
War	8.9	Specific personalities	13.3
Depression	6.5	Metaxas regime	13.3
State conditions or issues	5.7	Asked to run	13.3
		Specific election campaigns	3.3
		Refugee status	3.3

political men. In one case, education and employment were tied together: "It was natural to be interested in politics because of the education I had, and because of the state job I had filled." The legal profession is particularly intimate with the political world; apparently this connection seemed so obvious that no one in the sample mentioned it specifically. The initial decision to enter the legal profession was at least partially the result of an already aroused political interest. Occupational associations, especially the cooperative movement, were responsible for some interest in politics: "In the beginning I was interested in cooperatives, not politics." By and large, the influences in this category mentioned by Greek deputies can best be viewed as a stage on the path to political office. Instead of sources of political interest, they are indications of the time and origin of a deputy's orientation to a specifically political role—i.e., of his recruitment to politics.

The responses of American legislators and Greek deputies that were coded into the category of "events and conditions important as a source of political interest" are really not comparable. However, the comparative proportions of the responses in this category as a whole are significant (see Table 10.3). A substantial number of the Greek deputies were aroused by wars, foreign occupations, and the upheavals surrounding the population exchanges of the 1920's. It is not surprising that fewer Americans would be stimulated by public events. In the American context, only electoral campaigns and elections were important, and they were a major source of political interest to only a few.

Wahlke and his associates are not very helpful in explaining the responses of American legislators in the category of "personal predispositions." According to them, the majority simply said that they had long been interested in politics and "left it at that."[6] Very few Greek deputies responded in this

Table 10.4. Personal Predisposition and Political Socialization

Predisposition	Greece (N37)	United States (N224)
Long interest	13.5%	51.3%
Ambition, desire for power	16.2	7.1
Admiration for politician	29.7	14.7
Indignation	29.7	11.6
General sense of obligation	40.5	15.6
Sense of obligation to special group	32.4	4.5
Other	8.1	6.2

vague way (see Table 10.4). In neither case is desire for power admitted as a predisposition with much frequency; although this, or "ambition," may indeed influence many to enter politics, there would appear to be much reluctance to admit the fact publicly. Proportionately more Greek deputies noted "admiration for a politician" as a factor, but this is not surprising, given the personalist character of the Greek system. Substantial differences in response do appear in the next categories: indignation, and general or specific sense of obligation. The clientage system, characteristic of Greek politics at the parliamentary level, operates on the basis of mutual obligations. In the Greek setting, "obligation" has a much more specific meaning than it does in the American context. The responses here may be more appropriately characterized as orientations to political roles, rather than simply as indicators of political socialization. Although the factors noted here cannot be called "motivations," they do seem closely connected with political careers in a way that the other major sources of interest do not.

Adult socialization appears to be more important in modern settings (see Table 10.5). Over 75 per cent of the Greek deputies had developed political interests in childhood or youth. It is perhaps more surprising that even 23.6 per cent could have escaped developing an interest in politics before adulthood, given the difficulty of separating economic and social existence from political life in Greece. In a sample of German and French elites, Lewis Edinger and Donald Searing noted that adult socialization experiences were more useful than variables associated with earlier experiences in predicting elite attitudes on certain salient political issues.[7] For Greece, a transitional country, the nature of the salient political issues would in all probability be different; in this context, variables associated with earlier political socialization might well be crucial.

For those Greek deputies who placed the awakening of political interest

Table 10.5. Time of Earliest Political Interest

Time of initial interest	Greece (N55)	United States (N421)
Childhood	43.6%	37.3%
Youth	32.7	—
Adolescence	—	14.7
College or equivalent period	—	10.7
Adult	23.6	
After college, or equivalent period	—	16.6
At entry into politics	—	20.7

at adolescence or later, the major source of political interest varied. But in general, the character of the respondent's family determined how important later agents of political socialization were likely to be. Deputies found it easy to remember that their families had introduced them to politics, and took pride in saying so.

Differences in patterns of political socialization and recruitment can also be discerned among the different groups and sectors in the Greek political system (see Table 10.6). The empirical data presented here focus on the level of traditional politics, the parliament. Since the chamber of deputies in this period did not include many left-wing members, the sample does not include a sufficient number of EDA deputies to allow more than inferences and conjectures to be drawn.

The greater number of ERE deputies noting the family as a source of influence can be attributed to the ERE's being out of power. ERE candidates with the strongest ties to their constituencies, particularly family ties, were more likely to have been reelected; the EK contingent, as the governing party, included more deputies for whom family was not as paramount. Ideology was not a very significant source of political interest. This is not

Table 10.6. Major Source of Interest in Politics, by Party Affiliation

Source of interest	Number of deputies responding			
	ERE (N17)	EK (N32)	EDA (N4)	KP (N2)
Family	11	13	–	1
Political or civic participation	5	10	1	1
Events or conditions	8	18	3	1
Personal predispositions	8	23	4	2
Socioeconomic beliefs	–	1	1	1

*Table 10.7. Time of Earliest Political Interest
Recalled by Greek Deputies, by Party Affiliation*

Time	Number of deputies responding			
	ERE (N17)	EK (N32)	EDA (N4)	KP (N2)
Childhood	9	14	–	1
Youth	3	11	3	1
Adulthood	5	7	1	1

surprising, given the low ideological content of political conflict at the parliamentary level. During the formative years of most deputies in the sample, the parties of the Left were barely significant. Only three deputies used the questions as an opportunity to justify political interest by mentioning ideological factors; one, from the EDA, mentioned his syndicalist beliefs; the other two tried to give a vague liberalism or nationalism the status of ideology.

Most politicians in Greece seemed to have become interested in politics at an earlier age than the ordinary citizen. Some differences in the time of earliest political interest appear when the deputies are separated according to party affiliation (see Table 10.7). The limited sample casts doubt on any conclusions drawn for personnel from the minor parties. However, it is interesting that three of the four EDA deputies put the time of their earliest political involvement during adolescence. This period of their lives coincided with the most severe political and economic crisis of modern Greek history. The largest percentage of deputies recalled childhood as the time of earliest political interest, again reflecting the fact that Greek deputies seem to come from families heavily involved with politics.

We have already seen that great public events have had a significant role in socialization in Greece. Thirty of the deputies interviewed gave responses that could be classified in this category; their answers are listed by party in Table 10.8.

These various events, besides evoking political interest, have promoted cleavage in the society. The upheaval of the population exchanges often pushed some Greeks, particularly refugees, into leftist politics; at the same time, the impact of the refugees caused many native Greeks to adopt right-wing views. Reactions toward General Metaxas and his authoritarian regime differed. Several of the deputies interviewed became interested in politics because they approved of events; others became politically active in order to undermine the regime.

Table 10.8. Events or Conditions That Helped Develop Political Interest

	Number of deputies responding			
Event	ERE (N8)	EK (N18)	EDA (N3)	KP (N1)
Particular campaigns	–	1	–	–
War and occupation	1	3	1	1
Civil war	4	5	–	1
Local conditions	–	7	1	1
Personalities	1	3	–	–
Asked to run	3	–	–	–
Refugee status	–	1	1	1
Metaxas regime	2	1	1	–

I took part in the 1935 movement, and also in the anti-fascist activities against Metaxas, for which I was nearly exiled.

When I was twenty, I was connected with Metaxas, and I stayed with him until his death. This relationship led me into public life.

In 1935, just after the coup d'etat, when the victors turned against the rights of the people, my conscience was revolted; and I believed that I could only work for real democracy if I became involved in politics.

The occupation and the civil war had similar effects:

I was a student during World War I, and was pro-Venizelist; after World War II, I finally took a leftist position.

I entered politics because of my activities during the occupation. I returned after the war as an island hero, and was elected mayor with 98 per cent of the vote.

My first interest in politics was at the University during the occupation; I was involved in one of the many underground groups.

The category of "asked to run" reveals some notable differences. The number of ERE deputies giving this response reflected the efforts of Papagos and Karamanlis to build up their personal component in the political groupings they led. It was easier for the governing party to recruit than it was for the opposition. The EK under Papandreou had not had such an opportunity up to the time of the interviews.

Particular personalities have had a lasting impact on Greek political life. The significant figures in modern Greek history have been controversial; they have called forth devotion from admirers and hatred from opponents. Venizelos figures in the statements of several deputies, both those in the Center political grouping and those in the Right who had Center backgrounds. There has not been a similar commanding figure for the Right. Marshal

Table 10.9. *Personal Predisposition and Political Socialization*

Predisposition	Number of deputies responding			
	ERE (N8)	EK (N23)	EDA (N4)	KP (N2)
Long interest in politics	2	3	–	–
Ambition	1	4	–	1
Admiration for a politician	2	7	1	1
Indignation	2	6	2	1
General sense of obligation	4	9	1	1
Sense of obligation to special group	–	9	3	–
Other	1	1	–	–

Papagos might fit this role, and perhaps even Karamanlis; but those who would be influenced by them have not yet entered politics. Local conditions, generally economic deprivation, were mentioned by several deputies. However, all of them had only recently entered parliamentary politics. It would seem that this response was largely a justification for political involvement, rather than the actual agency that promoted political interest. On the whole, the responses indicate that no one set of events or conditions could be isolated as crucial. Their effect depended principally on the orientation of the individual deputy and his family.

The category of personal predespositions also showed marked differences in the responses of deputies from different parties (see Table 10.9). Of those who mentioned a long interest in politics, most had a history of family political involvement. Several deputies were quite frank in viewing a political career as a prime means of advancement for an ambitious man.

Personal advancement was part of it; I was fed up with military life.

From an early age I was ambitious to enter politics and play a role in public life.

However, the material advantages of public service—a substantial tax-free salary, privileges in transportation and the importation of autos, low-cost housing loans, and other benefits—were never specifically mentioned as goals. The personalist character of Greek politics is illustrated by the substantial number who mentioned admiration for a politician. The most frequently named figure was Venizelos, but other Center leaders were mentioned as well. Neither the Left nor the Right has produced leaders with the personal appeal of those from the Center, at least in recent times.

I ran with EPEK because I admired Plastiras and felt he was a genuine democrat.

Since I was interested in democracy, I became a follower of Alexander Papa-nastasiou.

One non-Left figure mentioned several times was Metaxas. However, those mentioning him were either distant relatives or came from the same island. Certainly, his appeal was not as general as that of the Center politicians. It should be noted that the widespread shifting from one political group to another in Greece has meant that deputies in nearly every part of the political spectrum can share a common admiration for the same man.

Indignation at the activities of local or national politicians was a predisposition in several cases:

I had not intended to be involved in politics, but as a servant of the city I had a quarrel with the mayor; I thought I would punish him by being involved in politics, so I ran and was elected.

After the war I was involved in the distribution of UNRRA aid in my district; this put some politicians in a difficult position, and they started chasing me. They forced my transfer, which I refused. I resigned from my civil-service position and decided to run for office.

It is difficult to separate the genuine expressions of obligation to the public from mere rhetoric. Several deputies who entered politics after being civil servants felt that they could do more for people as politicians than as bureaucrats. In the traditional sectors of Greek politics the powerholders are politicians, not bureaucrats. This kind of response seems to reflect both Greek preferences for political solutions and the realities of the Greek bureaucratic world.

I had been aware of the problems and demands of the people since my youth, when I began to work in the city offices of my home town. I felt I could do more in politics.

I worked in the office of the president of parliament, and the injustices of all government made me believe that perhaps I could help in some way to stop injustice and to raise the standard of living.

The same sentiment was echoed by an Athenian doctor: "I had always been concerned about the poor and unfortunate in my clinic, and I felt that a politician would have the power to do something about them." In some instances, the sense of obligation, a normal feature of Greek patronage politics, was engulfed in rhetoric:

I entered politics because I felt an obligation toward the Greek people to improve the standard of living, and because of the emotion caused by the affection of the people for my brother.

I felt a need to protect suffering man. I believe that politics is a sacred activity, and not just adventure.

As a child I became upset with the condition of the poor in comparison with my own family.

Several deputies mentioned their obligations to more specific groups, although for many of them the obligation seemed to result from participation in the organization they claimed to represent.

It was through the land-reform program that I entered politics, seeking rights for the cultivators.

During my long, violent fights as president of the union, I found that there was a need in the Vouli for the straight and honest voice that would come from the working classes and pensioners.

In 1926 I was present when the police attacked a labor meeting in which laborers were asking for an improvement in their humble conditions; that has deeply influenced my future course.

It is obvious from the foregoing analysis that the political interest of Greek deputies is awakened by a wide variety of experiences. It is less easy to discover how and why an individual becomes specifically oriented to a political career. At what point does a man perceive himself in a primarily political role, and at what point does he try to institutionalize this role through formal election to the parliamentary body? The responses to one of my interview questions, "What clinched your decision to run for public office yourself?" can be used to examine this question (see Table 10.10). First, the responses here are very similar to those elicited by the questions on major sources of

Table 10.10. Reasons for Political Career at the Moment of Entrance

Reason	Number of responses	Reason	Number of responses
Service	15	Asked by politician	7
Ideals	13	"Natural"	5
Family decision	10	Personal condition	3
Special interest pressure	8	Could win	2
Community pressure	6	Hopefulness	1
		Unknown	1

political interest. This, in itself, reaffirms the difficulty of separating political roles from others. As the vague categories of "ideals" and "service" indicate, some deputies had difficulty in pinpointing a particular time for the final decision. Some deputies ran because they were asked either by the party chief—at least this was the claim—or by the local party committee. However, not all requests came directly from the party; for example:

My compatriots were pressing me to run because the island of Syros had not had a spokesman in the Vouli for the last twelve years.

I was persuaded to enter politics by my present and former townsmen, who urged me to run even though I didn't know anything about the demands and interests of the people.

I was asked to run because it was felt that an engineer, with his knowledge of the more technical problems, was needed to offset the great number of lawyers.

For the rest, the decision to run for office was made because of a temporary condition, such as the imminence of an election, the availability of a place on the list, or the odds of success.

There was no trouble getting on the list because my family was part of the founding group of the Populist Party.

My standing for election was obligatory: since my brother had died, I had to stand in his place.

I decided to run for office in 1958 because I was assured of winning in a walk.

I ran because of the pressure of friends; they didn't want to be without a patron.

For many, political interest turned to active involvement only when one of these factors was present.

The responses of deputies from political groups that confined their activities to the parliamentary level were not significantly different. The variations in socialization patterns that did emerge centered on the importance of the family in the total process of political socialization. For some deputies, particularly those from families heavily involved in politics, family influence was predominant, and other experiences only reinforced it. Deputies coming from less political families were more affected by other kinds of socialization. The prevalence of either type of socialization pattern in the groups at the parliamentary level depended on the results of the previous election. More deputies from the out party tended to have socialization patterns emphasizing family influence, whereas the political group controlling the parliamentary institutions contained many deputies who had been influenced by other factors.

The sample for this survey was drawn from the traditional political milieu. The small number of EDA representatives included does not justify definitive statements about the attitudes of that entire organization. However, it is likely that the backgrounds of men attracted to a highly organized and ideologically oriented left-wing political group like the EDA would differ from the backgrounds of those in the traditional parliamentary groups. The limited evidence of the survey does provide some clues. None of the four EDA deputies named the family as a major source of political interest or mentioned childhood as the time of their earliest political interest. Dissatisfaction with the political system and a sense of obligation enunciated specifically in class terms were the major ingredients of their personal predispositions; other deputies, when they were dissatisfied at all, were usually indignant about specific minor events. Several groups in Greek society, refugees and urban labor in particular, are largely without clientage ties to the political system, and may be expected to be frustrated and dissatisfied with the traditional political groups. This would increase support for the EDA, and would probably create other groups ready to organize "combative" parties. In that event, adult experience and political indoctrination by the party would produce many more politicians whose socialization differs from that of the traditional political groups.

It is unclear whether the EDA deputies in the sample came to their beliefs because of their family situations or because they opposed family beliefs. In other words, it is not known whether their frustration came from the failure of the political system to meet specific demands. It is possible that dissatisfaction with the existing system could be transmitted through the family group, just as the more traditional political attitudes are transmitted in other Greek families. This dissatisfaction would surely be reinforced by the widespread discrimination against Greeks with leftist backgrounds.

Since this was a parliamentary survey, there are no responses from another major group, the professional military establishment. However, the importance of the family in socialization would almost certainly diminish with military education and adult experience in the military organization. The professional officer corps, unlike any other institution in contemporary Greece, is "total"; a cadet is separated from his family and from other nonmilitary groups at a relatively early age. Moreover, life in the military, unlike that in other work or social situations in Greek society, does not reinforce family influence and the relationships that extend from the family. The military is a part of Greek society not especially bothered by scarcity of resources; and its formal hierarchy is not dominated by family groups and clientage ties. One would expect professional military men to have different political attitudes and different perceptions of politics.

The varying importance of the family and of secondary structures illustrates the forces behind the dissensus in Greek society. It also indicates how different "communities" in Greece are perpetuated by the socialization process. In the traditional sector, family influence overwhelms secondary influences; in the more modern sectors, secondary influence is more significant. In Greece one's family exerts the greatest single influence on political socialization and recruitment, and we must examine its effects more closely.

FAMILY BACKGROUND

There has been a seeming resurgence of political dynasties in the United States and in other countries with democratic institutions.[8] However, inherited political position is generally associated with traditional political systems—with those societies in which ascriptive criteria, particularly family ties, have been used as qualifications for positions in modern representative institutions. Sir Lewis Namier, in his study of eighteenth-century British politics, divides a category of "predestined Parliament men" into "members of political families, born to hunt with certain parliamentary packs," and "country gentlemen with seats for heirlooms."[9] According to his data, only one-quarter of the members of the parliament elected in 1761 had no family connections.[10] In contrast, Austin Ranny, investigating political recruitment in contemporary Britain, notes a category of "hereditary seats" among Conservative constituencies, but does not suggest that they are a very high proportion of the total.[11] This category was apparently completely absent in Labour constituencies.

Mattei Dogan, in his extensive study of deputies in the Third and Fourth French Republics, also touches on the matter of political inheritance.[12] He found that about 100 of the 4,892 members during those periods were the sons of great political families dating from the Monarchy or the Empire; in addition, there were more than 300 provincial notables, who inherited a particular parliamentary seat as part of the famliy fortune. The first type of inheritance was common in the early years of the Third Republic; the second was significant throughout the Third Republic, but declined progressively after 1900.[13] The United States House of Representatives also contained a substantial membership drawn from families with traditions of officeholding in its early years, but the proportion has steadily dropped from that time to the present.[14] These data suggest that political inheritance is most common in societies with limited role differentiation. There, elite groups are not separate; political power, economic power, and social prestige tend to "agglomerate." However, as such a society becomes more complex, roles are increasingly differentiated, and the direct inheritance of political position becomes less common.

In the Greek setting, the actual inheritance of political position is common. At the national level, leadership in several major political groupings has passed from father to son or from relative to relative.[15] At the parliamentary level, a significant number of deputies have come from families with histories of political involvement. It seems likely that the networks of political influence at the provincial and local levels have similar family components.

Family and Parliamentary Position

In preparing this study, I examined the family backgrounds of deputies in selected past parliaments, as well as the family connections of those deputies selected for interviews from the 1964 parliament. The data on deputies from the earlier parliaments (1946 and 1958) came from published sources, parliamentary personnel records, and electoral lists. In each parliament examined, a large percentage of deputies had relatives in politics: 32.2 per cent in 1946, 34.6 per cent in 1958, and 40 per cent in 1964. Relationships were relatively easy to trace when political office passed from father to son; however, caution was necessary in ascribing relationship in other cases. Except for a few instances, it was impossible to be certain whether or not political backgrounds existed in the maternal line. This problem was avoided in the 1964 sample. In this group, 31 of the 55, or 56.4 per cent, noted that they had relatives who had been or were currently active in political life. The higher incidence is due primarily to the fact that information on political activity in the maternal line was available; this may also account for the higher percentage figure in the total 1964 parliament.

A high incidence of representatives drawn from political families active in politics is not in itself unusual. For example, among the Connecticut legislators studied by James Barber, some 63 per cent had relatives active in politics.[16] John Wahlke and his associates, surveying four American state legislatures, found that from 41 to 59 per cent of the members had politically involved families.[17] Since the level of differentiation is higher in these American states than in Greece, some further distinctions in the nature of "family political involvement" must be made. Dogan, after noting the different types of direct political inheritance, suggests that there can also be inheritance of a "social-psychological" nature, an inclination for politics that is produced by the socialization experience.[18] In this type of inheritance, the family may or may not have held offices directly; but the only advantage gained by the son, aside from an early interest in politics, is a name familiar to the electorate. Dogan classified about 750 of the 4,892 French deputies he studied in this category; about half of them also had relatives involved in politics at the parliamentary level.[19] The American data does not distinguish this form of inheritance, and is probably similar to the Greek data for this reason.

In modern settings, which have many alternative career opportunities, it seems likely that an individual could indeed "inherit" an interest in politics, and perhaps even a useful political name; however, an office would rarely pass from one family member to the next. Dogan notes in passing that this inheritance of inclination is renewed with each generation. Inheritance in the Greek context is more likely to involve an actual political position. There are few career opportunities in Greece, and political office itself is often the basis of family status and fortune. Family political activity implies office-holding—using office to secure favors for clients and using the votes of clients to secure office. For the most part, the results obtained in this study reflect direct inheritance, in which parliamentary seats have remained in the hands of one family or a small group of families.

In Greece, there seems to be little correlation between family political background and many of the variables that might be used as indicators of economic underdevelopment or of "traditional" cultural norms. In scattered areas, a high incidence of deputies from political families does seem related to social conservatism as indicated by high birth rates, a higher percentage of boys than girls in school, and illiteracy. In other places, mechanized agriculture or substantial industrial employment is associated with a decline in the number of deputies claiming family political backgrounds. But there is no uniform pattern. The indicators themselves depend on geographical factors, the complicated demographic history of modern Greece, and the varying regional cultural patterns. The usual indices of modernization do not explain the persistence of political inheritance in Greece.

Table 10.11 illustrates the regional differences in parliamentary recruitment from political families. Overall, there has been a gradual increase in the percentage of deputies coming from political families since 1946. It is difficult to explain this by correlating the results with socioeconomic variables. In some regions, such as Macedonia and Thrace, second-generation

*Table 10.11. Deputies from Political Families, by Percentage of
Regional Parliamentary Delegation*

Region	Parliament		
	1946	1958	1964
Athens-Piraeus	29.2%	32.5%	35.3%
Old Greece	34.1	34.3	40.0
Peloponnesus	44.8	51.0	63.6
Ionian Islands	54.5	45.4	44.4
Thessaly	44.8	45.8	50.0
Macedonia	14.4	18.6	22.0
Epirus	42.1	33.3	35.6
Crete	52.4	61.1	47.4
Aegean Islands	25.0	22.2	31.2
Cyclades	50.0	66.7	80.0
Thrace	5.9	7.1	30.8
Average	32.2	34.6	40.0

politicians have begun to appear only recently, since these regions had little opportunity for elective politics before their acquisition by the Greek kingdom. The most striking difference in family background is between the older parts of the kingdom and the new territories. There is also a significant difference between areas of great population gain such as Athens-Piraeus, and regions of population loss, such as the Cyclades. Basically, family background is less important in urban areas and in areas with substantial refugee resettlement. The type of patron-client relationship that characterizes the rest of Greece is not as common in these places. Moreover, the demands of the population in cities and in the areas of the greatest rural mobilization are harder to satisfy on an individual basis.

The use of family political involvement as an index of modernity needs to be qualified. First, the character of the traditional social structure is important. In the Greek case, the predominance of clientage relationships, even in the modern sectors of society, can account in part for the high incidence of inherited political position. In the Philippines, where similar clientage networks exist, direct political inheritance is also found. However, according to Jean Grossholtz, the practice of grooming someone from outside the family for office is more prominent.[20] Second, the manner in which parliamentary institutions are established in developing states may be critical. In Ceylon, many members of the parliament that was set up after independence came from families of traditional officeholders.[21] The uneventful transition from colonial status to independence allowed the older elites to secure new positions. However, in Ireland, where the independence struggle upset many traditional relationships, few Dáil members from 1920 to 1948 had family connections with the older political elite. Only 32 of the 518 members during this period inherited their seats directly; 12 of these were women elected in place of deceased male relatives.[22] Now, since the revolutionary generation has largely disappeared, more of the representatives may be inheriting their positions. Finally, the status of parliamentary office itself may be important. If this office is useful in maintaining family status in a constituency or personal status in society, particularly in a setting where opportunities are limited, political positions may be treated as family property. Beyond this, the electoral system may favor a party with strength in the areas where political inheritance is most common. This list of factors is meant to be suggestive, not exhaustive. Although inheritance of political position may be related to the process of modernization, many other intervening variables must be considered before it can be used as a reliable index of modernity.

Family and Initial Advantage

A Greek born into a political family automatically has an earlier awareness of politics through the normal process of socialization. When he comes of age, he is likely to have more specific advantages. In most cases, he will not have to create a network of clients by himself, but can use the organization already established by other members of his family. A candidate without this background will probably have to spend time in another occupation while he constructs his own political network. The man with political relatives will be more likely to receive a place on the ticket of the dominant political grouping in his area; he will not have to be content with minor party labels, since he will not have to develop and demonstrate his political capabilities.

Table 10.12. Family Connections and Age

Year	Age at entry			Age at election		
	With relatives	No relatives	Differ-ence	With relatives	No relatives	Differ-ence
1946 (N354)	38.8 yr.	33.4 yr.	−5.4 yr.	40.0 yr.	36.2 yr.	−3.8 yr.
1958 (N300)	36.8	41.3	4.5	41.1	46.7	3.6
1964 (N300)	36.6	40.4	3.8	40.3	45.8	5.5

Table 10.13. *Age Advantage of Deputies with Political Relatives, by Party Affiliation*

	1946		1958		1964	
Party	Entry	Election	Entry	Election	Entry	Election
Mainstream Right						
LK	2.9 yr.	5.8 yr.	–	–	–	–
ERE	–	–	4.7 yr.	2.1 yr.	7.3 yr.	8.5 yr.
Minor Right						
EPK	5.2	4.4	–	–	–	–
KP	–	–	–	–	−0.8	0.5
Mainstream Center						
PK	−6.8	−2.9	2.7	5.6	–	–
VenPK	4.5	2.2	–	–	–	–
EK	–	–	–	–	1.7	5.4
Minor Center						
EKE	2.8	7.3	–	–	–	–
SD	−0.2	0.8	–	–	–	–
PADE	–	–	3.0	9.0	–	–
Left						
EDA	–	–	6.2	5.7	4.7	11.7

Men from political families are more likely to enter politics at an earlier age, and to win elections at an earlier age, than other Greeks (see Table 10.12). In 1958 and 1964 deputies with political backgrounds had a pronounced advantage in both respects. (The figures for 1946 are unreliable because there were 43 deputies with relatives in politics for whom no entry age could be determined.) The same advantage existed in all but one minor political party, as shown in Table 10.13. The extreme advantage in the EDA figures for 1964 reflects advantages gained by early political awareness because of birth into a political family rather than a use of family connections. Table 10.14 considers only those who were victorious on their first try for

Table 10.14. *Average Age of Those Winning Elections on First Attempt*

	Age		Differ-
Parliament	With relatives	No relatives	ence
1946	40.8 yr. (N66)	43.0 yr. (N118)	2.2 yr.
1958	38.8 (N52)	44.2 (N86)	5.4
1964	37.7 (N54)	42.9 (N67)	5.2

parliamentary office. In all three parliaments those with family backgrounds had a slight edge.

Family and Political Party

Party affiliation is not particularly related to any family political background, except in the instance of a particular type of minor party. The minor parties that originate outside parliament most often have only a small family component. Generally, candidates are attracted to these parties because they have no family connections to facilitate entry into the major parties, or because they have ties of loyalty to the founder of the party. However, splinter groups that form in parliament and masquerade as separate parties at election time tend to be made up of deputies with long tenure, secure political bases, and substantial family connections.

The varying percentage of those with family political backgrounds in a given parliamentary delegation is related to that delegation's status as a governing party or a nongoverning party. The regional makeup of the party is also important. In general, a nongoverning major party seems to have a higher percentage of deputies with family connections. Family links are apparently more durable than those forged by other means, and the deputy with a family political background is less subject to sudden political upheavals (see Table 10.15). In 1964, when it was out of power, the ERE had a larger family component than in 1958; the reverse was true for the EK and its predecessor, the Liberals (PK). The PADE and ELK of 1958 were parliamentary splinters with a high family component. The KP in 1964 was a party largely outside the parliament. The 1946 distribution is more difficult

Table 10.15. Deputies from Political Families, by Party Affiliation

1946		1958		1964	
Party	Percentage	Party	Percentage	Party	Percentage
LK	50.0%	ERE	34.9%	ERE	47.0%
EPK	24.2	ELK	100.0	KP	20.0
EKE	27.8	PADE	40.0	EK	38.9
PK	24.4	PK	47.2	EDA	21.7
VenPK	56.5	EDA	27.8		
SD	30.4				
Minor	52.6				

Note: The parties for each parliament are listed in the approximate order of their self-assessed positions on the Right-Left spectrum.

to interpret, largely because the Metaxas period and the war, occupation, and civil war had broken up many traditional political networks. The high family component in the Populist Party (LK) was probably due to its regional base in the Peloponnesus. The Venizelist Liberals (Ven Phil) were the Cretan section of the prewar Liberal Party. These two political organizations represented the core of the prewar political groups. The other political organizations in 1946 were largely factions of the other two major groups. In order to present tickets in all constituencies, they simply took anyone who was willing to join the list. The contrast between the EDA and the major party groups is instructive. Although many EDA deputies did have family connections, they represented a much smaller percentage of their party.

Although the family component of the parties varies considerably from the Right to the Left and from major to minor political groups, being born into a political family is advantageous regardless of party affiliation. The individual politician is born into a political milieu; he takes his place in a particular network of influence, which may include both family clients in the local area and patrons in the capital. Usually, he will enter one of the major political groups, where his background can give him the greatest advantage (see Tables 10.12–10.14). As a result, the core of each major political group is composed of firmly entrenched deputies with substantial family connections and personal clientage networks. The minor groups are usually ephemeral, whereas the major groups continue despite changes in party names and hangers-on.

Surprisingly, family political background is more useful to left-wing candidates than to those from most other political groups, in terms of both age at entry into politics and age at election. The early introduction to politics in political families would account for some of the advantage. The frustrations and dissatisfactions that have made left-wing politics attractive may become apparent only in middle age. Perhaps more important, the EDA selects "typical" members of lower social groups as candidates. These are usually men with substantial local party experience and strong local ties, who are put on the electoral list largely for appearance. Occasionally, if the major political groups splinter, they are elected to parliament. But the core of the parliamentary delegation consists of party professionals.

As might be expected in a country characterized by personalist and ephemeral party groupings, party affiliation is given little credit for electoral victory but takes most of the blame for defeat. The 55 deputies in our sample were asked about the causes of their success or failure when they first ran;

Table 10.16. Deputies' Reasons for Success or Failure on First Candidature

Reasons for success (N23)	Responses	Reasons for Failure (N32)	Responses
Personal factors and qualities	5	Party affiliation	18
Respect of people, service	10	Youth	2
Family influence	7	Insufficient preparation	6
Party affiliation	3	Fraud	2
No answer	1	No answer	8

Note: Several deputies gave more than one reason.

their answers are summarized in Table 10.16. Personal character, respect from the voters, and family connections are given as the principal reasons for victory.* However, defeat is rarely ascribed to personal deficiencies. Since the party as an organization does little to help the individual candidates, it is not surprising that the deputies credit their personal victory to their own efforts and organizations. In most cases, a deputy considers that his personal qualities and his connections in his constituency are constant regardless of party label; if defeat comes, it must be because his party has allowed itself to be undercut by the electoral system or has become associated with inaction or maladministartion in the minds of the voters. In general, electoral defeat was assumed to mean that the candidate's personal qualities and organization did not outweigh the party albatross. None of these deputies considered the increasing number of voters outside the traditional clientage networks, who are more likely to vote on the basis of party leadership than on the basis of personal characteristics.

Family and Political Career

Once a Greek's political career has commenced, does his family, region of origin, or party aid in that career? The advantages connected with a family political background appear to be most important in beginning a political career; and Table 10.17 indicates that the "success ratio" (the number of times the candidate won divided by the number of times he ran) still favors those with relatives involved in politics. However, the differences between those with relatives and those without are not great. It would seem that once a deputy is elected, his new position compensates for family advantage. The figures for 1958 are heavily influenced by the abnormal victory of the EDA.

* Barber (in *The Lawmakers*) obtained responses to a similar question from Connecticut legislators. According to his separate figures for the four legislative types he delineates, only 12.5 per cent of these men attributed their election to their own efforts.

Table 10.17. Success and Family Political Background

Year	Success Ratios		
	.101–.400	.401–.700	.701–1.00
1958			
With relatives (N99)	16.1%	33.4%	50.5%
No relatives (N155)	21.2	49.6	29.1
1964			
With relatives (N119)	15.1	33.6	51.2
No relatives (N178)	24.7	33.1	42.2

Note: Does not include deputies winning the first time they were candidates.

In this instance many regular Left candidates won, largely because of the splintering of the Center. The importance in that year of the difference between the "success ratio" of those with family and those without family is unusual. The 1964 data are the more representative.

For the traditional sectors of Greek society, family is always important. The deputy with family political ties and personal clients is most likely to be an important figure in the Greek parliament and in the major political groups. His policy or issue orientation is usually minimal, and he concentrates on the satisfaction of unaggregated individual demands. However, family connections are not the only aid to forming these ties, or to political success in general. As we shall see in the next chapter, certain occupational backgrounds provide similar advantages.

11. Occupational Backgrounds and Local Connections

The fact that certain occupations lend themselves to political activity more than others is well established. An occupation that involves public contact, flexibility in the time and place of work, and relatively high status in the society is more likely to be selected by a person with political ambition, and it is more likely to inspire that ambition in the first place. However, other factors also seem to be relevant in determining the prevalence of particular occupational categories in the representative institutions of a given political system.

Data on the distribution of parliamentarians among occupational categories are available for many political systems, but comparisons are difficult. The general categories useful for analysis in one political system seldom fit the others. Different analysts may make distinctions in terms of intellectual and nonintellectual occupations, public and private affiliations, or amateur and professional status.[1] One fact seems clear: there is now a growing tendency for political systems to represent group interests rather than those of individuals. This is reflected in a changing distribution of deputies among the different occupational categories. Perhaps most striking is the rise in importance of pure political types—party or trade-union officials and specialists representing particular subject areas.

In general, the appropriateness of a given occupation to a political career in a particular system must be examined on three levels. First, practical considerations will intervene. Does the occupation facilitate a political career in terms of time and place of work, or in terms of useful skills? Is it useful for gaining support or recognition in the constituency, so that nomination can be secured? Finally, does it contribute to a successful performance of one's role in the parliamentary setting? These three dimensions, analytically separate but empirically muddled, are all likely to be considered by the ambitious man seeking political position, and by the voters as well.

One of the major factors influencing the pattern of political recruitment, particularly when it is considered in terms of occupation, is the degree of social and economic differentiation in the society. Differentiation is often related to the organizational complexity of political parties and other groups with specific economic and social interests. The very existence of party organizations, whatever their nature, has several consequences for political recruitment in general and for the utility of specific occupations in the process. A party must draw support from some part of the population, and must cater to the wishes of its supporters. The presence or absence of groups representing particular social or economic interests often determines the party's choice in these matters. Sometimes a particular interest group (for example, a trade union) may have extremely close ties to a party; in these cases, the pattern of party recruitment may reflect the common occupation of the supporting group.

Economic and social differentiation may be uneven within a given country; and the modes of organization, membership structures, and bases of support of different political groups may differ also. Parties with little organization are generally forced to seek candidates with some previous status in individual constituencies. Highly organized "modern" parties can select candidates without considering occupation and status, since the attributes of an individual candidate will often be less important to the voters than the party label he carries. If a party maintains a staff of professionals and depends on its formal members to handle volunteer organizational work, it may prefer to select candidates from its own cadre. However, if a party depends primarily on specific groups for support, it may be forced to include those groups in the nominating process. Finally the competition between parties may influence the type of candidates selected.

A change in economic or social differentiation in the society can easily change the status and political utility of specific occupations. At one time local notables may be accorded the highest social status and have a great effect on politics. Later, they may be replaced by entrepreneurs or merchants —who may give way, in turn, to professional politicians representing the managerial class in business or trade unions. In some settings, particular occupations may be crucial to politics, and hence to a political career, whereas in other settings they are not. For example, in France during the Third Republic journalists were crucial; this does not seem to have been the case elsewhere.[2] Teachers have been important in France and Italy, but they have been idenitfied with a different political group in each country.[3] Lawyers have dominated some settings—France, Italy, and the United States, for example—but have not been as important in Germany or Britain.[4] Some occupations are more adaptable than others. For example, lawyers, because of the instrumental character of their profession, can easily adjust to new levels of differentiation; they can defend traditional peasant interests and modern group interests equally well. This is true, to a lesser extent, of other intellectual occupations. However, it must also be recognized that recruitment to repersentative institutions from particular occupational categories may be maintained simply because of tradition and habit.

The electoral system, both the nominating procedures and the regulations surrounding the final choice, may affect political recruitment. The territorial size of a constituency and the number of individuals selected from it, as well as the particular method of selection, can also be important. For example, Benjamin Akzin argues that in Israel, which has a proportional representation system using the whole nation as a single constituency, candidates have little contact with individual voters and must rely on group ties.[5] On the other hand, Gerhard Loewenberg suggests that the recent slight rise in the number of lawyers in the German Bundestag may be attributed to the adoption of the single-member constituency, in which lawyers, as the chief local notables, have a better chance.[6] However, he observes that the German electorate is particularly responsive to candidates representing particular groups. Similarly, many members of the British parliament, particularly on the Labour side, are closely associated with group interests.[7]

Certain institutional features in a political system can have important consequences. For example, if the financial remuneration of a representative is slight, candidates must either be recruited from the wealthier sectors of the population or be supported by organized groups. Laws permitting parliamentarians to hold other public offices, either elective or administrative, influence the career choices of ambitious men, and thus affect the distribution of deputies across occupational categories. The number of career opportunities in the legislative setting itself may also be important. In addition, there is the question of where a parliamentary career may lead. Is the acquisition of a seat the climax of a career, or does it lead to higher office in the executive branches of government? In Britain there are many opportunities for members of the majority party when a government is formed. By contrast, there are very few such openings in the German system; as a result, the more ambitious persons may prefer to make a career in administration or in politics at the state level.[8] Mattei Dogan notes that many of the major political personalities in the Third French Republic were not found in the parliament.[9]

Another major factor in recruitment is the role and status of the legislature in the political system as a whole. In part, the status of a parliamentary career depends on its perceived importance in the system. If central bureaucratic structures are developed before a representative body exists, the role of the legislature as a policy-making body or as a defender of the individual against the state machinery may be less than if the developmental sequence had been reversed. For example, the lack of importance of the German Reichstag in the nineteenth century made it a poor career choice for ambitious citizens.[10] The substantial number of public officials in the Reichstag, and later in the Bundestag, as well as the large number of ex-officials in the Japanese Diet, may be related to the common perception of these institutions as outgrowths of the bureaucratic structures.[11] The decline of the legislatures noted in the last several decades may mean that positions of power outside the formal representative institutions, or even outside the government itself, have become more attractive. In some cases, where the representative institutions are viewed by the powerholders primarily as instruments for ratification and real power lies elsewhere, a broad spectrum of occupational categories may be recruited.

Representation refers to the processes through which representatives are chosen. Implicit in this concept is the suggestion that the manner of choosing representatives will influence the character of legislative decisions. In modern legislative bodies, the crucial question seems to center on whether group representation is considered legitimate, or conversely, whether individual demands for favors ought to be processed by legislators. Ultimately, the role and status of representative bodies, as perceived by the legislator and the public alike, may depend on the limits imposed by other sectors of the political system, and on the complexity of the society. In a complex society, characterized by "modern" political parties and well-defined and organized group interests, deputies may do little more than handle grievances from individual constituents, provided that group interests can be served by direct ties to the bureaucracy. If the bureaucratic structures are relatively immune to group penetration, individual deputies drawn from specific occupational categories may be needed. In a system where groups are poorly organized, the individual deputy may act primarily as a defender of individual interests against the state; in this case, a "professional" occupation may be most desirable. Most societies combine group and individual representation. Some groups will have ties to the bureaucracy, and others will not. Similarly, some individual demands may be handled by the bureaucrats, and others by representatives.

The relevance of particular occupational categories to politics sometimes depends on the functional relation of the political sphere to the society itself. If conflicts arising elsewhere in the social system are usually settled at the political level, more attention will be given to group representation. On the other hand, if politics are not important in the everyday life of the people, the occupational category from which a representative is drawn may make little difference. The resolution of conflicts between groups may call for different occupational specialties at the political level than the resolution of conflicts between specific groups and the state.

In Greece, most politicians are still recruited from the traditional "intellectual" occupations, particularly the law. This pattern is also found in similar settings elsewhere. Tarrow observes that representatives from southern Italy continue to be drawn from the traditional professions, despite changes in the character of representation elsewhere in Italy.[12] In Turkey, once the modernizing elite gave way, and once managed indirect elections were replaced by popular elections in a competitive political setting, lawyers and other professional men began to replace those with "official" occupations.[13] These data, as well as those to follow, indicate that particular occupations are more appropriate for representation at certain stages of differentiation, although the intervening variables in any given system may be crucial.[14]

TRADITIONAL OCCUPATIONS

The occupations most heavily represented in the Greek parliament have always been those with the highest traditional status. Under Turkish rule, a man's status in the community depended mostly on his relationship to the Ottoman authority, and this often depended on landholding. Although Greeks of all classes sought to possess land, no real landholding aristocracy developed; and after 1911, Greece had few large estates.[15] In part, the principle of state distribution of the public domain, the inheritance and dowry requirements, and the topography of the country discouraged the accumulation of land. In addition, the models of Greek civilization, whether classical or Byzantine, have been urban; there has been no tradition of the gentleman retiring to his country estate.[16]

The state structure of Greece was modeled on that of Western European states. Education, not landholding, became the mark of prestige and power; and after the University of Athens was established, the sons of the revolutionary elite were channeled into the professions, particularly the law. The educated man was admired because he alone was qualified for employment in the new state structure. He had power not only because he himself could attain official status, but because only an educated man had access to the equally educated men in the bureaucracy. In this way, the traditions of clientage and mutual obligation could be continued. In return for favors gained through state intervention, the rural Greek provided political support, which his patron used for personal advancement. Almost at once, the parliament came to be regarded as the major political institution—the goal of ambitious men.*

For much of Greek history, the only "professional" occupations were medicine and the law. These were admirably suited to traditional social structures because in each case the economic role merged into the political one. The stream of professionals produced by the University of Athens reached a flood stage just as the state administration began to extend into the countryside. The peasantry then needed patrons with new skills, and the new class of professionals needed support in order to attain political position in the society. The low degree of economic and social differentiation in Greek society has maintained the political importance of these traditional occupational categories into the present. The small size of the country, the failure of party organization, and the absence of group activity—all related in some way to this major factor—have inhibited the development of other avenues to a political career.

There are a number of excellent reasons for the widespread predominance of lawyers in representative bodies. Training in the law provides familiarity with the political and administrative processes of the state. It encourages the development of verbal skills, and provides practice in negotiation, compromise, and intercession. The law, as an instrumental profession, can serve the interests of individuals, specific groups, or social classes with equal ease; and the lawyer can be a protagonist of nearly every ideology, since his occupation is not grounded in any. In Greece, as elsewhere, a lawyer can leave his profession to enter politics, or can advantageously combine politics and the law.

---

* Cf. Grossholtz p. 238. The Greek pattern of political development in rural areas differs from that found by Grossholtz in the Philippines. She suggests that before World War II Filipino landlords controlled the peasantry through economic and social relationships. These were disrupted by the war, and by the rise of an entrepreneurial class. The entire social structure of the countryside was weakened, and the politicians stepped in. The Greek peasant was aware of his government earlier, and Greek politicians were in large measure drawn from the rural notables.

The nature of Greece's society and governmental structure give the Greek lawyer still more political advantages. The cultural importance of bargaining and negotiation in Greece, especially in dealings with authority, creates the need for an intermediary, a role the lawyer is superbly suited for. The lawyer, by virtue of his profession, has the skills necessary to create a political following. Moreover, his skills are needed at the national political level, as well as in the local setting. On the local level, lawyers are indispensable because they are concerned with the same matters of "kinship manipulation, petty favors, and land disputes" as their counterparts in southern Italy.[17] The lawyer, by virtue of his education alone, is likely to be a man of stature in the community; he will have social and professional contacts with provincial officials and other community leaders. A peasant, when searching for a *kumbaros*, would be likely to pick such a man.

Greek law is encumbered with many details and exceptions; an administrator must make constant decisions on which classificatory scheme is to be used, which method of computation to employ, and which of the multitude of provisions to enforce in a given case. This complexity, as well as the Greek tendency to concentrate all decision-making power at the top of the bureaucratic hierarchy, makes it necessary for the ordinary Greek to find someone who can speed up the administrative process and influence the decision to his advantage. A lawyer, because of his status, can bypass the crowd of lesser clerks present in most governmental offices. Since he often has a personal retinue of clients and friends, he can usually offer political aid to a deputy or a local official. He may be able to advise the provincial officials on their own legal problems, in return for administrative favors. Because he is of the same social status as the officials with whom he must deal, there are many informal occasions on which he can plead the causes of his clients; if favorable decisions are not made because of interest in the problems of the client, they may be made out of friendship for the lawyer.

It is difficult to determine precisely how many of the deputies in the parliaments considered in Table 11.1 actually practiced law and how many merely took a law degree before entering another occupation. In many respects the faculty of law in each of the two Greek universities corresponds to the generalized liberal arts curricula in the United States; it is the normal school for a young person to enter. Jurisprudence is commonly regarded as the key to advancement in the society. However, although the profession of law has more prestige than trade or business, it is overcrowded and poorly paid. Many deputies who have never practiced law may classify themselves

Table 11.1. Occupational Distribution in Four Greek Parliaments

Occupation	1936 (N300)	1946 (N354)	1958 (N300)	1964 (N300)
Professional				
Academic	0.7%	1.7%	4.3%	4.3%
Engineer	0.3	1.1	1.7	2.0
Journalist	3.7	3.1	5.3	5.7
Lawyer	45.6	50.8	40.0	40.3
Medical	11.3	15.2	12.7	10.7
Other technical	—	—	—	1.3
Politician	4.0	1.7	4.0	3.0
Official				
Civil servant	1.3	2.8	6.7	5.7
Military	8.0	7.6	5.7	6.7
Economic				
Banker	—	—	—	0.3
Businessman	3.3	2.5	5.3	4.7
Farmer	1.6	1.4	3.0	2.3
Industrialist	1.3	2.5	1.3	1.7
Landowner	2.3	3.1	2.3	1.3
Merchant	4.0	4.0	0.7	2.3
Shipowner	—	—	—	0.7
Unclassified				
Employee	4.0	1.7	4.7	3.0
Other	0.3	—	0.3	1.0
Unknown	8.3	0.6	2.0	3.0

Note: These figures were computed from deputies' responses to a question on their personnel records in the parliament. In some cases a deputy changed his occupation from one parliament to the next.

as lawyers to gain prestige, though actually having been engaged in other occupations. Law students also enter the civil service in great numbers. Here again, a deputy with a bureaucratic background often prefers to put law as his profession in the parliamentary records.

Although law is the most favored background for Greek politics, medical men are highly respected. The mere practice of their profession can create obligations that may be used politically; and the opportunities for a doctor to build a loyal clientele, especially in the rural areas, are second only to those of the provincial lawyer. Greek doctors, and even dentists, are admired for their education, and their high social status puts them on a par with provincial notables and gives them the same advantage that lawyers have in seeking favors. Most young doctors are reluctant to set up a practice in the rural areas because of the primitive facilities and because they prefer urban life. But even in Athens some doctors are able to acquire supporters from the provinces by treating villagers in their Athenian clinics—especially villagers from their home provinces. For the villagers, the clinic becomes a friendly place in the big city, and many of them may receive free medical care; naturally enough, the doctor is soon regarded as a patron.

Professional occupations may dominate the political scene in Greece, but there are some opportunities for those with other backgrounds. At certain times in Greek history the line between a military career and a political one was not sharply drawn. However, in recent years, military men have been required to resign from the armed forces before embarking on a parliamentary career. Retired officers in parliament occasionally express a military point of view, but they do not explicitly represent military interests. In several cases war heroes have retired from active service and entered the political arena, generally in the metropolitan constituencies. Military figures without this national renown may still have enough prestige to be relatively successful in rural politics. Moreover, there are some opportunities for the incumbents of particular military positions to build civilian clienteles if they desire to do so. The Greek use of universal military service means that nearly every family generates requests for deferments and transfers. Also, the Greek equivalent of the United States Army Corps of Engineers has a role in the construction of public works similar to that of its American counterpart, and this role can be used politically.

The graduates and students of law from the two universities have a near-monopoly of the higher civil-service positions. However, any civil-service career, even one at the lower levels, can be transformed into a parliamentary career. A young man from the provinces can often build up a substantial clientele simply by servicing hometown requests presented to his own agency and assisting former neighbors with problems involving other governmental departments. Toward anyone else, he adopts the haughtiness and obstructionism so common in the Greek bureaucracy. Eventually, those grateful for his assistance become his political capital; he may be able to use them to advance his civil-service career through political pressure, or he may finally have enough support to run for office.

Some particular occupations have unique political advantages. For example, in the Cyclades and in the Piraeus area shipowners have usually been involved in politics. Some shipowners come from the families of traditional notables; in other instances, their political success is due to their ability to offer employment in shipping lines. They may also grant voters free transportation—a particularly crucial commodity for the many Greeks living on the islands.

Although not every lawyer and doctor in parliament, nor every deputy with family political connections, may actually have a network of clients that keeps him in office, it is most probable that he does. Deputies with other ocupational backgrounds may also have clients, but they are less likely to. When the deputies in some recent parliaments are divided between those likely to have clientage networks based either on family political connections or occupations and those apparently unencumbered with such ties, the percentage of those with no obvious clientage support is modest: 23 per cent in 1946, 36 per cent in 1958, and 32 per cent in 1964.

OCCUPATION AND PARTY AFFILIATION

The pattern of occupational backgrounds is much the same in all the traditional political groupings. Occupations with a clientage-building potential clearly predominate, and each of the parties has a high proportion of deputies with legal or medical backgrounds. Even the distribution of deputies among other occupational categories varies only slightly. Table 11.2, illustrating the occupational distribution in four modern Greek parliaments, confirms these facts. Actually, this similarity in the groups primarily occupied with parliamentary politics is not surprising. The major party groupings draw their candidates and support from similar social and economic categories, and politicians think nothing of shifting from party to party. There is little or no effort to place group spokesmen in parliament. No group would be likely to have the political muscle to be successful; and in any case, parliament is not a crucial point of access for group demands. For most voters, a candidate should have a "traditional" political occupation, rather than one representative of the social or economic complexion of his constituency.

The left-wing parties, currently represented by the EDA, have a markedly different occupational distribution among their parliamentary deputies. This was especially true in 1936, but it also holds for the more recent delegations. The leftist party in 1936, the KKE, adopted a deliberate policy of nominating proletarians for parliamentary office, and 60 per cent of the KKE delegation classified themselves as workers or employees. In 1958, a year of almost accidental Left success, 16.4 per cent of the EDA parliamentary delegation had employee classifications. By 1964—a more normal year,

Table 11.2. Party Affiliation and Occupation

Occupation	1936				1946			1958					1964			
	Right	Center	Left	Other	Right	Center	Other	ERE	PK	PADE	EDA	ELK	ERE	EK	EDA	KP
Lawyer	49.0%	46.6%	6.7%	37.5%	52.2%	49.3%	42.8%	45.6%	47.2%	50.0%	24.0%	25.0%	43.5%	40.0%	27.3%	40.0%
Politician	4.8	3.8	—	—	1.4	2.1	—	1.8	13.9	10.0	2.5	25.0	2.0	4.1	18.2	—
Medical	11.7	12.0	—	12.5	12.1	20.7	—	13.4	13.9	—	12.6	—	8.9	11.0	9.1	—
Academic	—	0.8	6.7	—	1.4	1.4	14.3	2.3	—	10.0	8.9	50.0	5.9	2.9	22.7	20.0
Journalist	4.8	3.0	—	—	2.9	2.0	14.3	5.8	—	—	6.3	—	2.0	5.2	—	—
Civil servant	0.7	1.4	6.7	—	2.9	2.8	—	8.2	5.6	—	5.1	—	5.9	6.0	—	20.0
Military	7.6	9.8	—	—	7.2	7.8	14.3	7.0	2.8	10.0	3.7	—	7.9	6.4	4.5	—
Merchant	3.4	5.3	—	—	6.3	0.7	—	0.6	—	—	1.3	—	1.0	3.5	—	—
Businessman	4.1	2.2	—	12.5	2.9	2.1	—	7.0	5.6	10.0	1.3	—	7.9	2.9	4.5	—
Industrialist	1.4	1.4	—	—	1.9	3.6	—	1.8	2.8	—	—	—	—	2.9	—	—
Banker	—	—	—	—	—	—	—	—	—	—	—	—	—	0.6	—	—
Shipowner	—	—	—	—	—	—	—	—	—	—	—	—	1.0	0.6	—	—
Landowner	2.1	2.2	—	12.5	2.4	3.6	14.3	1.2	2.8	10.0	3.7	—	2.0	1.2	4.5	—
Farmer	0.7	0.8	13.3	12.5	1.4	1.4	—	1.8	2.8	—	6.3	—	1.0	2.9	—	—
Employee	—	2.2	60.0	—	2.4	0.7	—	0.6	—	—	16.4	—	2.0	3.5	4.5	—
Pensioner	—	—	—	—	—	—	—	—	—	—	1.3	—	—	—	—	—
Engineer	0.7	—	—	—	1.9	—	—	1.8	2.8	—	1.3	—	3.0	1.7	—	—
Other technical	—	—	6.7	—	—	—	—	—	—	—	—	—	1.0	1.2	—	20.0
Miscellaneous	—	—	—	—	—	—	—	—	—	—	—	—	1.0	0.6	4.5	—
Unknown	9.0	8.3	12.5	12.5	0.5	0.7	—	1.2	—	—	5.2	—	4.0	2.9	—	—

Note: These figures were computed from deputies' responses to a question on their personnel records in parliament. In some cases the deputy changed his occupation from one parliament to the next.

since the Left did not benefit from Center fragmentation—this particular occupational category had dropped significantly. Although the EDA now seems to make a practice of nominating workers or peasants for many parliamentary seats, these seats are in the marginal areas, where success is most unlikely. The smaller EDA delegation in the 1964 parliament, though still having significant differences from the parliamentary delegations of the other political groupings, does not contain many genuine proletarians.

The major characteristic of the EDA delegations is the relatively low percentage of lawyers and the broad representation of other occupations, including employees and farmers. Occupations calling for familiarity with modern communications media are also more common, reflecting the more modern character of the party. There is more emphasis on the propagandist and the legislative expert than on those occupations with built-in clientage networks. It should be noted in passing that there are several districts where attachment by the voter to the EDA runs through a patron in a traditional or legal occupation. By and large, however, the party is not tied to particular occupational classifications or to men with clientage networks; it can recruit any individual regardless of personal background and occupation, since the party itself draws voters.

LOCAL CONNECTIONS

The importance of clientage networks in Greek parliamentary politics is evident in the high percentage of deputies who represent the constituencies of their birth (see Table 11.3). If data on deputies with other types of local connections were available, the percentage of those supported in this way would undoubtedly be higher. Table 11.4 indicates that in the older portions of the country, this is the general pattern. Only Athens-Piraeus, with its recent urban influx, and Macedonia, Thrace, and the Aegean Islands, which have substantial refugee populations, are contrary to this generalization. The

Table 11.3. Deputies' Birthplace and Constituency

	Parliament		
Deputies	1946 (N354)	1958 (N300)	1964 (N300)
Those representing district of birth	69.5%	70.3%	65.0%
Those representing a different constituency	18.6	17.7	22.0
Refugees	9.8	12.0	10.7
Birthplace unknown	2.0	—	2.3

Table 11.4. Deputies Running in Districts of Birth, by Region

District	Parliament		
	1946 (N354)	1958 (N300)	1964 (N300)
Athens-Piraeus	33.3%	45.0%	37.2%
Old Greece	88.6	85.7	88.6
Peloponnesus	89.6	89.8	70.4
Ionian Islands	81.8	90.9	100.0
Thessaly	86.2	83.3	73.1
Macedonia	48.2	42.8	48.5
Epirus	78.9	86.7	85.7
Crete	95.2	94.4	84.2
Aegean Islands	87.5	77.8	97.5
Cyclades	100.0	83.3	80.0
Thrace	47.0	71.4	38.5

older, less urban, and more settled portions of the kingdom usually have above 80 per cent of their deputies elected from the district of their birth (see Table 11.4).

At first glance, comparative data from more developed countries do not diverge substantially from that noted above. Of the American state legislators examined by the authors of the *Legislative System*, 74 per cent were born in their states, and 56 per cent in the counties they represented.[18] The average would have been considerably higher, except that California was one of the four states examined. In Germany, another highly developed system, nearly 80 per cent of the Bundestag representatives elected in 1957 were residents of the districts that they won.[19] In France, according to Leo Hamon, if the district party organizations are strong, candidates from outside are generally discouraged; moreover, "The elector does not approve of changes of constituency."[20] And in the Italian parliament for 1946–58 there was almost complete identity between birthplace, place of upbringing, place of residence, and district represented.[21] However, the British experience shows that this association between candidates and their districts is not universal. Austin Ranney, using a much broader definition of connection, found that only about 30 per cent of the Conservative candidates from 1951 to 1961 had connections with their constituencies, with variations depending upon the type of election and the chances of victory in the constituency. Among Labour candidates, the connections of the candidate with his constituency ranged from 44 per cent in districts where success was very likely down to 20 per cent in districts likely to be lost.[22] Although these studies have not extended over long periods, the impression given is that these patterns are relatively stable. However, Frederick Frey, in his examination of members of the Turkish Grand National Assembly over several decades, finds substantial changes in the percentage of candidates with local connections. In the first several assemblies in the early 1920's the percentage of deputies born in the constituencies they represented remained relatively high, at 62 per cent. However, as the regime was consolidated, and as a nationally oriented elite took control, the number of deputies with local connections by birth diminished to 34 per cent.[23] The always latent localism began to reassert itself; and finally, after the introduction of the multi-party system in 1946 and the breakthrough of the opposition Democratic Party in 1950, the percentage of deputies with local connections increased, reaching 71 per cent in 1954.[24] "As the parties have moved into a situation of true inter-party competition—a situation of increased need for popular support and simultaneous uncertainty regarding that support—there has been an acute rise in localism within all political parties of Turkey."[25]

The data for Greece, Turkey, and the more developed systems suggests that the relationship between local constituency connections and political recruitment is complex and far from uniform. In Britain, it has long been customary for representatives to shift constituencies, and for constituencies to seek outside candidates. Since this is a long-standing practice, it cannot be solely due to the existence of highly disciplined parties. Moreover, Members are still expected to perform personal services for the inhabitants of the constituencies they represent.[26] In fact, Members from large urban centers seem to spend more time listening to constituents' grievances than those from the country.[27] By contrast Hamon observes that the French deputy from a rural constituency will have many requests for personal services from individual constituents, whereas a deputy from an urban setting is likely to have more from organized groups.[28] In Germany, although the Bundestag members have local ties, they tend to represent organized interests, no matter what the nature of their constituencies.[29] In all these systems, the particular relationship of the deputy with his constituency seems to depend on the perception of legislative role held by both the public and the deputy. Whether or not the patronage function is important seems to depend on this. The recognized points of access in the political system for organized groups will also be a factor in shaping the functions of the individual members of parliament. If organized groups in a constituency can work through local deputies, the recruitment of deputies is likely to reflect local interests of a group character.

The nature of the administrative system may also influence the perceptions of voters and parliamentarians. Where the bureaucracy is arbitrary or distant from the average citizen, the parliamentary figure is likely to be viewed as a middleman; for this function, the voter prefers someone he knows, and hence a premium is placed on local connections. Beyond these rather specific factors, past traditions, the size of the constituency, the nature of the electoral system, and the character of political party organization are all likely to be important.

In Greece (and probably in Turkey since local interests have become important in electoral politics) the relationship between deputy and voter is more direct than that in the Western European settings. It is usual for a deputy to have personal connections with many individuals in his district, and especially with local notables. This is relatively easy to do, since each deputy represents less than 30,000 citizens; the number of actual voters is, of course, much less. Since the constituencies follow provincial lines, the number of deputies elected by a constituency varies; but generally, in all but the largest metropolitan constituencies, the vote for any individual candidate is highly concentrated in the area of his birth.

PRE-LEGISLATIVE POLITICAL EXPERIENCE

The Greek political system is not structured to provide many opportunities for elective office. Only sporadically have local offices been elective; and the only consistent level of elective office is the parliament. A political career in Greece, then, cannot be viewed as either a "regimented, orderly life" or a "tangle of ladders, ropes, and runways that attract people from other activities at various stages of the process and lead others to a dead end or blind drop."[30] Although certain civil-service jobs or other public positions appointed on a political basis may lead to a political career, there are other avenues that seem more appropriate. Moreover, with the exception of the Left, party organization has been weak. This leaves each man free to find his own route to public office; he is not directed to particular channels. Under these conditions, the paths to a parliamentary career have usually been guided by family experience or other personal connections.

Given the dearth of elective offices in Greece, many of the data on pre-legislative officeholding in other political systems are not of much use. However, an examination of these data does suggest that the importance of local officeholding in political recruitment varies considerably from one system to the next. Perhaps the most important factor is simply the individual office seeker's perception of the career pattern most appropriate for him. Heinz Eulau, discussing four American states where the percentage of legislators without previous governmental experience ranged from 34 to 51 per cent, suggests that the more competitive the party system, the more likely it is for legislators to have had some prior governmental experience.[31] However, in the highly competitive British system almost two-thirds of the Conservative candidates and a bit over half of the Labour candidates had no experience in local office.[32] The base of a party's support and the place of the party in the system may determine career patterns. For example, in the recent Japanese data provided by Robert Scalapino and Junnosuke Masumi, 41 per cent of the Socialist deputies had previous governmental experience. A very small number had been national officials, and the rest had held local or prefectural elective office. In the Liberal Democratic Party, 34 per cent had had previous experience in local or prefectural office, but 26 per cent were in the ex-official category.[33] At least in part, this divergence in recruitment patterns is related to the relationship of the Japanese Socialist Party to the political system. Socialists are less likely to be admitted to administrative position and less likely to reach the top. The importance of local experience may depend on the character of the local office. If the voters regard a position as simply an appendage of the central administration rather than as a defender of local interests, it may be of limited utility in a political career, since any distrust of the central government may be transferred to the local office and its incumbent. Frey, in his study of Turkish deputies, found only a small percentage with experience in local office.[34] The local leaders, although connected with the higher government, were not necessarily the local officeholders.

A highly cohesive and disciplined political party may be able to prescribe appropriate career patterns for its recruits: apprenticeship in local or party offices, for example, or particular occupations and degrees of specialization. The usefulness of a particular career pattern can diminish in importance over time. In the German Bundestag, 24.4 per cent of the deputies who began their careers in the prewar period had held local elective office, whereas 58.1 per cent of those who began careers in the postwar period had such experience.[35] Dogan estimates that more than two-thirds of the French deputies from 1900 to 1940 had local office experience, but that this dropped to about 40 per cent during the Fourth Republic,[36] when party experience or resistance activity became more important.

The data from our sample of 55 deputies in Greece, as presented in Table

Table 11.5. Pre-legislative Political Experience

Experience	Number of Deputies (55)	Won First Time	Party Affiliation			
			ERE (17)	EK (32)	EDA (4)	KP (2)
No previous experience	23	10	6	15	2	–
Local government	11	4	4	6	1	–
Civil service, military	17	6	5	10	1	1
Political appointment	12	5	6	5	–	1

Note: Some deputies gave more than one response.

11.5 indicate that those with no previous political experience did as well or better than those with this experience. Perhaps most significant is that nearly half had no previous political experience in any elective, appointive, or civil-service position. Few significant conclusions can be drawn from the breakdown by party. The numbers involved for the EDA and the KP are too small for any comment. The divergencies between the career patterns of the other two parties are in part a result of the very long tenure of the Right and the more recent victory of the Center. The difference between EK and ERE deputies in the categories of "no previous experience" and "political appointment" is not as significant as it may appear because of this. Moreover, each of the two major party groupings includes a number of deputies who had switched from one group to the other.

According to modern Greek political lore, particular appointive offices on the national level can be useful for beginning a political career. The office of general secretary to a ministry is especially valued. This office, like the ministerial position itself, dispenses favors, and hence allows the incumbent to prepare for personal victory at the next election. However, general secretaries are appointed by the premier or the minister involved, and the offices are more likely to go to relatives of influential politicians or to defeated candidates from the winning party than to the ambitious person who is only beginning his political career. Information on these positions is very sketchy. The earliest listing of general secretaries available to me listed those in office in 1933.[37] At this time there were twelve, of whom four were involved in electoral politics prior to their appointments and three afterward. Only one of the general secretaries can be said to have had a substantial career in politics, and it is difficult to attribute it to his tenure as general secretary.

In lists for 1960, 1963, and 1964 the total number of secretaries increases.[38] In 1960 seven of the fourteen secretaries were "political"; four won at subsequent elections, always on the ERE list. In 1963, eight of the fourteen secretaries were politically involved; two went on to win elections in November of that year, although both had run unsuccessfully in the past. All eight were involved in the ERE, which was then in power, and their appointments were probably a reward for party service and a compensation for accidental defeat. There were thirteen secretaries in 1964, but only four had political backgrounds. Three of these had been involved in politics for a long time, although only one had ever been elected. Their political backgrounds varied considerably, ranging from minority-party to right-wing. The small number of "political" secretaries was at least partially due to the recent victory of the EK; several of the "nonpolitical" appointees had relatives active in parliamentary politics, and would probably run for parliamentary office eventually. Obviously, secretaryships will often advance a political career; however, the small number of positions open makes them an almost accidental route to parliamentary office.

Greek governments have traditionally appointed men to the office of nomarch in each of the provinces. The nomarch, in terms of function, is modeled after the French prefect, although he actually has somewhat less discretion than his French equivalent. In the recent past, efforts were made to create a cadre of nonpolitical officials. However, political necessity—both on the part of governments needing clients and on the part of a rural population more accustomed to political than bureaucratic solutions—has worked against this trend. According to the popular tradition of Greek politics, the position of nomarch is one of the most useful steps to a parliamentary career.

There are many individual cases of successful advancement from nomarch to deputy. Perhaps the most noteworthy example is the career of George Papandreou, whose early position as nomarch on the island of Lesbos enabled him to establish political ties there in addition to those in his native province. However, the data available, although spotty, indicate that this particular administrative office is not really very useful for beginning a political career (see Table 11.6). A nomarch, by virtue of his office, does have a few political resources. In most cases, however, he is not in office long enough to gather clients and challenge the political power of the sitting deputies. The average nomarch is usually more concerned with his relationship to the government in power and the local politicians. Moreover, the government will not usually appoint a nomarch who has family ties and personal friendships in the province. The sitting deputies from that region are likely to possess most of these resources.

Table 11.6. Nomarchs and Parliamentary Involvement

Year	Nomarchs	Number in Politics	Time of Involvement		
			Before appt.	After appt.	Both
1933	31	10	2	3	5
1960	49	17	16	1	–
1963	47	12	12	–	–
1964	49	17	16	1	–

Note: Compiled from incidental materials.

Of those occupying the position of nomarch in 1933, only three were ever really successful in parliamentary politics. One of them was elected 23 years later, on his first attempt; for the other two, the time in appointive office was merely an interlude in a lifetime of parliamentary politics. In 1960, only two of those entering the political arena were successful—one before his appointment as nomarch, and one after. The same pattern is found in the data for the other two years. In 1963, although several nomarchs came from political families, only one of the 17 involved in politics was elected to parliament. His success came shortly after his appointment as nomarch, but he had been running unsuccessfully for years. The 1964 nomarchs with political backgrounds had been uniformly unsuccessful in their previous attempts at parliamentary positions. In general, they came from all sectors of the political spectrum, and some had attempted to gain parliamentary office as early as 1932.[39]

Greek administrative appointments traditionally favor men from the older parts of the Greek state or from the strongholds of the major political groups—the Peloponnesus, continental Greece, the Cyclades, or Crete, for example. This tendency limits the usefulness of a nomarchy for future political purposes. In the older regions, the organizations of individual deputies are strong, and they are often inherited; thus the appointive nomarch is generally beholden to a local machine. In the newer parts of the kingdom, political organizations are more fragile, but the nomarch is an outsider who views his position primarily as an opportunity for personal enrichment. Some nomarchs have been successful in the quest for parliamentary office, but in general, the nomarch's office has had little relevance for the victory.

In our sample, 11 of the 55 deputies had experience in local government. All of these had entered parliamentary politics after World War II. There were four deputies who had served on city councils, three in Thessaloniki and one in Athens; the others had been mayors in smaller communities. Local officeholding did not seem to have had much relation to winning the parliamentary election. True, the position of mayor in Athens, and to a lesser extent in Thessaloniki, is hotly contested by all the parties. The mayor in these cities has little actual power; but there is enough prestige involved, especially in Athens, to entice deputies to resign from parliament in order to run. However, the same is not true in most Greek towns and cities. It was possible to secure lists of mayors for the years 1954, 1963, and 1964 (see Table 11.7).[40] In each of these years, the percentage of mayors who had been involved in parliamentary politics, either before election to the mayor's post or afterward, was relatively low: 21.6 per cent in 1954, 19 per cent in 1963, and 20.5 per cent in 1964. This is not surprising. In all but the largest cities a mayor is clearly identified with the interests of a particular community, rather than those of a whole constituency. Moreover, he is often chosen as mayor because of his presumed ties to the central government, not because of heartfelt support.

By and large, it would not seem that local office contributes significantly to later parliamentary success with the major traditional parties. However, a successful EDA member at the local level does appear to be groomed for eventual success on the parliamentary level. Moreover, the communities with EDA mayors were almost invariably urban or suburban districts where traditional clientage ties were minimal. This reflects the difference between the EDA's recruitment pattern and those of the more traditional political groupings. For the other political constellations, political control of a community may be useful. Mayors from these groups probably act as local influentials for their particular party; however, they are not any more likely to be involved in parliamentary politics than other community notables.

EDUCATIONAL ATTAINMENTS

Deputies are far more educated than the average Greek citizen, and there is some evidence that this has always been the case. This is consistent with data on the educational levels of representatives in virtually every other parliamentary body in the world. In Greece, it would be presumptious of someone with a limited education to seek public office. The educational attainments of the sample of 55 deputies are clearly above those of the general population.[41] The graduates of the two major educational institutions were in the majority: 27 deputies had attended the University of Athens, and

Table 11.7. Electoral Success of Greek Mayors

Attempts	Mayors in 1964 (N229)			Mayors in 1963 (N225)			Mayors in 1954 (N226) (Running before 1954)			Mayors in 1954 (Running after 1954)	
	N	Successes	Failures	N	Successes	Failures	N	Successes	Failures	Successes	Failures
Ran once	16	0	16	11	0	11	16	0	12	1	3
twice	11	3	19	9	0	18	12	0	17	2	5
three times	7	0	21	9	3	24	11	2	13	4	14
four times	4	1	15	6	1	23	4	0	11	3	2
five times	4	2	18	4	3	17	—	—	—	—	2
six or more times	5	27	10	2	8	8	6	12	12	13	—
TOTAL	47	33	99	41	15	101	49	14	65	23	26

another five had attended the University of Thessaloniki. Of these 32 deputies, 11 had done additional graduate work in either European or American universities. Seven deputies in the sample had received all of their advanced education abroad. Four additional deputies had attended the ASOEE, a school in Athens that offers advanced work in various commercial and technical fields. Two deputies were graduates of the military academy. The Polytechnic (Ethnikon Metsovion Polytechnion) is an engineering school of university quality; two deputies had degrees from that institution, and one of these had done additional work in Germany. Ultimately, of the sample of 55, only seven did not have some advanced training. Four of these were gymnasium graduates, and three had terminated their education at the elementary school level (one of these three had great difficulty in reading and writing).

There is little reason to believe that this sample was not representative of the entire parliamentary membership. Complete educational information was not available for everyone in the 1964 parliament, from which the sample was drawn, or for the other parliaments analyzed. However, educational background and occupation are closely related; and as we have seen the overwhelming majority of deputies in recent parliaments have been drawn from occupations requiring advanced education.

12. The Political Elite

Several scholars, most notably Pye and Verba, have suggested that the way political elites handle the particular "historical-situational" crises implicit in political development can determine the kind of political system that emerges.[1] Although the full list of relevant political phenomena varies from author to author, all theorists mention the crises of legitimacy, integration, and participation. The first refers to the development of loyalty to the major national symbols and the political elite, the second to the differentiation and extension of political structures, and the last to mass suffrage, or at least to a near universal suffrage that has political consequences. The magnitude and sequence of these crises both have important ramifications. Eric Nordlinger observes that "instead of attempting to identify a general pattern according to which political systems develop, we can look at the various developmental patterns and ask questions about their different consequences."[2] Certainly, the pattern of development in Greece has produced a system unlike most European ones. However, the developmental pattern and the consequent political system are inexplicable without a knowledge of the intervening variables through which change has been filtered.

The four general variables that seem significant in the Greek case have been noted in previous chapters: the character of the society, elite attitude and behavior (especially the prevailing perception of modernization), the international system, and the physical environment of the country. The manner in which the political system has handled the crises of legitimacy, integration, and participation, influenced by these intervening variables, can be examined by focusing on political recruitment.[3] Most commonly, studies of political recruitment examine the manner in which new social strata are admitted to or restricted from political roles. This requires that variables such as social background be described and related to particular leadership positions. However, one can also consider the recruitment function in terms of the performance of the whole political system. In this case, changes in the recruitment pattern over time are related to crises in the political system. This chapter, centered on recruitment to cabinet positions in Greece from 1843 to 1965, will use both modes of analysis. It will provide some clue to the "openness" of the Greek political elite by assessing the pattern of recruitment over time, as well as examining the relationship between recruitment patterns and critical periods of modern Greek history.

THE STRUCTURE OF OPPORTUNITY

In any examination of political recruitment, a knowledge of the opportunities offered by the political system is of great importance.[4] In Greece, aside from sporadic and short-lived efforts to elect mayors, only parliamentary offices have been filled by election since 1843. The size of the parliamentary body has varied, expanding as new territories and populations were added and fluctuating in response to changing electoral systems or new constitutions. Since the 1920's the number of elective places has generally remained between 250 and 300; only the 354-seat chamber elected in 1946 was an exception. We have already seen that in Greece the premiership and the cabinet offices are by far the most important political roles. The top leaders of the Greek political elite are those occupying ministerial office for long periods; a secondary level is composed of men who occupy these top offices intermittently; and the lowest level includes those who are never more than deputies. In this chapter we will examine only the top two groups.*

The Greek cabinet had eight portfolios from 1843 to 1910, with only occasional exceptions. The ministries of agriculture and national economy were added in 1910, in response to economic and social changes. The subsequent increase in state territory and population made it necessary to appoint governors-general for the new territories, who were given cabinet rank. New state concerns in health and welfare were also reflected in new cabinet positions. The period 1930–35 marked an uneasy truce between the major political groups; as Table 12.1 indicates, additional portfolios were added in an attempt to meet the interests of all factions. The Metaxas dictatorship from 1936 to 1941 needed a vast range of deputy ministers to deal with all sectors

---

* Data on the number of cabinet positions and the names of the incumbents up to 1926 is from Ktenavea, *Ai Hellenika Kuverneseis ai Ethnika Syneleuseis*; the post-1926 figures are from Ailianou, *The Greek Governments*.

Table 12.1. Greek Cabinet Size

Period	Number of cabinets	Average size	Period	Number of cabinets	Average size
1910–14	1	12.0	1940–44	4	24.0
1915–19	9	10.3	1945–49	11	32.0
1920–24	14	12.9	1950–54	7	29.4
1925–29	5	16.2	1955–59	4	25.2
1930–34	6	21.0	1960–64	7	24.0
1935–39	3	27.7			

of economic life, as well as additional territorial administrators with cabinet status. However, this period, as well as the period of exile governments from 1941 to 1946, is largely irrelevant to our study of political recruitment. The increase in ministerial positions in 1946–50 reflects the aftermath of the war and occupation, when government presence in every social sector and in every part of Greece was demanded. Even more, it reflects the fragmented character of the political realm at that time. Cabinet positions, after all, were the framework of coalition building, and were useful in bargaining. Since 1950 cabinet size has steadily diminished. The minor offices have been abolished, or have been combined with others; bargaining requirements have been met by new political resources derived from economic growth, the expansion of administrative regulations, and foreign assistance.

Compared with the larger Western European countries, Greece has a high ratio of ministerial offices to total population. Cabinets in the German Federal Republic have numbered about 20 portfolios.[5] French cabinets in the Fifth Republic have been of similar size, with perhaps six additional secretaries of state.[6] In Britain there are up to 40 men in the ministerial category and a substantial number of parliamentary secretaries, but the cabinet itself usually has only 15–20 members, depending on the preferences of the prime minister.[7] Greece resembles these countries in number of ministerial positions, but the total number of political opportunities in Greece is far fewer. Furthermore, opportunities in the nonpolitical sectors of Greek society are greatly restricted.

The number of top political roles in the Greek system is one indication of political opportunity, but it is also important to know the rate of turnover among the incumbents.[8] The graphs on page 299 illustrate the "openness" of the top political roles at different times; a ratio of new entrants to mem-

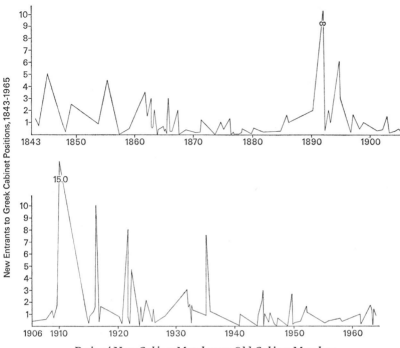

Ratio of New Cabinet Members to Old Cabinet Members

bers with experience in any prior cabinet was computed for each of the 148 cabinets from 1843 to 1965.* The rate of personnel carry-over from any one cabinet to its immediate successor was also analyzed; in only 45 per cent of the cabinets was there any carry-over at all.

The first years after 1843 were marked by relative cabinet stability, although many new faces appeared with each change. The key political figures cooperated to restrain the monarch, but they were still antagonistic. Each was supported by and sympathetic to a major European power; each had a regional base and a group of personal followers. Only 19 of the 45

---

* For the purposes of this analysis, modern Greek history was broken into six periods: 1843–78, 1878–1910, 1910–36, 1936–41, 1941–46, and 1946–65. The parliamentary institutions came into existence in 1843. By 1878, the last of the old leadership had disappeared, and the political system seemed to operate somewhat differently. The years 1909–10 marked a definite end of one era and the beginning of another with the premiership of Venizelos. The Metaxas dictatorship from 1936 to the occupation is also well defined, as is the period of exile regimes. The last period begins with the first postwar elections in 1946 and ends in the summer of 1965. Caretaker and temporary military cabinets have been included in the computations.

cabinets formed between 1843 and 1878 included ministers who had served in the cabinets immediately preceding; and most of the 19 were formed in the early years, when the circle of potential cabinet members was very small. This situation prevailed until the overthrow of King Otho in 1863. After this, cabinets collapsed at nearly every minor crisis, and new faces appeared around the cabinet table. Factions alternated in office because the pool of potential ministers was larger.

The original generation of Greek leaders was fading; the last of the old great men, Admiral Boulgares, died in 1878. The new elite was largely descended from the old competing leaders but tied more closely together because of similar education and intermarriage. Despite the rather closed nature of this elite, few men served in successive cabinets. Of the 32 ministries formed between 1878 to 1910, only five had any carry-over. The similar backgrounds of the top leaders did not prevent the formation of competing factions. The graph of this period shows several concentrated groups of new entrants after 1890; however, these were merely nonpolitical, caretaker cabinets who kept the government running just before an election. In general, the ministers in these caretaker cabinets did not differ from the regular politicians in socioeconomic background.

The prevailing recruitment pattern was abruptly broken in October 1910. The revolution of 1909, the political intervention of junior officers, and the premiership of Eleutherios Venizelos brought new men into top political roles. But recruitment soon grew more restrictive, and half of the 37 cabinets formed between 1910 and 1936 contained members of their predecessors. Although the system was generally stable, cabinet life was punctuated by short, violent periods of parliamentary breakdown and military intervention. The sudden jumps in the graph for this period indicate the temporary seizure of top offices by military officers in response to the domestic consequences of external events.

The period from 1936 to 1940 was abnormal. General Metaxas inherited a cabinet of practicing politicians, but later replaced them with men who had not held public office before. Most of these remained with Metaxas throughout his dictatorship and were inherited, in turn, by his successor in 1941. The exile governments of the war period were also abnormal. There was limited talent available, and it was difficult to assess political strength without a parliamentary setting. Each of the eight cabinets in 1941–46 contained members of the previous cabinet. From 1946 until 1965, a pattern of limited recruitment to top political roles was the rule. This pattern persisted both

Table 12.2. Individuals and Officeholding

Period	Ministers	Leaders	Per cent of minister-months held by leaders
1843–78	147	14	41.4%
1878–1910	116	12	47.7
1910–36	316	31	43.2
1946–65	337	35	44.8

Note: The total number of months available in each office was calculated, and was used as a base to compute individual tenures. Leaders are considered to be the top 10 per cent in terms of total time in office. The figures for the Metaxas dictatorship and the war years are omitted.

in 1946–52, a period of intense governmental instability, and in 1952–65, a period of fairly stable governments. Fifteen of the 24 cabinets after 1946 contained members inherited from immediate predecessors, but these instances were clustered at the beginning of the period, when political factionalization was most acute.

The total number of men attaining cabinet office in the Greek political system, shown in Table 12.2, is substantially higher than the totals in other countries. Unfortunately, there is no completely comparable study. In Britain from 1868 to 1955 there were 294 different incumbents with cabinet status.[9] In the United States, only 144 men and women held cabinet rank from 1900 to 1958; by contrast there were 121 individual ministers in France between 1947 and 1958.[10] As the table shows, Greece has had far more cabinet members during each of these periods. However, the opportunities are more apparent than real. Over 40 per cent of the available time in office was held by about 10 per cent of the men who had served as ministers. All in all, the opportunity for real political power in Greece is slight. There have always been few elective offices. Except in 1910, there has always been a small turnover in the higher positions; and within the top leadership group, most offices have been consistently held by a few durable figures.

EDUCATION AND OCCUPATION

The number of top roles in the Greek political system is limited, and the overall chances of recruitment are slight. Moreover, not everyone has an equal chance at even these few positions of leadership. Social backgrounds and career patterns can aid or hinder those who aim at being ministers, as well as those who merely want a lower parliamentary position. For one thing, sexual discrimination automatically excludes half the population. Traditional Greek attitudes toward the social roles of women were seriously altered only recently.[11] The part played by women in resistance movements during the Nazi occupation was perhaps the most important factor in this change. Nevertheless, women could not vote in national elections until 1958. In the short time since then, only one woman (the widow of a former premier) has attained cabinet rank, and very few have been elected as deputies.

Education also restricts eligibility for political roles. For Greeks, the important consideration is not necessarily education as training, but education as evidence of achieved status. It would not be appropriate to have a person of low status elected to high political position. The usefulness of higher education as an avenue to top political roles is recognized by Greeks at all social levels. Even so, few reach the ultimate threshold, the university.* Greece was one of the first nations to establish the principle of free public education, and she has had universal compulsory education to the sixth grade since 1911. Nevertheless, illiteracy is common. Children from the more prosperous regions or families have a definite advantage in the race for advancement through education.[12] The regional differential reflects the order in which the various areas were incorporated into the Greek state, as well as the gap between urban and rural areas. The initial capital investments in the older parts of the kingdom, especially the Peloponnesus, were not matched elsewhere. Two world wars, population exchanges, and a civil war have all ensured that school buildings and trained teachers are not uniformly available throughout the country.

The educational level of Greek cabinet ministers from 1843 to 1965, with the exception of those in the earliest period, was uniformly high (see Table 12.3).[13] In the early period, 53.8 per cent had university training or some advanced education. The educational achievements of the remainder, primarily revolutionary leaders, were unreported, but it is quite likely that these men had not received a formal education, since there were few institutions of higher education in Greece at that time. Taking the 147 ministers as a group, it is noteworthy that 38.7 per cent had received some education abroad. The majority of these had studied in France, with Italy and Germany following in importance. It is difficult to ascertain the quality and length of this education; however, the very facts of travel abroad and the acquisition of Western languages meant that these men had some familiar-

---

* Even as late as 1961–62, the major institutions of higher education, the University of Athens and the University of Thessaloniki, had enrollments of only 9,527 and 8,054, respectively. (*Statistical Yearbook of Greece*, 1963, p. 104.)

Table 12.3. Educational Background of Greek Cabinet Ministers, 1843–1965

Period	Military	Law	Medicine	Technical	Other	Gymnasium only	Studied abroad	Unknown
1843–78								
Ministers (147)	6.1%	38.7%	2.0%	2.1%	2.1%	2.7%	38.7%	46.2%
Leaders (14)	14.3	42.8	—	—	7.1	—	35.7	35.7
1878–1910								
Ministers (96)	28.1	52.0	2.1	4.1	—	1.0	51.0	12.5
Leaders (12)	16.7	58.3	8.3	—	—	8.3	50.0	8.3
1910–36								
Ministers (300)	16.6	53.6	7.3	6.3	1.7	2.2	37.0	12.7
Leaders (31)	16.1	77.4	3.2	3.2	—	—	61.3	—
1936–41								
Ministers (34)	20.5	29.4	5.9	2.9	2.9	5.9	29.4	32.3
1941–46								
Ministers (124)	16.1	48.4	7.2	5.6	3.2	1.6	39.5	17.7
1946–65								
Ministers (230)	10.4	58.2	8.7	8.7	1.3	0.4	33.8	12.2
Leaders (35)	5.7	80.0	5.7	8.6	—	—	57.2	—

Note: The computations on all ministers and on top leaders alone are not completely comparable. The overall trend is computed for all men who entered cabinet rank during a particular period. The top leadership is the top decile of this group, judged according to the number of minister-months held. These men may have entered politics in an earlier period. This accounts for the fact that the number of top leaders does not always equal 10 per cent of the total number of cabinet entrants.

ity with Western institutions and ideologies. In this early period, most students studied law, whether abroad or in Athens. There was little difference in educational background between the top political leadership and the average cabinet members.

Between 1878 and 1910, the educational level of entrants to the cabinet increased drastically, but the contrast between the total group and the top leadership remained slight. The percentage of ministers studying abroad increased; France and Germany were still the major centers of foreign study. There was a sharp increase in ministers with military educations. This did not reflect military intervention in politics; it was customary for the military ministries to be occupied by "uniformed politicians." Most cabinet ministers and leaders were educated, well traveled, and, as might be expected in a small country with few schools, friends and former classmates.

In the third period, the educational level of all cabinet entrants differs

only slightly from that of entrants in the previous period. The total number of men with military education decreased although a new category of
noncommissioned officers was added. The character of the education
changed; in particular, only 37 per cent had secured education abroad. However, the top leadership differed from both the total of cabinet entrants and
from the top leadership of previous periods. Legal educations and study
abroad were far more common. Although the events of 1909 brought new
men into the political arena, the leadership, even among the new men, came
from families wealthy enough to send their children abroad for study.

In the Metaxas period (1936–41) and in the era of exile governments
(1941–46) different patterns of educational achievement emerge. However,
the abnormal character of these periods makes the findings of lesser significance. During the Metaxas era, the military component reached 20 per
cent, and the antipolitical character of the regime was reflected in a decrease
in the number of men with legal training. Politicians were replaced by un-
knowns with little experience and parochial backgrounds. In the exile period
and the disturbed years immediately after the Nazi occupation, those with
greater personal resources—implying family wealth and a European education—were involved in government. Because of the number of temporary
figures in the ministries, the data for this period are also abnormal.

In the postwar period, the pattern of 1910–36 has been repeated. A third
of the entire group was educated abroad, primarily in France and Germany.
Law still held a paramount position, but other kinds of professional education, especially medicine and engineering, were increasingly common. (This
trend is particularly evident when the period 1946–65 is examined at five-
year intervals.) The contrast between the top leaders and the entire membership continued. Over half of the top leaders had been educated abroad;
and 80 per cent had legal educations.

Education is important for a political career not only because it marks one
off from the multitude, but because it qualifies a man for a "political" occupation. As we saw in Chapter 11, certain occupations are more appropriate
for political activity than others.[14] In transitional political systems most
people are subject-oriented; interests are rarely organized, and parties are
often short-lived and ill-defined. The deputy does not negotiate with other
"interests" on the parliamentary level, but intercedes with the administration for individual clients. In the Greek case, a lawyer or doctor, in the absence of a landed gentry, can fulfill the role of local notable; the patron-
client relationship is based on mutual service rather than land. Despite their

Table 12.4. *Occupational Background of Greek Cabinet Ministers, 1843–1965*

Period	Government Service			Professional				
	Mili-tary	Bureau-cratic	Poli-tics	Law	Other Profes-sions	Busi-ness	Other	Un-known
1843–78								
Ministers (147)	21.8%	27.9%	17.7%	6.1%	5.4%	5.4%	0.7%	14.9%
Leaders (14)	35.7	35.7	14.3	7.1	—	7.1	—	—
1878–1910								
Ministers (96)	25.0	13.5	18.8	13.5	9.4	12.5	—	7.3
Leaders (12)	8.3	33.3	16.7	16.7	8.3	8.3	—	8.3
1910–36								
Ministers (300)	18.6	18.0	4.3	22.0	18.7	8.7	0.3	9.3
Leaders (31)	12.9	12.9	12.9	42.0	12.8	6.4	—	—
1936–41								
Ministers (34)	26.4	2.9	5.9	17.6	14.7	8.8	2.9	20.6
1941–46								
Ministers (124)	16.1	16.1	2.4	20.1	21.4	8.9	1.6	13.7
1946–65								
Ministers (230)	16.9	19.1	2.2	32.6	20.0	4.3	1.8	3.0
Leaders (35)	20.0	20.0	—	43.0	11.5	—	5.8	—

modern characteristics, the intellectual professions operate in both the modern and traditional milieus. They have status because of modern education; this in turn, allows them to fill the traditional patronage role in the countryside. One would expect that occupation, like education, would be even more important to ministers than to deputies.

The information on occupation summarized in Table 12.4 reinforces the conclusions drawn from data on education. A major component of Greek cabinet membership in all periods had previously been involved in government service. In the first period, 67.4 per cent of all cabinet ministers had been bureaucrats, military men or politicians.[15] Only 6.1 per cent listed the law as their occupation. In the top leadership group, the government service category involved 85.7 per cent, largely because so many early leaders had been involved in the revolution. The combined government service category remained high among entrants to political positions in all subsequent periods, but there has been a steady increase in the number of practicing lawyers and members from the business sector. These figures are congruent with historical data suggesting that practicing lawyers were the main beneficiaries of the revolution of 1909.[16] Inspection of more detailed data for five-year intervals from 1946 to the present did not reveal any significant variations in these occupational patterns; however, it should be noted that the occupational distribution of ministers in the postwar years is very much like that of all deputies who served during the same period.

FAMILY AND REGIONAL BACKGROUND

We have already seen (Chap. 10) that certain ascriptive characteristics are important to a successful political career in Greece. There are two major factors: the first is kinship and family connection; the second, related to the first, is regional loyalty. The pervasiveness of the patron-client relationship in Greece accentuates the political importance of these factors. A man born into a political family will be able to utilize the clientage organization established by other members of his family. Political leadership based on long-standing clientage ties is generally less subject to sudden political upheavals. The longer and more certain a man's tenure, the greater his clientage network, and the better his chances of reaching the cabinet. Politicians from political families are particularly crucial in coalition building, which is especially important in Greece, where few individual parties remain strong for more than a few years. The small size of the Greek political system makes analysis of this factor possible; since parliament is the only political arena, it is possible to trace the involvement of individual families. In many cases biographical sources indicated family relationships. In the later periods, candidate lists, provincial electoral returns, and parliamentary personnel records were used. The problem was eased by the Greek practice of using the father's name as the second name of the child. No effort was made to trace political involvement in the maternal line, and thus the figures for family relationship are conservative. The results of the investigation are noted in Tables 12.5 and 12.6.

Before 1843, Greece had no constitution, and most of the government offices were staffed by Bavarians. Even so, many ministers between 1843 and 1878 had fathers who had been in politics; moreover, many ministers had been active in the revolution. By 1878, the sons of these men were entering politics. In fact, the fathers of one-third of the top leadership in this period had themselves held cabinet office. The disturbances of 1909 did bring new people to the top political level. A class of provincial lawyers, largely without family political connections, made their appearance. At the same time the percentage of ministers with relatives in politics diminished. How-

Table 12.5. Family Background of Greek Cabinet Ministers, 1843–1965

Period	Personally in revolution	Father in politics	Relative in politics	Total
1843–78				
Ministers (147)	30.6%	40.1%	6.8%	77.5%
Leaders (14)	35.7	21.4	—	57.1
1878–1910				
Ministers (96)	—	47.9	10.4	58.3
Leaders (12)	—	83.3	8.3	91.7
1910–36				
Ministers (300)	—	21.3	15.0	36.3
Leaders (31)	—	22.6	12.9	35.5
1936–41				
Ministers (34)	—	14.7	17.6	32.4
1941–46				
Ministers (124)	—	18.5	14.5	33.1
1946–65				
Ministers (230)	—	15.6	21.7	37.4
Leaders (35)	—	31.4	17.1	48.6

Table 12.6. Family Background of Greek Cabinet Ministers, 1946–65

Period	Father in politics	Relative in politics	Total
1946–51			
Ministers (86)	15.1%	30.2%	45.3%
Politicians (66)	19.7	28.8	48.5
1951–56			
Ministers (51)	11.8	19.6	31.4
Politicians (39)	15.4	20.5	35.9
1956–61			
Ministers (25)	12.0	24.0	36.0
Politicians (20)	15.0	25.0	40.0
1961–65			
Ministers (68)	20.6	19.1	39.7
Politicians (30)	30.0	16.7	46.7

Table 12.7. Regional Background of Greek Cabinet Ministers, 1843–1965

Period	Athens	Original kingdom	Ionian Islands	Thessaly	Epirus and Crete	Provinces of refugee settlement	Dodecanese Islands	Other	Unknown
1843–78									
Ministers (147)	2.0%	53.8%	6.8%	—	11.5%	4.0%	0.7%	12.2%	8.8%
Leaders (14)	7.1	57.1	—	—	7.1	7.1	—	14.3	7.1
1859 census	—	82.5	17.5	—	—	—	—	—	—
1878–1910									
Ministers (96)	21.9	50.9	10.4	1.0%	9.3	—	—	3.1	3.1
Leaders (12)	33.0	41.7	16.7	—	—	—	—	8.3	—
1907 census	9.1	62.3	9.7	17.4	1.6	—	—	—	—
1910–36									
Ministers (300)	18.6	39.0	6.0	4.7	6.3	5.3	0.7	7.7	11.7
Leaders (31)	22.6	29.1	3.2	9.7	12.9	3.2	—	16.1	3.2
1928 census	13.1	32.1	4.0	8.2	10.9	31.4	—	—	—
1936–41									
Ministers (34)	8.8	49.9	11.8	5.9	2.9	2.9	—	2.9	14.7
1941–46									
Ministers (124)	15.3	32.2	5.7	3.2	9.6	6.4	0.8	8.9	17.7
1946–65									
Ministers (300)	13.5	41.5	3.5	6.5	11.3	10.8	1.3	3.9	7.4
Leaders (35)	28.6	40.0	5.7	8.6	8.6	8.6	—	—	—
1961 census	22.0	24.7	2.5	8.3	10.0	29.9	1.6	—	—

Note: Thessaly includes part of the Epirus. The major areas of refugee settlement are Macedonia, Thrace, and the Aegean Islands. Between 1843 and 1910 the census data are somewhat unreliable.

ever, this change was only temporary, and after the confusion of the Metaxas period and the war years the number of hereditary politicians began to increase. When the years from 1946 to 1965 are broken into five-year segments, the percentage of all cabinet members with fathers or other relatives in politics is that shown in Table 12.6. However, when those who were members of caretaker cabinets and thus not active in elective office are eliminated, the percentages for the five-year periods become 48.5, 35.9, 40.0, and 46.7. Those from political families have increased their hold on the top political offices since the war. The number of ministers whose fathers were active in national politics may have declined, but the number with positions inherited from uncles, cousins, and brothers has increased.

Research on other political systems indicates that the high percentage of Greek leaders who originate in political families is not unique. An examination of the British political elite (which used an index of aristocratic descent, landownership, and public school education rather than one based on family connections alone) found that from 1868 to 1955, 50.5 per cent of the cabinet members were drawn from the traditional ruling class.[17] The authors of the *Legislative System* noted that in four American legislatures, the percentage of members with relatives in politics ranged from 41.0 to 59.0.[18] However, these data reflect political socialization, not inherited political position. Although impressionistic evidence suggests that inherited political position was important in nineteenth-century British and American national politics, it does not seem widespread today. In modern industrial societies offices are filled by recruitment through parties or other organizations. The clientage base of the hereditary politician has been eroded by mass education, economic development, and modern bureaucracies. In Greece, the necessity for a patron-client tie remains; in consequence, the percentage of politicians with inherited position is high. Without question, those raised in a political environment do have some advantage in future political careers; however, this advantage cannot compare with the inheritance of the office itself.

The advantages given by particular regional backgrounds are related to those given by family; and most Greek politicians retain ties to their place of birth, even if they actually live elsewhere. From the figures in Table 12.7, it is evident that families from the original parts of the Greek state have managed to dominate both elective and bureaucratic politics. The percentage of cabinet members from each major region of the original kingdom corresponded quite closely to the population distribution from 1843 to 1878 with one exception: the first addition, the Ionian Islands, had 17.5 per cent of the population but only 6.8 per cent of the ministers. In this earliest period, some 28.4 per cent of the ministers came from outside the state boundaries. However, the top leadership group was almost completely restricted to those with secure bases of political strength in the kingdom itself. In the following period the number of cabinet ministers born outside the national boundaries diminished considerably, but the new territories, including Thessaly and a part of the Epirus, were underrepresented. The original kingdom, including Athens, continued to be the dominant region.

In the third period, the population distribution of the Greek kingdom was much more complex. The addition of Crete, much of northern Greece, and the major Aegean islands, as well as the arrival of the refugees from Turkey and other Near Eastern areas, vastly increased the population. Nevertheless, the older parts of the kingdom continued to supply most cabinet ministers. Thessaly, Crete, and the Epirus were only somewhat slighted; but Macedonia and Thrace, where most of the refugees had settled, did not contribute more than 4 per cent of the ministers. The observations on the regional origins of the entire cabinet membership for this period also hold for the top leaders, making the slight to the newer areas even greater.

In the period from 1946 to 1965, the original kingdom and the Ionian Islands, excluding Athens, contributed 45.2 per cent of the ministers. In the past Athens had been overrepresented, but now it had less than its share of ministers. It must be noted, however, that many Athenians had been born elsewhere; and that politicians, like the people who elect them, had migrated to the city. The other slighted area continued to be Macedonia, although some of the ministers listed as "unknown" could have come from there. Again, this pattern was similar for both top leadership and the whole cabinet membership.

It is clear that refugees and persons born in areas recently added to the Greek state have not yet found their place in the top political stratum. The refugees, dispersed across the northern provinces, have not been able to enter politics as a bloc. Today, Macedonia, Thrace, and the urban constituencies are areas of substantial political competition, which results from weak clientage ties and a corresponding emphasis on personalities and issues. Few deputies from these areas can acquire enough tenure and influence in parliamentary politics to demand ministerial portfolios, especially since their constituencies are usually left-wing strongholds. Politicians from the older areas, with secure clientage networks, continue to dominate the traditional political groupings. They are the enduring part of any political constellation, and automatically receive a place at the cabinet table. Those elements most committed to substantial changes in the political system are not likely to appear.

GREEK POLITICS IN PERSPECTIVE

The critical periods in modern Greek history, which partly reflect crises of legitimacy, integration, and participation, are related to the patterns of political recruitment. A varied group of mountain chiefs, notables, phanariot princes, merchants, and sea captains participated in the war of independence, and eventually occupied the parliamentary institutions after 1843.[19] The members of this political elite, though holding divergent images of the future Greece, all utilized the central institutions imposed by foreign powers to maintain their traditional clientage networks. The state institutions, as they penetrated the countryside, were used more for patronage purposes than as instruments of central government control. Suffrage was extended at the same time as representative institutions were adopted; hence there was no crisis of participation. The individual voter—in reality a client belonging to the patronage network of a given political figure—was not a threat to the political elite, but the basis of its position. However, each voter was loyal to the incumbent of a public office, rather than to the office or the nation itself.

Until the end of the last century, the Greek kingdom could be viewed as an almost ideal state. Similar education, intermarriage, and a shared life in the Athenian social and political milieu had created a fairly homogeneous (though not cohesive) elite from the children of the early leaders. However, since the ties binding a citizen to the top political level were almost exclusively personal, the continuance of the system depended in large measure on the attitudes and behavior of that elite.

In the last decades of the nineteenth century the patriarchal character of the rural areas changed. Landowners sold their estates to the peasantry and moved to the cities. Agrarian discontent flared in Thessaly, the one area where absentee ownership remained common. Gradually, the peasant population increased, and land pressures became severe. The peasant was more in need of ties to influentials than before, since the state, through taxation and military recruitment, had begun to affect the rural population more directly. However, peasant requirements were often beyond the interests or ability of the traditional patron to handle. At the same time, the national university was producing a new class of professionals, mainly lawyers, who began to replace landowners as provincial notables. Other graduates, with no opportunities in the state services and no inclination to return to the country, settled down in Athens and became coffee-house agitators. The pressures for political office and the demands of a large voting population for the amelioration of individual grievances through political channels set the scene for crisis.

The revolution of 1909 was precipitated by external events. The decline of Turkey and the rise of other Balkan powers had created a need for a professional Greek military establishment. The state set up military academies and accepted foreign military missions, and soon the army appeared to be a modern, efficient force. Nevertheless, Greece was badly defeated by Turkey in 1897. The junior officers and noncoms, imbued with a sense of national mission not found in the traditional elite, became acutely aware of the deficiencies in the existing military establishment. The revolution of 1909, initiated by dissatisfied elements in the military and instructed by the Young Turk example, ultimately benefited the new class of provincial and Athenian professionals. It shattered the monopoly of the old elite and gave opportunities to the new men.

From 1910 to 1936, the Greek political elite was primarily composed of new men, without family ties to the earlier generations of political leaders. However, the chronic scarcity of resources, in Greece, although directing ambitious men to political office, also necessitated the retention of the prevailing political practices. Members of the major political groups were indistinguishable in their social background, and differed primarily in their regional origin. The jobs, the possibilities for administrative manipulation, and the public funds available to those in control of the state machinery were still used to build or maintain clientage networks. Political participants, for the most part, were still subject-oriented. Favors were bestowed by individuals, and no one benefited simply by being a citizen.

The knowledge that state regulations could be evaded through personal contacts further undermined loyalty to national symbols and obedience to national institutions. Since individual favors were tied to the actions of specific leaders, many Greeks equated loyalty to individuals with loyalty to the political system itself. The legitimacy of the system and the operation of the state institutions depended on good relations between the members of the political elite. However, leaders continually clashed over national identity, institutional forms, foreign alignments, and control of the state machinery. Since 1910, modern Greek history has been filled with crises of legitimacy and integration, all stemming from personal conflict. The political system has constantly been challenged and upset, either by the clashes of major figures or by domestic military pressures.

Besides the military, newer, less organized groups of refugees and other dissatisfied urbanites, uninvolved in the traditional political processes, became more important in the inter-war period. The crisis of 1936 and the ensuing dictatorship of General Metaxas can be related to a failure of recruitment, which was also a failure to settle basic questions of legitimacy and integration. The traditional political groups, held together by mutual necessity in the quest for scarce resources, could not accommodate Greeks who were not attached to the usual patronage structures. This failure provided opportunities for new political groups organized on other than clientage principles. The lassitude of the traditional politicians and the threat of a Communist outbreak provoked Metaxas to action, backed by the military.

After World War II, the sons and nephews of the beneficiaries of the revolution of 1909 began to enter politics. For most individual deputies, and for the political groups, the major concerns were still patronage and the pursuit of office. The majority of the Greek voters probably remained loyal to individual political figures. Social mobilization and the expansion of education produced more citizens who sought political careers, as well as more who wanted political solutions to their individual problems. However, as competition for political position increased, the number of political roles stayed substantially the same, and it became more and more necessary for an aspiring politician to have family political ties. This made it even more difficult for the newer groups in society to reach the top of the political system, and in turn inhibited their loyalty to the system and their obedience to its institutions.

Over the last several decades another level of politics has appeared in Greece. The elite at this extraparliamentary level has promoted a new image of modernity, chiefly tied to economic development. They have attempted to form modern organizations bound by associational ties rather than the loose groupings characteristic of traditional society. One extraparliamentary force, the left wing, has attracted many Greeks who were unaffiliated with the traditional leadership. Political office is important to the Left; at a minimum, it has sought to obtain recruitment to top political roles. However, leftists have also questioned the legitimacy of the entire political system by attacking the manner in which the state institutions operate. They have sought to eliminate the essential element of Greek politics—the clientage system based on the mutual obligations of individuals. The Left was viewed as a threat by the traditional parliamentary forces because the existence of universal suffrage might give it substantial power. The other extraparliamentary force, the Greek military establishment, had been freed from exclusive dependence on the traditional patron-client relationship by foreign military aid, both British and American. The military, too, was dissatisfied and fearful, distrusting both the Left and the parliamentary politicians. The politicians were unreliable because of the fragile bonds of personal loyalty that characterized their political groups. The larger concerns of the state, which the military saw itself as representing, seemed to be in constant confusion. The Left, should it realize its goals, would undermine the military as the symbol of national unity and disrupt its international affiliations.

The precarious relations among leaders representing these competing elites were shattered in the summer of 1965. The consequent unrest culminated in the military coup of April 1967. Since then, the military has attempted to eliminate both the parliamentary politicians and the Left as important political forces. It would seem that the destruction of the traditional political groups threatens the entire pattern of clientage relations in Greek society. Although the military leaders did not intend to do more than restore stability to Greek society, they may have cleared the way for new political groups with ideologies stressing new goals and institutions, whether under the auspices of the military or a renewed Left. On the other hand, the traditional pattern of clientage relations may penetrate the modern military organization. However, as social mobilization proceeds and as clientage ties weaken, an increasing proportion of the population would seem to be available for new political forms. No one can predict with precision what the future political pattern will be.

Whoever the ultimate victors in the political struggle may be, they will face a long-standing Greek problem. Political resources, largely produced by economic growth, must be increased to allow the increasing number of demands to be satisfied, either through the traditional patronage system or through some more rational set of priorities. Is this possible? Many observers seem to think so. Benjamin Ward concluded on the basis of various demographic and socioeconomic data from the mid-1950's, that the Greek population was "better prepared, both physically and mentally, than those of most developing countries to meet the heavy demands of modern society."[20] Richard Westebbe, using more recent data on economic growth, has suggested that "Greece has broken out of patterns characteristic of underdevelopment."[21] George Coutsoumaris, another prominent economist familiar with Greek affairs, reports that Greece "is on the way to a second stage of industrial development."[22]

This optimism is reinforced by a comparison of Greek development with that of Western Europe. The gross national product per capita in Greece during the early 1960's was equal to that in Great Britain about 100 years ago. Moreover, the rate of growth of both GNP per capita and government expenditure is now several times greater than it has been in Britain at any time during the last two centuries. In the last decade, the Greek economy has expanded at a rate equalled in only a few countries. This is especially evident when one examines the ratio of industrial income to gross national product, an important measure of economic structural change.

Unfortunately, economic growth in itself does not preclude relative scarcity. As Myron Weiner notes in regard to India, "The argument that economic growth provides government with greater revenue, thus enabling it to satisfy more of the demands made on it, assumes a constancy in demand for which there is neither historical precedent nor theoretical justification."[23] All evidence suggests that the rapid social mobilization of previously quiescent population sectors in Greece, partially due to economic growth itself, has caused a vast increase in the magnitude and variety of political demands. The Greek political system, traditionally the focus for all demands, cannot accommodate this increase. The structure of the consociational system imposes limits on flexibility in the allocation of resources; it does not allow easy access to the bargaining level for all segments of the Greek population. Ultimately, however, the basic limitation is still the limited quantity of Greek resources.

Obviously, Greece has insufficient supplies of the natural resources that are needed for development. Moreover, she is poorly located for trade with the industries and markets of Western Europe. In consequence, "The possibility of development of a significant industrial pole in Greece appears very small."[24] Although uneven internal development is not uncommon in any developing economy, the particular sectors that are most advanced in Greece are those least able to promote general development. Exports have not yet reached the level of imports, and industrial commodities account for a very small proportion of total exports. The major Greek exports are luxury goods that must cope with an elastic market and stiff competition. The Greek economy is tied to agriculture; but land scarcity, excessive farm fragmentation, rough terrain, and poor soil make any extensive development of commercial agriculture problematical. The few advantages enjoyed by Greece in international competition, her climate and her antiquities, though they attract tourists and revenue, have not been extensively exploited.[25] Plans for substantial long-term economic growth necessarily depend on conditions outside Greece. This limits the options available to the Greek political elite, and also relieves them of some responsibility.

As long as the available resources are unable to satisfy mounting demands, the Greek consociational system will probably be characterized by an unstable equilibrium as the major components compete for advantage; there will be a general malaise, with occasional chaotic outbursts. So far, the Greek system has not solved the basic questions of legitimacy, in that its people have never developed a loyalty to any office or institution for its own sake; moreover, the governmental institutions have never been able to cope with the demands of operation in a participatory democracy. These two failures have produced pressures that the political system is unable to bear. Conflict between traditional and modern, or parliamentary and extraparliamentary elements seems likely to continue for the indefinite future. What is more, this may indeed be the typical pattern of politics in many underdeveloped countries.

Appendixes

Appendix A:
Research Methods

For this study, I have used three general methods of investigation. First, techniques of ecological research were utilized to identify specific groups in society and to relate them to particular political groups. For the years before 1928, historical materials were used; after 1928, census data were available to identify patterns of refugee settlement and urbanization. These variables were used in my subsequent analysis of electoral data. Once particular groups in Greek society were identified, I attempted to determine the pattern of political recruitment by examining the social and political backgrounds of deputies from three Parliaments (1936, 1946, and 1964), using both published biographical data and the personnel records of the Parliament itself. Information on age, occupation, education, place of birth, and family political involvement was available from these sources. Perhaps the most serious lack was the absence of data on recruitment into the military and the bureaucracy. This deficiency was somewhat compensated for by a similar analysis of the backgrounds of all cabinet members from 1843 to 1965. Cabinets of a military or bureaucratic complexion, formed during the breakdown of normal parliamentary institutions, were analyzed along with the others. By and large, published biographical data was the basis for this analysis.

If one attempts to describe a political elite by concentrating on formal officeholders alone, it sometimes happens that the real powerholders in the society are neglected; however, this does not seem to be a problem in the Greek case. Judging from the number of aspirants for parliamentary office and from the fact that candidates come from all sectors of Greek society, the Greek parliament, because it normally does allocate resources for the whole society, contains the real holders of power in the Greek political system. Another possible deficiency in this type of analysis is the formal under-representation of emergent groups in the society, particularly the Left; this was overcome by an investigation of all candidates for election. The Greek

electoral system has usually been willing to recognize any group as a political party and to give it a chance at parliamentary seats.* My collation of
available data on all parliamentary candidates from 1926 to 1963 brought out
family political histories, individual political histories, and regional patterns
of candidate recruitment.

Finally, political socialization and recruitment were investigated through
interviews with a sample of deputies from the parliament elected in 1964.
The inspiration for these interviews came from the study made by John
Wahlke and his colleagues in *The Legislative System*. A sample of 55 was
drawn at random from the 300 members of the 1964 parliament. Five of
these could not be contacted or refused to cooperate, and five more deputies
with the same party affiliations and from the same constituencies were
selected as replacements. The sample matched the whole parliament very
closely in terms of party and age distribution, regional representativeness,
and occupation. The party distribution in the 1964 parliament was: 57%
EK, 34% ERE, 7.3% EDA, and 1.7% KP. The corresponding sample distribution was 58%, 31%, 7.4%, and 3.6%. Other statistical data are presented in Table A.

*Table A. Comparison of Selected Characteristics of Members of the
1964 Parliament and a Sample of 55 Deputies*

	Age		Region		Occupation	
	Parliament	Sample	Parliament	Sample	Parliament	Sample
N	293*	55	300	55	291*	55
Mean	5.61	5.74	6.64	6.13	5.81	5.31
Variance	3.85	3.63	6.49	5.46	2.88	2.58
Standard deviation	1.96	1.90	–	–	–	–

*Total less than 300 because some information was unavailable for some deputies.

The interviews took place in Athens, from September 1964 to March 1965.
In about one-third of the cases, I used the interview schedule (see p. 000) as
a written questionnaire. Otherwise, the interviews were conducted from the
schedule with the aid of an interpreter. (In six cases, I was able to conduct
interviews in English.) The interpreter, a young journalist working as the
parliamentary correspondent for a leading Athens daily closely linked with
the Papandreou forces, was invaluable in arranging meetings. The average
deputy was flattered that a journalist and an American scholar would want

* Of course this is only true when parliamentary institutions are operating. The Communist
Party was proscribed in 1947; however, this did not prevent its cadres from entering politics
under another label until the 1967 coup suspended all electoral activity.

to talk to him. Moreover, it was clear that talking with me was viewed as a favor to the journalist, who could, in return, mention the deputy favorably in a news account. Several deputies who were reluctant to participate were brought around by the implied threat of a news blackout of their parliamentary activities. The fact that the interpreter represented a pro-government newspaper did not seem to make any difference.

The interview schedule itself resembled that used by Wahlke *et al.*, but was shortened for several reasons. First, many of the Wahlke items were either irrelevant in the Greek context or beyond the scope of this study. Second, some of the questions could be viewed as too "personal" or too controversial in the Greek setting, even though they would be acceptable here. Finally, Greek deputies were generally much too busy to spend more than an hour with the author and the interpreter. The time factor finally forced us to leave some printed interview schedules for later return. Questions selected for inclusion were translated into Greek by the interpreter; another translation was made by a Greek trained in American social science. The two versions were compared, amended, and tried out on several deputies not part of the sample. They were printed in a form that could be used either as an interview schedule or as a questionnaire for later return.

By and large, the deputies did not understand the purpose of the interviews. After the interview had commenced, and the seemingly irrelevant and innocuous nature of the questions became evident, most deputies were quite relaxed. They enjoyed talking about themselves, but they would have been apprehensive about any questions calling for policy opinion. The introduction to the interview and the questionnaire stated that no names would be used, but few deputies believed that their responses would be secret. In fact, several were upset that we didn't want their names. One implied that he didn't intend to be "a mere number." Nearly every returned questionnaire was signed with a flourish.

THE INTERVIEW SCHEDULE

The present study is aimed at finding out why deputies decide to enter politics. The information and opinions you give will be tabulated along with responses from your colleagues. Finally, we will tabulate it with similar information about deputies from other countries. Of course, no names will be used, and what you say will be "off the record."

1. First, a few questions about your background.
   a. Where were you born?
   b. In what year?
   c. What is the name of your father?
   d. Are you married?
   e. How many children do you have, and what are their ages?

2. In what part of the country did you grow up?
   a. Did you spend most of the years when you were growing up in a city, town, or village?
   b. What was your father's occupation?

3. Now, would you tell me a little bit about your education—where you went to school?

4. What has been your own principal occupation?
   a. Has this been your occupation all your life?
   b. What other work have you done?
   c. In addition to your job as deputy, do you have any other current connections with a business firm, law office, or farm, etc.?

5. How did you become interested in politics? For example:
   a. What is your earliest recollection of being interested in it?
   b. What other members of your family or close relatives held elective office before you yourself did?
      (1) Do any of these relatives still hold elective office?
      (2) Do any of your wife's relatives hold elective office?
   c. What clinched your decision to stand for the Vouli yourself?
   d. When did you first stand for election? With which list? In which electoral district?
   e. Were you successful the first time you ran for the Vouli? To what do you ascribe your success or defeat?
   f. From your first election as deputy have you remained in the same party group? In the same election district?
   g. Have you ever held appointive positions in the civil service or in other public legal entities? If so, what?

6. Have you ever been a minister? In your opinion, what makes a deputy most eligible to be selected as a minister?

7. Now, a few questions about the job of being a deputy:
   a. How would you describe the job of being a deputy? What are the most important things you should do?
   b. Are there any important differences between what you think this job is and the way your constituents see it?
   c. How often do you visit your constituency? Approximately how many constituents visit you in Athens per week?

8. Is there any particular subject or field of interest in which you consider yourself particularly expert? I mean, when it comes to dealing with proposed legislation in that field? What is this?
   a. Is there any group within the population that you act as spokesman for?
   b. Are you a member or officer in any trade union, professional organization, commercial organization, or veterans' group?
   c. Do representatives of organized groups such as those mentioned above contact you to give you their opinions on proposed legislation?

9. Who are some of your closest personal friends in the Vouli—I mean the members you see most outside the Vouli, at lunch or on social occasions?*

10. In general, on what issues would you say your party differs from the others represented in the Vouli?

11. Do you consider yourself to be Orthodox, Orthodox who frequently goes to church, or something else?*

12. In regard to government and politics in general, what interests you most, and which interests you least: international affairs, national affairs, or local affairs?

* These questions, because of poor responses, were deleted after about 10 of the 55 interviews had been completed.

Appendix B:
Classification of Eparchies by Party Competition

In the following lists, the various Greek eparchies are grouped according
to their voting record for the eight elections that took place in the period
1946–63. The parties or groups of parties, categorized as Right or Center,
that received over half of the vote are considered the winners; and each
eparchy is classified by winner, although it may have returned some deputies from other political groups. In each category, eparchies are listed by
region. Urban eparchies (those with 50 per cent or more of the population
living in communes of 10,000 or over) are in italics. The regional classification used in Greek government documents is followed, except that the
Cyclades and the Dodecanese, because of their very different political histories, are separated from the Aegean Islands category. The transliteration
of Greek place-names follows Greek government usage.

One-party Right. In these eparchies groups defined as conservative won
all eight elections in the period 1946–63.
> Cyclades: Andros, Paros, Thera.
> Ionian Islands: Corfu, Paxoi.
> Old Greece: Aegina, Kythera, Troezenia.
> Peloponnesus: Epidavros-Limiras, Ghythion, Gortynia, *Kalamata*, Ky-
> nouria, Lakedaemon, Mantinia, Messini, Nauplia, Oety-
> los, Pylia, Trifylia.

One-party Center. Groups defined as "Center" won all eight elections.
> Crete: Apokoronon, Ierapetra, Kissamos, *Kydonia*, Malevizion, Mir-
> ambello, Monofatsion, Pedias, Selinon, Vianon.
> Dodecanese: Kalymnos. (Center won seven elections; the Dodecanese
> became part of Greece in 1950.)

One-party traditional. One set of political groups consistently received a
majority of votes in each election. However, the vote switched from Center

groups to conservative groups when the major political leader in the area switched.

Crete: Sfakia.
Cyclades: Kea.
Epirus: Arta, Dodoni, Konitsa, Metsovon, Paramythia, Pogonion.
Macedonia: Florina.
Thrace: Komotini, Samothraki, Sapae.
Thessaly: Skopelos.

One-party Right, one exception. The right-wing political groups captured the majority of votes in every election except one. The year of exception is noted in parentheses.

Cyclades: Milos (1950), Naxos (1950), *Syros* (1950), Tinos (1950).
Ionian Islands: Kranaea (1950), Zante (1951).
Macedonia: Grevena (1950), Kastoria (1950).
Old Greece: Attica (1951), Fthiotis (1950), Khalkis (1950), Misolon-
ghion (1950), Parnassis (1963), Spetsae (1950).
Peloponnesus: Argos (1950), Ermionis (1950), Kalavryta (1950), Kor-
inthia (1950), Megalopolis (1950).

One-party Right, two exceptions. The right-wing political groups cap-tured the majority of votes in every election except two. The years of ex-ception are noted in parentheses.

Ionian Islands: Ithaki (1961, 1963).
Macedonia: Almopia (1950, 1951), Arnaea (1950, 1951), Fyllis (1950,
1951), Khalkidiki (1950, 1951), Kilkis (1950, 1956), Ko-
zani (1950, 1951), Pangheon (1950, 1951), Sintiki (1950,
1951), Visaltia (1950, 1951), Voion (1950, 1951).
Old Greece: Hydra (1950, 1951), Karystia (1950, 1963), Naupactia
(1950, 1951).
Peloponnesus: Aighialia (1950, 1963).
Thrace: Orestias (1950, 1951), Souflion (1950, 1951).

Competitive districts, tendency Right. In these districts, the political groups of the Right have won five of the eight elections. There is no pattern to indicate that the districts have changed affiliation because of changing personnel, changing party labels, or any particular national issue.

Aegean Islands: Samos.
Ionian Islands: Sami.
Macedonia: Drama, Langadas, Serres.
Old Greece: Doris, Thebes, Trichonis.
Peloponnesus: Olympia.

Thessaly: Aghia, Almyros.

Thrace: Didymotichon.

Even districts. Each of the two major political groupings has won four elections in the period 1946–63.

Aegean Islands: Chios.

Epirus: Thyamis.

Macedonia: Eordaea, Paeonia, Yannitsa.

Old Greece: Evritania, Lokris, *Megaris*, Vonitsa-Xiromeron.

Peloponnesus: Ilia.

Thessaly: Elasson.

Competitive districts, tendency Center. In these districts, the political groups of the Center have won five of the eight elections.

Dodecanese: Rhodos. (Won five of seven elections; the Dodecanese did not become part of Greece until 1950.)

Epirus: Nikopolis-Parga.

Macedonia: Edessa, Pieria.

Old Greece: Domokos.

Peloponnesus: *Patras.*

Thessaly: Farsala, Kalambaka, Karditsa, Trikala.

Thrace: Xanthi.

One-party Center, two exceptions. The Center political groups captured the majority of votes in every election except two. The years of exception are in parentheses.

Aegean Islands: Limnos (1946, 1961).

Crete: Amarion (1952, 1956), Mylopotamos (1952, 1956).

Macedonia: Imathia (1946, 1958), Nestos (1946, 1952).

Old Greece: Istiaia (1946, 1958), Levadhia (1946, 1958), Valtos (1952, 1962).

Thrace: Alexandroupolis (1946, 1961).

One-party Center, one exception. The Center political groups captured the majority vote in every election except one.

Crete: Aghios Vasilios (1952), Kaenourghion (1958), Lasithion (1946), Pyrghiotissa (1958), *Rethymni* (1952), Sitia (1946), *Temenos* (1958).

Competitive three-party. These are districts in which any of the three major groupings have a chance at winning a majority. In ordinary circumstances, there is no majority, only a plurality.

Aegean Islands: Ikaria, Mithymni, Mytilini, Plomarion.

Ionian Islands: Levkas, Pali.

Macedonia: *Kavala, Naousa,* Thasos, Thessaloniki, *Thessaloniki City, Thessaloniki Suburbs.*

Old Greece: *Athens City, Athens Suburbs, Piraeus City, Piraeus Suburbs.*

Thessaly: *Larisa,* Tirnavos, *Volos.*

Unclassified. These are districts with substantial shifting of party label by deputies, but with unexplained victories by the opposite political group.

Dodecanese: Karpathos, Kos.

Epirus: Filiates, Margarition.

Appendix C:
Abbreviations of Greek Political Parties

Agrot   Agrotikon Komma (Agrarian Party). There have been many
          political groups using this label or variants of it. In the election
          of 1936, this party split into two fragments; the left-wing one
          was closely associated with the Communists. Since the war,
          three men with personal followings can be viewed as the suc-
          cessors to the prewar "right-wing" Agrarians: Alexander My-
          lonas, with strength in the Epirus; Augustos Pagoutsos in
          Thessaly (especially Trikala); and Alexander Baltadzis from
          Thrace. In 1946 and 1958 there were electoral alliances that
          combined the various Agrarian fragments. In other elections
          the factions have run independently or have joined with the
          larger political parties.

DE   Demokratiki Enosis (Democratic Union). The name used by
          Papandreou's Center coalition and the EDA during their elec-
          toral alliance in 1956.

DP   Demokratiki Parataksis (Democratic Front). A party formed
          by various left-wing groups, including remnants of the Com-
          munist Party, for the 1950 elections. This party was the prede-
          cessor of EDA.

DS   Demokratikos Sinaspismos (Democratic Coalition). A coali-
          tion of small Center groups led by Alexander Papanastassiou,
          George Papandreou, and George Kafandaris in 1936.

EDA   Eniaia Demokratiki Aristera (United Democratic Left).
          Formed in 1951 from several minor Left parties. It was gen-
          erally thought of as a substitute for the outlawed Communist
          Party. The EDA itself was outlawed by the military junta after
          April 1967.

EF Eleftherofronon (Free Opinion Party). Founded and led by General Ioannis Metaxas in the 1920's and 1930's. It was a minor right-wing personalist following in 1936.

EK Enosis Kendrou (Center Union). The Center party founded by Papandreou in 1961. This has remained the label for most of the Center since that time.

EKE Ethnikon Komma Ellados (National Party of Greece). A postwar party formed by Napoleon Zervas from the members of his wartime guerrilla group. It participated in the 1946 and 1950 elections, and then its cadres scattered to other parties, mainly in the Center.

ELK Enosis Laikou Komma (Union of Populist Parties). A splinter party that contested the 1958 elections. Its leaders were Stephanos Stephanopoulos, Panayotis Kanellopoulos, and Constantine Tsaldaris. It was mainly composed of right-wing notables from the Peloponnesus.

EPE Ethniki Politiki Enosis (National Political Union). A coalition composed of the Venizelist Liberals led by Sophocles Venizelos, George Papandreou and his Social Democrats, and Panayotis Kanellopoulos and his National Unity Party. It contested the 1946 election.

EPEK Ethniki Proodeftikon Enosis Kendrou (National Progressive Center Union). This was the label used by a Liberal coalition led by General Nicholas Plastiras and former premier Emmanuel Tsouderos in 1950 and 1951. The party has since merged into the EK, although the successors of the founders still maintain a party office.

EPEL Ethniki Parataksis Ergazomenou Laou (National Front of Working People). A coalition of small personalist parties that contested the 1950 election. Several leaders were former associates of General Metaxas.

EPK Ethnikon Phileleftheron Komma (National Liberal Party). Formed by Stulianos Gonatas from various Liberal Party elements in 1946. It lasted until 1950, when most of its members returned to the parent party.

ERE Ethniki Rizospastiki Enosis (National Radical Union). The political group founded in 1956 by Constantine Karamanlis. It was composed primarily of right-wing elements from the Greek Rally, although after 1956 many Center politicians were involved.

ES   Ellinikos Synagermos (Greek Rally). A political group created by Field Marshal Alexander Papagos in 1951. It won the elections of 1952 and passed from the scene in 1955 after the death of Papagos. Initially, its cadres came mainly from the Populist Party and some Center groups. Most of its deputies later went into the ERE.

GLRE   Geniki Laiki Rizospastiki Enosis (General Populist Radical Union). A 1936 right-wing political coalition including General George Kondylis and his National Radicals, John Theotokis and the National Populists, and John Rallis and some associated independents.

HPE   'Inomeni Parataksis Ethnikofronon (Coalition of Nationalists). A coalition of three parties that fought the 1946 election. It included the Populist Party led by Constantine Tsaldaris, the Reformist Party of Apostolos Alexandris, and the National Liberals of Stulianos Gonatas.

KGP   Komma Georgiou Papandreou (Party of George Papandreou). This was a continuation of Papandreou's prewar Democratic Socialist Party. It ran in 1950 and 1951, but won no seats in 1951. Papandreou himself collaborated with the Greek Rally in the election of 1952.

KKE   Kommounistikon Komma Ellados (Communist Party of Greece). This party was founded in 1918; with several lapses, it was active in Greek politics throughout the interwar period. It was outlawed (with other political parties) by Metaxas in 1936. Its cadres formed the key elements in the resistance movement and the ensuing civil war. It was again outlawed in 1947, and remains so today.

KP   Komma Proodeftikon (Progressive Party). This is a minor right-wing party founded by Spyros Markezinis after his departure from the Greek Rally in 1955. It was largely composed of personal followers who had been involved in his earlier party, the Neon Komma (New Party), which contested elections in 1950. It has participated in elections since 1956, usually in collaboration with one of the major political coalitions.

LK   Laikon Komma (Populist Party). This party can trace its ancestry to the personalist groups found in Greek politics in the last part of the nineteenth century; it did not take a cohesive form until the first decades of this century. Until 1951 it was one of the major political groups, but at that time most of its cadres shifted to the Greek Rally. The LK leader, Constantine Tsaldaris, continued the party office, but the LK has not been directly involved in electoral politics since it entered a coalition in 1961.

MEA   Metopon Ethnikis Anadimiourgias (National Regeneration Front). This was the label used by Panayotis Kanellopoulos for his political group in 1950. It was a successor to his National Unity Party.

MK   Metarruthmistikon Komma (Reformist Party). A Populist Party splinter led by a leading notable in Macedonia in 1936. It reappeared to join the Coalition of Nationalists in 1946, and then disappeared.

PADE   Proodeftiki Agrotiki Democratiki Enosis (Progressive Agrarian Democratic Union). A coalition of Right and Center personalities that contested the 1958 elections.

PAME   Pandemokratiki Agrotikon Metopon Ellados (Pan-democratic Agrarian Front of Greece). The label used by the EDA in the 1961 elections.

PAP   Politiki Aneksartitos Parataksis (Independent Political Front). A coalition of two personalist parties that contested the 1950 elections. One of the leaders, Constantine Maniadakis, had been in charge of internal security during the Metaxas regime.

PDK   Phileleftheron Demokratikon Kendrou (Liberal Democratic Union). A splinter from the Center Union founded by Stephanos Stephanopoulos and other notables after the termination of the Papandreou government in the summer of 1965. This party was composed of EK members who defied Papandreou and accepted posts in the later government.

PK   Phileleftheron Komma (Liberal Party). This was the party founded by Venizelos in 1910. It has gone through innumerable transformations, and its present lineal descendant is the EK.

SD   Demokratikon Socialistikon Komma (Democratic Socialist Party). Founded by George Papandreou in 1935, it ran in the

National Political Union in 1946 and was later changed to the George Papandreou Party.

VenPK   Venizelikon Phileleftheron Komma (Venizelist Liberal Party). This splinter group from the Liberal Party was formed by Sophocles Venizelos (the son of the former premier) to participate in the 1946 elections. At that time the PK itself was led by Themistocles Sofoulis. The splinter reentered the Liberal Party in 1947.

"X"   Komma Xiton Ethnikis Antistasseos ("X" National Resistance Party). Founded by General George Grivas in 1946, largely from extreme rightists in his own National Defense Battalion. The name was changed in 1950 to Ethnikon Agrotikon Komma Xiton ("X" National Agrarian Party). After 1950 the party disappeared.

Notes

Notes

Complete authors' names, titles, and publication data are given in the Bibliography, pp. 349–54.

Introduction

1. See Ginsburg, *Atlas of Economic Development*. On indices of birth or death rates, physicians per capita, and students in secondary or higher education per capita Greece ranks in the upper quartile of all nations, although below most Western European states. On other measures, such as gross national product, calories consumed per day, adult literacy, and the proportion of the population in cities of 20,000 or more, Greece is found in the second quartile.

2. Russett, pp. 28–30.

3. See S. P. Huntington, "Political Development and Political Decay," in Welch, pp. 207–9. See also Curtis, *Comparative Government and Politics*.

4. See de Schwienitz, *Industrialization and Democracy*.

5. Diamant, "The Nature of Political Development," in Finkle and Gable, p. 96.

6. Apter, "Political Systems," p. 2.

7. Almond and Powell, p. 22.

8. Riggs, pp. 416–23.

9. Apter, "Political Systems," pp. 8–9.

10. Riggs, pp. 39–40.

11. Almond and Powell, p. 34.

12. *Ibid.*, p. 35.

13. *Ibid.*, p. 285.

14. *Ibid.*, p. 25.

15. *Ibid.*, p. 19.

16. *Ibid.*, pp. 34, 285–86.

17. Apter, "Political Systems," p. 19.

18. *Ibid.*, p. 21.

19. Pye, "Typologies and Political Development," p. 10.

20. Arthur L. Kalleberg, "The Logic of Comparison: A Methodological Note on the Comparative Study of Political Systems," *World Politics*, XIX (Oct. 1966), p. 73.

21. Robert Brown, *Explanation in Social Science* (Chicago: Aldine, 1963), p. 171.

22. Lijphart, p. 7.

23. Riggs, p. 4.

24. *Ibid.*, Chap. 13.

25. *Ibid.*, Chap. 7.

26. *Ibid.*, p. 117.

27. Apter, "Political Systems," p. 1.

28. Apter, *Politics of Modernization*, p. vi.

29. *Ibid.*

30. Apter, "Political Systems," p. 21.

31. *Ibid.*, p. 20.

32. *Ibid.*, p. 11.

33. *Ibid.*, p. 19.

34. *Ibid.*, p. 27.

35. *Ibid.*, p. 19.

36. *Ibid.*, p. 22.

37. Apter suggests that this is characteristic of Latin America, where the government acts primarily as a mediator between power blocs.

38. Apter, "Political Systems," p. 17.

39. *Ibid.*, p. 22.

40. *Ibid.*, p. 20.

41. Apter, *Politics of Modernization*, p. 65.

42. Almond and Powell, p. 30. They seem to use "function" and "variable" interchangeably.

43. *Ibid.*, Chap. 8 and p. 190.

44. *Ibid.*, p. 195.

45. *Ibid.*, pp. 64–72, 47–48.

46. *Ibid.*, p. 23.

47. *Ibid.* See also the table on p. 217 and the illustration of relationships on p. 308.

48. *Ibid.*, p. 208.

49. *Ibid.*, Chaps. 9–10.

50. For a critique, see Lijphart, pp. 4–6, 13–14.

51. None of these authors elaborate the concept of regression or stagnation very satisfactorily. For a more complete discussion, see Samuel P. Huntington, *Political Order in Changing Societies* (New Haven: Yale University Press, 1968), Chap. 1; and S. N. Eisenstadt, "Breakdowns of Modernization" *Economic Development and Cultural Change*, Vol. 12, July 1964, pp. 345–67.

52. Apter, *Politics of Modernization*, p. 260.

53. Almond and Coleman, p. 33.

54. Godoy and Fortín, pp. 14–15.

55. Janowitz, p. 7.

56. *Ibid.*, p. 9. Janowitz notes that military traditions in the Ottoman Empire facilitated military intervention in politics. To some extent, Greece can be viewed as a part of that tradition.

57. The standard presentation is Duverger, *Political Parties*. See also Giovanni Sartori, "European Political Parties: The Case of Polarized Pluralism," in LaPalombara and Weiner, pp. 137–76.

58. LaPalombara and Weiner, p. 25.

59. *Ibid.*, p. 3.

60. *Ibid.*, p. 6.

61. See, for example, Namier, *The Structure of Politics at the Accession of George III*; and Rustow, *The Politics of Compromise: A Study of Parties and Cabinet Government in Sweden*.

62. LaPalombara and Weiner, p. 13.

63. *Ibid.*, p. 18.

64. Lijphart, pp. 3–44.

65. David Apter (in *The Political Kingdom in Uganda*) is cited by Lijphart as using the term "consociational" to apply to a system in which "constituent units do not lose their identity when merging in some form of union." By and large, the emphasis in the Apter formulation is on structural characteristics, which range from loose alliances to federalism.

66. Lijphart, "Typologies of Democratic Systems," pp. 22–23.

67. Lehmbruch, p. 3.

68. Binder, p. 54.

69. Horowitz, "Political Legitimacy," p. 48.

70. Janowitz, p. 29.

71. Stanley Hoffman, "Heroic Leadership: The Case of Modern France," in Edinger, p. 115. His concept of "homeorhetic change" is similar to the mechanism suggested here.

72. Pye, "Typologies and Political Development," p. 11.

73. Riggs, pp. 411–12.

74. Apter, "A Comparative Method for the Study of Politics," p. 223.

75. Almond and Powell, pp. 39–40.

76. See the Conclusion in Ward and Rustow, *Political Modernization in Japan and Turkey*.

77. Godoy and Fortín, p. 13.

78. For a similar application, see Grossholtz, p. 5.

79. Hoffman, in Edinger, p. 112.

80. Rosenau, p. 65.

81. Godoy and Fortín, p. 13.

82. For an excellent corrective to the usual assumptions, see Myrdahl, *Asian Drama*, Vol. I, Pt. III.

83. Apter, "Political Systems and Developmental Change," p. 18. He notes that the long-term prospect in modernizing countries is a constant shifting between bureaucratic and reconciliation types.

84. Lucian Pye, *Politics, Personality and Nation-Building* (New Haven: Yale University Press, 1962), p. 44.

85. Lester G. Seligman, "Elite Recruitment and Political Development," in Finkle and Gable, pp. 329–30.

86. See Almond, "A Developmental Approach to Political Systems," in Finkle and Gable, pp. 116–18.

87. Almond and Powell, p. 14.

88. Apter, *Politics of Modernization,*
pp. 131–37.
89. *Ibid.,* p. 137.
90. Riggs, Chap. 4.

1. The Character of Greek Society

1. This parliamentarian was one of our sample of 55.
2. Banfield, p. 87.
3. Tarrow, p. 59.
4. Banfield, p. 10.
5. Tarrow, p. 56.
6. Banfield, pp. 139–40.
7. Almond and Powell, p. 207.
8. Banfield, p. 17.
9. See, for example: Boorstin, *Colonial Experience* and *National Experiment*; and Potter, *People of Plenty.*
10. Pitt-Rivers, p. 139.
11. *Ibid.,* p. 154.
12. *Ibid.,* p. 108.
13. *Ibid.,* p. 141.
14. Tarrow, p. 68.
15. Wylie, p. 41.
16. Petropulos, p. 53.
17. *Ibid.,* p. 236.
18. Grossholtz, pp. 86–91, 184.
19. Almond and Powell, p. 209.
20. Tarrow, p. 56.
21. Sanders, p. 15.
22. Grossholtz, p. 90.
23. Sanders, p. 12.
24. Banfield, pp. 146–52.
25. Friedl, *Vasilika,* pp. 80–81.
26. *Ibid.,* p. 18.
27. Petropulos, p. 56.
28. Friedl, *Vasilika,* pp. 49–51.
29. Petropulos, p. 56.
30. Friedl, *Vasilika,* p. 31.
31. *Ibid.,* p. 14.
32. Friedl, "Hospital Care," p. 25.
33. Sanders, pp. 127–28.
34. Easton, p. 40.
35. Campbell, pp. 218–23.
36. Petropulos, p. 59.
37. Sanders, p. 283–94.
38. Friedl, *Vasilika,* pp. 34–35.
39. Friedl, "The Role of Kinship," p. 34.

40. Moustaka, p. 14.

2. The Development of the Modern Greek State

1. This chapter is a survey only. For more detailed accounts, see: Finlay, *History of the Greek Revolution*; Kaltchas, *Introduction to the Constitutional History of Modern Greece*; Petropulos, *Politics and Statecraft in the Kingdom of Greece, 1833–1843*; and Woodhouse, *The Greek War of Independence.*
2. Woodhouse, pp. 24–25.
3. *Ibid.,* p. 26.
4. *Ibid.,* p. 35.
5. *Ibid.*
6. Petropulos, pp. 38–39.
7. *Ibid.,* p. 36.
8. Kaltchas, pp. 9–10.
9. Petropulos, p. 102.
10. Woodhouse, p. 36.
11. Petropulos, p. 72.
12. *Ibid.,* pp. 48–49.
13. Woodhouse, pp. 43–47.
14. Forester, p. 9.
15. Petropulos, p. 41.
16. See, for example, Woodhouse, p. 41.
17. Petropulos, pp. 39–40.
18. *Ibid.,* p. 25.
19. *Ibid.,* p. 37.
20. *Ibid.,* p. 41.
21. Woodhouse, p. 57.
22. Petropulos, p. 29.
23. *Ibid.,* pp. 27–28.
24. *Ibid.,* p. 34.
25. Kaltchas, p. 30.
26. Petropulos, p. 33.
27. Kaltchas, p. 37.
28. Petropulos, p. 20.
29. Woodhouse, pp. 94–95.
30. Petropulos, p. 109.
31. *Ibid.,* p. 108.
32. Finlay, II, 109.
33. Petropulos, p. 119.
34. Finlay, II, 227.
35. Kaltchas, p. 37.
36. Petropulos, pp. 175–80.
37. *Ibid.,* p. 193.
38. *Ibid.,* p. 213.

Item	Average or percentage	Countries sampled	Rank of Greece
Population living in cities of over 20,000	37.4%	120	24
Average annual increase in population of cities over 20,000	0.6%	50	10
Percentage of population in armed forces (1959)	1.7%	88	13
Percentage of eligible population voting in election of 1958	73.3%	100	35
Newspaper circulation per 1,000 population	125.0	125	35
Items of domestic mail per capita	23.0	76	34
Radios per 1,000 population	89.9*	118	46
Annual cinema attendance per capita	6.3	104	46
Students in higher educational institutions per 1,000 students (1960)	320.0	105	39
Percentage of population 5–19 in primary and secondary schools	53.0%	125	49
Percent literacy in population 15 or older	80.0%	118	35

* *The average annual increase in radios per capita was 7.3%.*

39. *Ibid.*, p. 215.

40. *Ibid.*, pp. 270–71.

41. *Ibid.*, p. 373.

42. *Ibid.*, p. 441.

43. Kaltchas, p. 98.

44. Petropulos, p. 455.

45. Kaltchas, p. 111.

46. *Ibid.*

47. For the Cretan rebellion of 1866, see Stillman, *The Cretan Insurrection of 1866-7-8.* For the decade of the 1890's, see Howard, *Theatre of Life,* Vol. II; and Pallis, *The Cretan Drama: The Life and Memoirs of Prince George of Greece.*

48. Chandler, p. 199.

49. For a discussion of events causing the emancipation of women in a similar setting, see Frey, p. 151.

50. See: Eddy, *Greece and the Greek Refugees;* Pallis, *Greece's Anatolian Venture;* the League of Nations, *Greek Refugee Settlement;* and Pentzopoulos, *The Balkan Exchange of Minorities and Its Impact Upon Greece.*

51. McNeill, p. 51.

52. Woodhouse, p. 60.

53. Moustaka, *The Internal Migrant,* p. 62.

54. Russett, *et al., World Handbook of Political and Social Indicators.* According to these data, which rely on materials prior to 1961, Greece ranked in various aspects of modernization as shown in the tabulation above.

3. The International Factor

1. This is not to imply that systemic factors are not recognized in the study of comparative politics. Studies of individual countries, however, although paying homage to external variables, generally proceed on the assumption that domestic politics are self-contained.

2. For a good example, see Chaconas, *Adamantios Korais.*

3. Pallis, *Greece's Anatolian Venture,* p. 1.

4. Rosenau, p. 65.

5. Petropulos, p. 44.

6. Kaltchas, p. 87.

7. Petropulos, p. 48.

8. Kaltchas, p. 103.

9. Petropulos, pp. 145–46.

10. *Ibid.*, p. 166.

11. Kaltchas, p. 103.

12. Petropulos, p. 431.

13. Prince Alfred got 230,000 out of 240,000 votes. See Mavrogordato, p. 56.

14. Daphnes, *Ta Hellenika Politika Kommata,* Chap. 7.

15. Petropulos, pp. 434–38.

16. Levandis, p. ix.

17. Pepelasis, p. 173.

18. Levandis, p. ix.

19. Break and Turvey, p. 207.

20. For two views of Allied activities in Greece during World War I, see Thomson, *The Allied Secret Service in Greece*, and MacKenzie, *Greek Memories*.

21. Pentzopoulos, pp. 41–45.

22. Sakellaropoulos, *He Skia tes Duseos*.

23. See Barros, *The Corfu Incident of 1923*.

24. Xydis, p. 5.

25. *Ibid.*, Chaps. I and II.

26. *Ibid.*, p. 40.

27. *Ibid.*, p. 105.

28. *Ibid.*, p. 263.

29. Sweet-Escott, p. 63.

30. McNeill, p. 67.

31. Rousseas, p. 31.

32. McNeill, pp. 67–71.

33. Xydis, Chap. IV, describes the development of postwar territorial claims.

34. Rousseas gives an account of the coup and the events leading to it as a convinced Papandreou supporter. Later events have made his comments on the role of the monarch in the coup questionable.

35. Rousseas, pp. 31–35.

36. *New York Times*, May 21, 1967, p. 3.

37. Pentzopoulos, Chap. III.

38. Cited in Xydis, p. 57.

39. See Appendix A for the Interview Schedule.

40. Several deputies had photographic displays of themselves with prominent American or European political personalities in their offices.

41. Hanrieder, p. 977.

4. Consensus and Dissensus

1. Strong, p. 3.

2. Deutsch, *Nationalism and Social Communication*, p. 105.

3. Deutsch, *et al.*, pp. 26–41.

4. Deutsch, p. 188.

5. Fairchild, p. 6.

6. Petropulos, p. 20.

7. *Ibid.*, p. 35.

8. See Bent, *The Cyclades*.

9. Petropulos, p. 19.

10. Rodd, pp. 52–54.

11. See Kirkwall, *Four Years in the Ionian Islands*, Vols. I and II.

12. Rodd, p. 53.

13. See Chap. 2, Note 47.

14. See Wace and Thompson, *Nomads of the Balkans*; and Campbell, *Honour, Family and Patronage*.

15. During World War I, the clergy was split into pro-Venizelist and pro-Constantine factions. During the German occupation, several clerics were accused of collaboration. Similarly, in the civil-war period, there were several bishops involved in the Communist-dominated groups. In the recent upheaval, the church hierarchy was again reshuffled, at least in part for political reasons.

16. For an example, see Sanders, p. 25. He notes that the ancient god Helios has been replaced by St. Elijah.

17. *Ibid.*, p. 263.

18. *Ibid.*, p. 260.

19. *Ibid.*, p. 254.

20. Friedl, *Vasilika*, p. 56.

21. *Ibid.*, p. 46.

22. Peaslee, *Constitutions of Nations,* II, 91.

23. See Sanders, p. 251, for a table showing the distribution of hours among the various subjects in the Greek school curriculum.

24. Lasswell and Kaplan, p. 126.

25. Almond and Verba, pp. 17–18.

26. Munkman, p. 101.

5. Interest Groups

1. Almond and Powell, p. 75.

2. Weiner, pp. 37–38.

3. Tarrow, p. 40.

4. Almond and Powell, p. 78.

5. *Ibid.*

6. *Cf.* Grossholtz, p. 243.

7. Almond and Powell, pp. 76–77

8. Tarrow, p. 69.
9. Binder, p. 153.
10. LaPalombara, p. 285.
11. Weiner, p. 13.
12. Almond and Powell, p. 75.
13. Weiner, pp. 32–34.
14. LaPalombara, p. 196.
15. Grossholtz, p. 236.
16. Almond and Powell, p. 83.
17. Weiner, p. 16.
18. See Pepelasis, "The Legal System and the Economic Development of Greece."
19. Dahl, p. 226.
20. For a general survey, see Break and Turvey.
21. *Ibid.,* p. 121.
22. *Ibid.,* p. 38.
23. Strong, p. 119.
24. *Statistical Yearbook of Greece,* 1963, p. 261.
25. Alexander, p. 29.
26. *Ibid.,* p. 48.
27. Break and Turvey, pp. 24–28 and Chap. 7.
28. See Binder, p. 140, for a similar case.
29. Alexander, p. 77.
30. For more detailed information concerning the connections between Greek banking and industry, see Meynaud, pp. 356–65.
31. Psilos, pp. 204–5.
32. *Ibid.,* p. 187.
33. Bower and Bolitho, p. 56.
34. Break and Turvey, p. 35.
35. Kayser and Thomas, p. 222.
36. Pentzopoulos, p. 229.
37. *Statistical Yearbook of Greece,* 1961, p. 158.
38. *Ibid.,* 1963, p. 137.
39. Coutsoumaris, *Morphology of Greek Industry,* p. 65.
40. *Statistical Yearbook of Greece,* 1963, p. 143.
41. *Ibid.,* p. 261.
42. *Ibid.*
43. Kousoulas, p. 32.
44. Meynaud, p. 376.
45. Tarrow, p. 35.

46. Sanders, p. 209.
47. *Ibid.,* p. 238.
48. Weiner, p. 13.
49. Campbell, p. 230.
50. Sanders, p. 304.
51. Campbell, pp. 235–40.
52. Weiner, p. 31.
53. Grossholtz, p. 243.
54. Sanders, p. 198.
55. *Ibid.,* p. 199.
56. *Ibid.,* pp. 195–96.
57. Weiner, p. 120.
58. LaPalombara, pp. 83–84.
59. Weiner, p. 16.
60. Grossholtz, p. 243.
61. Weiner, p. 70.
62. Grossholtz, p. 6.
63. LaPalombara, p. 10.
64. Binder, p. 227.

6. Political Parties

1. LaPalombara and Weiner, p. 3.
2. *Ibid.,* p. 6.
3. *Ibid.,* p. 5.
4. *Ibid.,* p. 7.
5. Weber, "Politics as a Vocation," in Gerth and Wright, pp. 102–7; Duverger, pp. xxiii–xxxvii.
6. Petropulos, pp. 501–15.
7. See Daphnes, *Ta Hellenika Politika Kommata,* for a historical survey of Greek parties.
8. LaPalombara and Weiner, pp. 14–20.
9. *Ibid.,* p. 17.
10. For a thorough survey of the interwar period, see Daphnes, *He Hellas metaxu Duo Polemon.*
11. Riggs, p. 132.
12. The material on party organization is summarized from Meynaud, pp. 233–53 for the ERE and pp. 273–77 for the EK.
13. Interview with Panayotis Kanellopoulos, March 25, 1965.
14. For a full listing, see Meynaud, pp. 467–83.
15. See, for example: Weiner, p. 13; Key, p. 37; Tarrow, p. 78; and Clubok, "Political Party Membership and Sub-

leadership in Rural Japan," in Silberman and Harootunian, *Modern Japanese Leadership.*

16. Stycos, p. 59.

17. Friedl, *Vasilika*, pp. 94–96.

18. See Daphnes, *Ta Hellenika Politika Kommata*, pp. 179–90, for the period 1926–58. Data from official election returns were used for the years 1961 through 1964.

19. *Statistical Yearbook of Greece*, 1962, p. 316.

20. U.S. Department of State report, p. 14.

21. For a detailed, documented report (although from a partisan source) on the election irregularities in 1961, see *Mavri Biblos.*

22. Scalapino and Masumi, p. 67, note that the major difference between the two conservative parties in postwar Japan was also personal and factional.

23. Key, p. 304.

24. The survey of party policies is condensed from Meynaud, pp. 254–58 for the ERE and pp. 287–91 for the EK.

25. Heurtley, *et al.*, p. 169.

26. See, for example, the short summary prepared by Paul A. Samuelson, "The Greek Tragedy," *Newsweek*, May 22, 1967, p. 89.

27. Key, p. 307.

28. Russett, *et al.*, p. 108.

29. U.S. Department of State report, p. 14.

7. Politics at the Parliamentary Level

1. For a discussion of the decline of legislatures, see Hitchner and Levine, pp. 154–55.

2. Rose, p. 209.

3. Lijphart, p. 21.

4. Padgett, pp. 82–85.

5. Binder, p. 227.

6. *Ibid.*, Part VI.

7. Grossholtz, p. 6.

8. *Ibid.*, p. 124.

9. Riggs, pp. 232–33.

10. Couloumbis, p. 49.

11. Triantis, Part B, pp. 63–112.

12. See Pepelasis, pp. 173–98.

13. Coutsoumaris, *Morphology of Greek Industry*, p. 21.

14. *Statistical Yearbook of Greece*, 1961, p. 382.

15. Pepelasis, p. 195.

16. See Psilos, Chap. 8.

17. Break and Turvey, p. 60.

18. Riggs, p. 308.

19. Coutsoumaris, *Morphology of Greek Industry*, p. 137.

20. Thompson, p. 23.

21. Riggs, Chap. 9.

22. Break and Turvey, Chap. 2.

23. Riggs, pp. 304–6.

24. Binder, p. 229.

25. Petropulos, p. 214. The early Greek political leaders viewed rules, budgets, and changes of government in the same light as their modern heirs.

26. Wahlke, *et al.*, pp. 380–81.

27. *Ibid.*, p. 246.

28. *Ibid.*, pp. 465–68.

29. *Ibid.*, p. 467.

30. *Ibid.*, p. 247.

31. See Vouli Ton Hellenon, *To Syntagma tes Hellados kai O Kanonismos tes Voulis.*

32. Wahlke, *et al.*, p. 248.

33. *Ibid.*, pp. 277–80.

34. *Ibid.*, p. 272.

8. Politics at the Extraparliamentary Level

1. Janowitz, pp. 5–8.

2. Daphnes, *He Hellas metaxu Duo Polemon*, Vols. I and II.

3. O'Ballance, p. 156.

4. *Ibid.*

5. Janowitz, p. 47.

6. *Ibid.*, p. 74.

7. Meynaud, p. 340.

8. Kaltchas, p. 140.

9. Meynaud, p. 340.

10. Interview with Panayotis Kanellopoulos, March 25, 1965.

11. Kaltchas, p. 141.

12. For a full discussion of precedent and constitutional interpretation in light of the 1965 controversy, see *Foseis ten Politikin Krisin Pou Syneklonisi ten Hellada.*

13. Chandler, p. 21.

14. Kousoulas, p. 237.

15. Meynaud, pp. 195–97. This material was supplemental to an interview with the press secretary of the EDA.

16. EDA, *Weekly Press Bulletin* 227 (Feb. 11, 1965), p. 3.

17. Meynaud, p. 217.

18. As set forth in United Democratic Left, *For a National Democratic Change.* See also Meynaud, pp. 202–4.

19. Peaslee, p. 109.

20. EDA, *Weekly Press Bulletin* 278 (April 28, 1966), p. 7.

21. United Democratic Left, p. 19.

22. See, for example, S. G. Triantis, *Common Market and Economic Development.*

23. United Democratic Left, p. 56.

24. Burks, p. 70.

25. The figures for 1936–58 are found in Daphnes, *Ta Hellenika Politika Kommata*, pp. 184–90. The figures for 1961 through 1964 come from official election records.

26. The figures were: $N = 147$, $r = .27$, $P < .05$. Correlation analysis using area in cash crops such as wheat, tobacco, and cotton did not produce significant correlations. Even rural population per square kilometer is a poor indicator, since only 7 per cent of the variance is so explained.

27. Pentzopoulos, Chap. 4.

28. Alexander, p. 62.

29. Pentzopoulos, pp. 182–83.

30. Daphnes, *Ta Hellenika Politika Kommata*, Chap. 10.

31. Burks, p. 58.

32. Pentzopoulos, p. 189.

33. *Ibid.,* p. 186, provided figures for 1922–33. Figures for 1946, 1958, and 1964 were computed from biographical records in the personnel office of parliament. The data for 1936 were incomplete.

34. *Statistical Yearbook of Greece*, 1963, pp. 32–33. $N = 42$, $r = .22$.

35. Kayser and Thompson, p. 404. $N = 147$, $r = .010$.

36. Burks, p. 40.

37. Moustaka, pp. 69–70.

38. Calculated from election statistics in the period.

39. LaPalombara, p. 90.

40. Janowitz, p. 16.

41. *New York Times*, June 4, 1951, p. 11.

42. Couloumbis, p. 37.

43. Calculated from data in *Statistical Yearbook of Greece*, 1967, p. 330.

44. Couloumbis, p. 187.

9. Military Oligarchy: The Coup of 1967

1. See Janowitz, *The Military in the Political Development of New Nations.*

2. Rousseas, p. 28.

3. *Ibid.,* p. 30.

4. *Ibid.*

5. *Ibid.,* p. 39.

6. *Ibid.,* pp. 46–47.

7. *Christian Science Monitor*, Apr. 29, 1967, p. 4.

8. *New York Times*, Apr. 24, 1967, p. 1.

9. According to C. L. Sulzberger in the *New York Times*, May 3, 1967, p. 44.

10. *New York Times*, Mar. 3, 1968, p. 28.

11. *Time*, Apr. 28, 1967, p. 29.

12. Statement of Premier Kollias broadcast on the day of the coup. Quoted in *Keesing's Contemporary Archives*, Vol. XVI (1967–68), p. 22024.

13. *New York Times*, May 1, 1967, p. 2.

14. *Ibid.,* May 3, 1967, p. 4.

15. Horowitz, p. 270.

16. *New York Times*, May 6, 1967, p. 1.

17. *Ibid.,* May 12, 1967, p. 1.

18. See Rousseas, Part II; and *New York Times*, May 7, 1967, IV, 4.

19. *New York Times*, May 20, 1967, p. 14.

20. *Ibid.,* May 16, 1967, p. 18.

21. Rousseas, p. 27.

22. Smith Hempstone, "Greece," *Atlantic*, July 1967, p. 21.

23. *New York Times*, Apr. 26, 1967, p. 1.

24. *Ibid.*, Oct. 15, 1967, p. E5.

25. *Ibid.*, June 25, 1967, p. 20.

26. *Ibid.*, Apr. 28, 1967, p. 3.

27. *Ibid.*, Oct. 8, 1967, p. 1.

28. *Washington Post*, June 24, 1968, p. A21.

29. *New York Times*, June 1, 1967, p. 6.

30. *Christian Science Monitor*, Apr. 29, 1967, p. 4.

31. *New York Times*, May 6, 1967, p. 1.

32. Quoted by C. L. Sulzberger in the *New York Times*, May 7, 1967, p. 10.

33. *New York Times*, June 2, 1967, p. 16.

34. *Ibid.*, Oct. 8, 1967, p. 4.

35. *Ibid.*, May 15, 1967, p. 13.

36. *Ibid.*, May 11, 1967, p. 1.

37. *Ibid.*, May 3, 1967, p. 1.

38. *Ibid.*, Apr. 30, 1967, p. 1.

39. *Ibid.*, June 4, 1967, p. 1.

40. *Ibid.*, Mar. 3, 1968, p. 22.

41. *Ibid.*

42. *Ibid.*, June 3, 1967, p. 5.

43. *Ibid.*, June 15, 1967, p. 3.

44. *Ibid.*, June 27, 1967, p. 6.

45. *Ibid.*, June 25, 1967, p. 8.

46. *Christian Science Monitor*, Apr. 29, 1967, p. 4.

47. Psilos and Westebbe, p. 6.

48. Statement of Premier Kollias, printed in *Keesing's Contemporary Archives*, XVI (1967–68), p. 22025.

49. *New York Times*, May 15, 1967, p. 13.

50. *Ibid.*, May 28, 1967, p. 14.

51. *Ibid.*

52. *Ibid.*, May 7, 1967, p. 1.

53. Shils, "The Military in the Political Development of the New States," in Johnson, p. 58.

54. See Scalapino and Masumi, pp. 19–20.

55. *New York Times*, May 18, 1967, p. 12.

56. *Ibid.*, Apr. 28, 1967, p. 3.

57. *Ibid.*, May 28, 1967, p. 14.

58. Lucian Pye, "The Army in Burmese Politics," in Johnson, p. 232.

59. *Washington Post*, June 24, 1968, p. A21.

60. *New York Times*, May 9, 1967, p. 1.

61. *To Vima*, Oct. 1, 1968, p. 1.

10. Socialization and the Family

1. Pye, *Politics, Personality and Nation Building*, pp. 44–45.

2. Wahlke, *et al.*, pp. 77–78.

3. The comparative data in this and the following tables, unless otherwise noted, are drawn from Wahlke, *et al.*, Chap. 4. The states considered were New Jersey, California, Tennessee, and Ohio. The individual state totals were used to compute an overall average.

4. Wahlke, *et al.*, p. 82.

5. See Barber, *The Lawmakers*. This figure was computed from tables giving political background data for each of Barber's four types of legislators.

6. Wahlke, *et al.*, p. 91.

7. Edinger and Searing, p. 437.

8. The Kennedys, Rockefellers, and Roosevelts come immediately to mind. However, the most spectacular examples would seem to be in transitional societies: for example, the succession of Mrs. Indira Gandhi in India. D. S. Senanayake, the first prime minister of Ceylon, was succeeded first by his son and then by his nephew. When S. W. R. D. Bandaranaike died in the same office, having no brother and a young son, his wife became prime minister.

9. Namier, p. 4.

10. *Ibid.*, p. 168.

11. Ranney, p. 113.

12. Dogan, "Political Ascent in a Class Society," in Marvick, pp. 57–90.

13. *Ibid.*, pp. 84–85.

14. A. B. Clubok, Forrest Berghorn, and Norman Wilensky, "Family Relationships, Congressional Recruitment, and

Political Modernization." Unpublished paper, Department of Political Science, University of Florida.

15. Two cases have already been mentioned: Eleutherios Venizelos was succeeded by his son Sophocles as leader of the Liberals; more recently, Andreas Papandreou was gradually assuming more and more of his father's power.

16. Barber, *The Lawmakers*; compiled from background data given for his four legislative types.

17. Wahlke, *et al.*, p. 82.

18. Marvick, p. 85.

19. *Ibid.*

20. Grossholtz, p. 227.

21. Singer, pp. 101–2.

22. McCracken, p. 90.

11. Occupational Backgrounds and Local Connections

1. These particular distinctions are used, respectively, by the following authors: Dogan, "Political Ascent in a Class Society," in Marvick, pp. 57–90; Loewenberg, *Parliament and the German Political System*; and Buck, *Amateurs and Professionals in British Politics, 1918–1959*.

2. Marvick, p. 72.

3. *Ibid.*

4. See Loewenberg, pp. 109–10, for a summary.

5. Akzin, p. 577.

6. Loewenberg, p. 110.

7. Berrington and Finer, p. 610.

8. Loewenberg, p. 62.

9. Marvick, p. 90.

10. Loewenberg, p. 110.

11. Scalapino and Masumi, p. 176.

12. Tarrow, pp. 83–84.

13. Frey, p. 181.

14. The number of lawyers in the United States Congress—65 per cent in the Senate and 55 per cent in the House —is substantially higher than in most other western parliamentary bodies. However, there is a substantial difference between American lawyers and their

Greek counterparts in terms of differentiation and representation. See Loewenberg, p. 109.

15. Thompson, p. 20.

16. Ferriman, pp. 4–5.

17. Tarrow, p. 62.

18. Wahlke, *et al.*, p. 488.

19. Loewenberg, p. 75.

20. Hamon, p. 548.

21. Sartori, p. 587.

22. Ranney, pp. 38, 151.

23. Frey, p. 187.

24. *Ibid.*, p. 188.

25. *Ibid.*, p. 192.

26. Ranney, p. 78.

27. Berrington and Finer, p. 607.

28. Hamon, p. 557.

29. Loewenberg, p. 51.

30. Harold D. Lasswell, quoted in Wahlke, *et al.*, p. 73.

31. Wahlke, *et al.*, p. 96.

32. Ranney, pp. 108, 197.

33. Scalapino and Masumi, pp. 171, 173.

34. Frey, p. 98.

35. Loewenberg, p. 93.

36. Dogan, p. 79.

37. Compiled from incidental materials.

38. Calculated from data in *Odigos*, 1960, 1963, and 1964.

39. *Ibid.*

40. Calculated from data in *Odigos* for 1963 and 1964, and from records of the Ministry of the Interior for 1954.

41. In 1961, some 82 per cent of the Greek population was literate. *Statistical Yearbook of Greece*, 1963, p. 77. The same volume (p. 108) reported a total of 97,600 graduates of higher educational institutions, including teacher training institutes; of these, 56,600 were in the Athens metropolitan area.

12. The Political Elite

1. See Pye and Verba, *Political Culture and Political Development*.

2. Nordlinger, p. 496.

3. Portions of this chapter appeared in my article "Political Recruitment and Political Crises: The Case of Greece," *Comparative Political Studies*, I (Jan. 1969).

4. See Schlesinger, *Ambition and Politics*.

5. Heidenheimer, p. 127.

6. Blondel and Godfrey, p. 50.

7. Moodie, p. 75.

8. For an excellent discussion of turnover and opportunity, see Schlesinger, Chap. 3.

9. Guttsman, p. 79.

10. Edinger, p. 289.

11. Lerner, p. 399.

12. In 1961 there were 97,600 graduates of higher educational institutions, including teacher training institutes. Of these, 56,600 were in the Athens metropolitan area. *Statistical Yearbook of Greece*, 1963.

13. A total of 931 persons held cabinet rank from 1843 to 1965. Some social background information was secured for almost all of them. The gaps were largely in biographies for early ministers and for ministers who had served in nonpolitical, service governments. The calculation of general trends was made with data for the full cabinet membership. Biographical information on early cabinet ministers came from *Megale Hellenike Enkylopaideia*. For recent cabinet ministers, the 1962 and 1965 editions of *Ellinikon Who's Who* were used. The records in the personnel division of the Greek parliament were also used for data on ministers after 1936.

14. For additional discussion of occupation and politics, see Matthews, *U.S. Senators and Their World*, Chap. 2.

15. It is probable that the category of "politician" is a function of the biographical sources. When a biographer surveys a man's entire career, he is likely to classify the man as a politician; however, when a man has assessed his own occupation, as is the case for much of the recent source material used here, he is more likely to have listed one of the liberal professions.

16. See Daphnes, *Ta Hellenika Politika Kommata*, Chaps. 8–9.

17. Guttsman, p. 101.

18. Wahlke, *et al.*, p. 82.

19. Ward, p. 8.

20. *Ibid.*, p. 10.

21. Westebbe, p. 10.

22. Coutsoumaris, *Morphology of Greek Industry*, p. 249.

23. Weiner, pp. 238–39.

24. Triantis, p. 58.

25. *Ibid.*, p. 59.

Bibliography

Bibliography

Ailianou, Tsingou D. The Greek Governments and Presidencies of Parliament and Senate, 1926–1959. Athens, 1959.

Akzin, Benjamin. "The Knesset," *International Social Science Journal,* XIII, No. 4 (1961).

Alexander, Alec. Greek Industrialists. Athens: Center for Economic Research, 1964.

Almond, Gabriel A., and G. Bingham Powell, Jr. Comparative Politics: A Developmental Approach. Boston: Little, Brown, 1966.

———— and James S. Coleman, eds. The Politics of the Developing Areas. Princeton, N.J.: Princeton University Press, 1960.

———— and Sidney Verba. The Civic Culture. Princeton, N.J.: Princeton University Press, 1963.

Apter, David E. "Political Systems and Developmental Change." A paper presented at the Seventh World Congress of the International Political Science Association, 1967.

———— The Politics of Modernization (Phoenix ed.). Chicago: University of Chicago Press, 1967.

———— The Political Kingdom in Uganda: A Study in Bureaucratic Nationalism. Princeton, N.J.: Princeton University Press, 1961.

———— "A Comparative Method for the Study of Politics," *American Journal of Sociology,* LXIV (Nov. 1958).

Banfield, Edward C. The Moral Basis of a Backward Society (paperback edition). New York: Free Press, 1967.

Barber, James D. The Lawmakers. New Haven: Yale University Press, 1965.

Barros, James. The Corfu Incident of 1923. Princeton, N.J.: Princeton University Press, 1965.

Bent, J. Theodore. The Cyclades. London: Longmans, Green, 1885.

Berrington, H. B., and S. E. Finer. "The British House of Commons," *International Social Science Journal,* XII, No. 4 (1961).

Binder, Leonard. Iran: Political Development in a Changing Society. Berkeley: University of California Press, 1962.

Blondel, Jean, and E. Drexel Godfrey, Jr. The Government of France. New York: Crowell, 1968.

Boorstin, Daniel J. The Americans: The Colonial Experience. New York: Random House, 1958.

———— The Americans: The National Experiment. New York: Random House, 1965.

Break, George, and Ralph Turvey. Studies in Greek Taxation. Athens: Center for Economic Research, 1964.

Buck, Philip W. Amateurs and Professionals in British Politics, 1918–1959. Chicago: University of Chicago Press, 1963.

Burks, R. V. The Dynamics of Communism in Eastern Europe. Princeton, N.J.: Princeton University Press, 1961.

Campbell, J. K. Honour, Family, and Patronage. Oxford: Clarendon Press, 1964.
Carey, Andrew G., and Jane P. Clark Carey. The Web of Modern Greek Politics. New York: Columbia University Press, 1968.
Chaconas, Stephen C. Adamantios Korias. New York: Columbia University Press, 1942.
Chambers, William N. Political Parties in a New Nation: The American Experience, 1776–1809. New York: Oxford University Press, 1963.
Chandler, Geoffrey. The Divided Land. London: Macmillan, 1959.
Couloumbis, Theodore A. Greek Political Reaction to American and NATO Influences. New Haven: Yale University Press, 1966.
Coutsoumaris, George. Analysis and Assessment of the Economic Effects of US PL 480. Athens: Center for Economic Research, 1965.
——— The Morphology of Greek Industry. Athens: Center for Economic Research, 1963.
Curtis, Michael. Comparative Government and Politics. New York: Harper, 1968.

Dahl, Robert. Who Governs? New Haven: Yale University Press, 1961.
Daphnes, Gregory. He Hellas metaxu Duo Polemon, 1923–1940. Athens: Ikaros, 1955. 2 vols.
——— Ta Hellenika Politika Kommata. Athens: Galaxias, 1961.
de Schwienitz, Karl. Industrialization and Democracy. New York: Free Press, 1964.
Deutsch, Karl W. Nationalism and Social Communication (2d ed.). Cambridge, Mass.: M.I.T. Press, 1966.
——— et al. "Political Community and the North Atlantic Area," reprinted in *International Political Communities: An Anthology*. Garden City: Anchor Books, 1966.
Duverger, Maurice. Political Parties. New York: John Wiley and Sons, 1955.

Easton, David. A Systems Analysis of Political Life. New York: John Wiley and Sons, 1965.
Eddy, Charles B. Greece and the Greek Refugees. London: Allen and Unwin, 1931.
Edinger, Lewis J., ed. Political Leadership in Industrialized Societies. New York: John Wiley and Sons, 1967.
Edinger, Lewis J., and Donald D. Searing. "Social Background in Elite Analysis: A Methodological Enquiry," *American Political Science Review*, LXI (June 1967).

Fairchild, Henry Pratt. Greek Immigration to the United States. New Haven: Yale University Press, 1911.
Ferriman, Z. Duckett. Home Life in Hellas. London: Mills and Boon, 1910.
Finkle, Jason, and Richard Gable, eds. Political Development and Social Change. New York: John Wiley and Sons, 1966.
Finlay, George. History of the Greek Revolution. London: Blackwood, 1861. 2 vols.
Forester, Edward S. A Short History of Modern Greece (2d ed.). London: Methuen, 1958.
Foseis ten Politikin Krisin Pou Syneklonisi ten Hellada. Athens: Istorika Ekthoseis, 1965.
Frey, Frederick W. The Turkish Political Elite. Cambridge, Mass.: M.I.T. Press, 1965.
Friedl, Ernestine. "Hospital Care in Provincial Greece," *Human Organization*, XVI (winter 1958).

ORDER N.°	RECASENS, M. ROSA
	AL NOSTRE BARRI... DONES I HOMES D'ESPERANÇA.
DATE ORDERED	
DATE RECEIVED	BARCELONA : CLARET , 1994
	156 p. : (ELS DAUS ; 136)
PRICE	
938,00 Pts.	
COPIES RUSH	1.SOCIOLOGIA-CRISTIANISMO-CATALUÑA(ESPAÑA)-ESTUDIO
CONTROL N.°	
	84-7263-902-9 LC.CL. :HM

LIBRARY BOOK SUGGESTION

Date of request

(BLOCK CAPITALS ONLY)

AUTHOR (surname first) Legg.

TITLE Politics in Modern Greece

	No of copies	
PUBLISHER	Date of Publication	

JN5016.L4

Recommended by

Reserve for

Price			ISBN										
HBK													
PBK													
Branch	000	Loan	000		Fund								
Branch	000	Loan			Fund								
Branch	000	Loan			Fund								
Control No			0	8	0	4	7	0	7	0	5	7	

USE REVERSE FOR NOTES

Order No
869274

Date Ordered

Supplier Dan

Details found

Libertas
Card cat.

GBIP
BBIP
ABIP

12 AUG 1995

Record bought   Y   N

90039 revised 1/95

—— "The Role of Kinship in the Transmission of National Culture to Rural Villages in Mainland Greece," *American Anthropologist,* LXI (Feb. 1959).

—— Vasilika: A Village in Modern Greece. New York: Holt, Rinehart, and Winston, 1962.

Gerth, Hans, and C. Wright Mills, eds. From Max Weber: Essays in Sociology (Galaxy ed.). New York: Oxford University Press, 1958.

Ginsburg, Norton. Atlas of Economic Development. Chicago: University of Chicago Press, 1961.

Godoy, Horacio H., and Carlos Fortín. "Some Suggestions for a Typology of Latin American Political Systems." A paper presented to the Seventh World Congress of the International Political Science Association, 1967.

Greece, Parliament of. To Syntagma tes Hellados kai O Kanonismos tes Voulis. Athens, 1958.

Grossholtz, Jean. Politics in the Philippines. Boston: Little, Brown, 1964.

Guttsman, W. L. The British Political Elite. London: MacGibbon and Kee, 1963.

Hamon, Léo. "Members of the French Parliament," *International Social Science Journal,* XIII, No. 4 (1961).

Hanrieder, Wolfram F. "Compatibility and Consensus: A Proposal for the Conceptual Linkage of External and Internal Dimensions of Foreign Policy," *American Political Science Review,* LXI (Dec. 1967).

Heidenheimer, Arnold J. The Governments of Germany, 2d ed. New York: Crowell, 1966.

Heurtley, W. A., H. C. Darby, C. W. Crawley, and C. M. Woodhouse. A Short History of Greece from Early Times to 1964. Cambridge, Eng.: Cambridge University Press, 1965.

Hitchner, Dell G., and Carol Levine. Comparative Government and Politics. New York: Dodd, Mead, 1967.

Horowitz, Irving L. "Political Legitimacy and the Institutionalization of Crisis," *Comparative Political Studies,* I (Apr. 1968).

—— Three Worlds of Development. New York: Oxford University Press, 1966.

Howard, Esme (Lord Howard of Penrith). Theatre of Life, Vol. II. London: Hodder and Staughton, 1936.

Janowitz, Morris. The Military in the Political Development of New Nations. Chicago: University of Chicago Press, 1964.

Johnson, John J., ed. The Role of the Military in Underdeveloped Countries. Princeton, N.J.: Princeton University Press, 1962.

Kaltchas, Nicholas. Introduction to the Constitutional History of Modern Greece. New York: Columbia University Press, 1940.

Kayser, Bernard, and Kenneth Thompson. Economic and Social Atlas of Greece. Athens: Center for Economic Research, 1964.

Key, V. O., Jr. Southern Politics. New York: Knopf, 1949.

Kirkwall, Viscount. Four Years in the Ionian Islands, Vols. I and II. London: Chapman and Hall, 1864.

Kousoulas, Dimitrios. Revolution and Defeat. London: Oxford University Press, 1965.

Ktenavea, S. Ai Hellenika Kuverneseis ai Ethnika Syneleuseis Kai ta Dimopsifismeta apo to 1821 mechri Simeron. Athens, 1947.

LaPalombara, Joseph. Interest Groups in Italian Politics. Princeton, N.J.: Princeton University Press, 1964.
———— and Myron Weiner, eds. Political Parties and Political Development. Princeton, N.J.: Princeton University Press, 1966.
Lasswell, Harold D., and Abraham Kaplan. Power and Society. New Haven: Yale University Press, 1965.
League of Nations. Greek Refugee Settlement. Geneva, 1926.
Lehmbruch, Gerhard. "A Non-Competitive Pattern of Conflict Management in Liberal Democracies: The Case of Switzerland, Austria, and Lebanon." A paper presented at the Seventh World Congress of the International Political Science Association, 1967.
Lerner, Daniel. The Passing of Traditional Society. Glencoe, Ill.: Free Press, 1958.
Levandis, John A. The Greek Foreign Debt and the Great Powers, 1821–1898. New York: Columbia University Press, 1944.
Lijphart, Arend. "Typologies of Democratic Systems," *Comparative Political Studies,* I (Apr. 1968).
Loewenberg, Gerhard. Parliament in the German Political System. Ithaca: Cornell University Press, 1966.

MacKenzie, Compton. Greek Memories. London: Chatto and Windus, 1939.
Marvick, Dwaine, ed. Political Decision Makers. Glencoe, Ill.: Free Press, 1961.
Matthews, Donald R. U.S. Senators and Their World. Chapel Hill: University of North Carolina Press, 1960.
Mavri Biblos. Athens: Enosis Kendrou, 1962.
Mavrogordato, John. Modern Greece. London: Macmillan, 1931.
McCracken, J. L. Representative Government in Ireland. London: Oxford University Press, 1958.
McNeill, William H. Greece: American Aid in Action, 1947–1956. New York: Twentieth Century Fund, 1957.
Megale Hellenike Enkyklopaideia. Athens, 1933.
Meynaud, Jean. Les Forces politiques en Grece. Lausanne: Études de Science Politique, 1965.
Moodie, Graeme C. The Government of Great Britain (2d ed.). New York: Crowell, 1964.
Moustaka, Calliope. The Internal Migrant. Athens: Social Sciences Center, 1964.
Munkman, C. A. American Aid to Greece. New York: Praeger, 1958.
Myrdal Gunnar. Asian Drama: An Enquiry into the Poverty of Nations. New York: Random House, 1968.

Namier, Sir Lewis. The Structure of Politics at the Accession of George III. London: Macmillan, 1957.
Nordlinger, Eric A. "Political Development: Time Sequences and Rates of Change," *World Politics,* XX (Apr. 1968).

O'Ballance, Edgar. The Greek Civil War. New York: Praeger, 1966.
Odigos. Athens: published yearly by Ellinikos Organismos Dimosion Skheson "Orizon."

Padgett, L. Vincent. The Mexican Political System. Boston: Houghton Mifflin, 1966.
Pallis, A. A. Greece's Anatolian Venture and After. London: Methuen, 1937.

────── ed. The Cretan Drama: The Life and Memoirs of Prince George of Greece. New York: Robert Speller and Sons, 1959.

Peaslee, A. J. Constitutions of Nations, Vol. II. The Hague: Martinus Nijhoff, 1956.

Pentzopoulos, Dimitri. The Balkan Exchange of Minorities and Its Impact Upon Greece. Paris: Mouton, 1962.

Pepelasis, A. A. "The Legal System and the Economic Development of Greece," *Journal of Economic History,* XIX (June 1959).

Petropulos, John A. Politics and Statecraft in the Kingdom of Greece, 1833-1843. Princeton, N.J.: Princeton University Press, 1968.

Pitt-Rivers, J. A. The People of the Sierra (Phoenix ed.). Chicago: University of Chicago Press, 1961.

Potter, Charles M. People of Plenty. Chicago: University of Chicago Press, 1954.

Power, Leonard, and Gordon Bolitho. Otho I, King of Greece. London: Selwyn and Blount, 1899.

Psilos, Diomedes. Capital Market in Greece. Athens: Center for Economic Research, 1964.

────── and Richard M. Westebbe. Public International Development Financing in Greece. New York: Columbia University School of Law, 1964.

Pye, Lucian. Politics, Personality, and Nation-Building. New Haven: Yale University Press, 1962.

────── "Typologies and Political Development." A paper presented at the Seventh World Congress of the International Political Science Association, 1967.

────── and Sidney Verba. Political Culture and Political Development. Princeton, N.J.: Princeton University Press, 1965.

Ranney, Austin. Pathways to Parliament. Madison: University of Wisconsin Press, 1965.

Riggs, Fred. Administration in Developing Countries. Boston: Houghton Mifflin, 1964.

Rodd, Rennell. Customs and Lore of Modern Greece. London: David Stott, 1892.

Rose, Richard. Politics in England. Boston: Little, Brown, 1964.

Rosenau, James N. "Pre-Theories and Theories of Foreign Policy," in R. Barry Farrell, ed., *Approaches to Comparative and International Politics.* Evanston: Northwestern University Press, 1966.

Rousseas, Stephen. The Death of a Democracy: Greece and the American Conscience. New York: Grove Press, 1967.

Russett, Bruce M. International Regions and the International System: A Study in Political Ecology. Chicago: Rand McNally, 1967.

──────, Hayward Alker, Karl Deutsch, and Harold D. Lasswell. World Handbook of Political and Social Indicators. New Haven: Yale University Press, 1964.

Rustow, Dankwart. The Politics of Compromise: A Study of Parties and Cabinet Government in Sweden. Princeton, N.J.: Princeton University Press, 1955.

Sakellaropoulos, K. M. He Skia tes Duseos (2d ed.). Athens, 1961.

Sanders, Irwin T. Rainbow in the Rock. Cambridge, Mass.: Harvard University Press, 1962.

Sartori, G. "Parliamentarians in Italy," *International Social Science Journal,* XIII, No. 4 (1961).

Scalapino, Robert. Democracy and the Party Movement in Prewar Japan. Berkeley: University of California Press, 1953.

———— and Junnosuke Masumi. Parties and Politics in Contemporary Japan. Berkeley: University of California Press, 1962.

Schlesinger, Joseph A. Ambition and Politics. Chicago: Rand McNally, 1966.

Silberman, Bernard S., and H. D. Harootunian, eds. Modern Japanese Leadership. Tucson: University of Arizona Press, 1967.

Singer, Marshall. The Emerging Elite. Cambridge, Mass.: M.I.T. Press, 1964.

Statistical Yearbook of Greece, 1956 through 1967.

Stillman, W. J. The Cretan Insurrection of 1866–7–8. New York: Henry Holt, 1874.

Strong, Frederick. Greece as a Kingdom. London: Longman, Brown, Green, and Longmans, 1842.

Stycos, J. Mayone. "Patterns of Communication in a Rural Greek Village," *Public Opinion Quarterly*, XVI (spring 1952).

Sweet-Escott, Bickham. Greece: A Political and Economic Survey, 1939–1953. London: Royal Institute of International Affairs, 1954.

Tarrow, Sidney G. Peasant Communism in Southern Italy. New Haven: Yale University Press, 1967.

Thompson, Kenneth. Farm Fragmentation in Greece. Athens: Center for Economic Research, 1963.

Thomson, Sir Basil. The Allied Secret Service in Greece. London: Hutchinson, 1931.

Triantis, S. G. Common Market and Economic Development. Athens: Center for Economic Research, 1965.

United Democratic Left. For a National Democratic Change. Athens, 1961.

United States, Department of State. Greek Attitudes Towards the United States, USSR, Great Britain, and France, Report No. 3. New York: Columbia University Bureau of Applied Social Research, 1951.

Wace, A. J., and M. S. Thompson. Nomads of the Balkans. London: Methuen, 1914.

Wahlke, John C., Heinz Eulau, William Buchanan, and LeRoy C. Ferguson. The Legislative System. New York: John Wiley and Sons, 1962.

Ward, Benjamin. Greek Regional Development. Athens: Center for Economic Research, 1963.

Ward, Robert, and Dankwart Rustow. Political Modernization in Japan and Turkey. Princeton, N.J.: Princeton University Press, 1964.

Weiner, Myron. The Politics of Scarcity: Public Pressure and Political Response in India. Chicago: University of Chicago Press, 1962.

Welch, Claude, ed. Political Modernization. Belmont: Wadsworth, 1967.

Westebbe, Richard. Savings and Investment in Greece. Athens: Center for Economic Research, 1964.

Woodhouse, C. M. The Greek War of Independence. London: Hutchinson, 1952.

Wylie, Laurence. Village in the Vaucluse (rev. ed.). New York: Harper and Row, 1964.

Xydis, Stephen G. Greece and the Great Powers, 1944–1947. Thessaloniki: Institute for Balkan Studies, 1963.

Index

Index

litical recruitment, 210f, 254, 257, 308, 310

Regent, 232

Representational role orientation, 175, 181

Research methods, 319–21

Resistance movement, 58, 72, 147, 190, 196, 203. *See also* Civil war

Revenue, *see* Taxation

Revolution: of 1843, 55; of 1862, 56; of 1909, 128, 188, 194, 228, 300, 305–6, 312

Riggs, Fred W., 3–8 *passim*, 14, 20–26 *passim*, 129, 165, 172, 197

Right wing, 140f, 156, 189, 195; support for, 139, 153, 159–62, 324–27; political recruitment, 141–43, 148, 269, 284

"Ritualist" role orientation, 176, 178

Role conflict, 178–79, 182

Role orientations, 175–85, 251, 288

Roman Catholics, 88

Rosenau, James, 22

Rousseas, Stephen, 75

Royal Phalanx, 54

Rural Greek: contemporary period, 33–37, 76, 119–23, 128, 135, 169–70, 212, 311; nineteenth century, 43, 47f, 51, 82–86, 93. *See also* Agriculture

Russett, Bruce, 61

Russia, 42, 45f, 51, 64–68 *passim*, 71, 126. *See also* Soviet Union

Sacred Link of Greek Officers (IDEA), 216

Samos, 86

Sanders, Irwin, 39, 89, 119

Sartori, Giovanni, 197

Scalapino, Robert, 289

Scarcity, 23, 32, 39–40, 92, 99, 107, 118–22 *passim*, 138, 166. *See also* Natural resources

SD, *see* Democratic Socialist Party

Searing, Donald, 255

Security forces, *see* Battalions of National Security

Senate, Greek, 100

Serfdom, 47

Serbia, 43. *See also* Yugoslavia

Service occupations, 118

Shils, Edward, 241

Shipowners, 100, 106, 111, 113; and political careers, 281f, 284

Size, as a factor in development, 102, 107, 111, 118–24 *passim*, 159, 288

Social change: causes, 3–5, 13–14, 57–61, 158–59; and clientage system, 35–39 *passim*, 102, 123–24, 184–85, 220, 298; and the Left, 197, 202f, 206

Social mobilization, 82, 90–95 *passim*, 99, 128, 185f, 212, 214, 313ff

Socialists, 62, 196–97

Socialization: defined, 24; content, 34–37, 39–40, 86–92 *passim*, 158, 235–36; of deputies, 249–74, 301–11

Sofoulis, Themistocles, 332

Soviet Union, 72, 153, 202, 210, 215. *See also* Russia

Spandidakis, General, 231n

Sports associations, 104

Status distinctions, 47, 278–79

Stephanopoulos, Stephanos, 224, 329, 331

Strikes and demonstrations, 18, 101, 116f, 120, 207, 224f

Students, 213

Subject orientation, 119

Suffrage, 51, 56–57, 84f, 104, 126, 311

Tariffs, 100, 106, 171, 174, 205

Tarrow, Sidney, 31–35 *passim*, 102, 278

Taxation: character, 47–53 *passim*, 69, 84, 96, 112f, 135; and development, 105f, 156, 168–74 *passim*, 205, 241

TEA, *see* National Security Battalions

Teachers, 89, 135; in Europe, 275. *See also* Academic professions

Technical occupations, and political careers, 281, 284, 303–4

Territorial expansion, of Greece, 64–75 *passim*, 82–86 *passim*, 94–95, 194, 298

Technical Chamber, 100, 106–7

Their Majesties' Fund, 113, 193

Theodorakis, Mikis, 238

Theotokis, John, 330

Thessaloniki, 213, 226, 293

Thessaly, 58, 67, 70, 85, 161f, 194, 311; and political careers, 146, 267, 286, 308, 310

Thrace, 74, 86, 88, 161; and political careers, 146, 267, 285f, 310

Tobacco areas, 117, 123

Tourism, 62, 204, 239, 316

Trade agreements, 153

Trade unions: organization, 100, 112,